BERMUDA
24TH EDITION

Where to Stay and Eat
for All Budgets

Must-See Sights
and Local Secrets

Ratings You Can Trust

Fodor's Travel Publications   New York, Toronto, London, Sydney, Auckland
www.fodors.com

FODOR'S BERMUDA
Editor: Emmanuelle Morgen

Editorial Production: Ira-Neil Dittersdorf
Editorial Contributors: Satu Hummasti, Sue Johnston, Liz Jones, Jeannine Klein, Sandra Davis-Taylor, Judith Wadson, Sarah Titterton, Carla Zuill
Maps: David Lindroth, *cartographer;* Bob Blake and Rebecca Baer, *map editors*
Design: Fabrizio La Rocca, *creative director;* Guido Caroti, *art director;* Melanie Marin, *senior picture editor*
Production/Manufacturing: Angela L. McLean
Cover Photo (Couple wading in Bermuda surf): Homer Martin/Age Fotostock

ISBN 1-4000-1336-4

ISSN 0192-3765

Twenty-fourth Edition

SPECIAL SALES

Fodor's Travel Publications are available at special discounts for bulk purchases for sales promotions or premiums. Special editions, including personalized covers, excerpts of existing guides, and corporate imprints, can be created in large quantities for special needs. For more information, contact your local bookseller or write to Special Markets, Fodor's Travel Publications, 1745 Broadway, New York, New York 10019. Inquiries from Canada should be directed to your local Canadian bookseller or sent to Random House of Canada, Ltd., Marketing Department, 2775 Matheson Boulevard East, Mississauga, Ontario L4W 4P7. Inquiries from the United Kingdom should be sent to Fodor's Travel Publications, 20 Vauxhall Bridge Road, London SW1V 2SA, England.

AN IMPORTANT TIP & AN INVITATION

Although all prices, opening times, and other details in this book are based on information supplied to us at press time, changes occur all the time in the travel world, and Fodor's cannot accept responsibility for facts that become outdated or for inadvertent errors or omissions. So **always confirm information when it matters,** especially if you're making a detour to visit a specific place. Your experiences—positive and negative—matter to us. If we have missed or misstated something, **please write to us.** We follow up on all suggestions. Contact the Bermuda editor at editors@fodors.com or c/o Fodor's at 1745 Broadway, New York, New York 10019.

PRINTED IN THE UNITED STATES OF AMERICA

10 9 8 7 6 5 4 3 2 1

DESTINATION BERMUDA

With its fabulous beaches and coves, its turquoise waters and coral reefs, and its isolation in the Atlantic, Bermuda is the classic getaway destination. The island has long been a favorite of members of British royalty and celebrities looking to escape the public life—for at least a little while; and businesspeople from the East Coast looking for a serene vacation island that is still easy to reach. Travelers who return to Bermuda year after year appreciate its slow, even pace of life as much as its mild climate and fantastic hotels. For all intents and purposes, Bermuda is synonymous with gorgeous scenery, excellent golf, and an intriguing colonial history. And yet, if you ask a friend where the island—or, rather, the archipelago—is, he or she may not be able to reply confidently. Bermuda may have all the draws of the Caribbean—sun, surf, seafood, and sleeping late—but the island is actually hundreds of miles north of the Bahamas, and more than 500 mi east of the United States. Cape Hatteras, North Carolina, is the nearest point on the mainland. Bermuda is also Britain's oldest colony, and its most famous resort island, all because of the wreck of a New World–bound ship one fateful day in 1609 . . .

Karen Cure

Karen Cure, Editorial Director

CONTENTS

ABOUT THIS BOOK

There's no doubt that the best source for travel advice is a like-minded friend who's just been where you're headed. But with or without that friend, you'll have a better trip with a Fodor's guide in hand. Once you've learned to find your way around its pages, you'll be in great shape to find your way around your destination.

SELECTION
Our goal is to cover the best properties, sights, and activities in their category, as well as the most interesting communities to visit. We make a point of including local food-lovers' hot spots as well as neighborhood options, and we avoid all that's touristy unless it's really worth your time. You can go on the assumption that everything you read about in this book is recommended wholeheartedly by our writers and editors. Flip to **On the Road with Fodor's** to learn more about who they are. It goes without saying that no property mentioned in the book has paid to be included.

RATINGS
Orange stars ★ denote sights and properties that our editors and writers consider the very best in the area covered by the entire book. These, the best of the best, are listed in the **Fodor's Choice** section in the front of the book. Black stars ★ highlight the sights and properties we deem **Highly Recommended**, the don't-miss sights within any region. Fodor's Choice and Highly Recommended options in each region are usually listed on the title page of the chapter covering that region. Use the index to find complete descriptions. In cities, sights pinpointed with numbered map bullets ❶ in the margins tend to be more important than those without bullets.

SPECIAL SPOTS
Pleasures & Pastimes focuses on types of experiences that reveal the spirit of the destination. Watch for **Off the Beaten Path** sights. Some are out of the way, some are quirky, and all are worth your while. If the munchies hit while you're exploring, look for **Need a Break?** suggestions.

TIME IT RIGHT
Wondering when to go? Check **On the Calendar** up front and the Exploring chapter's **Timing** sections for weather and crowd overviews and best days and times to visit.

SEE IT ALL
For a good overview of Bermuda, use Fodor's exclusive **Great Itineraries** at the front of the book. In the Exploring chapter, **Good Walks** guide you to important sights in Hamilton, St. George's, and the Dockyard. ▶ indicates the starting points of walks and itineraries in the text and on the maps.

BUDGET WELL
Hotel and restaurant price categories from ¢ to $$$$ are defined in the opening pages of each chapter—expect to find a balanced selection for every budget. For attractions, we always give standard adult admission fees; reductions are usually available for children, students, and senior citizens. Look in **Discounts & Deals** in Smart Travel Tips for information on destination-wide ticket schemes. Want to pay with plastic? **AE, D, DC, MC, V** following restaurant and hotel listings indicate whether American Express, Discover, Diners Club, MasterCard, or Visa are accepted.

BASIC INFO
Smart Travel Tips lists travel essentials for the entire country. To find the best way to get around, see the transportation section; see individual modes of travel ("Bus Travel," "Moped & Scooter Travel") for details. We assume you'll check Web sites or call for particulars.

ON THE MAPS	Maps throughout the book show you what's where and help you find your way around. Black and orange numbered bullets ❶❶ in the text correlate to bullets on maps.
BACKGROUND	In general, we give background information within the chapters in the course of explaining sights as well as in CloseUp boxes and in Understanding Bermuda at the end of the book. To get in the mood, review the suggestions in Books & Movies.
FIND IT FAST	Within the Exploring Bermuda chapter, sights are grouped by location: first the cities and Dockyard, then the parishes. Where to Eat is also organized by location and then further divided by cuisine type. Where to Stay is organized by types of lodging. The Nightlife & the Arts and Beaches, Sports & the Outdoors chapters are arranged alphabetically by entertainment type. Within Shopping, a description of the island's main shopping districts is followed by a list of specialty shops grouped according to their focus. Heads at the top of each page help you find what you need within a chapter.
DON'T FORGET	Restaurants are open for lunch and dinner daily unless we state otherwise; we mention dress only when there's a specific requirement and reservations only when they're essential or not accepted— it's always best to book ahead. Hotels have private baths, phone, TVs, and air-conditioning and, unless stated otherwise, operate on the European Plan (a.k.a. EP, meaning without meals). We always list facilities but not whether you'll be charged extra to use them, so when pricing accommodations, find out what's included.

SYMBOLS

Many Listings

★ Fodor's Choice

★ Highly recommended

⊠ Physical address

⊹ Directions

⌖ Mailing address

☎ Telephone

🖷 Fax

⊕ On the Web

✉ E-mail

🎟 Admission fee

☉ Open/closed times

▶ Start of walk/itinerary

Ⓣ Bus stops

Outdoors

⛳ Golf

Hotels & Restaurants

🏨 Hotel

⇄ Number of rooms

♨ Facilities

🍽 Meal plans

✕ Restaurant

⌂ Reservations

👗 Dress code

✕🏨 Hotel with restaurant that warrants a visit

Other

☺ Family-friendly

🛈 Contact information

⇨ See also

✉ Branch address

☞ Take note

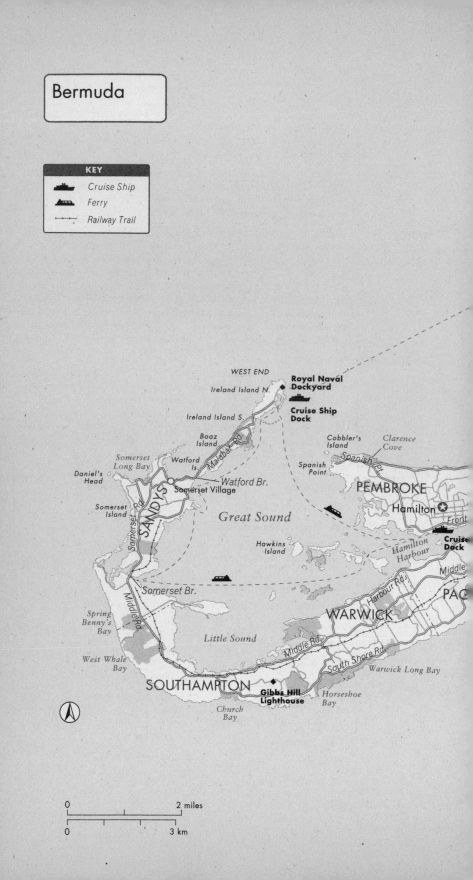

Bermuda

KEY
- Cruise Ship
- Ferry
- Railway Trail

WEST END

Ireland Island N.

Royal Naval Dockyard

Cruise Ship Dock

Ireland Island S.

Boaz Island

Cobbler's Island

Clarence Cove

Somerset Long Bay

Watford Is.

Spanish Point

Spanish Pt.

PEMBROKE

Daniel's Head

Watford

Malabar Rd.

Watford Br.

Somerset Village

Hamilton ✪

Somerset Island

SANDYS

Somerset Rd.

Great Sound

Front St.

Cruise Dock

Hawkins Island

Hamilton Harbour

Somerset Br.

Middle Rd.

PAG

Spring Benny's Bay

Middle Rd.

Little Sound

Harbour Rd.

WARWICK

West Whale Bay

Middle Rd.

South Shore Rd.

Warwick Long Bay

SOUTHAMPTON

Gibbs Hill Lighthouse

Horseshoe Bay

Church Bay

0   2 miles

0   3 km

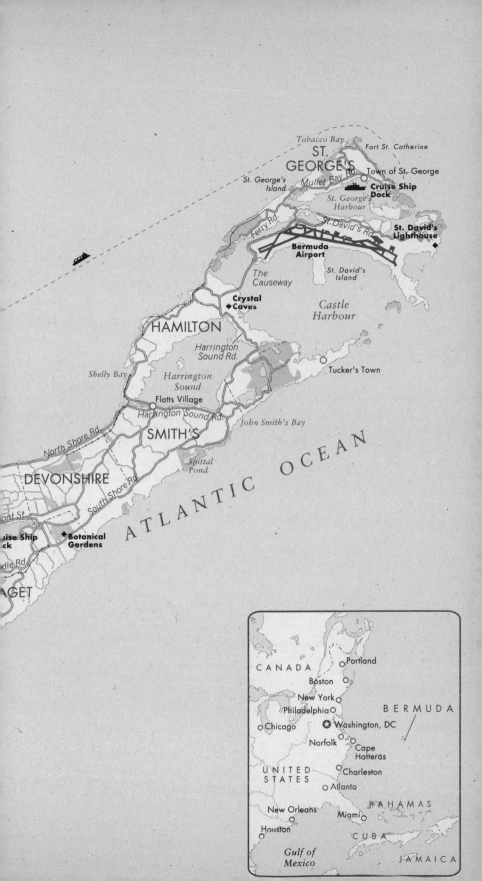

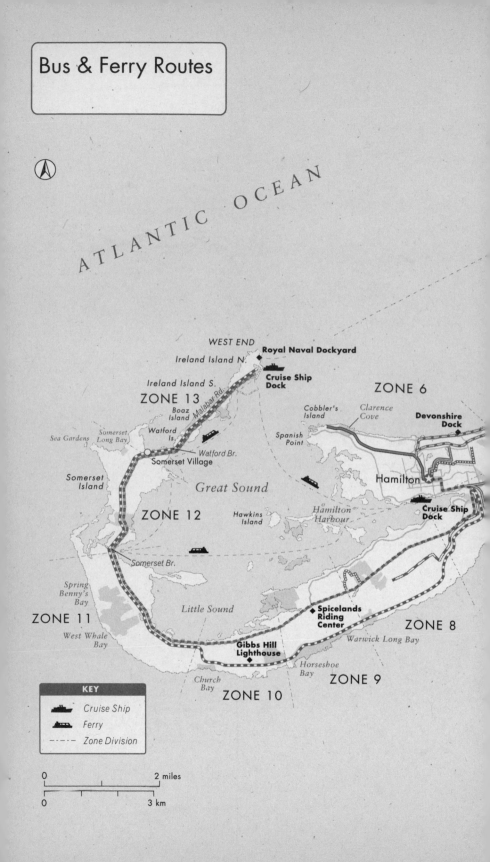

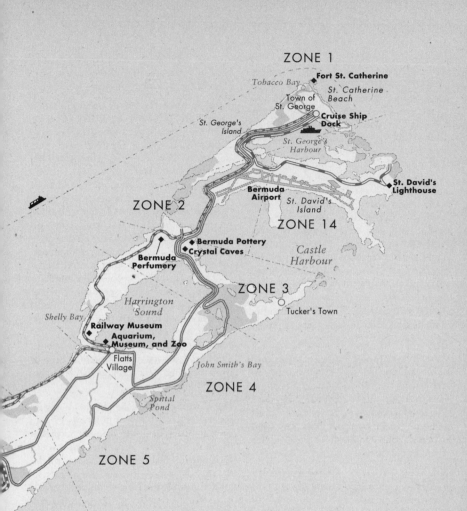

ZONE 1

Tobacco Bay

Fort St. Catherine

St. Catherine Beach

Town of St. George

St. George's Island

Cruise Ship Dock

St. George's Harbour

St. David's Lighthouse

ZONE 2

Bermuda Airport

St. David's Island

ZONE 14

Castle Harbour

◆ Bermuda Pottery
Crystal Caves

Bermuda Perfumery

Harrington Sound

ZONE 3

Tucker's Town

Shelly Bay

Railway Museum
Aquarium, Museum, and Zoo

Flatts Village

John Smith's Bay

ZONE 4

Spittal Pond

ZONE 5

ZONE 7

BUS ROUTES		
≡≡≡≡	**1**	*Hamilton–Castle Harbour/St. George's*
≈≈≈≈	**2**	*Hamilton–Ord Road*
―――	**3**	*Hamilton–Grotto Bay*
────	**4**	*Hamilton–Spanish Point*
━━━━	**5**	*Hamilton–Pond Hill*
───	**6**	*St. George's–St. David's*
▪▪▪▪	**7**	*Hamilton–Sonesta*
		Hamilton–Somerset/Dockyard
▬▬▬▬	**8**	*Hamilton–Somerset*
		Hamilton–Dockyard
═══	**8c**	*Hamilton–Cedar Hill*
⁞⁞⁞⁞	**9**	*Hamilton–Prospect*
∿∿∿∿	**10**	*Hamilton–St. George's*

ON THE ROAD WITH FODOR'S

A trip takes you out of yourself. Concerns of life at home completely disappear, driven away by more immediate thoughts—about, say, what marvels will beguile the next day, or where you'll have dinner. That's where Fodor's comes in. We make sure that you know all your options, so that you don't miss something that's around the next bend just because you didn't know it was there. Because the best memories of your trip might well have nothing to do with what you came to Bermuda to see, we guide you to sights large and small all over the island. You might set out to relax on the beach and practice your golf swing, but back at home you find yourself unable to forget exploring historic Fort St. Catherine or climbing to the top of Gibb's Hill Lighthouse. With Fodor's at your side, serendipitous discoveries are never far away.

Our success in showing you every corner of the archipelago is a credit to our extraordinary writers. Although there's no substitute for travel advice from a good friend who knows your style, our contributors are the next best thing—the kind of people you would poll for travel advice if you knew them.

A native Canadian, Sue Johnston has lived in Bermuda since 1995, spending much of that time exploring the island in a bid to understand it. Naturally, we asked her to update the Exploring and Understanding Bermuda chapters. When she's not enjoying the casual outdoor lifestyle of her home-away-from-home, Sue writes articles for *The Bermudian* and *Bermudian Business* magazines, among other publications, and she teaches communication courses. Sue served as the communication director for the Bermuda National Trust in 1999.

Liz Jones moved to Bermuda from Britain in 1973 to marry a Bermudian. After lecturing on English and writing at Bermuda College for 12 years, she decided to practice what she preached and become a freelance writer. Liz contributes regularly to *The Bermudian* magazine, *Mid-Ocean News,* and *RG,* the Royal Gazette's monthly magazine. She also co-authored the books *Bermuda Recollections* and *Moods of Bermuda.* Liz inspected the

Bermuda grass of the island's eight golf courses for our Golf chapter.

Jeannine Klein arrived in Bermuda from Canada in 2000 to work for a local television station, but she soon found her true calling as a senior reporter with the *Bermuda Sun* newspaper. Jeannine covers political, environmental, transportation, and business news, and she produces a weekly "After Dark" insert for the paper's lifestyle section. Her extreme resourcefulness and her extensive knowledge of Bermuda's inner workings and infrastructure made her the perfect updater for the Smart Travel Tips chapter. After many cold years growing up on the Canadian prairies, Jeannine cannot get enough of the sun and sea, but she's also a devoted shopper, known to regularly pound the pavement on her lunch hours to find the newest clothes and shoes before her size sells out. She found it difficult to restrain herself from spending while doing research for the Shopping chapter.

Our cruising expert, Sandra Davis-Taylor toured and sailed on numerous cruise ships to provide us with detailed, nitpicky descriptions about each line and vessel. Once she reached Bermuda, she then made the rounds of the hotels and guest houses, and even took the time to dip into a few spas. Sandra has been a freelance writer and photojournalist since 1982, before which time she held executive marketing positions in the hotel and airline industries in the United States and the Caribbean. Sandra's articles have appeared in *Sky-Writings,* Air Jamaica's in-flight magazine; *BeWe Beat,* BWIA's Pan-Caribbean in-flight magazine; *Caribbean Lifestyles*; and *Showboats International.*

Bermuda-born Judith Wadson, our restaurant updater and an acclaimed chef in her own right, has reviewed Bermuda restaurants and up-and-coming culinary stars for numerous publications, including *The New York Times, The Robb Report,* and *Yachting* magazine, where she worked as a staff photographer and writer. She also authored the book *Bermuda: Traditions and Tastes,* about the island's gastronomic heritage.

Life-long Bermudian and adventure-seeker Sarah Titterton revised the Beaches, Sports & the Outdoors chapter, after which she took off on a two-month cruise in a tall ship to study oceanography. Sarah contributes regularly to *The Royal Gazette* newspaper, and she has also written for BlackandCoke.com, a Bermudian entertainment Web site.

Carla Zuill, a feature writer for *The Royal Gazette*, is a lifelong resident of Bermuda, though she took a break from the island just long enough to earn a degree in journalism from the University of Georgia. She lent us her native point of view for the upfront What's Where, Great Itineraries, When to Go, On the Calendar, and Pleasures & Pastimes sections. Her own favorite pastimes include basking on Bermuda's beautiful beaches, taking her infant daughter to the aquarium, and trying out a different restaurant each week. When asked what she enjoys best about living on the island, Carla said: "Swimming every summer day in our crystal-clear waters!"

When the 1610 Bermuda Company divided up the islands of Bermuda among its seven original shareholders, Bermuda's parishes, or districts, were delineated into shares (25 acres per share) and tribes (50 shares per tribe). The parishes are named after these early Bermuda Company investors—Sandys, Southampton, Warwick, Paget, Pembroke, Devonshire, Smith's, Hamilton, and St. George's—who were, as in "Humpty Dumpty," all the king's men: aristocrats, knights, some members of parliament, who financed or played a role in Bermuda's colonization. Although the names are still used colloquially as a reference point, sometimes indicating where one's family is from (and has been for centuries), the function of these property lines today is mostly historical.

Hamilton

Hamilton, Bermuda's capital since 1815, has most of the island's government buildings. Here you can watch Parliament in session or visit the grand City Hall, home to two major art galleries. The city is also one of the island's three cruise-ship ports and a departure point for ferries heading to other parts of the island. The soaring Cathedral of the Most Holy Trinity, seat of the Anglican Church of Bermuda, is in Hamilton, as is Fort Hamilton, a moated fortress with underground passageways. But most people know Hamilton as the hub of shopping and dining, with colorful Front Street as the main thoroughfare.

St. George's

Bermuda's original capital (from the early 17th century until 1815) is steeped in history. Settled in 1609, it was the second English settlement in the New World, after Jamestown, Virginia. Today its alleys and walled lanes are packed with small museums and historic sights, including King's Square, where cedar replicas of the stocks, pillory, and ducking stool once used to punish criminals now serve as props. St. George's was named as a UNESCO World Heritage Site in 2000.

The West End & Dockyard

The West End of Bermuda encompasses Somerset and Ireland islands, bucolic areas of nature reserves, wooded areas, and beautiful bays and harbors. When you cross Somerset Bridge, you are, as Bermudians say, "up the country." It is a rural area of small farms and open space, craggy coastlines, gentle beaches, and parks and nature preserves. Picturesque Somerset Village looks much as it did in 1962 when it was featured in _A Touch of Mink,_ starring Doris Day and Cary Grant—a town of quiet streets and charming old buildings skirting lovely Mangrove Bay. In addition, a big attraction is the Royal Naval Dockyard, a former bastion of the Royal British Navy and now a major tourist center with a maritime museum, shopping arcade, crafts market in the Old Cooperage building, and a number of restaurants and pubs. On most days you can see artisans at work on their crafts—quilts, candles, banana leaf dolls, miniature furniture, hand-painted fabrics, and more. The Bermuda Arts Center and Bermuda Clayworks Pottery are also nearby.

The Western Parishes

Sandys, Southampton, and Warwick comprise the western parishes. The southern part of Sandys is lovely and rural, with beautiful Ely's Harbor a local favorite boating and diving spot. The northern part of the parish stretches into what locals call the West End—Somerset and Ireland islands are actually part of Sandys Parish. Southampton Parish is known for its beautiful pink sand beaches, manicured golf courses, and the elegant resorts that line them. Warwick's claim to fame is the Warwick Long Bay beach, the Bermuda's longest, which is open to the public and has a coral outcrop close to shore. Warwick is somewhat isolated from restaurants and nightlife, however.

The Central Parishes

Paget, Pembroke, and Devonshire are Bermuda's middle parishes, though Paget is sometimes lumped in with the western parishes and Devonshire is sometimes called an eastern parish. Pembroke is home to the city of Hamilton and is the most populous parish. Paget has some of Bermuda's best south-shore beaches and resort hotels. It's also a stone's throw from Hamilton, the ferries, and lots of restaurants. Devonshire's draws include Ocean View Golf Course, nature reserves, and the arboretum.

The Eastern Parishes

Like their counterparts at the opposite end of the island, the eastern parishes—Hamilton Parish, Smith's Parish, and St. George's Parish—couldn't be called lively, although the international airport is here and a host of guest houses surround Harrington Sound. This is a historic area, and the attractions and landscape here tell the complex story of Bermuda's founding and settlement. Historical Flatts Village is the de facto center of Smith's Parish, which borders Harrington Sound and is home to the Bermuda Aquarium, Spittal Pond, and Verdmont, an 18th-century estate. Crystal Caves and Bailey's Bay are the landmarks of Hamilton Parish. St. George's Parish has Tucker's Town, an affluent area of residential estates, plus plenty of historical sites, like Fort St. Catherine and St. David's Lighthouse.

Bermuda in 5 Days

On an island with as many gorgeous beaches and historic homes as Bermuda, you risk seeing half of everything or all of nothing. So use the efficient itinerary below to keep you on track as you explore both the famous sights and those off the beaten path. Although Bermuda is a tiny island, you can have the time of your life on its 22 square mi.

Day 1: Take a bus or taxi into Hamilton to explore the city's cultural offerings and do some shopping. You might also save a trip to Hamilton for a rainy day, if one is in the forecast. The city is a good place to visit on a rainy day—yes, it does rain in Bermuda—because it offers lots of indoor activities and the sidewalks along Front Street are protected by wooden balconies and arcaded buildings.

Start your day with a stroll along Front Street, taking the time to look into the many small shops you find along the way. When you reach City Hall, stop in for a visit to the Bermuda National Gallery, with its European paintings, and the Bermuda Society of Arts Gallery, with its local art and photography exhibits. Afterward, return to Front Street, where you can have lunch in one of restaurants overlooking the harbor.

After lunch, take a taxi or long walk to the Bermuda Underwater Exploration Institute, where multimedia displays and scale models of sunken ships provide a real sense of Bermuda's underwater environment. Taking tea is the perfect way to end your afternoon. Walk over to the Fairmont Hamilton Princess, the eye-catching pink hotel and a Hamilton landmark since it was built in 1884. You can sit in the posh dining room or at the bar overlooking Hamilton Harbour, as waiters in formal attire bring you tea and scones. If you'd rather skip tea, take a walk or rest on a park bench at Albuoy's Point, at the foot of Front Street, where you can watch the rosy evening sky and the boats coming into the harbor.

Day 2: Catch a ferry to the Royal Naval Dockyard on the West End to absorb some of the island's history and culture, and for more shopping. You can bask in the sun on the ferry's upper deck and get a fantastic view of the harbor and curving land before you reach your destination. While in Dockyard, tour the Commissioner's House to learn about Bermuda's naval history and visit the dolphins in the keep of the Maritime Museum. Save an hour or two to see the shops and crafts stands in the Clocktower Mall, which is big enough to be delightfully uncrowded.

After working up a hearty appetite, lunch at the Frog & Onion Pub is a must. From fish-and-chips to bangers and mash, there's always something on the menu that will grab your attention. By mid-afternoon, catch a bus or a ferry back into Hamilton in time to see the gombey dancers perform at the No.1 Shed, near the ferry terminal, and to see the sights and browse the shops along Front Street. You might catch the sunset at Albuoy's Point.

Day 3: Spend a day at the beach! With hundreds of beaches to choose from you could lose the better part of the day running from one to another, being mesmerized at each by the sight of shimmering water, startling cliffs and rock formations, or undulating sand dunes. But the best way to enjoy the beach, as everyone knows, is to choose one and stay put, bringing along water, sunblock, and a few good books. See Chapter 6, Beaches, Sports & the Outdoors, for descriptions of Bermuda's beaches and water sports outfitters. After a satisfying Bermuda break-fast, you might head out to Warwick Long Bay or Horseshoe Bay, both of which are off South Shore Road in Southampton Parish. Both also have beautiful pink-and-white coral sand and a tempting wave-riding surf. Or, consider traveling north to Shelly Bay Beach, near Flatts Village. Shelly Bay has shallow water and great breezes for windsurfing.

Day 4: On your fourth day, visit the island's East End, and be sure to pack a swimsuit. Start in the town of St. George's, a UNESCO World Heritage Site. In the old town square, you will find tiny shops and informative historical plaques. Don't miss St. Peter's Church and Somers Garden. In the afternoon, take a minibus to pristine Tobacco Bay Beach, where you can rent snorkeling equipment and discover some of Bermuda's beautiful coral and fish. You also can also kick back under an umbrella. Or, for a more active afternoon, walk from Tobacco Bay to Fort St. Catherine. The fort overlooks St. Catherine's beach, where the survivors from the *Sea Venture* scrambled ashore on July 28, 1609. You can return to St. George's for your evening meal.

Day 5: One of the best ways to get to know Bermuda is by taking a long bicycle or scooter ride, stopping at various sights along the way. If you don't feel like contending with traffic, hire a taxi and take a driving tour of the island. Must-see sights include Gibb's Hill Lighthouse, for the best view of the island and a perfectly wonderful afternoon tea; Fort Hamilton in Somerset; Verdmont House in Smith's; the Botanical Gardens in Paget; and Paget Marsh. A tour of the island outside its major communities is sure to show you that Bermuda is another world.

If You Have More Time

With more than five days in Bermuda, you'll have time to take part in a few water-based activities. You can sign up with a deep-sea fishing charter company, a scuba- or helmet-diving outfitter, or a sea-kayaking tour. More time on the island will also permit you to play tennis or golf, and to visit one or more of the island's exceptional health spas. History buffs may want to spend more time at Verdmont House, the Museum of the Bermuda Historical Society, the Bermuda National Trust Museum at the Globe Hotel, and the Bermudian Heritage Museum. Shoppers can revisit Hamilton, St. George's, and the Dockyard, and beach lovers can get in some extra R&R.

If You Have 3 Days

If you are going to Bermuda for a long weekend, your focus should be on Hamilton, the Royal Naval Dockyard, St. George's, and the beach or golf course, depending on your interests. You can see Hamilton and Dockyard in one day if you don't spend too much time shopping or in the museums, and a trip to St. George's could be squeezed into a half day. Three days in Bermuda will give you a satisfying taste of the island that will likely tempt you to start planning your next trip there.

WHEN TO GO

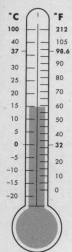

In summer, Bermuda teems with activity. Hotel barbecues and evening dances complement daytime sightseeing trips, and public beaches never close. The pace slows considerably in the off season (November through March). A few hotels and restaurants close; some of the sightseeing, dive, snorkeling, and water-skiing boats are dry-docked; and only taxis operate tours of the island. Most hotels remain open, however, and slash their rates by as much as 40%. The weather at this time of year is often perfect for golf and tennis, and you can still rent boats, tour the island, and take advantage of sunny days, shops, restaurants, and walking tours.

Climate

Bermuda has a remarkably mild climate that seldom sees extremes of either heat or cold. In winter (December through March), temperatures range from around 55°F at night to 70°F in the early afternoon. High, blustery winds can make the air feel cooler, however, as can Bermuda's high humidity. The hottest part of the year is between May and mid-October, when temperatures range from 75°F to 85°F. It's not uncommon for the temperature to reach 90°F in July and August. The summer months are somewhat drier, but rainfall is spread fairly evenly throughout the year. Bermuda depends solely on rain for its supply of fresh water, so residents usually welcome the brief storms. In August and September, hurricanes moving northward from the Caribbean sometimes batter the island and cause flight delays.

📷 Forecasts **Weather Channel Connection** ☎ 900/932-8437, 95¢ per minute from a Touch-Tone phone 🌐 www.weather.com.

BERMUDA

Jan.	68F	20C	May	76F	24C	Sept.	85F	29C
	58	14		65	18		72	22
Feb.	68F	20C	June	81F	27C	Oct.	79F	26C
	58	14		70	21		70	21
Mar.	68F	20C	July	85F	29C	Nov.	74F	23C
	58	14		76	24		61	16
Apr.	72F	22C	Aug.	86F	30C	Dec.	70F	21C
	59	15		76	24		61	16

ON THE CALENDAR

Heritage, music, theater, dance, and sports festivals are scheduled year-round in Bermuda, and you can find great room-and-festival hotel deals if you shop around.

ONGOING

Mar.–Oct.

The Ceremony is usually performed twice monthly by the Bermuda Regiment Band, the Bermuda Islands Pipe Band with Dancers, and members of the Bermuda Pipe Band. The historic ceremony is performed alternately on Front Street in Hamilton, King's Square in St. George's, and Dockyard in the West End. There are no performances in August.

WINTER

December

In the Christmas Boat Parade, lighted yachts and boats of many sizes float along in Hamilton Harbour, followed by a fireworks extravaganza. It takes place on the second Saturday of the month.

Usually held on the first Sunday in December, Father Christmas visits Front Street in the Hamilton Jaycees Santa Claus Parade. Santa is accompanied by marching bands, majorettes, and floats.

The Bermuda Aquarium, Natural History Museum & Zoo (☎ 441/293–2727) also has an annual yuletide "do," with children's games, a crafts workshop, and a visit with Santa in the Zoo Garden.

The Bermuda National Trust Annual Christmas Walkabout in St. George's (☎ 441/236–6483), a festive early-evening open-house event, features traditional Christmas decorations, musicals in the State House, monologues at the Globe Hotel, and historic readings at the Town Hall.

Boxing Day (Dec. 26) is a public holiday, when you'll find a variety of sports events, and various Gombey Dancing troupes performing around the Island.

St. George's New Year's Eve Celebration (☎ 441/297–1532) in King's Square and on Ordnance Island has food stalls, rides for children, and continuous entertainment by local musicians. A midnight countdown and dropping of the "onion" are followed by fireworks.

January

Bermuda International Race Weekend (☎ 441/236–6086) kicks off the third weekend of the month. The event begins Friday night with the popular Front Street Mile. It also includes marathon and half-marathon races and a fitness-and-charity 10-km walk. Most races are open to all. Top international runners participate.

Thousands of residents attend performances put on by the Bermuda Festival (☎ 441/235–1291). This two-month program attracts internationally known artists for concerts, dance, and theater.

The Annual Regional Bridge Tournament, (☎ 441/295–5161), sponsored by the Bermuda Unit of the American Contract Bridge League, is held at the Fairmont Southampton Princess the last week of January.

	At the **Annual Photographic Exhibition** (☎ 441/292–3824), held during the third week of the month in the Bermuda Society of the Arts gallery, you can see the work of local amateur and professional photographers, including many underwater shots.
Jan.–Mar.	The **Regimental Musical Display** (☎ 441/238–2470) is a captivating re-creation of a retreat ceremony, performed in Hamilton by the Bermuda Regiment Band and the Bermuda Islands Pipe Band with Dancers.
February	The **Bermuda International Open Chess Tournament** (☎ 441/238–2313) is open to both residents and visitors.
	The **Annual Bermuda Rendezvous Bowling Tournament** (☎ 441/236–5290), sanctioned by the ABC and WIBC, is open to all bowlers. Cash prizes are awarded.

SPRING

March	The **Bermuda All Breed Championship Dog Shows and Obedience Trials** (☎ 441/291–1426) draw dog lovers from far and wide to the Botanical Gardens in Paget. The event is held again in November.
	The **Bermuda Super Senior Invitational Tennis Tournament** (☎ 441/296–0834) is a USTA-sanctioned event held at the Coral Beach & Tennis Club in Paget. It is held during the second week in March.
	See a range of equestrian events at the **Bermuda Horse & Pony Association Spring Show** (☎ 441/234–0485), including dressage, jumping, Western, and driving classes, at National Equestrian Centre.
	The **Bermuda Men's Amateur Golf Championship** (☎ 441/295–9972) is played at the Mid Ocean Club in Tucker's Town.
	The **Bermuda Cat Fanciers Association Championship Cat Show** features pedigree felines and household pets judged at various locations. Contact Morag Smith (☎ 441/238–0112) or Diana Plested (☎ 441/295–5723).
Mar.–Apr.	The **Palm Sunday Walk** (☎ 441/236–6483) is an annual 6–8 mi stroll. Each year an alternate route is taken.
	Good Friday is a public holiday and traditionally a kite-flying day.
	Enjoy a spectacular display of locally made kites at the **Bermuda Kite Festival** (☎ 441/295–0729), held at Horseshoe Bay in Southampton.
April	The **Annual Exhibition** (☎ 441/236–4201), similar to a county or state fair, brings entertainment, exhibits, and plays reflective of Bermuda's agricultural and cultural heritage to the Botanical Gardens in Paget. The three-day event is usually held the third weekend in April.
	The **Peppercorn Ceremony** (☎ 800/223–6106) celebrates—amid great pomp and circumstance—the payment of one peppercorn in rent to the government by the Masonic Lodge of St. George No. 200 of the Grand Lodge of Scotland for its headquarters in the Old State House in St. George's.
	The **XL Capital Bermuda Open** (☎ 441/296–2554) is an ATP Tour, USTA–sanctioned event of the world's top professionals.

The **Annual Fun Run/Walk Around Harrington Sound** (☎ 441/293–7074) invites walkers, joggers, runners, bikers, rollerbladers—whatever—to go the 7- to 8-mi distance around the Sound.

The popular seven-day **Bermuda International Film Festival** (☎ 441/293–3456) screens independent films in three theaters. Filmmakers are on hand to answer questions. It usually kicks off during the second week of April.

Apr.–May

The **Garden Club of Bermuda** (☎ 441/295–9155) leads tours through private houses and gardens.

International Race Week (☎ 441/295–2214) pits Bermudians against sailors from around the world in a series of races on the Great Sound. Contact the Sailing Secretary of the Royal Bermuda Yacht Club.

May

May is **Bermuda Heritage Month** (☎ 441/292–9447), when a host of commemorative, cultural, and sporting activities is scheduled. The climax is Bermuda Day (May 24), a public holiday that includes a parade to the National Stadium, a cycling race, a half-marathon (13 mi) for Bermuda residents only, and Bermuda dinghy races in St. George's Harbour.

The **Bermuda End-to-End Scenic Railway Trail Walk for Charities** is a terrific way to see the Island and meet active residents. The 26-mi course begins in King's Square, St. George's, and finishes with a range of festivities at the Royal Naval Dockyard. An alternative, 15-mi course begins at Albuoy's Point, Hamilton. You can sign up 30 minutes before either starting point.

The **Bermuda Senior Amateur Championships for Men and Ladies** (☎ 441/295–9972) are played on a different course each year. Women must be at least 50 years old, men at least 55.

ZooDoo Day (☎ 441/293–7074) at the Bermuda Aquarium, Museum & Zoo has free admission, fun, games, and gift stalls.

SUMMER

June

For **Queen Elizabeth II's Birthday,** a public holiday in mid-June, military marching bands parade down Hamilton's Front Street.

The **Bermuda Angler's Club International Light Tackle Tournament** (☎ 441/296–4767 days; 441/236–6565 evenings), played out the first or second week of the month, draws a large crowd to its 5 PM weigh-in.

Free **Open Air Pops Concerts** (☎ 441/238–1108) are presented by the Bermuda Philharmonic Society at King's Square, St. George's, and the Clocktower Mall at Dockyard.

The **Bermuda Amateur Stroke Play Championship for Men and Ladies** (☎ 441/295–9972) are simultaneous events played at the Port Royal Golf Course. Men and women play 72- and 54-hole strokes, respectively.

July

Played at the Mid Ocean and Port Royal golf courses, the **Atlantic International Junior Championship** (☎ 441/295–5111) is a 72-hole stroke play junior golf tournament.

July–Aug.	The **Cup Match Cricket Festival** (☎ 441/234–0327 or 441/297–0374) is a two-day-long festival centered on the match between arch rivals Somerset and St. George's cricket clubs. The festival is held on the weekend of Emancipation Day, a public holiday, either the last Thursday and Friday in July or the first Thursday and Friday in August.
	The **Sea Horse Anglers' Club Annual Bermuda Billfish Tournament** (☎ 441/292–7272) is a favorite among fishermen.
August	Landlubbers in homemade contraptions compete in the hilarious **Non-Mariners Race** (☎ 441/236–3683) in Mangrove Bay. If it floats, you are disqualified.

FALL

September	**Labour Day** brings a number of activities, including a march from Union Square in Hamilton to Bernard Park. Local entertainers and food stalls selling local fare are part of the festivities.
	The **Bermuda Mixed Foursomes Amateur Golf Championship** (☎ 441/295–9972) is a 36-stroke play competition for couples at Port Royal Golf Course. Handicap limit: men 24, ladies 36.
	The **Annual Bermuda Triathlon** (☎ 441/293–2765) is open to visiting and local teams who compete in a 1-mi swim, 15-mi cycle, and 6-mi run.
	The **Bermuda Masters International Golf Classic** (☎ 800/648–1136) is played at Port Royal and Castle Harbour.
November	**Remembrance Day** is a public holiday in memory of Bermuda's and its allies' fallen soldiers. A parade with Bermudian, British, and U.S. military units, the Bermuda Police, and war veterans' organizations takes place on Front Street in Hamilton.
	The **Reconvening of Parliament** (☎ 441/292–7408), on the first Friday in November, is preceded by the arrival of His Excellency the Governor, in plumed hat and full regalia, at the Cabinet Building in Hamilton. Arrive by 10:30 to secure a place to stand.
	The **Bermuda Four Ball Stroke Play Amateur Championships for Men and Ladies** (☎ 441/295–9972) are simultaneous events at the Port Royal Golf Course.
	The **World Rugby Classic** (☎ 441/295–6574 ⊕ www.worldrugby.bm) pits international rugby players against the best players from Bermuda in a series of matches at the National Sports Center (Frog Lane, Devonshire).

PLEASURES & PASTIMES

Beaches The fine, pink sand of Bermuda's beaches—a result of shell particles, calcium carbonate, and bits of crushed coral mixed with sand—is an island trademark. This unique mixture also provides Bermuda's beaches with a startling characteristic—even during the summer months, the sand remains cool. Add to this the beaches' picturesque surroundings, which include dramatic cliff formations, coconut palms, and gently rolling dunes sloping into crystal-clear waters. The island's 34 beaches range from long, unbroken expanses of shoreline, such as that at Warwick Long Bay, to small, secluded coves divided by rock cliffs, such as those at Whale Bay Beach and Jobson's Cove.

Cricket The popularity of cricket in Bermuda begins to sink in only when you consider that the annual Cup Match Cricket Festival, a two-day event that pits the west side of the island against the east, is treated as a national holiday. Traditionally held the Thursday and Friday before the first Monday in August, Cup Match draws an average of 12,000 spectators, including zealous supporters who "decorate" the batsman by running out onto the field and slipping a little cash in his pocket. The event is also home to the Crown & Anchor tent packed with gambling tables, the only legal betting event on Bermuda's calendar. Other cricket games are held throughout the summer, from April through September.

Shopping For shoppers, Bermuda has everything from sophisticated department stores and designers' boutiques to art galleries with works by local artists, and comestible souvenirs, like Outerbridge's Sherry Peppers and Gosling's Black Seal rum. For high end gifts, look for European-made crystal and china, British-made clothing (especially woolen sweaters), and fine jewelry. Duty-free gold items, particularly watches, can sell for up to 20% less than in the U.S. On the artsy side, galleries throughout the island sell sculptures and paintings, hand-blown glass, handmade dolls, and other works by Bermudian artists and artisans.

Snorkeling & Diving Reefs, shipwrecks, underwater caves, spectacular coral and marine life, and warm, clear water combine to make Bermuda an ideal place for underwater exploration. The many sheltering reefs hide parrot fish, angelfish, trumpet fish, and grouper. Divers can enjoy a visibility range of 70 feet to 150 feet, the longest in the western Atlantic.

FODOR'S CHOICE

The sights, restaurants, hotels, and other travel experiences on these pages are our writers' and editors' top picks—our Fodor's Choices. They're the best of their type in the area covered by the book—not to be missed and always worth your time. In the destination chapters that follow, you will find all the details.

LODGING

$$$$	**The Fairmont Hamilton Princess**, Hamilton. Superbly located in downtown Hamilton—right on the harbor—and in business since 1884, the traditional and formal Princess is regarded as the mother of Bermuda's tourism industry.
$$$$	**The Reefs**, Southampton Parish. The pink lanais of this small, casually elegant resort jut out from the cliffside to overlook Christian Bay. The spectacular Point Suites at the tip of the property seem almost to hover over the ocean.
$$$–$$$$	**Horizons & Cottages**, Paget Parish. Lush, romantic gardens weave around this hilltop Relais & Châteaux cottage colony, which overlooks breathtaking views of the south shore. The grand main house was part of an 18th-century plantation.
$$$–$$$$	**Waterloo House**, Hamilton. An enchanting Relais & Chateaux property, Waterloo House is in an early-19th-century, white-column manse facing Hamilton Harbour. An alfresco luncheon or candlelit dinner on the Poinciana Terrace, on the water's edge, is a must-do.
$$–$$$	**Grotto Bay Beach Resort**, Bailey's Bay, Hamilton Parish. An aquarium, two underground caves for exploration and swimming, plus superior children's programs make Grotto Bay, on 21 oceanfront acres, an exciting family destination. The enclosed bay with three private beaches offers some of the most protected ocean waters in Bermuda.

BUDGET LODGING

$	**Oxford House**, Hamilton. Warmth and comfort radiate from this stately, colonial-style town house, now a family-run B&B with traditional, antique furnishings in individually decorated rooms. You can walk to downtown Hamilton in five minutes.
¢	**Salt Kettle House**, Hamilton. The cozy guest house, with its water views, fireside lounge, and hearty English breakfast, attracts repeat visitors year after year.

RESTAURANTS

$$$$	**Horizons**, Paget Parish. Chef Anton Mosimann's contemporary, healthy, fusion cuisine makes this restaurant, in the cottage colony of the same name, one of the hottest reservations in town.
$$$$	**Waterlot Inn**, Southampton Parish. Superior French cuisine and a 1670 manor-house setting combine to make this restaurant, at the Fairmont Southampton hotel, one of the island's finest.
$$$–$$$$	**Newport Room**, Southampton Parish. One of Bermuda's only authentic French restaurants, and certainly the island's best, the Fairmont Southampton's Newport Room holds promises of foie gras, rich yet light sauces, and delicate soufflés.

$$$–$$$$	**Tom Moore's Tavern,** Bailey's Bay, Hamilton Parish. This superb restaurant, in a house built in 1652, get its name from the poet who frequented it in 1804. Today it serves fabulous Bermuda seafood garnished with sophisticated European imports.
$$$–$$$$	**Waterloo House,** Hamilton. Exquisite Continental cuisine makes this restaurant, in the premier Relais & Châteaux hotel of the same name, one of Bermuda's finest restaurants.
$$–$$$	**Ascots,** Pembroke Parish. The chef and manager at this restaurant in the Royal Palms Hotel, insist on the freshest of local and imported ingredients, which are then combined to create contemporary, innovative dishes with complex and subtle tastes.
$$–$$$	**Seahorse Grill,** Paget Parish. The rockin', hoppin' Seahorse, in Elbow Beach Hotel, is nothing like the old-fashioned, austere dining rooms of Bermuda's other exceptional restaurants. Its menu showcases a fusion of international cuisines and Bermudian ingredients in light, healthy preparations.

BUDGET RESTAURANTS

$	**Black Horse Tavern,** St. David's. It's worth driving all the way out to the little East End community of St. David's for the classic Bermudian seafood served at this casual pub. Go for the curried conch stew, Bermuda lobster, amberjack, rockfish, or—a true Bermuda original—shark hash.
¢–$	**Aggie's Garden & Waterside Café,** Hamilton. This quirky little restaurant, with harborfront garden dining, serves fresh, local produce shaped into appealing sandwiches, soups, and salads.

AFTER HOURS

The Deep, Paget Parish. Top island DJs, a long champagne and wine list, and a double-level, stainless-steel design make The Deep Bermuda's most happenin' nightclub.

Hubie's Bar, Hamilton. A landmark cultural center, Hubie's hosts jazz jam sessions, open-mike poetry, and the occasional rock group. Everyone from college students to members of parliament comes here to loosen up.

Jasmine, Southampton Parish. You can dance to live music, drink cocktails in the lounge, or schmooze over light meals at one of the island's trendiest bars in the Fairmont Southampton.

BEACHES

Horseshoe Bay Beach, Southampton Parish. This quintessential Bermudian beach has it all: acres of pink sand, clear-blue waters, a vibrant social scene, rental facilities, and even a "baby beach" off one end of it. Lush, green South Shore Park lays behind the beach.

Elbow Beach, Paget Parish. Part of this stretch of glorious pink sand is reserved for Elbow Beach Hotel guests, but the rest is large enough to accommodate a devoted public without getting as crowded as Horseshoe Bay Beach. It's also a fantastic snorkeling spot.

CRUISES

Celebrity Cruises, to Bermuda. Celebrity makes cruising to Bermuda luxurious and affordable at the same time, with seven-night trips departing almost every week in summer and starting at prices as low as $700. The *Horizon* and *Zenith* are sleek, modern ships with relatively large cabins, plenty of natural light, and multiple decks with every kind of entertainment option.

"Don't Stop the Carnival Party" Cruise, from Hamilton to Hawkins Island. It's not a cruise to Bermuda, but rather a two-hour, 200-person bacchanal on a boat departing from Albuoy's Point and heading out to Hawkin's Island, complete with live music, gombey dancers, a barbecue buffet, and plenty of rum swizzles.

Silversea Cruises, to Bermuda. Although Silversea travels to Bermuda only a few times each year, those cruises are among the most lavish and sophisticated in the wide world of cruising. Every room on the *Silver Cloud, Silver Wind,* and *Silver Whisper* feels like the captain's cabin: opulent and spacious, with verandahs and water views. Ship restaurants serve fine, fresh meals, and entertainment is specially designed for each cruise.

Wildcat Adventure Tours, from Hamilton and St. George's. Spirited tour guides accompany you on this two-hour high-speed cruise around the entire country. You'll see some spectacular views as well as the homes of the rich and famous (including mayor of New York, Mike Bloomberg). The bright-yellow Wildcat catamaran is one of the most recognized boats on the island, so you're likely to get a few waves from other boaters.

GOLF

Mid Ocean Club, Tucker's Town. If you can find a way in via an introduction by a member, you'll find yourself playing a course that is consistently ranked among the world's top 50 golf courses. Babe Ruth, Michael Douglas, Michael Jordon, and Michael Bloomberg have all played here.

Port Royal Golf Course, Southampton Parish. Accessible, inexpensive, and overlooking gorgeous Whale Bay, this classic Bermudian public course is a Jack Nicklaus favorite and has a faithful following among local golfers.

MUSEUMS

Bermuda Maritime Museum and Dolphin Quest, Dockyard. Even if you're not a history buff, you can spend a fascinating day at the fortress that contains the Maritime Museum. The coastal scenery is spectacular and the grounds offer surprises at every turn—you may even get an up-close view of a dolphin.

Bermuda Aquarium, Museum & Zoo, Flatts Village. The aquarium's wonderful North Rock exhibit is as close as you can get to a scuba dive without getting wet.

NATURE

Paget Marsh, Paget Parish. Those who travel the boardwalk trail over Paget Marsh understand what Bermuda was like before man arrived—no colorful hibiscus or majestic palms, but an inside look at the island's sensitive original ecosystem.

OUTDOOR ACTIVITIES

Diving with Blue Water Divers Ltd., off the south shore. Make the most of an underwater exploration of the ancient, eerie shipwrecks off the south shore with this well-reputed outfitter, based in Elbow Beach Hotel.

Snorkeling in Church Bay, Southampton Parish. The little coves and crannies of this jewel of a bay, the locals' favorite place to snorkel, simply beg to be discovered and explored.

SHOPPING

A. S. Cooper Man, Hamilton. This branch of the classy department store stocks the best selection of men's clothes on the island. This is where to get your classic Bermuda shorts.

Bermuda Arts Centre, Dockyard. A contemporary art gallery in an old, stone Dockyard building makes the perfect setting for traditional and experimental Bermudian art, from paintings to sculpture to jewelry.

Calypso, Hamilton. Fashionistas adore Calypso for its sophisticated collection of designer clothes, including the island's largest selection of swimwear, and Italian-made shoes and handbags. Everything looks like it comes straight out of *Harper's Bazaar.*

Dockyard Glassworks and Bermuda Rum Cake Company, Dockyard. This is *the* place to shop for souvenirs, even if you don't buy anything. The combination bakery and glassmaking studio is a destination in and of itself, notwithstanding the wonderful wares. You can watch glass-blowers at work and taste different flavors of rum cake, and the friendly staff will pack and deliver purchases.

Trimingham's, Hamilton. If you only have time to go to one store in Bermuda, go to Trimingham's, the largest department store on the island, with everything from crystal and china to clothing, souvenirs, and jewelry.

Windjammer Gallery, Hamilton. You can wander at your leisure among the high-quality paintings in this quaint cottage, surrounded by a tranquil garden. Purchases can be shipped to your home.

VIEWPOINTS

Gibb's Hill Lighthouse, Southampton Parish. Even if you're not interested in climbing the 180 or so steps to get to the top of the lighthouse, you can still get a brilliant view of Bermuda's hills, dotted with white-roof houses, and the magnificent south shore, dotted with white boats and sails. Plus, you can sit down to a perfectly brewed cup of tea and home-baked scone.

SMART TRAVEL TIPS

The 180 islands that compose Bermuda are divided into nine parishes: Sandys (pronounced Sands), Southampton, Warwick, Paget, Pembroke, Devonshire, Smith's, Hamilton, and St. George's. Their import is pretty much historical these days, although they often appear on addresses following or in lieu of the street. It can get confusing, however, since Hamilton is both a city and a parish. The City of Hamilton is actually in Pembroke Parish. St. George is a city within the parish of the same name. We indicate Hamilton Parish and St. George's Parish when we refer to a property that falls outside the respective city proper.

Although the numbering of houses is becoming more common, many houses still are known only by their picturesque names, and buildings in Hamilton are numbered rather whimsically. In fact, some Front Street buildings have two numbers, one of them an old historic address that has nothing to do with the building's present location. Fortunately, almost all Bermudians can give you precise directions.

AIR TRAVEL

Nonstop service to Bermuda is available year-round on major airlines from Atlanta, Boston, Newark (NJ), New York City, Toronto, and London, and seasonally from Charlotte, Fort Lauderdale, Philadelphia, Washington, D.C., and Halifax. Travelers from Australia and New Zealand must fly to Bermuda via London, New York, or Toronto. Most flights arrive around noon, making for particularly long waits to get through immigration; however, British Airways flights, and one American Airlines flight from New York, arrive later in the evening. Fares from New York City may be found for under $300, while fares from Toronto typically cost $300 to $500, and those from Gatwick start at $700.

BOOKING

When you book, **look for nonstop flights** and **remember that "direct" flights stop at least once.** Try to avoid connecting flights, which require a change of plane. Two airlines may operate a connecting flight jointly, so ask whether your airline operates every segment of the trip; you may find that the carrier you prefer flies you only part of the way. To find more booking tips and to check prices and make online flight reservations, log on to www.fodors.com.

CARRIERS

American flies nonstop to Bermuda twice daily from New York and once daily from Boston during high season, April through October. Frequency drops from November to March. Continental flies daily from Newark, New Jersey. Delta has one daily flight from Atlanta and one from Boston. US Airways flies daily from New York, nonstop April through September, connecting in Philadelphia during low season. It also offers seasonal nonstop flights from Boston, Washington, D.C., Charlotte, and Fort Lauderdale. Air Canada has one daily flight from Toronto, plus a weekly seasonal flight from Halifax. British Airways flies in from London's Gatwick Airport four times per week in high season and three times per week in low season.

🛪 Major Airlines **Air Canada** ☎ 888/247-2262 ⊕ www.aircanada.com. **American** ☎ 800/433-7300 ⊕ www.aa.com. **Continental** ☎ 800/231-0856 ⊕ www.continental.com. **Delta Airlines** ☎ 800/241-4141 ⊕ www.delta.com. **US Airways** ☎ 800/428-4322 ⊕ www.usairways.com.
🛪 From the U.K. **British Airways** ☎ 0181/897-4000 ⊕ www.ba.com.

CHECK-IN & BOARDING

Flights to Bermuda are occasionally delayed or cancelled due to high winds or crosswinds, particularly in the late summer and fall. Before you leave home for the airport, you should always **call to confirm whether or not there are Bermuda-bound delays.**

You should also **find out your carrier's check-in policy.** Plan to arrive at the airport about two hours before your scheduled departure time for flights from the United States or Canada and 2½ to 3 hours ahead for flights from other countries. You may need to arrive earlier if you're flying from one of the busier airports or during peak air-traffic times. To avoid delays at airport-security checkpoints, try not to wear any metal. Jewelry, belt and other buckles, steel-toe shoes, barrettes, and underwire bras are among the items that can set off detectors.

Assuming that not everyone with a ticket will show up, airlines routinely overbook planes. When everyone does, airlines ask for volunteers to give up their seats. In return, these volunteers usually get a several-hundred-dollar flight voucher, which can be used toward the purchase of another ticket, and are rebooked on the next flight out. If there are not enough volunteers, the airline must choose who will be denied boarding. Bermuda-bound travelers are rarely bumped, even during the island's busiest summer season. Instead, when overbooking occurs, some airlines switch to a larger aircraft. In the event that passengers are bumped, however, the first to go are typically those who checked in late and those flying on discounted tickets, so **check in and get to the gate as early as possible.**

Have your passport or government-issued photo ID handy. Bermuda is rather scrupulous about ID, and you'll be asked to show your passport when checking in and again when boarding.

At many airports outside Bermuda, travelers with only carry-on luggage can bypass the airline's front desk and check in at the gate. But in Bermuda, everyone checks in at the airline's front desk. U.S. customs has a desk here, too, so you won't have to clear customs at home when you land. Passengers returning to Britain or Canada will need to clear customs and immigration on arrival.

CUTTING COSTS

The least-expensive airfares to Bermuda are priced for round-trip travel and must usually be purchased in advance. Airlines generally allow you to change your return date for a fee; most low-fare tickets, however, are nonrefundable. It's smart to **call a number of airlines and check the Internet;** when you are quoted a good price, **book it on the spot**—the same fare may not be available the next day, or even the next hour. Always **check different routings** and look into using alternative airports. Also, price off-peak flights, which may be significantly less expensive than others. Travel agents, especially low-fare specialists (⇨ Discounts and Deals), are helpful.

Consolidators are another good source. They buy tickets for scheduled flights at reduced rates from the airlines, then sell them at prices that beat the best fare available directly from the airlines. Sometimes you can even get your money back if you need to return the ticket. Carefully read the fine print detailing penalties for changes and cancellations, purchase the ticket with a credit card, and **confirm your consolidator reservation with the airline.**

🔢 Consolidators AirlineConsolidator.com ☎ 888/468-5385 ⊕ www.airlineconsolidator.com; for international tickets. **Best Fares** ☎ 800/576-8255 or 800/576-1600 ⊕ www.bestfares.com; $59.90 annual membership. **Cheap Tickets** ☎ 800/377-1000 or 888/922-8849 ⊕ www. cheaptickets.com. **Expedia** ☎ 800/397-3342 or 404/728-8787 ⊕ www.expedia.com. **Hotwire** ☎ 866/468-9473 or 920/330-9418 ⊕ www. hotwire.com. **Now Voyager Travel** ⊠ 45 W. 21st St., 5th floor, New York, NY 10010 ☎ 212/459-1616 🖷 212/243-2711 ⊕ www.nowvoyagertravel.com. **Onetravel.com** ⊕ www.onetravel.com. **Orbitz** ☎888/656-4546 ⊕ www.orbitz.com. **Priceline. com** ⊕ www.priceline.com. **Travelocity** ☎ 888/ 709-5983; 877/282-2925 in Canada; 0870/111-7060 in the U.K. ⊕ www.travelocity.com.

ENJOYING THE FLIGHT

State your seat preference when purchasing your ticket, and then repeat it when you confirm and when you check in. For more legroom, you can request one of the few emergency-aisle seats at check-in, if you are capable of lifting at least 50 pounds—a Federal Aviation Administration requirement of passengers in these seats. Seats behind a bulkhead also offer more legroom, but they don't have underseat storage. Don't sit in the row in front of the emergency aisle or in front of a bulkhead, where seats may not recline.

Ask the airline whether a snack or meal is served on the flight. If you have dietary concerns, **request special meals when booking.** These can be vegetarian, low-cholesterol, or kosher, for example. It's a good idea to pack some healthful snacks and a small (plastic) bottle of water in your carry-on bag. On long flights, try to maintain a normal routine, to help fight jet lag. At night, **get some sleep.** By day, **eat light meals, drink water** (not alcohol), and **move around the cabin** to stretch your legs. For additional jet-lag tips consult *Fodor's FYI: Travel Fit & Healthy* (available at bookstores everywhere).

Smoking policies vary from carrier to carrier. Many airlines prohibit smoking on all of their flights; others allow smoking only on certain routes or certain departures. Ask your carrier about its policy.

FLYING TIMES

Flying time to Bermuda from New York, Newark, Boston, Philadelphia, and Baltimore is about 2 hours; from Atlanta, 2¾ hours; from Toronto, 3 hours; and 7 hours from London Gatwick.

HOW TO COMPLAIN

If your baggage goes astray or your flight goes awry, complain right away. Most carriers require that you **file a claim immediately.** The Aviation Consumer Protection Division of the Department of Transportation publishes *Fly-Rights*, which discusses airlines and consumer issues and is available on-line. You can also find articles and information on mytravelrights.com, the Web site of the nonprofit Consumer Travel Rights Center.

🔢 Airline Complaints Aviation Consumer Protection Division ⊠ U.S. Department of Transportation, C-75, Room 4107, 400 7th St. SW, Washington, DC 20590 ☎ 202/366-2220 ⊕ airconsumer.ost.dot.gov. **Federal Aviation Administration Consumer Hotline** ⊠ for inquiries: FAA, 800 Independence Ave. SW, Washington, DC 20591 ☎ 800/322-7873 ⊕ www.faa.gov.

AIRPORTS & TRANSFERS

Bermuda's gateway is Bermuda International Airport (BDA), on the east end of the island, approximately 9 mi from Hamilton and 17 mi from Somerset.
🔢 Bermuda International Airport (BDA) ⊠ 2 Kindley Field Rd., St. George's ☎ 441/293-1640 ⊕ www.bermudaairport.com.

TRANSFERS

Taxis, readily available outside the arrivals gate, are the usual and most convenient way to leave the airport. The approximate fare (not including tip) to Hamilton is $22; to St. George's, $12; to south-shore hotels, $30; and to Sandys (Somerset), $35. A surcharge of 25¢ is added for each piece of luggage stored in the trunk or on the roof. Fares are 25% higher between midnight and 6 AM and all day on Sunday and public holidays. Depending on traffic, the driving time to Hamilton is about 30 minutes; to Sandys, about one hour.

Bermuda Hosts Ltd. provides transportation to hotels and guest houses aboard air-conditioned 6- to 25-seat vans and buses. Reservations are recommended.
🔢 Bermuda Hosts Ltd. ☎ 441/293-1334 🖷 441/ 293-1335. **The Bermuda Industrial Union Taxi**

Co-op ☎ 441/292-4476. Bermuda Taxi Radio Cabs ☎ 441/295-4141. Island Wide Taxi Services ☎ 441/292-5600. Sandys Taxi Service ☎ 441/234-2344.

DUTY-FREE SHOPPING

Although you can certainly find discounts in china, crystal, woolens, and other European imports, duty-free shopping in Bermuda is limited. To qualify for duty-free (or in-bond) liquor prices, you'll have to buy at least two liters or five 75-centiliter bottles. However, each U.S. citizen (21 and older) may only bring back 1 liter of alcohol duty-free. You can arrange for duty-free liquor you buy at stores to be delivered to the airport, or you can purchase it at the airport itself.

BIKE TRAVEL

You'll be in the minority if you choose to ride around Bermuda since most two-wheelers on the island are mopeds. Traffic and high winds can make biking on island roads dangerous. In addition, steep hills and winding roads (particularly those going north–south) mean that bikers need a lot of pedal power. However, bicycling on the Railway Trail, which is closed to vehicular traffic, is particularly rewarding. "The Bermuda Railway Trail Guide" is free at all Visitors Service Bureaus. Day rates for rentals range from $15 to $25. If possible, try to reserve bikes a few days in advance.

BIKES IN FLIGHT

Most airlines accommodate bikes as luggage, provided they are dismantled and boxed; check with individual airlines about packing requirements. Some airlines sell bike boxes, which are often free at bike shops, for about $15 (bike bags can be considerably more expensive). International travelers often can substitute a bike for a piece of checked luggage at no charge; otherwise, the cost is about $100. U.S. and Canadian airlines charge $40–$80 each way.

BOAT & FERRY TRAVEL

The Bermuda Ministry of Transport maintains excellent, frequent, and on-time ferry service from Hamilton to Paget and Warwick (the pink line), Somerset and the Dockyard in the West End (the blue line), Rockaway in Southampton (the green line), and, weekdays in summer only, the Dockyard and St. George's (the orange line).

FARES & SCHEDULES

A one-way adult fare to Paget or Warwick is $2.50; to Somerset, the Dockyard, or St. George's, $4. The last departures are at 9:45 PM mid-April through mid-November, 9 PM mid-November through mid-April. Sunday ferry service is limited and ends around 7 PM. You can bring a bicycle on board free of charge, but you'll pay $4 extra to take a motor scooter to Somerset or the Dockyard, and scooters are not allowed on the smaller Paget and Warwick ferries. Neither bikes nor scooters are allowed on ferries to St. George's. Discounted one-, three-, and seven-day passes are available for use on both ferries and buses. They cost $11, $23, and $36, respectively. The helpful ferry operators can answer questions about routes and schedules and can even help get your bike on board. Schedules are published in the phone book, posted at each landing, and are also available at the ferry terminal, central bus terminal, visitor services bureaus, and most hotels.
🚩 **Ministry of Transport, Department of Marine and Ports Services** Hamilton Ferry Terminal: ✉ 8 Front St., near Queen St. ☎ 441/295-4506 ⊕ www.seaexpress.bm.

BUSINESS HOURS

BANKS & OFFICES

Most branches of the Bank of Bermuda are open weekdays from 9 to 4:30 and Saturday from 11 to 1. All branches of the Bank of Butterfield are open Monday through Thursday from 9 to 3:30 and Friday from 9 to 4:30. Bermuda Commercial Bank (at 43 Victoria Street in Hamilton) operates Monday through Thursday from 9:30 to 3 and Friday from 9:30 to 4:30. Capital G Bank (at 25 Reid Street in Hamilton) is open weekdays from 8:30 to 4:30 and Saturday from 8:30 to 3:30.

GAS STATIONS

Many gas stations are open daily from 7 AM to 9 PM, and a few stay open until midnight. The island's only 24-hour gas station is Esso City Auto Market in Hamilton, near the Bank of Butterfield, off Par-La-Ville Road.

MUSEUMS & SIGHTS

Hours vary greatly, but museums are generally open Monday through Saturday from 9 or 9:30 to 4:30 or 5. Some close on Saturday. Check with individual museums for exact hours.

PHARMACIES

Pharmacies are open Monday through Saturday from 8 AM to 6 or 8 PM, and sometimes Sunday from around 11 to 6 PM.

SHOPS

Most stores are open Monday through Saturday from around 9 until 5 or 6. Some of the larger department stores, like Trimingham's, are open until 9 PM on Friday. Some Hamilton stores keep evening hours when cruise ships are in port. Dockyard shops are generally open Monday through Saturday from 10 to 5, Sunday from 11 to 5. Otherwise, most shops are closed on Sunday. Those that are open—mainly grocery stores and pharmacies—have abbreviated hours.

BUS TRAVEL

Bermuda's pink-and-blue buses travel the island from east to west. To find a bus stop outside Hamilton, look for either a stone shelter or a pink-and-blue striped pole. For buses heading to Hamilton, the top of the pole is pink; for those traveling away from Hamilton, the top is blue. Remember to **wait on the proper side of the road.** Driving in Bermuda is on the left. Bus drivers will not make change, so **purchase tickets or discounted tokens** or carry plenty of coins.

In addition to public buses, private minibuses serve St. George's. The minibus fare depends upon the destination, but you won't pay more than $5. Minibuses, which you can flag down, drop you wherever you want to go in this parish. They operate daily from about 7:30 AM to 9 PM. Smoking is not permitted on buses.

FARES & SCHEDULES

Bermuda is divided into 14 bus zones, each about 2 mi long. Within the first three zones, the rate is $3 (coins only). For longer distances, the fare is $4.50. If you plan to travel by public transportation often, buy a booklet of tickets (15 fourteen-zone tickets for $25.50, or 15 three-zone tickets for $16). You can also buy a few tokens, which, unlike tickets, are sold individually. Tickets, tokens, and one-, three-, and seven-day adult passes ($11, $23, and $36, respectively; good for ferry service as well) are available at the central bus terminal. Tickets and passes are also sold at the Visitors Service Bureau in Hamilton, post offices, and at many hotels and guest houses. Passes for children (ages 5–16) are $6, $11, or $16. Passes are accepted on both buses and ferries.

Hamilton buses arrive and depart from the Central Bus Terminal. A small kiosk here is open weekdays from 7:15 to 5:30, Saturday from 8:15 to 5:30, and Sunday and holidays from 9:15 to 4:45; it's the only place to buy money-saving tokens.

Buses run about every 15 minutes, except on Sunday, when they usually come every half hour or every hour, depending on the route. Bus schedules, which also contain ferry timetables, are available at the bus terminal in Hamilton and at many hotels. The timetable also offers an itinerary for a do-it-yourself, one-day sightseeing tour by bus and ferry. Upon request, the driver will be happy to tell you when you've reached your stop. **Be sure to greet the bus driver when boarding**—it's considered rude in Bermuda to ask a bus driver a question, such as the fare or details on your destination, without first greeting him or her. Exact change for the buses is essential.

🚌 **Public Transport Bermuda** Central Bus Terminal: ✉ Washington and Church Sts., Hamilton ☎ 441/292-3851 ⊕ www.bermudabuses.com. **St. George's Minibus Service** ☎ 441/297-8199.

CAMERAS & PHOTOGRAPHY

Photo processing is very expensive in Bermuda, so develop your film when you get home. Photography is forbidden in the Senate Chamber, Sessions House, and in the courts, but the rest of Bermuda offers plenty of wonderful photo opportunities. Horseshoe Bay, the view from Gibb's Hill Lighthouse, and the small coves near Warwick Long Bay make lovely subjects. If you are driving a motor scooter along South Shore Road, you might be tempted to snap a picture of the southern beaches. Locals are usually very friendly and will not hesitate to take your photo if you ask. The *Kodak Guide to Shooting Great*

Travel Pictures (available at bookstores everywhere) is loaded with tips.

F Photo Help **Kodak Information Center** ☎ 800/242-2424 ⊕ www.kodak.com.

EQUIPMENT PRECAUTIONS

Don't pack film and equipment in checked luggage, where it is much more susceptible to damage. X-ray machines used to view checked luggage are extremely powerful and therefore are likely to ruin your film. Try to ask for hand inspection of film, which becomes clouded after repeated exposure to airport X-ray machines, and **keep videotapes and computer disks away from metal detectors.** Always **keep film, tape, and computer disks out of the sun.** Carry an extra supply of batteries, and be prepared to turn on your camera, camcorder, or laptop to prove to airport security personnel that the device is real.

FILM & DEVELOPING

Although a roll of color print film costs about the same as in the U.S. ($7–$8 for a 36-exposure roll), developing that film is another story. If you're in a hurry to see what you shot, plan to dish out a whopping $28 per roll for 36 exposures, whether or not you choose speedy three-hour processing.

VIDEOS

Blank NTSC videotapes run about $3 each for six hours of tape and $4 for eight hours.

CAR TRAVEL

You cannot rent a car in Bermuda. Bermuda has strict laws governing against overcrowded roads, so even Bermudians are only allowed one car per household. A popular albeit somewhat dangerous alternative is to rent mopeds or scooters (⇨ Moped & Scooter Travel), which are better for negotiating the island's narrow roads.

CHILDREN IN BERMUDA

When children need a break from the beach or pool, there is plenty to see and do in Bermuda, from the carriage and maritime museums to the aquarium and botanical gardens. Places that are especially appealing to children are indicated by a rubber-duckie icon (🐤) in the margin.

BABY-SITTING

For baby-sitters, check with your hotel desk. The charge averages around $15 per hour per child. These rates may go up after midnight and they may vary depending on the number of children. Sitters may expect paid transportation.

FLYING

If your children are two or older, **ask about children's airfares.** As a general rule, infants under two not occupying a seat fly at greatly reduced fares or even for free. But if you want to guarantee a seat for an infant, you have to pay full fare. Consider flying during off-peak days and times; most airlines will grant an infant a seat without a ticket if there are available seats. When booking, **confirm carry-on allowances** if you're traveling with infants. In general, for babies charged 10% to 50% of the adult fare you are allowed one carry-on bag and a collapsible stroller; if the flight is full, the stroller may have to be checked or you may be limited to less.

Experts agree that it's a good idea to use safety seats aloft for children weighing less than 40 pounds. Airlines set their own policies: if you use a safety seat, U.S. carriers usually require that the child be ticketed, even if he or she is young enough to ride free, because the seats must be strapped into regular seats. And even if you pay the full adult fare for the seat, it may be worth it, especially on longer trips. Do **check your airline's policy about using safety seats during takeoff and landing.** Safety seats are not allowed everywhere in the plane, so get your seat assignments as early as possible.

When reserving, **request children's meals or a freestanding bassinet** (not available at all airlines) if you need them. But note that bulkhead seats, where you must sit to use the bassinet, may lack an overhead bin or storage space on the floor.

FOOD

Bermuda has no fast-food chains, except for a lone Kentucky Fried Chicken, but children will have no trouble finding familiar menu items in welcoming settings, especially at the more casual restaurants.

SUPPLIES & EQUIPMENT

Major American brands of baby formula, disposable diapers, and over-the-counter children's medications are widely available. However, prices are steep.

COMPUTERS ON THE ROAD

You should have no trouble bringing a personal laptop through customs into Bermuda, though you may have to open and turn it on for inspection by security officers. It would be a good idea to bring proof of purchase with you so you will not run into any difficulty bringing the computer back to the States, especially if it is a new machine.

Most hotels charge connection fees each time a laptop is hooked up to the Internet ($3 to $10), with additional charges (10¢ to 30¢ per minute) during the connection. The Fairmont Southampton and the Newstead Hotel both have fully equipped business centers where guests can use hotel computers for Internet access (connection charges still apply).

CONSUMER PROTECTION

Whether you're shopping for gifts or purchasing travel services, **pay with a major credit card** whenever possible, so you can cancel payment or get reimbursed if there's a problem (and you can provide documentation). If you're doing business with a particular company for the first time, **contact your local Better Business Bureau and the attorney general's offices** in your state and (for U.S. businesses) the company's home state as well. Have any complaints been filed? Finally, if you're buying a package or tour, always **consider travel insurance** that includes default coverage (⇨ Insurance).

🚩 BBBs Council of Better Business Bureaus ⊠ 4200 Wilson Blvd., Suite 800, Arlington, VA 22203 ☎ 703/276-0100 🖷 703/525-8277 ⊕ www. bbb.org.

CUSTOMS & DUTIES

When shopping, **keep receipts** for all purchases. Upon reentering the country, **be ready to show customs officials what you've bought.** Pack purchases together in an easily accessible place. If you think a duty is incorrect, appeal the assessment. If you object to the way your clearance was handled, note the inspector's badge number. In either case, first ask to see a supervisor. If the problem isn't resolved, write to the appropriate authorities, beginning with the port director at your point of entry.

IN AUSTRALIA

Australian residents who are 18 or older may bring home A$400 worth of souvenirs and gifts (including jewelry), 250 cigarettes or 250 grams of cigars or other tobacco products, and 1,125 ml of alcohol (including wine, beer, and spirits). Residents under 18 may bring back A$200 worth of goods. Members of the same family traveling together may pool their allowances. Prohibited items include meat products. Seeds, plants, and fruits need to be declared upon arrival.

🚩 **Australian Customs Service** ⊕ Regional Director, Box 8, Sydney, NSW 2001 ☎ 02/9213-2000 or 1300/363263; 02/9364-7222 or 1800/803-006 quarantine-inquiry line 🖷 02/9213-4043 ⊕ www. customs.gov.au.

IN BERMUDA

On entering Bermuda, you can bring in duty-free up to 50 cigars, 200 cigarettes, and 1 pound of tobacco; 1 liter of wine and 1 liter of spirits; and other goods with a total maximum value of $30. To import plants, fruits, vegetables, or pets, you must get an import permit in advance from the Department of Environmental Protection. Merchandise and sales materials for use at conventions must be cleared with the hotel concerned before you arrive.

🚩 **Department of Environmental Protection** ⊠ HM 834, Hamilton HM CX ☎ 441/236-4201 🖷 441/232-0046 ⊕ www.animals.gov.bm.

IN CANADA

Canadian residents who have been out of Canada for at least seven days may bring in C$750 worth of goods duty-free. If you've been away fewer than seven days but more than 48 hours, the duty-free allowance drops to C$200. If your trip lasts 24 to 48 hours, the allowance is C$50. You may not pool allowances with family members. Goods claimed under the C$750 exemption may follow you by mail; those claimed under the lesser exemptions must accompany you. Alcohol and tobacco products may be included in the seven-day and 48-hour exemptions but not in the 24-hour exemption. If you meet the age requirements of the province or territory through which you reenter Canada, you may bring in, duty-free, 1.5 liters of wine *or* 1.14 liters (40 imperial ounces) of liquor *or* 24 12-ounce cans or bottles of beer or ale. Also, if you meet the local age requirement for tobacco products, you may bring in, duty-free, 200 cigarettes and 50 cigars. Check ahead of time with the Canada Customs and Revenue Agency or the Department of Agriculture for policies regarding meat products, seeds, plants, and fruits.

You may send an unlimited number of gifts (only one gift per recipient, however) worth up to C$60 each duty-free to Canada. Label the package UNSOLICITED GIFT—VALUE UNDER $60. Alcohol and tobacco are excluded.

Canada Customs and Revenue Agency ✉ 2265 St. Laurent Blvd., Ottawa, Ontario K1G 4K3 ☎ 800/461-9999, 204/983-3500, or 506/636-5064 🌐 www.ccra.gc.ca.

IN NEW ZEALAND

All homeward-bound residents may bring back NZ$700 worth of souvenirs and gifts; passengers may not pool their allowances, and children can claim only the concession on goods intended for their own use. For those 17 or older, the duty-free allowance also includes 4.5 liters of wine or beer; one 1,125-ml bottle of spirits; and either 200 cigarettes, 250 grams of tobacco, 50 cigars, *or* a combination of the three up to 250 grams. Meat products, seeds, plants, and fruits must be declared upon arrival to the Agricultural Services Department.

New Zealand Customs ✉ Head office: The Customhouse, 17-21 Whitmore St., Box 2218, Wellington ☎ 09/300-5399 or 0800/428-786 🌐 www.customs.govt.nz.

IN THE U.K.

From countries outside the European Union, including Bermuda, you may bring home, duty-free, 200 cigarettes or 50 cigars; 1 liter of spirits or 2 liters of fortified or sparkling wine or liqueurs; 2 liters of still table wine; 60 ml of perfume; 250 ml of toilet water; plus £145 worth of other goods, including gifts and souvenirs. Prohibited items include meat products, seeds, plants, and fruits.

HM Customs and Excise ✉ Portcullis House, 21 Cowbridge Rd. E, Cardiff CF11 9SS ☎ 0845/010-9000 or 0208/929-0152; 0208/929-6731 or 0208/910-3602 complaints 🌐 www.hmce.gov.uk.

IN THE U.S.

U.S. residents who have been out of the country for at least 48 hours may bring home, for personal use, $800 worth of foreign goods duty-free, as long as they haven't used the $800 allowance or any part of it in the past 30 days. This exemption may include 1 liter of alcohol (for travelers 21 and older), 200 cigarettes, and 100 non-Cuban cigars. Family members from the same household who are traveling together may pool their $800 personal exemptions. For fewer than 48 hours, the duty-free allowance drops to $200, which may include 50 cigarettes, 10 non-Cuban cigars, and 150 ml of alcohol (or 150 ml of perfume containing alcohol). The $200 allowance cannot be combined with other individuals' exemptions, and if you exceed it, the full value of all the goods will be taxed. Antiques, which the U.S. Bureau of Customs and Border Protection defines as objects more than 100 years old, enter duty-free, as do original works of art done entirely by hand, including paintings, drawings, and sculptures. This doesn't apply to folk art or handicrafts, which are in general dutiable.

You may also send packages home duty-free, with a limit of one parcel per addressee per day (except alcohol or tobacco products or perfume worth more than $5). You can mail up to $200 worth of goods for personal use; label the package PERSONAL USE and attach a list of its contents and their retail value. If the package contains your used personal belongings, mark it AMERICAN GOODS RETURNED to avoid paying duties. You may send up to $100 worth of goods as a gift; mark the package UNSOLICITED GIFT. Mailed items do not affect your duty-free allowance on your return.

To avoid paying duty on foreign-made high-ticket items you already own and will take on your trip, register them with Customs before you leave the country. Consider filing a Certificate of Registration for laptops, cameras, watches, and other digital devices identified with serial numbers or other permanent markings; you can keep the certificate for other trips. Otherwise, bring a sales receipt or insurance form to show that you owned the item before you left the United States.

U.S. Bureau of Customs and Border Protection ✉ for inquiries and equipment registration, 1300

Pennsylvania Ave. NW, Washington, DC 20229
🌐 www.customs.gov ☎ 877/287-8667, 202/354-1000 ✉ for complaints, Customer Satisfaction Unit, 1300 Pennsylvania Ave. NW, Room 5.5D, Washington, DC 20229.

DISABILITIES & ACCESSIBILITY

Hamilton, the Dockyard, and St. George's have sidewalks with sloping ramps (though not on every street corner), but sidewalks are not prevalent elsewhere on the island. Businesses are not required by law to provide access for people with disabilities, but most try to follow the guidelines of the Americans with Disabilities Act (ADA).

If you plan to bring a guide dog to Bermuda, you must **obtain a permit in advance.** Application forms are available from all Bermuda Department of Tourism offices. Once your application is approved, the Department of Agriculture and Fisheries will send an import permit to the traveler; the permit must accompany the dog at the time of arrival. The Bermuda Chapter of the Society for the Advancement of Travel for the Handicapped produces information sheets for travelers with disabilities. You can also get this information at any Bermuda Department of Tourism office.

🔷 Local Resources Bermuda Chapter of the **Society for the Advancement of Travel for the Handicapped (SATH)** ✉ 347 5th Ave., Suite 610, New York, NY 10016 USA ☎ 212/447-7284. **Bermuda Physically Handicapped Association (BPHA)** ✉ Base Gate, 1 South Side, St. David's Island, DD 03 🔷 Box HM 8, Hamilton, HM AX ☎ 441/293-5035; 441/293-8148 after 5 PM 🖨 441/293-5036 🌐 www.bermuda-online.org/BPHA.htm.

LODGING

The most accessible lodgings are the large resorts, such as Elbow Beach and the Fairmont resorts.

RESERVATIONS

When discussing accessibility with an operator or reservations agent, **ask hard questions.** Are there any stairs, inside *or* out? Are there grab bars next to the toilet *and* in the shower/tub? How wide is the doorway to the room? To the bathroom? For the most extensive facilities meeting the latest legal specifications, **opt for**

newer accommodations. If you reserve through a toll-free number, consider also calling the hotel's local number to confirm the information from the central reservations office. Get confirmation in writing when you can.

SIGHTS & ATTRACTIONS

Hamilton is hilly and difficult to navigate for people with physical disabilities. City Hall; the Bermuda National Gallery; and the Bermuda Aquarium, Museum, and Zoo are the city's most wheelchair-friendly sights. St. George's and the Dockyard have cobblestone walks, but are otherwise wheelchair friendly. Horseshoe Beach is the easiest to visit in a wheelchair as taxis can drive up right to the sand. Most beaches have ramps and rest rooms that accommodate people with disabilities.

TRANSPORTATION

Public buses in Bermuda are not equipped for wheelchairs. However, the Bermuda Physically Handicapped Association (BPHA) has volunteer-operated buses with hydraulic lifts. Make arrangements in advance.

🔷 Complaints **Aviation Consumer Protection Division** (⇨ Air Travel) for airline-related problems. **Departmental Office of Civil Rights** ✉ for general inquiries, U.S. Department of Transportation, S-30, 400 7th St. SW, Room 10215, Washington, DC 20590 ☎ 202/366-4648 🖨 202/366-9371 🌐 www.dot.gov/ost/docr/index.htm. **Disability Rights Section** ✉ NYAV, U.S. Department of Justice, Civil Rights Division, 950 Pennsylvania Ave. NW, Washington, DC 20530 ☎ ADA information line 202/514-0301; 800/514-0301; 202/514-0383 TTY; 800/514-0383 TTY 🌐 www.ada.gov. **U.S. Department of Transportation Hotline** ☎ for disability-related air-travel problems, 800/778-4838 or 800/455-9880 TTY.

TRAVEL AGENCIES

In the United States, the Americans with Disabilities Act requires that travel firms serve the needs of all travelers. Some agencies specialize in working with people with disabilities.

🔷 Travelers with Mobility Problems **Access Adventures/B. Roberts Travel** ✉ 206 Chestnut Ridge Rd., Scottsville, NY 14624 ☎ 585/889-9096 🌐 www.brobertstravel.com ✉ dltravel@prodigy.net, run by a former physical-rehabilitation counselor. **CareVacations** ✉ No. 5, 5110-50 Ave., Leduc, Alberta, Canada, T9E 6V4 ☎ 780/986-6404 or 877/478-7827 🖨 780/986-8332 🌐 www.carevacations.

com, for group tours and cruise vacations. **Flying Wheels Travel** ✉ 143 W. Bridge St., Box 382, Owatonna, MN 55060 ☎ 507/451-5005 🖷 507/451-1685 ⊕ www.flyingwheelstravel.com.

DISCOUNTS & DEALS

Be a smart shopper and **compare all your options** before making decisions. A plane ticket bought with a promotional coupon from travel clubs, coupon books, and direct-mail offers or purchased on the Internet may not be cheaper than the least expensive fare from a discount ticket agency. And always keep in mind that what you get is just as important as what you save.

DISCOUNT RESERVATIONS

To save money, **look into discount reservations services** with Web sites and toll-free numbers, which use their buying power to get a better price on hotels, airline tickets (⇨ Air Travel), even car rentals. When booking a room, always **call the hotel's local toll-free number** (if one is available) rather than the central reservations number—you'll often get a better price. Always ask about special packages or corporate rates.

When shopping for the best deal on hotels and car rentals, **look for guaranteed exchange rates,** which protect you against a falling dollar. With your rate locked in, you won't pay more, even if the price goes up in the local currency.
🖪 Airline Tickets **Air 4 Less** ☎ 800/AIR4LESS; low-fare specialist.
🖪 Hotel Rooms **Accommodations Express** ☎ 800/444-7666 or 800/277-1064 ⊕ www. accommodationsexpress.com. **Turbotrip.com** ☎ 800/473-7829 ⊕ www.turbotrip.com.

PACKAGE DEALS

Don't confuse packages and guided tours. When you buy a package, you travel on your own, just as though you had planned the trip yourself. Fly/drive packages, which combine airfare and car rental, are often a good deal. In cities, ask the local visitor's bureau about hotel packages that include tickets to major museum exhibits or other special events.

ECOTOURISM

Bermudians are, on the whole, extremely proud of their island and fairly fanatical about protecting its natural beauty. Still, the concept of "ecotourism" has yet to find a firm footing. Although the government has been extremely successful in such endeavors as limiting cruise-ship traffic, banning rental cars, and protecting the offshore reef environment, the typical Bermuda vacation still consists of days by the pool or beach, a few rounds of golf or some watersports, shopping, and (for the adventurous) zipping around from sight to sight on a moped.

ELECTRICITY

Local electrical current is the same as in the United States and Canada: 110 volt, 60 cycle AC. All appliances that can be used in North America can be used in Bermuda without adapters. Winter storms bring occasional power outages.

EMERGENCIES

🖪 Doctors & Dentists Referral **Government Health Clinic** ✉ 67 Victoria St., Hamilton ☎ 441/236-0224 🖷 441/292-7627.
🖪 Emergencies **Air/Sea Rescue** ☎ 441/297-1010 🖷 441/297-1530 ⊕ www.rccbermuda.bm ✎ info@rccbermuda.bm. **Police, fire, ambulance** ☎ 911.
🖪 Hospitals **King Edward VII Memorial Hospital** ✉ 7 Point Finger Rd., outside Hamilton near the Botanical Gardens ☎ 441/236-2345 🖷 441/236-3691.
🖪 Pharmacies **Clarendon Pharmacy** ✉ Clarendon Bldg., Bermudiana Rd., Hamilton ☎ 441/295-9137. **Collector's Hill Apothecary** ✉ South Shore Rd. and Collector's Hill, Smith's ☎ 441/236-9878. **Hamilton Pharmacy** ✉ Parliament St., Hamilton ☎ 441/295-7004 or 441/292-7986. **Paget Pharmacy** ✉ Rural Hill Plaza, Middle Rd., Paget ☎ 441/236-2681. **Phoenix Centre** ✉ 3 Reid St., Hamilton ☎ 441/295-3838 or 441/295-0698. **Robertson's Drug Store** ✉ York St. and Customs House Sq. ☎ 441/297-1736. **White's Pharmacy** ✉ 22 Middle Rd., Warwick ☎ 441/238-1050. **Woodbourne Chemist** ✉ Gorham Rd., Pembroke, on outskirts of Hamilton ☎ 441/295-1073 or 441/295-2663.

ETIQUETTE & BEHAVIOR

Bermudians tend to be quite formal in attire as well as in personal interactions. Casual dress, including bathing suits, is acceptable at hotels and resorts, but locals seldom venture into Hamilton in anything less than long shorts and sports shirts for men, and slacks-and-blouse combinations or dresses for women. Most restaurants and clubs request that men wear jackets, and more formal establishments require ties during dinner.

In downtown Hamilton, the classic Bermuda shorts are often worn by banking and insurance executives, but the outfit always includes high black socks, dress shoes, and jacket and tie. When it comes to dress, **err on the formal side.** It is an offense in Bermuda to appear in public without a shirt, even for joggers. This rule may seem arcane, but most Bermudians appreciate this decorum. This also holds true for the beach—thong bathing suits and topless sunbathing are not acceptable.

Courtesy is the rule when locals interact among themselves. In business and social gatherings **use the more formal Mr. and Ms. instead of first names,** at least until a friendship has been established, which sometimes takes just a few minutes. Always greet bus drivers with a friendly "Good morning" or "Good afternoon" when you board public buses. This is an island custom, and it's nice to see each passenger offer a smile and sincere greeting when boarding and exiting the bus. In general, respect and appreciation are shown quite liberally to public servants in Bermuda. Although one underlying reason may be the fact that the residents of this small island seem to know one another, and personal greetings on the streets are commonplace, it also seems that a genuinely upbeat and friendly attitude is part of the national character.

GAY & LESBIAN TRAVEL

Bermuda remains socially conservative in many respects, so same-sex couples may encounter some initial uncomfortable moments. However, discriminating against anyone based on sexual orientation is against the law. The Web site www.gaybermuda.com offers information on what to do and where to go.

⚑ Gay- & Lesbian-Friendly Travel Agencies **Different Roads Travel** ✉ 8383 Wilshire Blvd., Suite 520, Beverly Hills, CA 90211 ☏ 323/651-5557 or 800/429-8747 (Ext. 14 for both) ☐ 323/651-3678 ✍ lgernert@tzell.com. **Kennedy Travel** ✉ 130 W. 42nd St., Suite 401, New York, NY 10036 ☏ 212/840-8659, 800/237-7433 ☐ 212/730-2269 ⊕ www.kennedytravel.com. **Now, Voyager** ✉ 4406 18th St., San Francisco, CA 94114 ☏ 415/626-1169 or 800/255-6951 ☐ 415/626-8626 ⊕ www.nowvoyager.com. **Skylink Travel and Tour** ✉ 1455 N. Dutton Ave., Suite A, Santa Rosa, CA 95401 ☏ 707/546-9888 or 800/225-5759 ☐ 707/636-0951; serving lesbian travelers.

HEALTH

Sunburn and sunstroke are legitimate concerns if you're traveling to Bermuda in the summer. On hot, sunny days, **wear a hat, a beach cover-up, and lots of sunblock.** These are essential for a day on a boat or at the beach. Be sure to take the same kind of precautions on overcast summer days—some of the worst cases of sunburn happen on cloudy afternoons when sunblock seems unnecessary. Drink plenty of water and, above all, **limit the amount of time you spend in the sun** until you become acclimated.

The Portuguese man-of-war occasionally visits Bermuda's waters, so **be alert when swimming,** especially in summer or whenever the water is particularly warm. This creature is recognizable by a purple, balloonlike float sack of perhaps 8 inches in diameter, below which dangle 20- to 60-inch tentacles armed with powerful stinging cells. Contact with the stinging cells causes immediate and severe pain. Seek medical attention immediately: a serious sting can send a person into shock. In the meantime—or if getting to a doctor will take a while—treat the affected area liberally with ammonia. Although usually encountered in the water, Portuguese men-of-war may also wash up on shore. If you spot one on the sand, steer clear, as the sting is just as dangerous out of the water.

DIVERS' ALERT

Do not fly within 24 hours of scuba diving.

MEDICAL PLANS

No one plans to get sick while traveling, but it happens, so **consider signing up with a medical-assistance company.** Members get doctor referrals, emergency evacuation or repatriation, hot lines for medical consultation, cash for emergencies, and other assistance.

⚑ Medical-Assistance Companies **International SOS Assistance** ⊕ www.internationalsos.com ✉ 8 Neshaminy Interplex, Suite 207, Trevose, PA 19053 ☏ 215/245-4707 or 800/523-6586 ☐ 215/244-9617

✉ Landmark House, Hammersmith Bridge Rd., 6th fl., London, W6 9DP ☎ 20/8762-8008 🖷 20/8748-7744 ✉ 12 Chemin Riantbosson, 1217 Meyrin 1, Geneva, Switzerland ☎ 22/785-6464 🖷 22/785-6424 ✉ 331 N. Bridge Rd., 17-00, Odeon Towers, Singapore 188720 ☎ 6338-7800 🖷 6338-7611.

HOLIDAYS

On Sundays and national public holidays, all shops, businesses, and many restaurants in Bermuda close. Buses and ferries run on limited schedules. Most entertainment venues, sights, and sports outfitters remain open. When holidays fall on a Saturday, government and commercial offices close the following Monday, but restaurants and shops remain open. National public holidays are New Year's Day, Good Friday, Bermuda Day (in late May), Queen's Birthday (in mid June), Emancipation Day/Somers Day (in late July), Labour Day (in early September), Remembrance Day (in early November), Christmas, and Boxing Day (Dec. 26).

INSURANCE

The most useful travel-insurance plan is a comprehensive policy that includes coverage for trip cancellation and interruption, default, trip delay, and medical expenses (with a waiver for preexisting conditions).

Without insurance you'll lose all or most of your money if you cancel your trip, regardless of the reason. Default insurance covers you if your tour operator, airline, or cruise line goes out of business. Trip-delay covers expenses that arise because of bad weather or mechanical delays. Study the fine print when comparing policies.

If you're traveling internationally, a key component of travel insurance is coverage for medical bills incurred if you get sick on the road. Such expenses aren't generally covered by Medicare or private policies. U.K. residents can buy a travel-insurance policy valid for most vacations taken during the year in which it's purchased (but check preexisting-condition coverage). British and Australian citizens need extra medical coverage when traveling overseas.

Always **buy travel policies directly from the insurance company**; if you buy them from a cruise line, airline, or tour operator that goes out of business you probably won't be covered for the agency or operator's default, a major risk. Before making any purchase, **review your existing health and home-owner's policies** to find what they cover away from home.

🔢 Travel Insurers In the U.S.: **Access America** ✉ 6600 W. Broad St., Richmond, VA 23230 ☎ 800/284-8300 🖷 804/673-1491 or 800/346-9265 ⊕ www.accessamerica.com. **Travel Guard International** ✉ 1145 Clark St., Stevens Point, WI 54481 ☎ 715/345-0505 or 800/826-1300 🖷 800/955-8785 ⊕ www.travelguard.com. 🔢 In the U.K.: **Association of British Insurers** ✉ 51 Gresham St., London EC2V 7HQ ☎ 020/7600-3333 🖷 020/7696-8999 ⊕ www.abi.org.uk. In Canada: **RBC Insurance** ✉ 6880 Financial Dr., Mississauga, Ontario L5N 7Y5 ☎ 800/565-3129 🖷 905/813-4704 ⊕ www.rbcinsurance.com. In Australia: **Insurance Council of Australia** ✉ Insurance Enquiries and Complaints, Level 3, 56 Pitt St., Sydney. NSW 2000 ☎ 1300/363683 or 02/9251-4456 🖷 02/9251-4453 ⊕ www.iecltd.com.au. In New Zealand: **Insurance Council of New Zealand** ✉ Level 7, 111-115 Customhouse Quay, Box 474, Wellington ☎ 04/472-5230 🖷 04/473-3011 ⊕ www.icnz.org.nz.

MAIL & SHIPPING

Allow 7 to 10 days for mail from Bermuda to reach the United States, Canada, or the United Kingdom and about two weeks to arrive in Australia or New Zealand.

OVERNIGHT SERVICES

Overnight courier service is available to or from the continental United States through several companies. Service between Bermuda and Canada takes one or two business days, depending on the part of Canada; between Bermuda and the United Kingdom, generally two business days; and between Bermuda and Australia or New Zealand, usually three.

In Bermuda, rates include pickup from anywhere on the island. Prices for a document up to the first pound range from $26 to $37 to the United States, from $30 to $38 to Canada, and from $35 to $42 to the United Kingdom, Australia, or New Zealand. For the fastest delivery, your pickup request must be made before about 10 AM. Note that pickups (and drop-off locations) are limited on Saturdays, and there is no service on Sunday. Also, packages sent to Bermuda may take a day longer than documents.

🔢 Major Services **DHL Worldwide Express** ☎ 441/441/295-3300. **Federal Express** ☎ 441/295-3854.

International Bonded Couriers ☎ 441/295-2467.
Mailboxes Unlimited Ltd. ☎ 441/292-6563. Sprint
International Express ☎ 441/296-7866. United
Parcel Service ☎ 441/295-2467.

POSTAL RATES

Airmail postcards and letters for the first
10 grams to the United States and Canada
cost 70¢. Postcards to the United Kingdom
cost 80¢, letters 85¢ for the first 10 grams.
Postcards to Australia and New Zealand
cost 90¢, letters 95¢ for the first 10 grams.

RECEIVING MAIL

If you have no address in Bermuda, you
can have mail sent care of General Delivery, General Post Office, Hamilton HM
GD, Bermuda.

SHIPPING PARCELS

Through Parcel Post at Bermuda's post office, you can send packages via either International Data Express (which takes
from 2 to 4 business days to the United
States and Canada and from 3 to 7 days
to the United Kingdom, Australia, and
New Zealand) or Air Parcel Post (which
takes from 7 to 10 business days to the
United States, Canada, and the United
Kingdom, or two weeks to Australia and
New Zealand).

For the first 500 grams, International Data
Express rates are $25 to the United States
and Canada, $30 to the United Kingdom,
and $38 to Australia or New Zealand. Air
Parcel Post rates run $7.65 for the first
500 grams to the United States, $9.10 to
Canada, $11.95 to the United Kingdom,
and $14.95 to Australia or New Zealand.

Most of Bermuda's largest stores offer
shipping of purchases. Some may ask you
either to buy insurance or to sign a waiver
absolving them of any responsibility for
potential loss or damage.
📶 Post Office **International Data Express** ☎ 441/
297-7802. **Parcel Post** ☎ 441/297-7875.

MEDIA

E-MAIL

If your hotel doesn't hook you up, you
may send and receive e-mail for about $12
per hour at a few places around the island,
two of which are also restaurants.
📶 E-mail Services **Freeport Seafood Restaurant**
✉ 1 Freeport Rd., Dockyard, Sandys ☎ 441/234-

1692 ✎ freeport@ibl.bm. **Internet Lane** ✉ 22
Reid St., Hamilton ☎ 441/296-9972 ⊕ www.
internetlane.net. **M. R. Onions Restaurant and
Bar** ✉ Par-La-Ville Rd., Hamilton ☎ 441/292-5012
🖴 441/292-3122 ⊕ www.bermuda.bm/onions.
Twice Told Tales Bookstore ✉ Parliament St.,
near Reid St., Hamilton ☎ 441/296-1995 🖴 441/
296-6339 ✎ pfowkes@ibl.bm.

NEWSPAPERS & MAGAZINES

The *Royal Gazette,* Bermuda's only daily
newspaper, is considered the paper of
record. Established in 1828, it is published Monday through Saturday and offers a comprehensive mix of international
hard news along with sports, business,
and features. Its weekly sister paper, the
Mid-Ocean News, is more community
oriented, with extensive coverage of local
arts, theater, politics, and overseas travel.
Published twice a week, the *Bermuda Sun*
also focuses on local politics, trends,
and events.

Appearing monthly in the *Royal Gazette,*
RG magazine is a high-quality glossy, with
topical features. *The Bermudian,* the island's oldest monthly, is another glossy,
highlighting the people, food, homes, gardens, and heritage of Bermuda.

Six times per year, both the *Bottom Line*
and *Bermudian Business* publish business
news, commentary, and analysis.

RADIO & TELEVISION

Dial Mix 106 (106.1 FM) for calypso, reggae, and soca, plus R&B, adult contemporary, local jazz, and European classical.
For country music, listen to 1450 Country
(1450 AM), which also has a midday call-
in talk show covering hot local issues.
Z2 (1340 AM) surrounds its talk shows
with Billboard Top 100 and country-and-
western tunes. You can hear more Top 100
rock, R&B, hip-hop, and reggae on Power
95 (94.9 FM). Gospel, easy listening, and
religious talk are the sounds on ZFB 1230
AM. Conservative programs can be found
on the Bible Broadcasting Network (1280
AM), an all-Christian radio station. The
Government Emergency Broadcast Station
(1610 AM) is used in case of a storm.

In addition to a slew of cable television
stations (mainly from the United States),
Bermudian sets can be tuned in to ZBM
("Zed BM"), the CBS affiliate, on TV
channel 9 or cable 3; ZFB ("Zed FB"), the

ABC affiliate, on TV channel 7 or cable 2; and VSB, the NBC affiliate, on TV channel 11 or cable 4. Along with the nightly news, local programming, which is interspersed with the networks' offerings, might include a cooking show, a cricket or football (soccer) match, or a program on health awareness.

MONEY MATTERS

Since Bermuda imports everything from cars to cardigans, prices are very high. At an upscale restaurant, for example, you're bound to pay as much for a meal as you would in New York, London, or Paris: on average, $60 to $80 per person, $120 with drinks and wine. There are other options, of course; the island is full of coffee shops, where you can eat hamburgers and french fries with locals for about $9. The same meal at a restaurant costs about $15.

A cup of coffee costs between $1.50 and $3; a mixed drink from $5 to $8; a bottle of beer from $3 to $6; and a can of soda about $1.50. A 15-minute cab ride will set you back about $25 including tip. A 36-exposure roll of 35mm 100 ASA print film costs $7 to $8. A pack of cigarettes costs between $5 and $7. Prices throughout this guide are given for adults. Substantially reduced fees are almost always available for children, students, and senior citizens. For information on taxes, *see* Taxes.

ATMS

ATMs are found all over Bermuda, in shops, arcades, supermarkets, the airport, and two of the island's banks. Both the **Bank of Bermuda** and the **Bank of Butterfield** are affiliated with the Cirrus and Plus networks. Note that both banks' ATMs only accept personal identification numbers (PIN) with 4 digits.

CREDIT CARDS

Most shops and restaurants accept credit and debit cards, but some hotels insist on cash or traveler's checks, so check in advance whether your hotel takes credit cards. The most widely accepted cards are MasterCard, Visa, and American Express. Discover and Diners Club are welcomed to a much lesser degree. Throughout this guide, the following abbreviations are used: AE, American Express; D, Discover;

DC, Diners Club; MC, MasterCard; and V, Visa. Most 800 numbers still incur a toll when dialing from Bermuda, so you may want to call your company collect.
🔢 Reporting Lost Cards **American Express** ☎ 800/441-0519. **Diners Club** ☎ 800/234-6377. **Discover** ☎ 800/347-2683. **MasterCard** ☎ 800/622-7747. **Visa** ☎ 800/847-2911.

CURRENCY

The Bermudian dollar is on par with the U.S. dollar, and the two currencies are used interchangeably. (Other non-Bermudian currency must be converted.) You can use American money anywhere, but change is often given in Bermudian currency. Try to avoid accumulating large amounts of local money, which is difficult to exchange for U.S. dollars in Bermuda and expensive to exchange in the United States.

CURRENCY EXCHANGE

If you need to exchange Canadian dollars, British pounds, or other currencies, for the most favorable rates **change money through banks**. Although ATM transaction fees may be higher abroad than at home, ATM rates are excellent because they're based on wholesale rates offered only by major banks. You won't do as well at exchange booths in airports or rail and bus stations, in hotels, in restaurants, or in stores. To avoid lines at airport exchange booths, get a bit of local currency before you leave home.
🔢 Exchange Services **International Currency Express** ✉ 427 N. Camden Dr., Suite F, Beverly Hills, CA 90210 ☎ 888/278-6628 orders 🖶 310/278-6410 🌐 www.foreignmoney.com. **Thomas Cook International Money Services** ☎ 800/287-7362 orders and retail locations 🌐 www.us.thomascook.com.

TRAVELER'S CHECKS

Traveler's checks are widely accepted throughout Bermuda. Lost or stolen, they can usually be replaced within 24 hours. To ensure a speedy refund, buy your own traveler's checks. Don't let someone else pay for them, as irregularities like this can cause delays. The person who bought the checks should make the call to request a refund.

Some hotels take personal checks by prior arrangement (a letter from your bank is sometimes requested).

MOPED & SCOOTER TRAVEL

Because car rentals are not allowed in Bermuda, you might decide to get around by moped or scooter. Bermudians routinely use the words "moped" and "scooter" interchangeably, even though they are different. You must pedal to start a moped, and it carries only one person. A scooter, on the other hand, which starts when you put the key in the ignition, is more powerful and holds one or two passengers.

Think twice before renting a moped, as accidents occur frequently and are occasionally fatal. The best ways to avoid mishaps are to drive defensively, obey the 20-mph (35-kph) speed limit, remember to **stay on the left-hand side of the road**—especially at traffic circles—and avoid riding in the rain and at night.

Helmets are required by law. Mopeds and scooters can be rented from cycle liveries by the hour, the day, or the week. The liveries will show first-time riders how to operate the vehicles. Rates vary so it is worth calling several liveries to see what they charge. Single-seat scooter rentals cost from $35 to $53 per day or from $136 to $181 per week. Some liveries tack a mandatory $20 insurance-and-repair charge on top of the bill, while others include the cost of insurance, breakdown service, pickup and delivery, and a tank of gas in quoted price. A $20 deposit may also be charged for the lock, key, and helmet. You must be at least 16 and have a valid driver's license to rent. Major hotels have their own cycle liveries, and all hotels and guest houses will make rental arrangements. Gas for cycles runs from $3 to $4 per liter, but you can cover a great deal of ground on the full tank that comes with the wheels.

ROAD CONDITIONS

Roads are narrow, winding, and full of blind curves. Whether driving cars or scooters, Bermudians tend to be quite cautious around less-experienced visiting riders, but crowded city streets make accidents all the more common. Local rush hours are Monday through Friday, from 7:30 AM to 9 AM and from 4 PM to 5:30 PM. Road are often bumpy, and they may be slippery under a morning mist or rainfall. Street lamps are few and far between outside of the cities, so be especially careful driving at night.

RULES OF THE ROAD

The speed limit is 35 kph (21 mph), except in the World Heritage Site of St. George's, where it is a mere 25 kph (about 15 mph). The limits, however, are not very well enforced, and the actual driving speed in Bermuda hovers around 50 kph (30 mph). Police seldom target tourists for parking offenses or other driving infractions. Bermuda's seat-belt law does not apply to taxis or buses. Drunk driving is a serious problem in Bermuda, despite stiff penalties. The blood-alcohol limit is 0.08. The courts will hand down a $1,000 fine for a driving-while-intoxicated infraction, and also take the driver off the road for about one year.

⑦ Rental Companies Eve's Cycle Livery ⊠ Middle Rd., Paget ☎ 441/236-6247. **Oleander Cycles** ⊠ Valley Rd., Paget ☎ 441/236-5235 ⊠ Gorham Rd., Hamilton ☎ 441/295-0919 ⊠ Middle Rd., Southampton ☎ 441/234-0629 ⊠ Dockyard, Sandys ☎ 441/234-2764. **Wheels Cycles** ⊠ 117 Front St., Hamilton ☎ 441/292-2245.

PACKING

Bermudians dress more formally than most Americans. **Leave your cutoffs, short shorts, and halter tops at home.** In the evening, many restaurants and hotel dining rooms require men to wear a jacket and tie and women to dress comparably, so bring a few dressy outfits. Some hotels have begun setting aside one or two nights a week for "smart casual" attire, when jacket-and-tie restrictions are loosened. In this case, women should be fine with slacks or a skirt and a dressy blouse or sweater. Bermudian men often wear Bermuda shorts (and proper kneesocks) with a jacket and tie.

During the cooler months, bring lightweight woolens or cottons that you can wear in layers to accommodate vagaries of the weather. A lightweight jacket is always a good idea. Regardless of the season, **pack a swimsuit, a beach-wear cover-up, sunscreen, and sunglasses,** as well as a raincoat (umbrellas are typically provided by hotels). Comfortable walking shoes are a must. If you plan to play tennis, be aware that many courts require proper whites and that tennis balls in

Bermuda are extremely expensive. Bring your own tennis balls if possible.

In your carry-on luggage, **pack an extra pair of eyeglasses or contact lenses and enough of any medication** you take to last a few days longer than the entire trip. You may also ask your doctor to write a spare prescription using the drug's generic name, as brand names may vary from country to country. In luggage to be checked, **never pack prescription drugs, valuables, or undeveloped film.** And don't forget to carry with you the addresses of offices that handle refunds of lost traveler's checks. Check *Fodor's How to Pack* (available at on-line retailers and bookstores everywhere) for more tips.

To avoid customs and security delays, carry medications in their original packaging. Don't pack any sharp objects in your carry-on luggage, including knives of any size or material, scissors, and corkscrews, or anything else that might arouse suspicion.

To avoid having your checked luggage chosen for hand inspection, don't cram bags full. The U.S. Transportation Security Administration suggests packing shoes on top and placing personal items you don't want touched in clear plastic bags.

CHECKING LUGGAGE

In Bermuda you board and deplane via a staircase. Let this be your guide when deciding how much to carry on.

You're allowed to carry aboard one bag and one personal article, such as a purse or a laptop computer. Make sure what you carry on fits under your seat or in the overhead bin. Get to the gate early, so you can board as soon as possible, before the overhead bins fill up.

Baggage allowances vary by carrier, destination, and ticket class. On international flights, you're usually allowed to check two bags weighing up to 70 pounds (32 kilograms) each, although a few airlines allow checked bags of up to 88 pounds (40 kilograms) in first class. Some international carriers don't allow more than 66 pounds (30 kilograms) per bag in business class and 44 pounds (20 kilograms) in economy. On domestic flights, the limit is usually 50 to 70 pounds (23 to 32 kilograms) per bag. In general, carry-on bags

shouldn't exceed 40 pounds (18 kilograms). Most airlines won't accept bags that weigh more than 100 pounds (45 kilograms) on domestic or international flights. Check baggage restrictions with your carrier before you pack.

Airline liability for baggage is limited to $2,500 per person on flights within the United States. On international flights it amounts to $9.07 per pound or $20 per kilogram for checked baggage (roughly $640 per 70-pound bag), with a maximum of $634.90 per piece, and $400 per passenger for unchecked baggage. You can buy additional coverage at check-in for about $10 per $1,000 of coverage, but it often excludes a rather extensive list of items, shown on your airline ticket.

Before departure, **itemize your bags' contents** and their worth, and label the bags with your name, address, and phone number. (If you use your home address, cover it so potential thieves can't see it readily.) Include a label inside each bag and **pack a copy of your itinerary.** At check-in, **make sure each bag is correctly tagged** with the destination airport's three-letter code. Because some checked bags will be opened for hand inspection, the U.S. Transportation Security Administration recommends that you leave luggage unlocked or use the plastic locks offered at check-in. TSA screeners place an inspection notice inside searched bags, which are re-sealed with a special lock.

If your bag has been searched and contents are missing or damaged, file a claim with the TSA Consumer Response Center as soon as possible. If your bags arrive damaged or fail to arrive at all, file a written report with the airline before leaving the airport.

Bermuda-bound airlines commonly accept golf club bags in lieu of a piece of luggage, but there are fairly stringent guidelines governing the maximum amount of equipment that can be transported without an excess baggage fee. The general rule of thumb is one covered bag containing a maximum of 14 clubs, 12 balls, and one pair of shoes.

🚩 Complaints **U.S. Transportation Security Administration Consumer Response Center** ☎ 866/ 289-9673 ⊕ www.tsa.gov.

PASSPORTS & VISAS

When traveling internationally, **carry your passport**, even if you don't need one (it's always the best form of ID), and **make two photocopies of the data page** (one for someone at home and another for you, carried separately from your passport). If you lose your passport, promptly call the nearest embassy or consulate and the local police.

U.S. passport applications for children under age 14 require consent from both parents or legal guardians; both parents must appear together to sign the application. If only one parent appears, he or she must submit a written statement from the other parent authorizing passport issuance for the child. A parent with sole authority must present evidence of it when applying; acceptable documentation includes the child's certified birth certificate listing only the applying parent, a court order specifically permitting this parent's travel with the child, or a death certificate for the nonapplying parent. Application forms and instructions are available on the Web site of the U.S. State Department's Bureau of Consular Affairs (⊕ www.travel.state.gov).

ENTERING BERMUDA

Citizens of the United State or Canada should **bring a passport to ensure quick passage through immigration and customs.** You do not need a passport to enter Bermuda if you plan to stay less than six months, but you must have onward or return tickets and proof of identity, such as an original or certified copy of your birth certificate with raised seal, or another certificate of citizenship (Naturalization Certificate, Alien Registration Card, or a Reentry Permit), and a photo ID.

Citizens of the United Kingdom and other countries must have a valid passport to enter Bermuda.

PASSPORT OFFICES

The best time to apply for a passport or to renew is in fall and winter. Before any trip, check your passport's expiration date, and, if necessary, renew it as soon as possible.
▪ Australian Citizens **Passports Australia** ☎ 131-232 ⊕ www.passports.gov.au.
▪ Canadian Citizens **Passport Office** ✉ to mail in applications: 200 Promenade du Portage, Hull,

Québec J8X 4B7 ☎ 819/994-3500, 800/567-6868, 866/255-7655 TTY ⊕ www.ppt.gc.ca.
▪ New Zealand Citizens **New Zealand Passports Office** ☎ 0800/22-5050 or 04/474-8100 ⊕ www.passports.govt.nz.
▪ U.K. Citizens **U.K. Passport Service** ☎ 0870/521-0410 ⊕ www.passport.gov.uk.
▪ U.S. Citizens **National Passport Information Center** ☎ 900/225-5674 or 900/225-7778 TTY (calls are 55¢ per minute for automated service or $1.50 per minute for operator service); 888/362-8668 or 888/498-3648 TTY (calls are $5.50 each) ⊕ www.travel.state.gov.

SAFETY

Don't wear a money belt or a waist pack, both of which peg you as a tourist. Distribute your cash and any valuables (including your credit cards and passport) between a deep front pocket, an inside jacket or vest pocket, and a hidden money pouch. Do not reach for the money pouch once you're in public.

Bermuda is a small affluent country and as a consequence has a low crime rate. Serious crimes against visitors—or anyone, for that matter—are rare. Still, **exercise the usual precautions with wallets, purses, cameras,** and other valuables, particularly at the beach. If you are driving a bike, always travel with your purse or bag concealed inside the seat. Always lock your moped or pedal bike, and store valuables in your room or hotel safe. Although an ocean breeze through a screen door is wonderful, **close and lock your hotel room's glass patio door** while you're sleeping or out of your room. After sunset, stick to the main streets in Hamilton and St. George's. Court Street in Hamilton is a little rough even in the daytime. Use common-sense precautions as you would in any unfamiliar environment, and be alert while walking at night.

SENIOR-CITIZEN TRAVEL

Special rates are available for seniors traveling on Bermuda's public ferries and buses, and some pharmacies and department stores offer discount days for seniors.

To qualify for age-related discounts, **mention your senior-citizen status up front** when booking hotel reservations (not when checking out) and before you're seated in restaurants (not when paying the bill). Be sure to have identification on hand. When renting a car, ask about promotional car-rental discounts, which can be cheaper than senior-citizen rates.

⚏ **Educational Programs Elderhostel** ✉ 11 Ave. de Lafayette, Boston, MA 02111-1746 ☎ 877/426-8056; 978/323-4141 international callers; 877/426-2167 TTY 🖶 877/426-2166 ⊕ www.elderhostel.org.

STUDENTS IN BERMUDA

There are no youth hostels, YMCAs, or YWCAs on the island. During Bermuda Spring Break Sports Week, however, special student rates are offered at some hotels and guest houses, restaurants, pubs, and nightclubs.

⚏ **IDs & Services STA Travel** ✉ 10 Downing St., New York, NY 10014 ☎ 212/627-3111, 800/777-0112 24-hr service center 🖶 212/627-3387 ⊕ www.sta.com. **Travel Cuts** ✉ 187 College St., Toronto, Ontario M5T 1P7, Canada ☎ 800/592-2887 in the U.S., 416/979-2406 or 866/246-9762 in Canada 🖶 416/979-8167 ⊕ www.travelcuts.com.

TAXES

Hotels add a 7.25% government tax to the bill, and most add a 10% service charge or a per diem dollar equivalent in lieu of tips. Other extra charges sometimes include a 5% "energy surcharge" (at small guest houses) and a 15% service charge (at most restaurants).

A $29 airport departure tax and a $4.25 airport security fee are built into the price of your ticket, while cruise lines collect $60 in advance for each passenger.

TAXIS

Taxis are the fastest and easiest way around the island—and also the most costly. Four-seater taxis charge $4.80 for the first mile and $1.68 for each subsequent mile. Between midnight and 6 AM, and on Sunday and holidays, a 25% surcharge is added to the fare. There is a 25¢ charge for each piece of luggage stored in the trunk or on the roof. Taxi drivers accept only American or Bermudian cash, but not bills larger than $50, and they expect a 15% tip. You can phone for taxi pick-up, but you may wait awhile while the cab navigates through Bermuda's heavy traffic. Don't hesitate to hail a taxi on the street.

For a personalized taxi tour of the island, the minimum duration is three hours, at $30 per hour for one to four people and $42 an hour for five or six, excluding tip.

⚏ **Cab Companies The Bermuda Industrial Union Taxi Co-op** ☎ 441/292-4476. **Island Wide Taxi Services** ☎ 441/292-5600. **Bermuda Taxi Radio Cabs** ☎ 441/295-4141; 441/295-0041 to arrange taxi tours. **Sandys Taxi Service** ☎ 441/234-2344.

TELEPHONES

Telephone service in Bermuda is organized and efficient, though service may be interrupted during storms.

AREA & COUNTRY CODES

The country code for Bermuda is 441. When dialing a Bermuda number from the United States or Canada, simply dial 1 + 441 + local number. You do not need to dial the international access code (011). The country code is 1 for the United States and Canada, 61 for Australia, 64 for New Zealand, and 44 for the United Kingdom.

CELL PHONES

Most travelers can use their own cell phones in Bermuda, though you should check with your provider to be sure. Cell phone rentals are available from stores in Hamilton and St. George's.

⚏ **Rentals All Talk** ✉ 27 York St., town of St. George's ☎ 441/297-3151 **BermudaCellRentals.com** ✉ The Armoury Bldg., 37 Reid St., Hamilton ☎ 441/232-2355 **Internet Lane** ✉ The Walkway, 22 Reid St., Hamilton ☎ 441/296-9972

DIRECTORY & OPERATOR ASSISTANCE

When in Bermuda, call ☎ 411 for local phone numbers. To reach directory assistance from outside the country, call ☎ 441/555-1212.

INTERNATIONAL CALLS

Most hotels impose a surcharge for long-distance calls, even those made collect or with a phone card or credit card. Many toll-free 800 or 888 numbers in the United States aren't honored in Bermuda. Consider buying a prepaid local phone card rather than using your own calling card. In many small guest houses and apartments the phone in your room is a private line from which you can make only collect, credit-card, or local calls. Some small hotels have a telephone room or kiosk where you can make long-distance calls.

You'll find specially marked AT&T USADirect phones at the airport, the cruise-ship dock in Hamilton, and King's Square and Ordnance Island in St. George's. You can also make international calls with a calling card from the main post office. You can make prepaid international calls from the Cable & Wireless Office, which also has international telex, cable, and fax services Monday through Saturday from 9 to 5.

To call the United States, Canada, and most Caribbean countries, simply dial 1 (or 0 if you need an operator's assistance), then the area code and the number. For all other countries, dial 011 (or 0 for an operator), the country code, the area code, and the number. Using an operator for an overseas call is more expensive than dialing direct. For calls to the United States, rates are highest from 8 AM to 6 PM and discounted from 6 PM to 8 AM and on weekends.

🔁 **To Obtain Access Codes AT&T USADirect** ☎ 800/872-2881. **MCI Call USA** ☎ 800/888-8000 or 800/888-8888. **Sprint Express** ☎ 800/623-0877. 🔁 **International Calls Main post office** ✉ Church and Parliament Sts., Hamilton ☎ 441/295-5151. **Cable & Wireless Office** ✉ 20 Church St., opposite City Hall, Hamilton ☎ 441/297-7000

LOCAL CALLS

To make a local call, simply dial the seven-digit number.

LONG-DISTANCE SERVICES

AT&T, MCI, and Sprint access codes make calling long-distance relatively convenient, but you may find the local access number blocked in many hotel rooms. First ask the hotel operator to connect you. If the hotel operator balks, ask for an international operator, or dial the international operator yourself. One way to improve your odds of getting connected to your long-distance carrier is to travel with more than one company's calling card (a hotel may block Sprint, for example, but not MCI). If all else fails, call from a pay phone.

🔁 **Access Codes AT&T Direct** ☎ 800/872-2881. **MCI WorldPhone** ☎ 800/888-8000. **Sprint International Access** ☎ 800/623-0877.

PHONE CARDS

Buy a prepaid a phone card for long distance calls. They can be used with any touch-tone phone in Bermuda, although they can only be used for calls outside Bermuda. Rates are often significantly lower than dialing direct, but the down side is that some hotels will charge you for making the call to your card's 800 number. Phone cards are available at pharmacies, shops, and restaurants. The phone companies Cable & Wireless, TeleBermuda, and Logic Communications sell prepaid calling cards in denominations of $5 up to $50. The cards can be used around the world as well as in Bermuda.

🔁 **Phone Card Companies Cable & Wireless** ☎ 441/297-7022. **Logic Communications** ☎ 441/296-9600. **TeleBermuda** ☎ 441/296-9000.

PUBLIC PHONES

You'll find pay phones similar to those in the United States on the streets of Hamilton, St. George's, and Somerset as well as at ferry landings, some bus stops, and public beaches. Deposit 20¢ (U.S. or Bermudian) before you dial. Most hotels charge from 20¢ to $1 for local calls.

TIME

Bermuda is in the Atlantic Time Zone. Bermuda observes Daylight Saving Time (from the first Sunday in April to the last Sunday in October), so it's always one hour ahead of U.S. Eastern Standard Time. Thus, for instance, when it is 5 PM in Bermuda, it is 4 PM in New York, 3 PM in Chicago, and 1 PM in Los Angeles. London is four hours, and Sydney 14 hours, ahead of Bermuda.

TIPPING

A service charge of 10% (or an equivalent per diem amount), which covers everything from baggage handling to maid service, is added to your hotel bill. Most restaurants tack on a 15% service charge; if not, a 15% tip is customary (more for exceptional service). Porters at the airport expect about a dollar a bag, while taxi drivers usually receive 15% of the fare. Tip bartenders and hairdressers 15% to 20%, if the charge is not already included on your bill. It's customary to tip the person who bags your groceries $1 or $2 for their efforts. For a small purchase, spare change is fine. Although tipping is not expected for tour and museum guides, a few dollars in thanks for a job well done is always appreciated.

TOURING

GARDEN & WILDLIFE TOURS

Free 75-minute guided tours of the Botanical Gardens depart from the visitor center Tuesday, Wednesday, and Friday at 10:30 AM. You can tour the Premier's official residence in the gardens Tuesday and Friday at 2 PM.

In the 1960s, passionate environmentalist David Wingate began restoring the uninhabited Nonsuch Island to its 17th-century glory. Today the 15-acre nature reserve, which lies northeast of Bermuda, is a living museum of the original flora and fauna encountered in Bermuda by the first settlers. On the Nonsuch Island Field Trip, you can learn about the ecological relationships of Bermuda's various indigenous wildlife. Tours, lasting 4 hours and costing $75 per person, depart from the Bermuda Biological Station for Research (BBSR) every Thursday at 9 AM, returning at 1:30 PM. Ordnance Island in St. George's is the second pick up point with departures at 9:15 AM and returns at 1:15 PM. All proceeds will help support environmental research and educational programs at BBSR.

In spring, the Garden Club of Bermuda arranges tours ($15) to three different houses each Wednesday afternoon from 1 to 4.

The enjoyable walking tours organized by Native Adventures allow you to experience Bermuda's natural beauty and remote corners through the eyes of professional photographer, Tamell Simons. He leads 2½- and 5-hour tours that include transportation, and cost $65 and $100, respectively.
⏵ Botanical Gardens ☎ 441/236-5291 or 441/236-4201. **Nonsuch Island Field Trip** Bermuda Biological Institute, ✉ 17 Biological La., Ferry Reach, St. George's Parish ☎ 441/297-1880. **Garden Club of Bermuda** ☎ 441/295-1480. **Native Adventures** ☎ 441/295-2957.

HISTORICAL & SOCIAL TOURS

The Bermuda Department of Tourism publishes brochures with self-guided tours of Hamilton, St. George's, the West End, and the Railway Trail. Available free at all Visitor Service Bureaus and at hotels and guest houses, the brochures also contain detailed directions for walkers and cyclists as well as historical notes and anecdotes. The BDT also coordinates walking tours of Hamilton, St. George's, Spittal Pond Nature Reserve, the Royal Naval Dockyard, and Somerset. The tours of Hamilton and St. George's, as well as most of the Royal Naval Dockyard tours, take in historic buildings, while the Spittal Pond and Somerset tours focus on the island's flora.

Out & About Bermuda leads walking tours through some of Bermuda's most scenic nature reserves, parks, residential neighborhoods, and historic areas. The tours are conducted for 2 to 6 people and cost $20 per person or $30 per couple.

Tim Rogers Tours are run by a witty British transplant who has lived on Bermuda for more than a decade. Rogers leads exceptional walks (and seated talks) about various Bermuda topics that other historians or guides sticking to their textbooks may be hesitant to relay. His humorous and conversational tours yield intriguing historical material on piracy, local ghosts and lore, and the island's more interesting architectural motifs. A 90-minute walking tour costs $65 per couple and $10 extra for each additional person. Special group rates are also available.

The Walking Club of Bermuda is an exercise club that provides visitors with a social opportunity to meet Bermudians while seeing the island. Walks are of varied length and refreshments included in the fee are served afterward. A $20 yearly membership fee is required for regulars, but donations are welcome for non-members at the beginning of the walk.
⏵ Bermuda Department of Tourism (BDT) ☎ 441/292-0023 ⏷ www.bermudatourism.com. **Out & About Bermuda** ☎ 441/295-2595 ⏷ www.bermudashorts.bm/outandabout. **Tim Rogers Tours** ☎ 441/234-4082 🖷 441/238-2773. **The Walking Club of Bermuda** Laura Gorham ☎ 441/236-6034 ✉ ltgorham@ibl.bm ⏷ www.walk.free.bm.

HORSE-DRAWN CARRIAGE TOURS

You can hire carriages on Front Street in Hamilton—a Bermuda tradition among the just-married. Rates for a one- or two-horse carriage for up to four passengers are $30 for 30 minutes. Each adult is charged an additional $5 per half hour when more than five people ride in one carriage.

TAXI & MINIBUS TOURS

For an independent tour of Bermuda, a taxi is a good but more expensive alternative to a group tour. A blue flag on the hood of a cab indicates that the driver is a qualified tour guide. These cabs can be difficult to find, but most of their drivers are friendly, entertaining—they sometimes bend the truth for a good yarn—and well informed about the island and its history. Ask your hotel to arrange a tour with a knowledgeable driver.

Cabs seat four or six, and the legal rate for island tours (minimum three hours) is $30 per hour for one to four passengers and $42 per hour for five or six passengers. Two children under 12 equal an adult.
▤ Taxi & Minibus Tour Operators **Bee-Line Transport Ltd.** ☐ Box HM 2270, Hamilton HM ☎ 441/293-0303 ⅏ 441/293-8015. **Bermuda Hosts Ltd.** ☐ Box CR 46, Crawl, Hamilton CR ☎ 441/293-1334 ⅏ 441/293-1335. **Destination Bermuda Ltd.** ☐ Box HM 1822, Hamilton HM HX ☎ 441/292-2325 ⅏ 441/292-2252. **Radio Taxis** ☐ Box HM 2252 Hamilton HM ☎ 441/295-0041 ⅏ 441/295-3988.

TOURS & PACKAGES

Because everything is prearranged on a prepackaged tour or independent vacation, you spend less time planning—and often get it all at a good price.

BOOKING WITH AN AGENT

Travel agents are excellent resources. But it's a good idea to collect brochures from several agencies, as some agents' suggestions may be influenced by relationships with tour and package firms that reward them for volume sales. If you have a special interest, **find an agent with expertise in that area**; the American Society of Travel Agents (ASTA; ⇨ Travel Agencies) has a database of specialists worldwide. You can log on to the group's Web site to find an ASTA travel agent in your neighborhood.

Make sure your travel agent knows the accommodations and other services of the place being recommended. Ask about the hotel's location, room size, beds, and whether it has a pool, room service, or programs for children, if you care about these. Has your agent been there in person or sent others whom you can contact?

Do some homework on your own, too: local tourism boards can provide information about lesser-known and small-niche operators, some of which may sell only direct.

BUYER BEWARE

Each year consumers are stranded or lose their money when tour operators—even large ones with excellent reputations—go out of business. So **check out the operator.** Ask several travel agents about its reputation, and try to **book with a company that has a consumer-protection program.** (Look for information in the company's brochure.) In the United States, members of the National Tour Association and the United States Tour Operators Association are required to set aside funds to cover payments and travel arrangements in the event that the company defaults. It's also a good idea to choose a company that participates in the American Society of Travel Agents' Tour Operator Program; ASTA will act as mediator in any disputes between you and your tour operator.

Remember that the more your package or tour includes, the better you can predict the ultimate cost of your vacation. Make sure you know exactly what is covered, and **beware of hidden costs.** Are taxes, tips, and transfers included? Entertainment and excursions? These can add up.
▤ Tour-Operator Recommendations **American Society of Travel Agents** (⇨ Travel Agencies). **National Tour Association (NTA)** ✉ 546 E. Main St., Lexington, KY 40508 ☎ 859/226-4444 or 800/682-8886 ⅏ 859/226-4404 ⊕ www.ntaonline.com. **United States Tour Operators Association (USTOA)** ✉ 275 Madison Ave., Suite 2014, New York, NY 10016 ☎ 212/599-6599 ⅏ 212/599-6744 ⊕ www.ustoa.com.

TRANSPORTATION AROUND BERMUDA

Despite its small size, Bermuda does pose some transportation problems. Because rental cars are not allowed, you'll have to travel by bus, taxi, ferry, moped, bike, or horse-drawn carriage, or on foot. More than 1,200 mi of narrow, winding roads and a 20-mph speed limit make moving around the island a time-consuming process. Mopeds (⇨ Moped & Scooter Travel) are a somewhat stressful and dangerous way to travel. Ferries (⇨ Ferry Travel), on the other hand, offer clean, relaxing jaunts and are an inexpensive way to see the island from the water. Traveling the length of this long, skinny island by bus (⇨ Bus Travel) takes a long time. The trip from St. George's to Hamilton takes an hour, and the journey onward to the West End takes another hour, though an express bus from Hamilton to the West End takes only 40 minutes. Hiring a taxi (⇨ Taxis) can cut down the amount of time you spend on the road, but it costs significantly more. Fortunately, Hamilton, St. George's, and Somerset are all manageable on foot.

TRAVEL AGENCIES

A good travel agent puts your needs first. Look for an agency that has been in business at least five years, emphasizes customer service, and has someone on staff who specializes in your destination. In addition, **make sure the agency belongs to a professional trade organization.** The American Society of Travel Agents (ASTA)—the largest and most influential in the field with more than 20,000 members in some 140 countries—maintains and enforces a strict code of ethics and will step in to help mediate any agent-client disputes involving ASTA members if necessary. ASTA (whose motto is "Without a travel agent, you're on your own") also maintains a Web site that includes a directory of agents. (If a travel agency is also acting as your tour operator, see Buyer Beware in Tours and Packages.)

⁊ Local Agent Referrals American Society of Travel Agents (ASTA) ✉ 1101 King St., Suite 200, Alexandria, VA 22314 ☎ 703/739-2782; 800/965-2782 24-hr hot line ⎙ 703/739-3268 ⊕ www. astanet.com. **Association of British Travel Agents** ✉ 68-71 Newman St., London W1T 3AH ☎ 020/7637-2444 ⎙ 020/7637-0713 ⊕ www.abta.com. **Association of Canadian Travel Agencies** ✉ 130 Albert St., Suite 1705, Ottawa, Ontario K1P 5G4 ☎ 613/237-3657 ⎙ 613/237-7052 ⊕ www.acta.ca. **Australian Federation of Travel Agents** ✉ Level 3, 309 Pitt St., Sydney, NSW 2000 ☎ 02/9264-3299 ⎙ 02/9264-1085 ⊕ www.afta.com.au. **Travel Agents' Association of New Zealand** ✉ Level 5, Tourism and Travel House, 79 Boulcott St., Box 1888, Wellington 6001 ☎ 04/499-0104 ⎙ 04/499-0786 ⊕ www. taanz.org.nz.

VISITOR INFORMATION

Learn more about foreign destinations by checking government-issued travel advisories and country information. For a broader picture, consider information from more than one country.

⁊ In Bermuda Bermuda Department of Tourism ✉ Global House, 43 Church St., Hamilton ☎ 441/292-0023 ✉ ferry terminal, Front St., Hamilton ☎ 441/295-1480 ✉ King's Sq., St. George's ☎ 441/297-1642 ⊕ www.bermudatourism.com. **St. George's Foundation** ✉ Stewart Hall, 5 Queen St., St. George's ☎ 441/297-8043 ⊕ www.stgeorgesfoundation.com ⊕ www. bermudaworldheritage.com.

⁊ In Canada Bermuda Department of Tourism ✉ 1200 Bay St., Suite 1004, Toronto, Ontario M5R 2A5 ☎ 416/923-9600 ⎙ 416/923-4840.

⁊ In the U.K. Bermuda Department of Tourism ✉ BCB Ltd., 1 Battersea Church Rd., London SW11 3LY ☎ 020/7771-7001 ⎙ 020/7771-7037.

⁊ In the U.S. Bermuda Department of Tourism ✉ 205 E. 42nd St., 16th fl., New York, NY 10017 ☎ 800/223-6106 ⎙ 212/983-5289.

⁊ Government Advisories U.S. Department of State ✉ Overseas Citizens Services Office, Room 4811, 2201 C St. NW, Washington, DC 20520 ☎ 202/647-5225 interactive hot line; 888/407-4747 ⊕ www.travel.state.gov; enclose a cover letter with your request and a business-size SASE. **Consular Affairs Bureau of Canada** ☎ 800/267-6788 or 613/944-6788 ⊕ www.voyage.gc.ca. **U.K. Foreign and Commonwealth Office** ✉ Travel Advice Unit, Consular Division, Old Admiralty Building, London SW1A 2PA ☎ 020/7008-0232 or 020/7008-0233 ⊕ www. fco.gov.uk/travel. **Australian Department of Foreign Affairs and Trade** ☎ 02/6261-1299 Consular Travel Advice Faxback Service ⊕ www.dfat.gov.au. **New Zealand Ministry of Foreign Affairs and Trade** ☎ 04/439-8000 ⊕ www.mft.govt.nz.

WEB SITES

Do check out the World Wide Web when planning your trip. You'll find everything from weather forecasts to virtual tours of famous cities. Be sure to **visit Fodors.com** (⊕ www.fodors.com), a complete travel-planning site. You can research prices and book plane tickets, hotel rooms, rental cars, vacation packages, and more. In addition, you can post your pressing questions in the Travel Talk section. Other planning tools include a currency converter and weather reports, and there are loads of links to travel resources.

One of the best Bermuda sites is ⊕ www. bermuda-online.org. It's supported by the *Royal Gazette* and has information on every aspect of Bermuda from local history to transportation. The Department of Tourism's Web page at ⊕ www. bermudatourism.com is good for vacation-planning. A popular site is ⊕ www. bermuda.com—it has a good search engine and links to a number of Bermuda-related Web pages. Another good site is the Bermuda Hotel Association's ⊕ www. experience-bermuda.com. Its monthly events calendar has a search function that allows users to find events by date or type. There is also a good selection of maps and details on numerous attractions. Gay visitors to Bermuda might find www. gaybermuda.com useful for finding gay-friendly hotels and nightlife venues. BlackandCoke.com is an online guide to entertainment events in Bermuda, with a complete listing of the island's bars, clubs, and pubs.

CRUISING TO BERMUDA

FODOR'S CHOICE
Celebrity Cruises
Silversea Cruises

HIGHLY RECOMMENDED
Norwegian Cruise Lines
Seven Seas Cruises

Updated by
Sandra Davis-
Taylor

BERMUDA IS ONLY A TWO-HOUR FLIGHT from most East Coast cities, but nothing quite compares with sailing up to this crown colony. Most ships make seven-night loops from New York, with three nights at sea and four tied up in port. Three Bermuda harbors serve cruise ships: Hamilton (the capital), St. George's, and King's Wharf at the Royal Naval Dockyard.

Ships generally call in Bermuda during the week and sail to and from the island on the weekends, with the exception of the *Seven Seas Navigator* and occasionally one of Silversea Cruises' ships. While in Bermuda the ships act as a hotel. Some ships may call at only one port city, such as the capital Hamilton, while others may split their time between Hamilton and St. George's or the Dockyard in the West End. In any case, you'll have access to the entire island by taxi, moped, or shore excursion. Departure points for Bermuda cruises run the length of the Eastern Seaboard, including Baltimore, Boston, Cape Canaveral, Fort Lauderdale, Miami, New York, and Philadelphia. Special departures are sometimes scheduled from other Mid-Atlantic ports, so check with the cruise line or your travel agent. The Bermuda cruise season runs from April through October.

CHOOSING A CRUISE

Your choice of cruise line to Bermuda is made a bit easier by the government's limitation of nine ships to the island. Although most ships to Bermuda are big, floating-resort type vessels, each has its own personality depending on amenities, theme, and, of course, passengers.

Your cruise experience will be shaped by several factors. To determine whether a particular ship's style will suit you, you need to do a bit of research: Is there a full program of organized activities each day? What happens in the evening? What kind of entertainment is offered after dark? How often will you need to dress up for dinner?

Space and passenger-to-crew ratios are equally important. The latter indicates the number of passengers served by each crew member—the lower the ratio, the better the level of service. The space ratio (the gross tonnage of a ship divided by its passenger capacity) allows you to compare ships' roominess. The higher the ratio, the more spacious the vessel feels: at 40:1 or higher a ship will feel quite roomy. Less than 25:1 will cramp anyone's style.

Cost

For one all-inclusive price, a cruise gives you what many call the trip of a lifetime. The only extras are tips, shore excursions, shopping, bar bills, and other incidentals.

The per diem—the average daily price per passenger, based on double occupancy—will vary dramatically and is subject to discounting. The cost of a cruise on a luxury line like Seven Seas Cruises may be five or more times the cost of a cruise on a mainstream line such as Carnival. When you cruise will also affect your costs: published brochure rates are usually highest during the peak season. However, you can reduce this cost in several ways. If you shop around and book early you will undoubtedly pay less. If you take a cruise during the off-season, especially during hurricane season (October), you will generally pay less. Sometimes you can buy a last-minute cruise at substantial savings if the ship hasn't booked all its cabins. Frequent cruisers also get discounts from their preferred cruise lines.

When booking your cruise, consider any extra expenditures, such as airfare to the port city. Only the most expensive cruises include airfare, but virtually all cruise lines offer air add-ons, which may be less expensive than the current lowest airline fare. Shore excursions in Bermuda begin at less than $35 for the cheapest one-hour city tour. Most snorkeling and diving trips cost $40 for adults and $25 for children. On-board incidentals, including drinks (both alcoholic and non-alcoholic), activity fees (you pay to use that onboard climbing wall), use of special restaurants, spa services, and even cappucinos, will add many extras onto your shipboard account. And don't forget to budget in a little shopping, whether you intend to buy inexpensive souvenirs or pricey duty-free luxuries.

Tipping is another extra. At the end of the cruise, it's customary to tip your room steward, server, and the person who buses your table. You should expect to pay an average of $7.50 to $11 per person per day in tips. Some lines are moving away from the traditional method of tipping. Norwegian Cruise Lines, for example, gives you the option of adding a flat $10 per day to your onboard account to cover tips; Seven Seas Cruises has tipping-optional policies, though most passengers tip anyway. Each ship offers guidelines.

Accommodations

Cabin Size

The term "stateroom," used on some ships, is usually interchangeable with "cabin." Price is directly proportional to size and location, and most cabins are tiny. The higher you go in the ship, the larger the quarters tend to be; outside cabins (those with windows) are generally bigger than inside ones (no windows).

Suites are the roomiest and best-equipped accommodations, but they may differ in size, facilities, and price even on the same ship. Steward service may be more attentive to passengers staying in suites; top suites on some ships are even assigned private butlers. Most suites have a sitting area with sofa and chairs, and some have two bathrooms, occasionally with a whirlpool bath. The most expensive suites may be priced without regard to the number of passengers occupying them.

Location

Today's cruise ships have stabilizers that make seasickness mostly a problem of the past. However, if you are very susceptible to motion sickness, try to book a cabin amidship, close to the middle of the ship. The bow (front) and stern (back) pitch up and down on the waves far more than the hull amidships (middle). Ships also experience a side-to-side motion known as roll. The closer your deck is to the true center of the ship—which is halfway between the bottom of the hull and the highest deck and midway between the bow and the stern—the less you will feel the ship's movement. Some cruise lines charge more for cabins amidships; most charge more for higher decks.

Outside cabins have portholes or windows (which cannot be opened). Upper-deck views from outside cabins may be partially obstructed by lifeboats or overlook a public promenade. Because outside cabins are more desirable, newer ships are configured with only or mostly outside cabins; outside cabins on upper decks are increasingly being built with private verandas. Cabins that overlook a public promenade have mirrored windows, so that passersby can't see in by day; after dark, you'll need to draw your curtains.

Inside cabins on older vessels are often smaller and oddly shaped. On newer ships, the floor plans of inside cabins are virtually identical to those of outside cabins. As long as you don't feel claustrophobic without a window—and most cruise lines hang curtains on the wall to create the illusion—inside cabins are generally an excellent value.

Cruise brochures in print and online show a ship's layout deck by deck, and include the approximate location and shape of every cabin and suite. Use the deck plan to make sure the cabin you choose is not near public rooms or the ship's engine, both of which can be noisy; and make sure that you're close to stairs or an elevator if you want to avoid walking down a long corridor every time you return to your cabin. If you can access detailed layouts of typical cabins, you can determine what kind of beds each cabin has, whether it has a window or a porthole, and what furnishings are provided.

Sharing

Most cabins are designed to accommodate two people. When more than two share a cabin, the third and fourth passengers are usually offered a substantial discount, thereby lowering the per-person price for the room for the entire group. An additional discount is sometimes offered when children share a cabin with their parents. There's usually a premium on smaller, one-person cabins—when you can find them. When none is available, as is frequently the case, passengers traveling on their own must pay a single supplement, which usually ranges from 125% to 200% of the double-occupancy per-person rate. On request, many cruise lines will find same-sex roommates for singles; each then pays the per-person, double-occupancy rate.

THE BERMUDA CRUISE FLEET

To avoid overcrowding, the Bermudian government limits the number of regular cruise-ship visits to the island. Cruise lines with weekly sailings are Carnival Cruise Lines, Celebrity Cruises, Norwegian Cruise Line, Seven Seas Cruises, and Royal Caribbean International. Silversea Cruises travels to Bermuda from New York City less frequently.

Mainstream Cruise Lines

Generally speaking, the mainstream lines have two sizes of ships—cruise liner and megaship—in their fleets. Cruise liners have plentiful outdoor deck space, and most have a wraparound outdoor promenade deck that allows you to stroll or jog the ship's perimeter. In the newest cruise liners, traditional meets trendy. You find atrium lobbies and expansive sun and sports decks, picture windows instead of portholes, and cabins that open onto private verandahs. Depending on their size, cruise liners carry 500 to 1,500 passengers.

If you're into big, bold, brassy, and non-stop activity, megaships offer it all. The centerpiece of most is a three-, five-, or seven-story central atrium. These giant vessels are most easily recognized by their profile: the hull and superstructure rise as many as 14 stories out of the water, and are capped by a huge sun or sports deck with a jogging track and swimming pool, which may be Olympic-size. Some megaships have a wraparound promenade deck. Picture windows are standard equipment, and cabins in the top categories have private verandahs. From their casinos and discos to their fitness centers, everything is bigger and more extravagant than on other ships. You may want to re-think a cruise aboard one of these ships if you want a little downtime, since you'll be joined by 1,500 to 3,000 fellow passengers.

Carnival Cruise Lines

Carnival is the largest and most successful cruise line in the world, carrying more passengers than any other. Today's Carnival is a vastly different company from the one launched in 1972 (with one refitted transatlantic ocean liner), but it is still know for high standards set into place by entrepreneur Ted Arison, who made a vacation experience once reserved for the very rich widely accessible.

Carnival throws a great party, and the ships are like floating theme parks. Activities and entertainment are nonstop, beginning just after sunrise and continuing well into the night. On-board dining has been upgraded in recent years, with food that is plentiful, diverse, and well presented. Dinner in the main dining room is served at 6 PM and 8 PM seatings, though food is served throughout the day. There's even 24-hour room service. Carnival cruises are popular with young, single cruisers as well as with those older than 55. Parents cruising with their children also appreciate the line's affordability.

Gratuities are customarily given on the last evening of the cruise, but they may be prepaid at a rate of $9.75 per passenger per day. Carnival recommends the following tips: cabin steward $3.50 per day; dining room team service, $5.50 per day; alternative dining service 75¢ per day. A 15% gratuity is automatically added to bar and beverage tabs. ⌂ *Carnival Cruise Lines, 3655 N.W. 87th Ave., Miami, FL 33178-2428* ☎ *305/599–2600, 800/438–6744, or 800/327–9501* ⊕ *www.carnival.com.*

Legend and Pride. Sister ships to Carnival's *Spirit*, the *Pride* and *Legend* were introduced in 2001 and 2002, respectively, with notable design improvements over previous lines. For example, all staterooms aboard these superliners are located above ocean level, making for a smoother cruise. Cabins are spacious and comfortable, with ample drawer and closet space, and in-cabin TVs show first-run films. Most have ocean views, and of those 80% have balconies. Other innovations include eye-popping, 11-story atriums, two-level promenades, wide decks, shopping malls, and reservations-only supper clubs. Terrific children's programs make this a good ship for any family vacation. These *Spirit*-class ships, cruising at 22 knots, are also faster than most other ships of their size. Choose between a seven-day cruise to Bermuda (four days in port) on the *Pride* and a six-day cruise (three days in port) on the *Legend*. Both dock at historic King's Wharf, in the Dockyard, a centuries-old port city with exceptional shopping and dining, plus a number of interesting sites and landmarks. ⇨ *1,062 cabins, 2,124 passengers (2,667 at full-occupancy), 13 passenger decks* ර *Dining room, 3 restaurants, pizzeria, in-room safes, 4 pools, fitness classes, gym, hair salon, 5 outdoor hot tubs, spa, 16 bars, casino, cinema, dance club, showroom, video game room, children's programs (ages 2–15), laundry facilities, laundry service, computer room, no-smoking rooms* ▭ *AE, D, MC, V.*

Celebrity Cruises

Fodor'sChoice
★

Celebrity has made a name for itself based on sleek ships and superior food. Each ship has its own particular style and layout, with a level of refinement rare on most large ships. In just a short time Celebrity has won the admiration of its passengers and its competitors—who have copied its occasional adults-only cruises, nouvelle cuisine, and cigar clubs, and hired its personnel (a true compliment). Celebrity has risen above typical mass-market cruise cuisine by hiring Chef Michel Roux as a consultant. Menus are creative, and all food is prepared from scratch using only fresh produce and herbs, aged beef, and fresh fish—even the ice cream onboard is homemade. Entertainment choices range from Broadway-style productions, captivating shows, and lively discos to Monte Carlo–style casinos and specialty lounges.

Celebrity attracts everyone from older couples to honeymooners. Summertime children's programs are as good as those on any upscale cruise line. Service is friendly and first class—rapid and accurate in the dining rooms. Waiters, stewards, and bartenders are enthusiastic, take pride in their work, and try to please.

Tip your cabin steward/butlers $3.50 per day; chief housekeeper 50¢ per day; dining room waiter $3.50 per day; assistant waiter $2 per day; and restaurant manager 75¢ per day, for a total of $10.25 per day. A 15% service charge is added to all beverage checks. For children under 12, or the third or fourth person in the stateroom, half of the above amounts is recommended. Gratuities are typically handed out on the last night of the cruise, or they may be charged to your shipboard account. ⌖ *Celebrity Cruises, 1050 Caribbean Way, Miami, FL 33132-2096* ☎ *305/539–6000 or 800/646–1456* 🖷 *800/437–5111* ⊕ *www.celebritycruises.com.*

Horizon and Zenith. Big when they were built but just midsize now, these sister ships offer a somewhat more intimate alternative to the expansive megaships. Interiors are indisputably gracious, airy, and comfortable, with a design that makes the most of natural light through expansive, strategically placed windows. Wide corridors, broad staircases, seven elevators, and well-placed signs make it easy to get around. Nine passenger decks give ample breathing space. Cabins are modern and fairly roomy, with reasonably large closets and bathrooms. There are two seatings each for breakfast, lunch, and dinner. Celebrity avoids theme dinners—common on other lines—in favor of theme midnight buffets, served four nights a week. Both ships take seven-night, round-trip cruises to Bermuda from New York City. ⇴ *677/687 cabins (Horizon/Zenith), 1,374/1,374 passengers, 9/9 passenger decks* ♨ *Dining room, 2 restaurants, food court, ice cream parlor, pizzeria, in-room safes, minibars, 2 pools, fitness classes, gym, hair salon, 3 outdoor hot tubs, sauna, spa, steam room, 7/9 bars, casino, cinema, dance club, showroom, video game room, children's programs (ages 3–17), dry-cleaning, laundry service, computer room, no-smoking rooms* ▱ *AE, MC, V.*

Norwegian Cruise Line

★ Norwegian Cruise Line (NCL) was established as Norwegian Caribbean Lines in 1966, when one of Norway's oldest and most respected shipping companies, Oslo-based Klosters Rederi A/S, acquired the *Sunward* and repositioned the ship from Europe to the then-obscure Port of Miami. For the next several years, NCL was the leader in the cruise-vacation industry with its fleet of sleek, new ships. In 1979 NCL purchased the former *France* and rebuilt the grand ocean liner in Bremerhaven, Germany, for Caribbean cruising. The rechristened *Norway* then assumed the honored position as flagship of the fleet. The late 1980s brought new ships and a new corporate name, as Norwegian Caribbean Lines became Norwegian Cruise Line in 1987. NCL has continued its expansion by acquiring lines, stretching and refurbishing older ships, and building new megaships.

As Princess did with its Personal Choice concept, NCL created a sensation in the industry with the concept of "Freestyle Cruising," which eliminates dinner table and time assignments and dress codes. The line has even loosened the rules on disembarkation, which means passengers can relax in their cabins until it's time to leave the ship (instead of gathering in a lounge to wait for their numbers to be called). NCL's passenger list usually includes seniors, families, and younger couples, mostly from the U.S. and Canada.

A full-time Bermuda concierge is staffed on all trips to the island. There are lectures and seminars about the history and heritage of the island, and the concierge can assist with restaurant reservations. As part of the "Freestyle Dining" program, NCL provides you with a $25 lunch voucher to use shore side (a $5 charge will be added to each guest's onboard account), and for just $5 more, the voucher can be upgraded to a $50 dinner voucher for use at one of Bermuda's top restaurants.

NCL applies a service charge to passengers' shipboard accounts: $10 per passenger per day for those 13 and older, and $5 per day for children (ages 3–12). These automatic tips can be increased, decreased, or removed. A 15% gratuity is added to bar tabs and spa bills. ⌒ *Norwegian Cruise Line, 7665 Corporate Center Dr., Miami, FL 33126* ☎ *305/436–4000 or 800/327–7030* ⊕ *www.ncl.com.*

Norwegian Sea. The *Norwegian Sea,* one of the older ships in the fleet, completed a multimillion-dollar refurbishment project in January 2003. Enhancements include a new restaurant, new carpeting, upholstery, wood floors, and granite floors and countertops. All cabins were updated with new bedding, curtains, and towels. Standard cabins are small and awkwardly fitted with twin beds in an L-shape; tiny bathrooms have little counter space, though all have hair dryers. Service is friendly, warm, and efficient, as it is on all NCL ships, but there aren't the extensive public amenities you usually find on big ships. ↩ *763 cabins, 1,518 passengers, 9 passenger decks* ♿ *2 dining rooms, 2 restaurants, food court, ice cream parlor, in-room safes, 2 pools, fitness classes, gym, hair salon, 2 hot tubs, sauna, spa, 8 bars, casino, cinema, dance club, showroom, video game room, children's programs (ages 2–17), dry-cleaning, laundry service, no kids under 6 months* ▤ *AE, D, MC, V.*

Norwegian Majesty. The *Norwegian Majesty* was lengthened in 1999 with the insertion of a prefab midsection that added 110 feet to its length and 203 cabins; about 71% are outside. During the conversion, all interiors were spruced up and refurbished. Some of the standard cabins are fairly small, and all have showers but not bathtubs. Most oceanview staterooms have refrigerators. Lower beds in most staterooms can be combined to form a queen-size bed. ↩ *731 cabins, 1,462 passengers, 9 passenger decks* ♿ *Dining room, 5 restaurants, food court, ice cream parlor, in-room safes, some refrigerators, 2 pools, fitness classes, gym, hair salon, 2 hot tubs, sauna, spa, 8 bars, casino, cinema, dance club, showroom, video game room, children's programs (ages 2–17), dry-cleaning, laundry service, computer room, no-smoking rooms* ▤ *AE, D, MC, V.*

Royal Caribbean International

Imagine if the Mall of America were sent to sea. That's a fair approximation of what the megaships of Royal Caribbean Cruises (RCL) are all about. These giant vessels are indoor/outdoor wonders, with every conceivable activity in a resort-like atmosphere, including atrium lobbies, shopping arcades, large spas, and expansive sundecks. The centerpiece of Royal Caribbean's megaships is the central atrium, a hallmark that has been duplicated by many other cruise lines. The brilliance of this design is that all the major public rooms radiate from this central point, so you can learn your way around within minutes of boarding. Royal Caribbean is one of the best-run and most popular cruise lines.

While the line competes directly with Carnival for passengers—active couples and singles in their 30s to 50s, as well as a large family contingent—there are distinct differences of ambience and energy. Royal Caribbean is a bit more sophisticated and subdued than Carnival, even while delivering a good time on a grand scale.

Royal Caribbean suggests the following tips per passenger. Dining room waiter, $3.50 a day; stateroom attendant, $3.50 a day; assistant waiter, $2 a day. Gratuities for headwaiters and other service personnel are at your discretion. A 15% gratuity is automatically added to your beverage and bar bills. All gratuities may be charged to your onboard account. ☐ *Royal Caribbean International, 1050 Caribbean Way, Miami, FL 33132* ☎ *305/539–600 or 800/327–6700* ⊕ *www.royalcaribbean.com.*

Nordic Empress. This distinctive-looking ship, with huge aft bay windows, was specifically designed for the short (three- to four-day) cruise market and splits its year between Bermuda and the Caribbean. A simple design with a single main corridor makes it easy for passengers to learn their way around. The interior, filled with large and festive public rooms, is a glittering combination of art deco and futuristic designs; the six-story atrium is dazzling and well-lit, with lots of glass, chrome, and cascading waterfalls. A triple-level casino and a sensational double-decker dining room with a fantastic view of the sea round out a very tidy ship. Standard cabins are small at 117 square feet, and the bright decor can't make them feel any larger; most have twin beds convertible to a queen. On seven-night round trips to Bermuda, the ship docks at Kings' Wharf and Hamilton. ⌁ *801 cabins, 1,602 passengers (2,020 at full occupancy), 12 passenger decks* ♿ *Dining room, restaurant, in-room safes, 2 pools, fitness classes, gym, hair salon, 4 hot tubs, sauna, 4 bars, casino, cinema, dance club, showroom, video game room, children's programs (ages 3–17), dry-cleaning, laundry facilities, Internet, no-smoking rooms* ▤ *AE, D, MC, V.*

Luxury Cruise Lines

Ultra-luxury cruise lines to Bermuda, which include Seven Seas Cruises and Silversea Cruises, offer high staff-to-guest ratios for personal service, superior cuisine in a single seating, and a highly inclusive product with few on-board charges. These small and midsize ships offer much more space per passenger than you will find on the mainstream lines' vessels. If you consider travel an entitlement rather than a luxury and frequent exclusive resorts, then you will appreciate the extra attention and the higher level of comfort that these luxury cruise lines can offer.

Seven Seas Cruises

★ Seven Seas Cruises (formerly Radisson Seven Seas Cruises) is part of Carlson Hospitality Worldwide, one of the world's major hotel and travel companies. The cruise line was formed in December 1994 with the merger of the one-ship Diamond Cruises and Seven Seas Cruises lines. From these modest beginnings, SSC has grown to become the world's largest luxury line. The spacious ocean-view cabins have the industry's highest percentage of private balconies; you'll always find open seating at dinner (which includes complimentary wine); there's a strict no-tipping policy; and activities tend to be oriented toward exploring the destinations on the itinerary. SSC manages to provide a high level of service and sense of intimacy on midsize ships, which have the stability of larger vessels. Passengers tend to be older, affluent, and active—ready participants in the cruise line's excellent, unique shore excursions, such as the Art of Watercolors excursion, for which passengers are invited to take a painting class with a Bermudian artist. Other excursions include the Elbow Beach Escape, a day on one of Bermuda's prettiest beaches, including bottled water and beach umbrellas; and From Farm to Table, a tour of one of Bermuda's farms led by a Bermudian chef. ⌂ *Seven Seas Cruises, 600 Corporate Dr., Suite 410, Fort Lauderdale, FL 33334* ☎ *954/776–6123, 800/477–7500, or 800/285–1835* ⊟ *954/772–3763* ⊕ *www.rssc.com.*

Seven Seas Navigator. The spacious *Navigator* is a midsize ship with a big-ship feel. Every stateroom is a superbly appointed, ocean-view suite ranging from 300 to over 1,000 square feet—90% with private teak balconies. All standard suites have walk-in closets and marble bathrooms with separate tub and shower, cotton bathrobes, hair dryers, TV/VCRs, refrigerators stocked with soft drinks, and bar set up upon embarkation. At 300 square feet, even the smallest stateroom is sufficiently roomy for comfortable en suite dining—course-by-course, ordered from the Compass Rose dining room. There is one crew member for every 1.5 passengers. Round trips to Bermuda are for seven nights, departing from New York on Wednesday and docking in downtown Hamilton on Friday and Saturday nights, and in St. George's on Sunday. ⇨ *251 cabins, 490 passengers, 8 passenger decks ⚓ Dining room, restaurant, in-room safes, minibars, in-room VCRs, pool, fitness classes, gym, hair salon, outdoor hot tub, sauna, spa, steam room, 4 bars, casino, cinema, dance club, showroom, dry-cleaning, laundry service, no kids under age 1, no-smoking rooms* ⊟ *AE, D, MC, V.*

Silversea Cruises

Fodor'sChoice
★   Silversea Cruises straddles the line that separates ocean-liner and luxury-yacht cruising. Its ships have full-size showrooms, domed dining rooms, and a selection of bars and shops; yet all cabins are outside suites, most have private verandahs, and space- and crew-to-passenger ratios are among the best at sea. Silversea ships have larger swimming pools and more deck space than other cruise yachts (but no retractable marina at the stern). Another of the line's selling points is its all-inclusive packaging, which includes gratuities, port charges, transfers, some shore excursions, and all beverages. All packages include economy airfare to the port of embarkation and a pre-cruise hotel room. Perhaps more compelling than the line's relatively low prices is its flair for originality. An extravagant red-carpet galley luncheon is served once each cruise. And Silversea's shore excursions are specially designed—you might, for example, join a tour of local art galleries guided by an historian and antiques specialist. ⌂ *Silversea Cruises, 110 E. Broward Blvd., Fort Lauderdale, FL 33316* ☎ *954/522–4477 or 800/722–9955* ⊕ *www. silversea.com.*

Silver Cloud, Silver Wind, Silver Whisper. Silversea's ships have the feel of a private yacht but with much more spaciousness, including larger public rooms and a two-tier showroom with a moveable stage. The sleek decor is meant to evoke the great steamships of the past. The restaurant has brass sconces, wood paneling, and brass-ringed portholes; diners sit in high-backed chairs at small tables adorned by crisp, white tablecloths and set with Christofle silver, fine porcelain, and European crystal. All cabins, the most exquisitely appointed in the industry, are outside suites (larger on the *Silver Whisper*) with walk-in closets and marble baths, and most open onto a teak verandah with floor-to-ceiling glass doors. Creature comforts include fine bedding (Frette linens and down pillows), Bulgari toiletries, stocked refrigerators, and a daily-replenished fruit basket. Silversea's vessels alternate regularly on trips to Bermuda, and they typically dock in Hamilton Saturday through Monday. ⇨ *148/148/194 cabins (Silver Cloud/Silver Wind/Silver Whisper),*

296/296/388 passengers, 6/6/7 passenger decks & Dining room, restaurant, in-room safes, refrigerators, in-room VCRs, pool, fitness classes, gym, hair salon, 2 hot tubs, sauna, spa, steam room, 3 bars, casino, showroom, dry-cleaning, laundry facilities, laundry service, computer room = AE, D, MC, V.

SHORE EXCURSIONS

Shore excursions are optional tours organized by the cruise line and sold aboard the ship. Most tours last two to three hours and all are meant to optimize your time on the island—the cruise line does the research about what to see and do, and you just go along for the ride. You'll pay more for these tours than if you booked them independently, but with only two or three days in port, the convenience is worth the price. Fees are generally $30–$40 per person for island tours, $40 for snorkeling trips, and $60–$100 for diving trips. Approximate durations and adult prices are listed for tours—prices for children are usually much less. For exact durations and prices, consult your cruise line. The luxury lines, Seven Seas Cruises and Silversea Cruises, offer their own unique shore excursions through special arrangement with on-shore operators and tourist agencies.

Of course, you are always free to explore on your own. With its excellent taxi service, Bermuda is a good island for hiring a car and driver.

Going Ashore

Ships calling in Bermuda pull up along the pier, so you can walk right off the ship to the center of town and major attractions. In Hamilton, for instance, passengers walk off the ship right onto Front Street, with its shops and restaurants. Before anyone is allowed to walk down the gangway, however, the ship must be cleared for landing. Immigration and customs officials board the vessel to examine passports and sort through red tape. It may be more than an hour before you're allowed ashore. You will be issued a boarding pass, which you'll need to get back on board.

Returning to the Ship

Cruise lines are strict about sailing times, which are posted at the gangway and elsewhere and announced in the daily schedule of activities. Be sure to be back on board at least a half hour before the announced sailing time or you may be stranded. If you are on a shore excursion that was sold by the cruise line, however, the captain will wait for your group before casting off. That is one reason many passengers prefer ship-packaged tours.

If you're not on one of the ship's tours and the ship sails without you, immediately contact the cruise line's port representative, whose phone number is often listed on the daily schedule of activities. You may be able to hitch a ride on a pilot boat, although that is unlikely. Passengers who miss the boat must pay their own way to the next port.

Bicycling

The Railway Trail. With traffic such as only a tiny island can have, high winds, and steep, narrow roads, Bermuda is not the easiest place in the world to bicycle. That said, a ride on the Railway Trail is one of the quintessential Bermuda experiences. Restricted to pedestrian, bicycle, and scooter traffic, the trail is mostly paved and runs intermittently for almost the length of the island along the route of the old Bermuda Railway. ⊙ 2–3 hrs ▧ $50.

On the Water

Boating & Sailing. Take your own rental boat to a secluded cove for swimming, snorkeling, or basking in the sun. The boats, 18 feet long at most, range from sailboats (typically tiny Sunfish) to motorboats (13-foot Boston Whalers) to pedal boats. ☉ *2–8 hrs* ▣ *$65–$165.*

Calypso Cruise. Boogie to live calypso music and sip rum swizzles on a cruise that departs Albuoy's Point in Hamilton every Tuesday and Thursday at 2 PM. When the boat reaches Hawkin's Island, everybody jumps off for a sobering swim. ☉ *3 hrs* ▣ *$60.*

Charter Boats. More than 20 large power cruisers and sailing vessels, piloted by local skippers, are available for charter. From 30 feet to 60 feet long, charter sailboats can carry up to 30 passengers. ☉ *4–8 hrs* ▣ *$500–$1,650.*

"Don't Stop the Carnival Party" Cruise. Bermuda's biggest floating party, this tropical-theme cocktail cruise to Hawkin's Island leaves Albuoy's Point daily except Thursday and Sunday, with 200 passengers aboard, including bawdy carnival entertainers in colorful costumes. Dinner is from a gargantuan buffet, and drinks are from a well-stocked open bar. ☉ *3½ hrs* ▣ *$85.*

Kayaking. Paddle in protected coves or the open ocean, depending on your skill level, accompanied by a skilled guide and trainer. ☉ *3 hrs* ▣ *$50.*

Fishing

Deep-Sea Fishing. Most charter-fishing captains go to the reefs and deep water to the southwest and northwest of the island, where the fishing is best. Half-day or full-day charters are offered by most operators, but full-day trips offer the best chance for a big catch. No license is required, but restrictions apply, particularly regarding the fish you can keep. For instance, only Bermudians with commercial fishing licenses are allowed to take lobsters. There's also a prohibition against keeping spearguns. ☉ *4–8 hrs* ▣ *$1,000–$1,800.*

Horseback Riding

South Shore Park Ride. Between South Road and the Warwick beaches, sandy trails, most of which are open only to walkers or horseback riders, wind through strands of dune grass and oleander, and over coral bluffs to the beach. ☉ *1½ hrs* ▣ *$60.*

Island Sights

Art & Architecture Walking Tour. You'll see Hamilton's loveliest structures on this tour, which stops at the Bermuda National Gallery, the cathedral on Church Street, and several other buildings, before ending at Waterloo House, a harborside hotel. ☉ *2½ hrs* ▣ *$65.*

Carriage Ride. Climb into a horse-drawn carriage for a ride down Front Street in Hamilton. The old-fashioned wooden carriages are a romantic way to tour the island. A one-horse carriage can carry up to four people, while a two-horse carriage can carry 6 to 8. ☉ *½ hr* ▣ *$20.*

Nonsuch Island Eco-Adventure. After a 15-minute boat ride from St. George's to uninhabited Nonsuch Island, you'll spend the day watching wildlife in a uniquely Bermudian natural setting. The island offers a rare glimpse of what Bermuda was like when settlers first arrived in 1609. ☉ *4 hrs* ▣ *$75.*

Undersea Creatures

Helmet Diving. Walk on the bottom of the sea, play with fish, and learn about coral, all without getting your hair wet. Helmets cover your head and feed you air from the surface. ☉ *25 min* ✉ *$40.*

Scuba Diving. Bermuda has all the ingredients for classic scuba diving— reefs, wrecks, underwater caves, a variety of coral and marine life, and clear, warm water (at least, May through October). ☉ *2–4 hrs* ✉ *$60–$100.*

🖑 **Snorkeling.** Equipment, lessons, and an underwater guided tour are included in this family favorite, but the underwater cameras are extra. ☉ *4 hrs* ✉ *$40.*

🖑 **Swim with the Dolphins.** The excellent Dolphin Quest program at King's Wharf allows you to interact with friendly bottlenose dolphins. ☉ *½–1 hr* ✉ *$75–$265.*

BEFORE YOU GO

Once you have chosen your cruise and signed on to go, it's time to get ready. Preparations for a cruise may involve many distinct tasks, but none of them is difficult, especially if broken down into manageable steps. Most important, allow plenty of time to get ready so you don't get harried in the last couple of weeks.

Tickets, Vouchers & Other Travel Documents

After you make the final payment to your travel agent, the cruise line will issue your cruise tickets and vouchers for airport-to-ship transfers. Depending on the airline, and whether you have purchased an air-sea package, you may receive your plane tickets or charter-flight vouchers at the same time; you may also receive vouchers for any shore excursions, although most cruise lines issue these aboard ship. Should your travel documents not arrive when promised, contact your travel agent or call the cruise line directly. If you book late, tickets may be delivered directly to the ship.

Passports & Visas

Read your cruise documents carefully to see what you'll need for embarkation. (You don't want to be turned away at the pier!) Most cruise lines that sail to Bermuda require passengers to have a valid passport.

What to Pack

Certain packing rules apply to all cruises: always take along a sweater in case of cool evening breezes or overactive air-conditioning. A rain slicker usually comes in handy, too, and make sure you take at least one pair of comfortable walking shoes for exploring port towns. Men who want to participate in formal night activities should pack a dark suit, a tuxedo, or a white dinner jacket. Women should pack one long gown or cocktail dress for every two or three formal evenings on board. Life onboard most ships is much more casual than it once was, but there's always a dress-up evening that you can attend or skip.

Generally speaking, plan on one outfit for every two days of cruising, especially if your wardrobe contains many interchangeable pieces. Ships often have convenient laundry facilities. And don't overload your luggage with extra toiletries and sundry items; they are easily available in port and in the ship's gift shop (although usually at a premium price).

Cabin amenities typically include soap, and often shampoo, conditioner, and other lotions and potions.

Electrical outlets in cabins on all ships sailing weekly to Bermuda are compatible with U.S.–purchased appliances, such as hair dryers and electric shavers.

Take an extra pair of eyeglasses or contact lenses in your carry-on luggage. If you have a health problem that requires a prescription drug, pack enough to last the duration of the trip or have your doctor write a prescription using the drug's generic name (brand names can vary from country to country). Always carry prescription drugs in their original packaging to avoid problems with customs officials.

Accessibility Issues

The latest cruise ships have been built with the needs of travelers with disabilities in mind, and many older ships have been modified to accommodate them. But several cruise lines operate older ships that have not been modified or do not have elevators: the tall sailing ships and explorer-type vessels are not the easiest ships to navigate if you are in a wheelchair. The key areas to be concerned about are public rooms, outer decks, and, of course, your cabin.

If you need a specially equipped cabin, book as far in advance as possible and ask specific questions of your travel agent or a cruise-line representative. Specifically, ask how your cabin is configured and equipped. Is the entrance level or ramped? Are all doorways at least 30 inches wide (wider if your wheelchair is not standard)? Are pathways to beds, closets, and bathrooms at least 36 inches wide and unobstructed? In the bathroom, are there 42 inches of clear space in front of the toilet and are there grab bars behind and on one side of it and in the bathtub and shower? Are elevators wide enough to accommodate wheelchairs?

The best cruise ship for passengers who use wheelchairs is one that ties up right at the dock at every port, at which time a ramp or even an elevator is always made available. Unfortunately, it's hard to ascertain this in advance, since a ship may tie up at the dock at one port on one voyage and, on the next, anchor in the harbor and have passengers transported to shore via tender. Ask your travel agent to find out which ships are capable of docking. If a tender is used, some ships will have crew members carry the wheelchair and passenger from the ship to the tender. Other ships will refuse to take wheelchairs on tenders, especially if the water is choppy.

ARRIVING & DEPARTING

If you have purchased an air-sea package, you will be met by a cruise-company representative when your plane lands at the port city and then shuttled directly to the ship in a bus or minivan. Some cruise lines arrange to transport luggage between airport and ship so passengers don't have to hassle with baggage claim at the start of a cruise or with baggage check-in at the end. If you decide not to buy the air-sea package but still plan to fly, ask your travel agent if you can use the ship's transfer bus. Otherwise, you will have to take a taxi to the ship.

If you live close to the port of embarkation, bus transportation may be available. This is often the case on cruises to Bermuda for passengers who live on the East Coast. Another option for those who live close to their point of departure is to drive to the ship. The major U.S. cruise ports all have parking facilities.

Embarkation

Check-In

On arrival at the dock, you must check in before boarding your ship. An officer will collect or stamp your ticket, inspect or even retain your passport or other official identification, ask you to fill out a tourist card, check that you have the correct visas, and collect any unpaid port or departure tax.

Seating assignments for the dining room are often handed out at this time, too, although most cruise ships are now offering you the opportunity to dine when and with whom you like in any of several restaurants aboard. You may also register your credit card to open a shipboard account, or that may be done later at the purser's office.

After this you will be required to walk through a metal detector and pass your hand baggage through an x-ray inspection. These are the same security checks used in airports, so ask to have your photographic film inspected by hand.

Although it takes only five or ten minutes per family to check in, lines are often long, so aim for off-peak hours. The worst time tends to be immediately after the ship begins boarding. The later it is, the less crowded. For example, if boarding begins at 2 PM and continues until 4:30, lines are shorter after 3:30.

Boarding the Ship

Before you walk up the gangway, the ship's photographer will probably take your picture. There's no charge unless you buy the picture (usually $7 to $8). On board, stewards may serve welcome drinks in souvenir glasses—for which you're usually charged between $3 and $5.

You will be escorted to your cabin by a steward, who will carry your hand luggage. The rest of your bags will either be inside your cabin when you arrive or will come shortly thereafter. If your bags don't arrive within a half hour of sailing, contact the purser. If you are among the unlucky few whose luggage doesn't make it to the ship in time, the purser will trace it and arrange to have it flown to the ship in Bermuda.

ON BOARD

Checking Out Your Cabin

The first thing to do upon arriving at your cabin or suite is to make sure that everything is in order. In most modern ships, beds can be pushed together to create one single bed or moved apart for two. However, if you wanted a double bed and there are two twin beds instead, you can ask your cabin steward to set up the beds the way you would like them or to move you to another room. Unless the ship is full, you can usually persuade the chief housekeeper or hotel manager to allow you to change cabins. It is customary to tip the stewards who assist you.

Because your cabin is your home-away-from-home for a few days or weeks, everything should be to your satisfaction. Take a good look around. Is the cabin clean and orderly? Do the toilet, shower, and faucets work? Check the telephone and television. Again, major problems should be addressed immediately. Minor concerns, such as a shortage of bath towels or pillows, can wait until the frenzy of embarkation has subsided.

Your dining-time and seating-assignment card may be in your cabin if it wasn't handed to you upon embarkation. Now is the time to check it and immediately request any changes. The maître d' usually sets up shop in one of the public rooms specifically for this purpose.

Shipboard Accounts

Cruise ships operate as cashless societies. Passengers charge onboard purchases and settle their accounts at the end of the cruise with a credit card, traveler's checks, or cash. You can sign for wine at dinner, drinks at the bar, shore excursions, gifts in the shop—virtually any expense you may incur aboard ship. On some lines, an imprint from a major credit card is necessary to open an account. Otherwise, a cash deposit may be required and a positive balance maintained to keep the shipboard account open. Either way, you will want to open a line of credit soon after settling in, if an account was not opened for you at embarkation. This can easily be arranged by visiting the purser's office in the central atrium or main lobby. On most ships, you can now view your account at any time on your in-cabin television. To make your stay aboard as seamless—and as cashless—as possible, many cruise lines now add dining room gratuities at a set rate to your onboard account. Some lines offer access to personal records via Internet; you can alter automatic tips, for example, before your cruise begins.

Tipping

For better or worse, tipping is an integral part of the cruise experience. Most companies pay their cruise staff nominal wages and expect tips to make up the difference. Most cruise lines have recommended tipping guidelines, and on many ships "voluntary" tipping for beverage service has been replaced with a mandatory 15% service charge, which is added to every bar bill. On the other hand, the most expensive luxury lines include tips in the cruise fare and may prohibit crew members from accepting additional gratuities.

Some large cruise lines now add dining room tips of $10 to $12 a person per day directly to your bill. That sum is intended to cover all your dining room service, except perhaps the wine steward and the maître d'; it may also include your room steward. Ask the purser if tips are being added to your bill and which personnel will receive them—waiter, busboy, and room steward/stewardess are all expecting tips. You may adjust tips up or down.

Where to Eat

Cruise ships serve food nearly around the clock. There may be up to four breakfast options: early morning coffee and pastries on deck, breakfast in bed through room service, buffet-style breakfast in the cafeteria, and sit-down breakfast in the dining room. There may also be two or three choices for lunch, mid-afternoon hors d'oeuvres, and midnight buffets. You may eat whatever is on the menu, in any quantity, at any meals. Room service is traditionally, but not always, free.

Restaurants

The chief meals of the day are served in the main dining room, which on most ships can accommodate only half the passengers at once. Meals are therefore usually served in early (or main) and late (or second) seatings. Early seating for dinner is generally between 6 and 6:30, late seating between 8 and 8:30.

Most cruise ships have a buffet-style restaurant, usually near the swimming pool, where you can eat lunch and breakfast. On many of the newer ships, that room, nearly always located on the Lido Deck near the swimming pool, becomes a casual, waiter-service dining room at dinner. Those dining rooms, often having grilled specialties, are popular on nights when the ship has been in port all day. Many ships provide self-serve coffee or tea in their cafeteria around the clock, as well as midnight buffets. Some ships, particularly newer ones, also have alternative specialty restaurants for which a reservation must be made. You might have to pay a fee for grilled steak or Asian cuisine. On-demand food shops may include pizzerias, ice-cream parlors, and caviar or cappuccino bars; there may be an extra charge at these facilities, too.

Smoking is usually banned in main dining rooms. At least one cruise line—Carnival—now has a non-smoking ship. Smoking policies vary and change; contact your cruise line to find out what the situation will be on your cruise.

Seatings

When it comes to your dining-table assignment, you should have options on four important points: early or late seating; smoking or no-smoking section (if smoking is allowed in the dining room); a table for two, four, six, or eight; and special dietary needs. When you receive your cruise documents, you will usually receive a card asking for your dining preferences. Fill this out and return it to the cruise line, but remember that you will not get your seating assignment until you board the ship. Check it out immediately, and if your request was not met, see the maître d'. Usually there is a time and place set up for changes in dining assignments.

On some ships, seating times are strictly observed. Ten to 15 minutes after the scheduled mealtime, the dining-room doors are closed, although this policy is increasingly rare. On other ships, passengers may enter the dining room at their leisure, but they must be out by the end of the seating. When a ship has just one seating, passengers may enter any time the kitchen is open.

Seating assignments often apply only to dinner. Most ships have open seating for breakfast or lunch, which means you may sit anywhere at any time the meal is served. Smaller or more luxurious ships offer open seating for all meals.

Several large cruise lines now offer several restaurant and dining options and have eliminated pre-assigned seating, so you can dine with whom you like at any table that's available and at any time the dining room is open.

CHANGING TABLES Dining is a focal point of the cruise experience, and your companions at meals may become your best friends on the cruise. However, if you're traveling on a ship that assigns you to a table where you dine every night with the same people and you find you don't enjoy their company, the maître d' can usually move you to another one if the dining room isn't completely full (a tip helps). He will probably be reluctant to comply with your request after the first full day at sea, however, because the waiters, busboys, and wine steward who have been serving you up to that point won't receive their tips at the end of the cruise. Be persistent if you are truly unhappy.

Cuisine

Most ships serve food geared to the American palate, but there are also theme dinners featuring the cuisine of a particular country. Some European ships, especially smaller vessels, may offer a particular cuisine throughout the cruise—Scandinavian, German, Italian, or Greek, perhaps—depending on the ship's or the crew's nationality. The quality of cruise-ship cooking is generally good, but even a skilled chef is hard put to serve 500 or more extraordinary dinners per hour. Presentation is often spectacular, especially at gala midnight buffets.

There is often a direct relationship between the cost of a cruise and the quality of its cuisine. The food is very sophisticated on some (mostly expensive) lines, among them Silversea Cruises. In the more moderate price range, Celebrity Cruises has gained renown for the culinary stylings of French chef Michel Roux, who acts as a consultant to the line.

Special Diets
With notification well in advance, many ships can provide a kosher, low-salt, low-cholesterol, sugar-free, vegetarian, or other special menu. However, there's always a chance that the wrong dish will somehow be handed to you. Especially when it comes to soups and desserts, it's a good idea to ask about the ingredients.

Large ships usually offer an alternative "light" or "spa" menu based upon American Heart Association guidelines, using leaner cuts of meat, low-cholesterol or low-sodium preparations, smaller portions, salads, fresh-fruit desserts, and healthy garnishes. Some smaller ships may not be able to accommodate special dietary needs. Vegetarians generally have no trouble finding appropriate selections.

Wine
Wine at meals costs extra on most ships; prices are usually comparable to those in shoreside restaurants and are charged to your shipboard account. A handful of luxury vessels include both wine and liquor. On some lines, you can also select the wines you might like for dinner before leaving home and they will appear at your table and on your bill at the end of the cruise.

The Captain's Table
It is both a privilege and a marvelous experience to be invited to dine one evening at the captain's table. Although some seats are given to celebrities, repeat passengers, and passengers in the most expensive suites, other invitations are given at random to ordinary passengers. You can request an invitation from the chief steward or the hotel manager, although there is no guarantee you will be accommodated. The captain's guests always wear suits and ties or dresses, even if the dress code for that evening is casual. On many ships, passengers may also be invited to dine at the other officers' special tables, or officers may visit a different passenger table each evening.

Room Service
A small number of ships have no room service at all, except when the ship's doctor orders it for an ailing passenger. Many offer only breakfast (Continental on some, full on others); most, however, have selections that you can order around the clock, although menus may be abbreviated at some hours. Many ships now offer unlimited round-the-clock room service. There usually is no additional charge other than for beer, wine, or spirits delivered to your room.

Bars, Lounges & Entertainment
Many larger ships have several showrooms and a variety of bars, ranging from sports bars to piano bars and mirrored-floors-and-strobe-light dance bars. Entertainment and ballroom dancing may go late into the night; adult midnight comedy shows are popular on many ships. Elsewhere, you may find a disco, nightclub, or cabaret, usually built around a bar and dance floor. Music is provided by a piano player, a disc jockey,

or by performing ensembles such as country-and-western duos, a harpist and violinist, or jazz combos.

Bars

A ship's bars, whether adjacent to the pool or attached to one of the lounges, tend to be its social centers. Except on a handful of luxury-class ships where everything is included in the ticket price, bars operate on a pay-as-it's-poured basis. Rather than demand cash after every round, however, most ships allow passengers to charge drinks to an account.

In international waters there are, technically, no laws against teenage drinking, but almost all ships require passengers to be over 18 or 21 to purchase alcoholic beverages. Many cruise ships have chapters of Alcoholics Anonymous (a.k.a. "Friends of Bill W.") or will organize meetings on request. Look for meeting times and places in the daily program slipped under your cabin door each night or delivered to the cabin by the steward.

Entertainment

The main entertainment lounge or showroom schedules nightly musical revues, magic acts, comedy performances, and variety shows, all included in the price of the cruise. During the rest of the day the room is used for group activities, such as talks or bingo games. Generally, the larger the ship, the bigger and more impressive the productions. Newer ships have elaborate showrooms that often span two or three decks. Some are designed like an amphitheater, others have two levels—a main floor and a balcony. Seating is sometimes in clusters of armchairs set around cocktail tables. Other ships have more traditional theater-style seating.

Casinos

Once a ship is 12 mi off the U.S. shore it is in international waters and gambling is permitted. (Some "cruises to nowhere," in fact, are little more than sailing casinos.) All ocean liners, as well as many cruise yachts, have casinos. On larger vessels, they usually have poker, baccarat, blackjack, roulette, craps, and slot machines. House stakes are much more modest than those in Las Vegas or Atlantic City. On most ships the maximum bet is $200. Some ships allow $500. Payouts on the slot machines are generally much lower, too. Credit is never extended, but many casinos have handy ATMs that dispense cash (for a hefty fee).

Children are officially barred from the casinos, but it's not uncommon to see them playing the slots rather than the adjacent video machines. Most ships offer free individual instruction and off-hours gambling classes. Casinos are usually open from early morning to late at night, although you may find only unattended slot machines before evening. By law, casinos are always closed while at port in Bermuda.

Game Rooms

Most ships have a room with card tables and board games. These rooms are for serious players and are often the site of friendly round-robin competitions and tournaments. Most ships furnish everything for free (cards, chips, games, and so forth), but a few charge $1 or more for each deck of cards. Be aware that professional cardsharps and hustlers have been fleecing passengers almost as long as there have been ships. There are small video arcades on most medium and large ships. Family-oriented ships often have a computer learning center.

Bingo & Other Games

Daily high-stakes bingo games are often even more popular than casinos. You can play for as little as $1 a card. Most ships have a snowball bingo game with a jackpot that grows throughout the cruise into hundreds or even thousands of dollars.

Another popular cruise pastime is the so-called "horse races." Fictional horses are auctioned off to "owners." Individual passengers can buy a horse or form "syndicates." Bids usually begin at around $25 and can top $1,000 per horse. Races are then "run" according to dice throws or computer-generated random numbers. Audience members bet on their favorites.

Library
Many cruise ships have a library with up to 1,500 volumes, from the latest best-sellers to reference works. Many shipboard libraries also stock videotapes for in-cabin VCRs.

Movie Theaters
Most vessels have a room for screening movies. On older ships and some newer ones, this is often a genuine cinema-style movie theater, although on other ships it may be just a multipurpose room. Films are frequently one or two months past their first release date but not yet available on videotape or cable TV. Films rated "R" are edited to minimize sex and violence. Over the course of a weeklong voyage a dozen films may be screened, each repeated several times. Theaters are also used for lectures, religious services, and private meetings.

With a few exceptions, ocean liners equip their cabins with closed-circuit TVs showing movies (continuously on some newer ships), shipboard lectures, and regular programs (thanks to satellite reception). Ships with in-cabin VCRs usually provide a selection of movies on videocassette at no charge (a deposit is sometimes required).

Sports & Fitness

Swimming Pools
All but the smallest ships have at least one pool. Some are elaborate affairs with water slides or retractable roofs; hot tubs and whirlpools are quite common. Pools may be filled with fresh water or salt water; some ships have one of each. While in port or during rough weather pools are usually emptied or covered with canvas. Many are too narrow or too short to allow swimmers more than a few strokes in any direction; none have diving boards, and not all are heated. Often there are no lifeguards. Wading pools are sometimes provided for small children.

Sun Deck
The top deck on a cruise ship is usually called the Sun Deck or Sports Deck. On some ships, this is where you'll find the pool and hot tubs. Nearby are volleyball, table tennis, shuffleboard, and other such sports. Often, at twilight or after the sun goes down, the Sun Deck is used for dancing, barbecues, limbo contests, or other social activities.

Exercise & Fitness Rooms
Most newer ships and some older ships have well-equipped fitness centers, and some have full-fledged spas. Exercise rooms are equipped with bodybuilding equipment, stationary bicycles, rowing machines, treadmills, and the like. Aerobics classes are offered several times a day. An upper-deck fitness center often has an airy and sunny view of the sea; an inside, lower-deck health club is often dark and small unless it is equipped with an indoor pool or beauty salon.

Promenade Deck
Many vessels designate certain decks for fitness walks and may post the number of laps per mile. Fitness instructors may lead daily walks around

the Promenade Deck. A number of ships discourage jogging and running on the decks or ask that no one take fitness walks before 8 AM or after 10 PM, so as not to disturb passengers in cabins. With the advent of the megaship, walking and jogging have in many cases moved up top to tracks on the Sun or Sports deck.

Shipboard Services

Communications

SHIPBOARD   Most cabins have loudspeakers and telephones. Generally, the loudspeakers cannot be switched off because they are used for broadcast of important notices. Telephones are used to call fellow passengers, order room service, summon a doctor, request a wake-up call, or speak with the ship's officers or departments.

SHIP TO SHORE   Internet centers are very popular aboard ship in part because e-mailing, although not cheap, is still less costly than phoning to keep in touch. Ships charge connection fees of 50¢ to $1 per minute, in addition to one-time activation fees of $3.95 to $10.95. Most cruise lines also offer packages that let you use the Internet for set blocks of time. For example, 100 minutes online costs $55 to $75, and 250 minutes costs $100 to $150. Norwegian Cruise Lines ships are among those with wireless Internet capability, and you may bring along your own laptop with a wi-fi card or rent a laptop from the ship; you generally pay for a block of time or pay a fee for unlimited access.

Satellite facilities make it possible to call anywhere in the world from most ships. Most are also equipped with fax machines, and some provide credit card–operated phones. It may take as long as a half hour to make a connection, but unless a storm is raging outside, conversation is clear and easy. Newer ships are generally equipped with direct-dial phones in every cabin for calls to shore. Be warned: the cost of communication, regardless of the method, can be quite expensive—up to $15 a minute. If possible, wait until you go ashore to call home. Cell phones can be used on ships, although reception depends on your distance from shore and whether your cell phone provider has service to the area where you are cruising. It's much cheaper to wait until you arrive in Bermuda to call home. Once ashore you can use your calling card or a prepaid phone card to make calls from a public phone.

Laundry & Dry Cleaning

All but the smallest ships and shortest cruises offer laundry service and self-service laundry machines. Valet laundry service includes cabin pickup and delivery and usually takes 24 hours. If you choose this service, remember that the cost of washing your shirts, shorts, socks, and so forth can add up quickly. Some ships also offer dry-cleaning services, but a concern for the environmental effect of the chemicals used in dry-cleaning is beginning to limit those services, so don't count on it.

Hair Salons

Hair salons are a standard feature on all ships sailing to Bermuda. Book your appointment well in advance, especially before such popular events as the farewell dinner.

Film Processing & Supplies

Cruise ships carry a supply of film and batteries to fit most recent cameras. However, you're less likely to find slide film, black-and-white film, and batteries for older cameras aboard. Either bring an adequate supply from home or pick up a fresh stock while in Bermuda. Cruise ships can usually process and print your film overnight, again provided you're shooting standard color prints.

Photographer

The staff photographer, a near-universal fixture on cruise ships, typically shoots pictures of passengers on the gangway upon embarkation, outside the dining room, and on many shore excursions. The thousands of photos snapped over the course of a cruise are displayed publicly in special cases every morning and are offered for sale, usually for $6 to $8 for a 5"×7" color print or $12 to $15 for an 8"×10". If you want a special photo or a portrait, the photographer is usually happy to oblige. Many passengers choose to have a formal portrait taken before the captain's farewell dinner, the dressiest evening of the cruise. The ship's photographer usually anticipates this demand by setting up a studio near the dining room entrance.

Religious Services

Most ships may provide nondenominational religious services on Sundays and religious holidays, and a number offer Catholic Masses daily and Jewish services on Friday evenings. The kind of service held depends upon the clergy the cruise line invites on board. Usually religious services are held in the library, the theater, or one of the private lounges, although a few ships have actual chapels—and some offer a wedding chapel and full wedding services.

Health & Safety at Sea

Fire Safety

The greatest danger facing cruise-ship passengers is fire. All of the ships reviewed in this book must meet international standards for fire safety, which require sprinkler systems, smoke detectors, and other safety features. However, these rules are designed to protect against loss of life. They do not guarantee that a fire will not happen. In fact, fire is a relatively common occurrence on cruise ships. The point here is not to create alarm, but to emphasize the importance of taking fire safety seriously.

Once settled into your cabin, find your life vests and review the emergency instructions posted inside the cabin door or near the life vests. Make sure your vests are in good condition and learn to secure the vest properly. Make certain the ship's purser knows if you or your companion has a physical infirmity that may hamper a speedy exit from your cabin. In case of an emergency, the purser can quickly dispatch a crew member to assist you. If you are traveling with children, be sure that child-size life jackets are placed in your cabin.

Within 24 hours of embarkation you will be asked to attend a mandatory lifeboat drill. Listen carefully. If you have any questions, ask them. If you are unsure how to use your vest, now is the time to ask. Only in the most extreme circumstances will you need to abandon ship, but it has happened. The few minutes you spend learning the right procedure may serve you well in a mishap.

Crime

Most people never have a problem with crime aboard cruise ships, but you should exercise the same precautions aboard that you would at home. Keep your valuables out of sight. On big ships virtually every cabin has a small safe in the closet. Don't carry too much cash ashore, use credit cards whenever possible, and keep your money in a secure place, such as a front pocket that's harder to pick. Single women traveling with friends should stick together, especially when returning to their cabins late at night. And be careful about whom you befriend, as you would anywhere, whether it's a fellow passenger or a member of the crew. Don't be paranoid, but do be prudent.

Health Care

Quality medical care at sea is another important safety issue. All big ships are equipped with medical infirmaries to handle minor emergencies. However, these should not be confused with hospitals. There are no international standards governing medical facilities or personnel aboard cruise ships, although the American Medical Association has recommended that such standards be adopted. If you have a preexisting medical condition, discuss your upcoming cruise with your doctor. Pack an extra supply of any medicines you might need. Once aboard, see the ship's doctor and alert him or her to your condition, and discuss treatments or emergency procedures before any problem arises. Passengers with potentially life-threatening conditions should seriously consider signing up with a medical evacuation service, and all passengers should review their health insurance to make sure they are covered while on a cruise.

If you become seriously ill or injured and happen to be near a major city, you may be taken to a medical facility shoreside. But if you're farther afield, you may have to be airlifted off the ship by helicopter and flown either to the nearest American territory or to an airport where you can be taken by charter jet to the United States. Many standard health insurance policies, as well as Medicare, do not cover these or other medical expenses incurred outside the United States. You can, however, buy supplemental health insurance to cover you while you're traveling.

The most common minor medical problems confronting cruise passengers are seasickness and gastrointestinal distress. Modern cruise ships, unlike their transatlantic predecessors, are relatively motion-free vessels with computer-controlled stabilizers, and they usually sail in relatively calm waters. If, however, you do feel queasy, you can always get seasickness pills aboard ship.

Outbreaks of food poisoning happen from time to time aboard cruise ships. Episodes are random. They can occur on ships old and new, big and small, budget and luxury. The Centers for Disease Control and Prevention (CDC) monitors cruise-ship hygiene and sanitation procedures, conducting voluntary inspections twice a year of all ships that sail regularly from U.S. ports (this program does not include ships that never visit the United States). For a free listing of the latest ship scores, write the CDC's **National Center for Environmental Health** (Vessel Sanitation Program, (✉ 1015 North America Way, Room 107, Miami, FL 33132 ☎ 888/232–3299 for fax-back service ⊕ www.cdc.gov). If you use the fax-back service, request publication 510051.

A high score on the CDC report isn't a guarantee that you won't get sick. Outbreaks have taken place on ships that consistently score very highly. Conversely, on some ships that score very poorly passengers never get sick. So use these scores as a guideline and factor them in with other considerations when choosing your ship.

DISEMBARKATION

The last night of your cruise is full of business. On most ships you must place everything except your hand luggage outside your cabin door, ready to be picked up by midnight. Color-coded tags, distributed to your cabin in a debarkation packet, should be placed on your luggage before the crew collects it. The color of your tag will later determine when you leave the ship and help you retrieve your luggage on the pier.

Your shipboard bill is left in your room during the last day; to pay the bill (if you haven't already put it on your credit card) or to settle any questions, you must stand in line at the purser's office. Some lines close down their computer files for the cruise by 9 or 10 AM to prepare for the next cruise and may be unable to credit your account with any disputed charges, requiring you to contact your credit card company or the cruise line later for a refund. Tips to the cabin steward and dining staff are distributed on the last night of the cruise or are automatically added to your onboard account. On many ships, you can review your account on your in-cabin television and change those tips in any way you like, up or down. You may also make changes to or discuss your bill at the purser's office at any time during the cruise.

On the morning the cruise ends, in-room breakfast service may not be available because stewards are too busy, but you will usually find breakfast being served in both the formal dining room and at the ship's buffet dining area. Most passengers clear out of their cabins as soon as possible, gather their hand luggage, and stake out a chair in one of the public lounges to await the ship's clearance through customs. Be patient—it takes a long time to unload and sort thousands of pieces of luggage. Passengers are disembarked by groups according to the color-coded tags placed on luggage the night before. Those with the earliest flights get off first. If you have a tight connection, notify the purser before the last day, and he or she may be able to arrange faster debarkation for you.

Customs & Duties

U.S. Customs

Before a ship lands, each individual or family must fill out a customs declaration, regardless of whether anything was purchased abroad. If you have less than $400 worth of goods, you will not need to itemize purchases. Be prepared to pay whatever duties are owed directly to the customs inspector, with cash or check.

U.S. Customs preclears a number of ships sailing in and out of certain ports. It's done on the ship before you disembark. In other ports you must collect your luggage from the dock and then stand in line to pass through the inspection point. This can take up to an hour.

DUTIES FOR U.S. CITIZENS For general customs and duty information, *see* Customs & Duties *in* Smart Travel Tips A to Z. Duties are the same for returning cruise passengers as for all other travelers, with a few exceptions. On certain Caribbean itineraries that include a visit to Bermuda, you may be entitled to bring back $600 worth of goods duty-free, as opposed to the usual $400.

DUTIES FOR NON-U.S. CITIZENS If you hold a foreign passport and will be returning home within hours of docking, you may be exempt from all U.S. Customs duties. Everything you bring into the United States must leave with you when you return home. When you reach your own country, you will have to pay appropriate duties there.

SENDING PACKAGES HOME You may also send packages home duty-free, with a limit of one parcel per addressee per day (except alcohol or tobacco products or perfume worth more than $5). You can mail up to $200 worth of goods for personal use; and $100 worth of goods as a gift. Mailed items do not affect your duty-free allowance on your return.

EXPLORING BERMUDA

FODOR'S CHOICE

Bermuda Aquarium, Museum & Zoo, *in Flatts Village*

Bermuda Maritime Museum and Dolphin Quest, *at the Royal Naval Dockyard*

Gibb's Hill Lighthouse, *in Southampton Parish*

Paget Marsh, *in Paget Parish*

HIGHLY RECOMMENDED

Bermuda National Trust Museum at the Globe Hotel, *in St. George's*

Cathedral of the Most Holy Trinity, *in Hamilton*

City Hall & Arts Centre, *in Hamilton*

Fort Hamilton, *in Pembroke Parish*

Fort St. Catherine, *in St. George's Parish*

Museum of the Bermuda Historical Society/Bermuda Public Library, *in Hamilton*

Ordnance Island, *in St. George's*

Spittal Pond, *in Smith's Parish*

St. Peter's Church, *in St. George's*

Tucker House, *in St. George*

Verdmont, *in Smith's Parish*

Revised by Sue
Johnston

HEDGES OF HIBISCUS and oleander line Bermuda's streets, while prettily painted limestone buildings sit primly before well-tended gardens. You may hear the cry of a kiskadee and, on warm evenings, the chirping of tiny tree frogs. On the breeze, depending on the season, is the fragrance of frangipani, freesia, lily, or rosemary. Touring Bermuda, whether by foot, taxi, motor scooter, or horse-drawn carriage, is a multisensory pleasure.

Hamilton, the capital, has Bermuda's principal harbor and most of the island's shops. The town is also the main departure point for sightseeing boats, ferries, and the pink-and-blue buses that ramble all over the island. The town of St. George's, at the island's East End, was Bermuda's first capital and is a UNESCO World Heritage Site. At the West End you'll find the sleepy village of Somerset and the Royal Naval Dockyard, a former British naval shipyard, now home to the Bermuda Maritime Museum and an arts, crafts, and shopping center.

Hamilton, St. George's, and Dockyard can all be explored easily on foot. The rest of the island, however, is best discovered by taxi, motor scooter, or bicycle (only if you're fit—Bermuda is hilly). The main roads connecting the parishes are: North Shore Road, Middle Road, South Shore Road, and Harbour Road, whose names can help you find your bearings. Almost all traffic traversing the island's 22-mi length uses these roads, although some 1,200 smaller ones crisscross the land.

Consider buying the Heritage Passport for $37.50 if you plan to visit five or more of the following attractions: the Bermuda National Gallery; Bermuda Underwater Exploration Institute; Bermuda Maritime Museum; Fort St. Catherine; Bermuda National Trust Museum in the Globe Hotel; Verdmont; Tucker House; and Bermuda Aquarium, Museum & Zoo. The pass gets you into all eight attractions in any four-day period for one price. You can buy the Heritage Passport at any of the Visitors Service Bureaus and at the attractions themselves.

HAMILTON

Bermuda's capital since 1815, the City of Hamilton is a small, bustling harbor town. If you've never been to Bermuda, it's easy to confuse Hamilton, the town, with the parish of the same name, but the city is actually in Pembroke Parish, while Hamilton Parish is farther northeast. Hamilton the city is the economic and social center of Bermuda, with busy streets lined with shops and offices. The thriving international-business community works in such industries as financial and investment services, insurance, telecommunications, global management of intellectual property, shipping, and aircraft and ship registration. International influences, from both business and tourism, have brought a degree of sophistication unusual in so small a city. There is a handful of museums and galleries to explore; however, the favorite pastimes are shopping in Hamilton's numerous boutiques and dining in its many upscale restaurants.

Numbers in the text correspond to numbers in the margin and on the Hamilton, Town of St. George's, West End, and Parishes maps.

a good
walk

Any tour of Hamilton should begin on **Front Street ①**, a pretty, busy thoroughfare lined with small, colorful buildings, many with balconies and arcades. The **Visitors Service Bureau** ➤, near the Ferry Terminal, is a good starting point. Turn left after leaving the bureau and follow Point Pleasant Road to the waterside park for a splendid view of Hamilton Harbour at **Albuoy's Point ②**. From here, retrace your steps and pass the Ferry Terminal Building, where passengers board sightseeing boats to

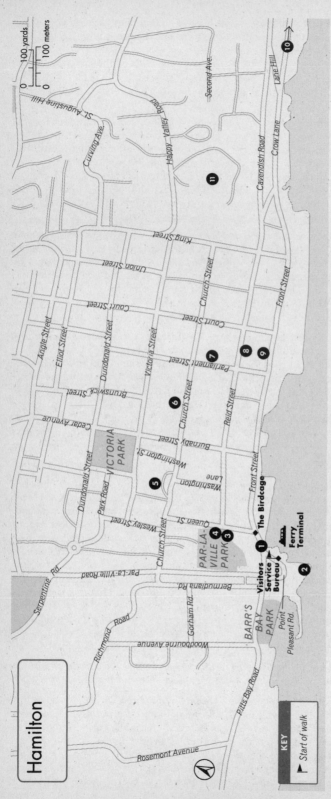

Hamilton

100 yards
100 meters

St. Augustine Hill

Curving Ave.

Happy Valley Road

Second Ave.

Lane Hill

Crow Lane

Cavendish Road

⑪

King Street

Union Street

Church Street

Front Street

Court Street

Court Street

Angle Street

Elliot Street

Dundonald Street

Victoria Street

Parliament Street

⑦

⑧

⑨

Brunswick Street

⑥

Church Street

Reid Street

Cedar Avenue

Burnaby Street

VICTORIA PARK

Dundonald Street

Park Road

Washington St.

Washington Lane

Front Street

⑤

Queen St.

Wesley Street

Church Street

④
③

PAR-LA-VILLE PARK

Par-La-Ville Road

Bermudiana Rd.

Serpentine Rd.

Richmond Road

Gorham Rd.

Woodbourne Avenue

Pitts Bay Road

Rosemont Avenue

The Birdcage

① Visitors Service Bureau

Ferry Terminal

②

BARR'S BAY PARK

Point Pleasant Rd.

KEY

▲ Start of walk

Albuoy's Point **2**

Bermuda Underwater Exploration Institute (BUEI) **10**

Cabinet Building **8**

Cathedral of the Most Holy Trinity **6**

Cenotaph **9**

City Hall & Arts Centre . . .**5**

Fort Hamilton **11**

Front Street **1**

Museum of the Bermuda Historical Society/Bermuda Public Library **4**

Perot Post Office **3**

Sessions House **7**

tour the island's waterways. Just beyond the docks is a large pink building called the No. 1 Shed, one of the island's several terminals for the elegant cruise ships that call at Bermuda.

Back on Front Street, at Queen Street, you'll see the Birdcage, a traffic box named for its designer, Michael "Dickey" Bird. Continue up Queen Street to view the restored, 19th-century **Perot Post Office ❸**. Just beyond it is the **Museum of the Bermuda Historical Society/Bermuda Public Library ❹**. Follow Queen Street away from the harbor to Church Street to reach the **City Hall & Arts Centre ❺**, which houses the Bermuda National Gallery, the Bermuda Society of Arts Gallery, and a performing arts center.

From the City Hall steps, turn east (left) on Church Street and pass the Hamilton Bus Terminal. One block further, you'll see the imposing **Cathedral of the Most Holy Trinity ❻**. Just beyond the cathedral, near the corner of Church and Parliament streets, is **Sessions House ❼**. If you continue down Parliament to Front Street, you'll see the **Cabinet Building ❽** and, in front of it, the **Cenotaph ❾**. From here, have a leisurely stroll past (or into) the Front Street shops and perhaps have tea upstairs at Trimingham's or Cooper's department stores.

If you're up for a longer walk (about 15 minutes east from the Cenotaph) or are travelling by scooter or taxi, head to the **Bermuda Underwater Exploration Institute (BUEI) ❿**. Pedestrians can follow the sidewalk on the south (water) side of Front Street to BUEI. Scooters and cars have to go a roundabout way as BUEI is accessible only when you're coming inbound to Hamilton. To get there, drive out of town on Front Street, go around the traffic circle, and exit at the lane signposted for the BUEI.

Fort Hamilton ⓫ is another worthwhile destination, though the road to it, north on King Street, then a sharp right on Happy Valley Road, is a bit too steep for casual walkers. The fort has a moat, beautiful grounds, underground passageways, and great views of Hamilton and its harbor. If you're on a motorbike, one-way streets mean you should reach the fort via Court Street, turning right on Church Street, then left on King. Then you negotiate a 270-degree turn at Happy Valley Road and follow the signs to the fort.

TIMING   You can see Hamilton in less than an hour, but give yourself a day if you're going to take in some of the museums, Fort Hamilton, and the Bermuda Underwater Exploration Institute. Serious shoppers should reserve a half day to explore the shops.

What to See

❷ **Albuoy's Point.** Hamilton Harbour is dotted with tiny islands, and its blue waters are graced with the sails of pleasure craft and passenger ferries. Ringside seats for this show are the benches beneath the trees at Albuoy's Point, a small waterside park. Nearby is the **Royal Bermuda Yacht Club**, founded in 1844 and granted the use of the word "Royal" by Prince Albert in 1845. Today international yachting celebrities hobnob with local yachtsmen and business executives at the club's 1930s headquarters. If you are here between April and November, you might see one of the many club-sponsored racing events, such as the Newport–Bermuda Ocean Yacht Race in June or the Gold Cup International Match Race Tournament in October. ✉ *Off Front St.*

off the beaten path

BARR'S BAY PARK – West of Albuoy's Point, just beyond Bermudiana Road on Pitts Bay Road (a continuation of Front Street), steps and a ramp lead from the street to this park, with its vast expanse of green grass, its vistas, and its benches for taking it all in.

🖐 ⑩ **Bermuda Underwater Exploration Institute.** The harborside BUEI's Ocean Discovery Centre has numerous multimedia and interactive displays designed to acquaint you with the vast deep and its inhabitants. You can board a diving capsule and step out amidst the sights and sounds of the ocean floor—including treasures from sunken ships—all without getting wet. Never heard of a bathysphere? See a replica of this deep-sea diving vehicle, which allowed oceanographer William Beebe and Otis Barton to venture ½ mi down into the deep in 1934. Or take up conchology, the study of shells—the BUEI holds one of the world's finest shell collections. Films and lectures are scheduled daily, and the on-site waterside restaurant, La Coquille, is a lovely place for lunch. Children will have a hard time leaving the gift shop without a souvenir in hand. ⊠ *40 Crow La., off E. Broadway* ☎ *441/292–7219* 🖶 *441/236–6141* ⊕ *www.buei.bm* 🎫 *$9.75* ☉ *Daily 9–5.*

❽ **Cabinet Building.** Bermuda's Senate, the upper house of Parliament, sits in the dignified Cabinet Building, built in 1938. A most rewarding time to visit is at the formal opening of Parliament, traditionally on the first Friday of November. His Excellency the Governor, dressed in a plumed hat and full regalia, arrives on the grounds in a landau drawn by magnificent black horses and accompanied by a police escort. A senior police officer, carrying the Black Rod made by the Crown jewelers, then asks the Speaker of the House, elected representatives, and members of the Senate Chamber to convene. The governor presents the Throne Speech from a tiny cedar throne, dating from the 1600s, which is carved with the words "Cap Josias Forstore Govornour of the Sumer Islands Anodo 1642" (Josias Foster was governor in 1642). At other times of the year, visit on a Wednesday to watch the Senate in action. ⊠ *Front St. at Parliament St.* ☎ *441/292–5501* ⊕ *www.gov.bm* 🎫 *Free* ☉ *Weekdays 9–5.*

★ ❻ **Cathedral of the Most Holy Trinity.** Designed in early-English style with Gothic-revival flourishes, this Anglican cathedral was constructed of Bermuda limestone and imported materials from France, Nova Scotia, and Scotland. The cathedral was completed in 1911, the replacement for an earlier church destroyed by an arsonist in 1884. It has a copper roof, unusual in Bermuda's sea of white-topped buildings. Inside, the clerestory in the nave is supported by piers of polished Scottish granite, and the choir stalls and bishop's throne are carved of English oak. Of the lovely stained-glass windows, note especially the Angel Window on the east wall of the north transept, which was made by local artist Vivienne Gilmore Gardner. After exploring the interior, you can purchase tickets to climb the 150-odd steps (143 feet) of the tower, from the top of which you can see beautiful views of the town. ⊠ *Church St.* ☎ *441/292–4033* 🎫 *Tower $3* ☉ *Church daily 8–4:45 and for Sun. services, tower weekdays 10–3.*

(need a break?) **The Spot** (⊠ 6 Burnaby St. ☎ 441/292–6293) has been around since the 1940s and its recipe for success has hardly changed. Old-fashioned deli sandwiches—try the turkey—are served all day, from Monday to Saturday, 6:30 AM to 10 PM. Bacon-and-eggs breakfasts are also available.

La Baguette Delicatessen (⊠ 16 Burnaby St. ☎ 441/296–1129), a couple of doors down from The Spot, makes Euro-style sandwiches for up to $7, and the house specialty is chili with onions and cheddar.

❾ **Cenotaph.** This memorial to Bermuda's war dead stands in front of the Cabinet Building. Made of Bermuda limestone, it is a replica of the cenotaph in London, England. Since it was built, in 1920, every Remembrance Day (November 11), the governor and other dignitaries lay wreaths at its base.

★ ⑤ **City Hall & Arts Centre.** Set back from the street behind a fountain and lily pond, City Hall, built in 1960, houses Hamilton's administrative offices as well as two art galleries and a performance hall. Rather than a clock, its tower has a wind vane—not a surprise in a land where the weather is as important as the time. The statues of children playing in the fountain are by local sculptor Desmond Fountain, whose lifelike characters you may encounter elsewhere in your Bermuda travels. The building was designed by Bermudian architect Will Onions, a champion of balanced simplicity. Massive cedar doors open into a large lobby with great chandeliers and high ceilings. Mayors, past and present, look back at you from the walls. The city offices, to your right, hold the Benbow Stamp Collection and exhibits of Bermuda antiques. The City Hall Theatre, to the left, is a major venue for concerts, plays, and dance performances. A handsome cedar staircase leads upstairs, past a large portrait of Her Royal Majesty Queen Elizabeth II, to two second-floor art galleries. (An elevator gets you there, too.)

On the first landing, in the East Exhibition Room, is the **Bermuda National Gallery** (☎ 441/295–9428 ⊕ www.bermudanationalgallery. com ☞ $3), the home of Bermuda's national art collection. The permanent exhibits, with artwork from the 16th century to the 21st, include European and Bermudian paintings, African masks and sculpture, and photographs by internationally known artists, such as Bermudian Richard Saunders (1922–1987). The fine and decorative art pieces in the Bermuda Collection reflect the country's multicultural heritage. Temporary exhibits are a major part of the museum's program, and on any given day you can see a selection of local artists' work as well as a visiting exhibit from another museum. If you visit on a Wednesday, you may find a noon-time lecture taking place, or, on Thursday at 10, join a guided tour.

Further up the stairs, in the West Wing, the **Bermuda Society of Arts Gallery** (☎ 441/292–3824 ☞ Free, donations accepted) displays work by its members. Its frequently changing juried shows attract talented local painters, sculptors, and photographers. Many of the pieces are for sale. ⊠ *17 Church St.* ☎ *441/292–1234* ⊘ *City Hall weekdays 9–5; National Gallery and Society of the Arts Mon.–Sat. 10–4.*

need a break? **Paradiso Café** (⊠ 7 Reid St. ☎ 441/295–3263), at the entrance to Washington Mall, is a hip lunch spot that serves sandwiches and wraps, desserts, and espresso coffees, including an attractive, layered mochachino.

Windsor Garden (⊠ Windsor Place Mall, Queen St. ☎ 441/295–4085) is a good place to pause, take a breath, and have a cool drink or reviving cup of coffee before returning to your shopping spree. Sandwiches and diet-busting pastries are also served.

★ ♻ ⑪ **Fort Hamilton.** The imposing old fortress has a moat, 18-ton guns, and underground passageways that were cut through solid rock by Royal Engineers in the 1860s. Built to defend the west end's Royal Naval Dockyard from an attack by land, it was outdated even before its completion, though it remains one of the finest surviving examples of a mid-Victorian polygonal fort in Bermuda. Not a history buff? The fort offers splendid views of the capital and the harbor as well as lovely gardens. On Mondays at noon, from November to May, bagpipes may echo through the grounds as the Bermuda Islands Pipe Band performs its skirling ceremony. One-way streets make getting to the fort by scooter a bit challenging. From downtown Hamilton head north on Queen Street, turn right on Church Street, then turn left to go up the hill on King Street. Make a sharp right turn (270°) onto Happy Valley Road and follow the signs. Pedestrians may walk along Front Street to King Street. ⊠ *Happy Valley Rd.* ☎ *No phone* ☞ *Free* ☉ *Daily 9:30–5.*

❶ **Front Street.** Hamilton's main thoroughfare runs alongside the harbor. Front Street bustles with small cars, motor scooters, bicycles, buses, pedestrians, and the occasional horse-drawn carriage. When cruise ships are in port, Front Street's colorful little buildings, containing shops, galleries, and restaurants, fairly burst with shoppers and sightseers. Don't overlook small offshoots and alleyways, like Chancery Lane, Bermuda House Lane, and the Walkway, where you'll stumble upon even more hidden-away boutiques. A good place to start a walking tour of Hamilton is at the ☞ Visitors Service Bureau on Front Street near the cruise ship terminal on the harbor.

★ ❹ **Museum of the Bermuda Historical Society/Bermuda Public Library.** Mark Twain admired the giant rubber tree that stands on Queen Street in the front yard of this Georgian house, once the home of Hamilton's first postmaster, William Bennet Perot, and his family. (There's no known connection to former U.S. presidential candidate Ross Perot, although he does have a house in Bermuda.) Although charmed by the tree, which had been imported from Demerara (now Guyana) in the mid-19th century, Twain lamented that it didn't bear fruit in the form of hot-water bottles and rubber overshoes. The library, upon which Twain had no comment, was founded in 1839 and its reference section has virtually every book ever written about Bermuda, as well as a microfilm collection of Bermudian newspapers dating back to 1784. The library entrance is to the right of the museum entrance.

Established in 1955, the museum is filled with household goods and other artifacts, including an 18th-century sedan chair, depicting the history of life in Bermuda. One display is full of tools and trinkets made by and belonging to Boer War prisoners who were exiled on several of Bermuda's islands in 1901 and 1902. If you're lucky, author and Boer War expert Colin Benbow will be on hand to show you around the museum. Portraits of Sir George Somers and his wife, painted around 1605, and of Postmaster Perot and his wife hang in the entrance hall. Ask to see the copy of the letter George Washington wrote in 1775 "to the inhabitants of Bermuda," requesting gunpowder for use in the American Revolution. ⊠ *13 Queen St.* ☎ *441/295–2905 library; 441/295–2487 museum* ☞ *Free, donations accepted* ☉ *Library weekdays 9–6, Sat. 9–5; museum Mon.–Sat. 9:30–3:30* ☞ *Tours by appointment.*

❸ **Perot Post Office.** Bermuda's first postage stamps originated in this carefully restored two-story building, which dates from around 1840 and still operates as a post office. Bermuda's first postmaster, William Bennet Perot, was appointed in 1818. Perot would meet arriving steamers, collect the mail, stash it in his beaver hat, and then stroll around Hamilton to deliver it, greeting each recipient with a tip of his hat. To post a letter, residents came and paid Perot, who hand-stamped each one. He began printing stamps in 1848 and, though thousands of Perot-era Bermuda stamps were printed, only 11 exist today. ⊠ *Queen St.* ☎ *441/295–5151* ☞ *Free* ☉ *Weekdays 9–5.*

THE BERMUDA TRIANGLE DEMYSTIFIED

BEWITCHINGLY BEAUTIFUL BERMUDA is one of the few places in the modern world that still remain wrapped in an aura of superstitious mystery. The Bermuda Triangle—sometimes called the Devil's Triangle, Limbo of the Lost, the Twilight Zone, and Hoodoo Sea—covers some 500,000 square mi of the Atlantic Ocean. Its apexes are most commonly defined as Bermuda, the southernmost tip of Florida, and San Juan, Puerto Rico, although some place a boundary closer to Chesapeake Bay than to Miami. It seems to have been christened in February 1964, when Vincent Gaddis wrote an article titled "The Deadly Bermuda Triangle" for Argosy magazine.

Long before the myth of the Bermuda Triangle became popular, Bermuda had already earned a reputation as an enchanted island. It was nicknamed "The Devil's Islands" by early sea travelers, frightened by the calls of cahow birds and the squeals of wild pigs that could be heard on shore. But perhaps the most damning tales were told by sailors terrified of shipwreck on Bermuda's treacherous stretch of reefs. The island's mystical reputation was perhaps immortalized in Shakespeare's The Tempest, a tale of shipwreck and sorcery in "the still-vexed Bermoothes."

The early origin of the Triangle myth stretches as far back as Columbus, who noted in his logbook a haywire compass, strange lights, and a burst of flame falling into the sea. Columbus, as well as other seamen after him, also encountered a harrowing stretch of ocean now known as the Sargasso Sea. Ancient tales tell of sailboats stranded forever in a windless expanse of water, surrounded by seaweed and the remnants of other unfortunate vessels. It is true that relics have been found in the Sargasso Sea—an area of ocean in between Bermuda and the Caribbean—but the deadly calm waters are more likely the result of circular ocean currents sweeping through the North Atlantic rather than paranormal activity.

In the past 500 years at least 50 ships and 20 aircraft have vanished in the Triangle, most without a trace—no wreckage, no bodies, no nothing. Many disappeared in reportedly calm waters, without having sent a distress signal. Among the legends is that of the Mary Celeste, a 103-foot brigantine found floating and abandoned in 1872. But the real mystery of the Mary Celeste is that she turns up in Triangle tales at all. The ship was actually found off the coast of Portugal. Then there is the case of Flight 19. At 2:10 on the afternoon of December 5, 1945, five TBM Avenger Torpedo Bombers took off from Fort Lauderdale, Florida, on a routine two-hour training mission. Their last radio contact was at 4 PM. The planes and 27 men were never seen or heard from again. The official navy report said the planes disappeared "as if they had flown to Mars."

The bizarre disappearances attributed to the Triangle have been linked to everything from alien abduction to sorcery. Although the mystery has not yet been completely solved, there are scientific explanations for many of the maritime disasters that have occurred in the Triangle. The most obvious answers are linked to extreme weather conditions with which any Bermudian fisherman would be well acquainted. "White squalls"— intense, unexpected storms that arrive without warning on otherwise clear days—are probable culprits along with waterspouts, the equivalent of sea tornadoes. The most recent scientific theory on the infamous Triangle suggests that the freakish disappearance of ships and aircraft could be the result of large deposits of methane gas spewing up from the ocean floor. Huge eruptions of methane bubbles may push water away from a ship, causing it to sink. If the highly flammable methane then rises into the air, it could ignite in an airplane's engine— causing it to explode and disappear.

Fact or fiction, the Bermuda Triangle is a part of local lore that won't disappear anytime soon. But don't let the legend scare you away—the Triangle isn't the only thing that makes this island seem magical.

— Kim Dismont Robinson

Next to the Perot Post Office is the Queen Street entrance to **Par-la-Ville Park** (there's another entrance on Par-la-Ville Road). Paths wind through the luxuriant gardens, and the park benches are ideal for picnicking or enjoying a short rest. At the park's west entrance is a fine example of a Bermuda moongate.

You might pick up your picnic at the **Lemon Tree Café** (⊠ Queen St. ☎ 441/292–0235) right beside the Par-la-Ville Park entrance. Monday through Saturday, from breakfast to late afternoon, talented chefs whip together hot meals, sandwiches, and wicked French pastries to enjoy on the patio or take away.

❼ **Sessions House.** The eye-catching Italianate edifice called Sessions House, built in 1819, is where the House of Assembly (the lower house of Parliament) and the Supreme Court convene. Bermuda has one elected official for every 745 registered voters—approximately 14 times as many politicians per capita as Europe or North America. The Florentine towers and colonnade, decorated with red terra-cotta, were added to the building in 1887 to commemorate Queen Victoria's Golden Jubilee. The Victoria Jubilee Clock Tower made its striking debut at midnight on December 31, 1893. Bermuda's Westminster-style Parliament meets on the second floor, whereas the Supreme Court is on the lower floor. You're welcome to watch the ceremonious and colorful (i.e., robes and full wigs) proceedings inside; call in advance to find out when sessions are scheduled. ⊠ *Parliament St. between Reid and Church Sts.* ☎ *441/292–7408* ⊕ *www.gov.bm* ⊡ *Free* ☉ *Weekdays 9–12:30 and 2–5.*

ST. GEORGE'S

The settlement of Bermuda began in what is now the town of St. George's nearly 400 years ago, when the *Sea Venture* was shipwrecked on Bermuda's treacherous reefs on its way to the colony of Jamestown, Virginia. No trip to Bermuda is complete without a visit to this historic town and UNESCO World Heritage Site. The town is an outstanding example of an early English settlement in the New World, with old walled lanes and alleys that beckon to be explored.

a good walk

Start your tour in **King's Square** ⑫ ▶, perhaps stopping in the Visitors Service Bureau to pick up maps and brochures. Stroll out onto **Ordnance Island** ⑬ to see the dunking stool and a replica of the *Deliverance II*. Behind you, just up the street is the **Bermuda National Trust Museum at the Globe Hotel** ⑭, and across the square is the **Town Hall** ⑮. Venturing up King Street, notice the fine Bermudian architecture of **Bridge House** ⑯. At the top of King Street is the **Old State House** ⑰, the oldest stone house in Bermuda.

Walk up Princess Street to Duke of York Street and turn right, following the sidewalk to the **Bermudian Heritage Museum** ⑱. Across Duke of York Street, you'll find the beautiful **Somers Garden** ⑲, the alleged burial site of the heart of Sir George Somers. After walking through the garden, climb the steps to Blockade Alley, where you'll see, on a hill ahead, the **Unfinished Church** ⑳. To your left are Duke of Kent Street, Featherbed Alley, and the **St. George's Historical Society Museum** ㉑. Around the corner is the **Featherbed Alley Printery** ㉒. Cross Clarence Street to Church Street and then turn right on Broad Alley to reach the **Old Rectory** ㉓. Straight ahead (as straight as you can go among these twisted alleys) is Printer's Alley, where Joseph Stockdale published Bermuda's first newspaper, on January 17, 1784. The short street connecting Printer's Alley with Old Maid's Lane is **Nea's Alley** ㉔, which looks like something out of a tale retold by the Brothers Grimm.

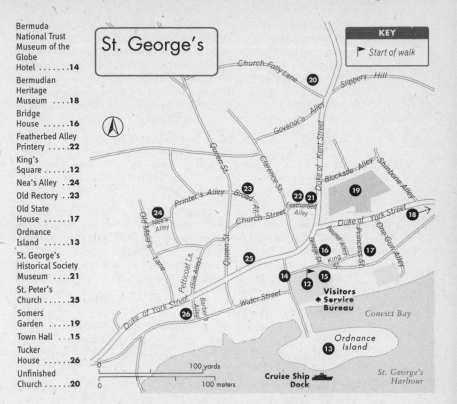

Return to Church Street and enter the yard of **St. Peter's Church** ㉕, an architecturally significant Anglican church. (The main entrance is on Duke of York Street.) From the church, continue down Duke of York Street to Barber's Alley, turning left to reach **Tucker House** ㉖, a historical home and museum filled with antiques.

TIMING Plan to spend a full day in St. George's, which, though small, holds many places of historical interest, and museums, gardens, and shops. They say you can't get lost in St. George's—but you can lose track of time.

What to See

★ ⑭ **Bermuda National Trust Museum at the Globe Hotel.** Governor Samuel Day built this house in 1700. Later, during the American Civil War, Confederate Major Norman Walker was stationed in the building. From there, Walker coordinated the flow of guns, ammunition, and war supplies through Union blockades in American ports. The house saw service as the Globe Hotel during the mid-19th century and became a National Trust property in 1951. A video, *Bermuda, Centre of the Atlantic,* explains the history of Bermuda, and an exhibit entitled "Rogues & Runners: Bermuda and the American Civil War" describes St. George's when it was a port for Confederate blockade runners. ⊠ *Duke of York St.* ☎ *441/297–1423* ⊕ *www.bnt.bm* ☒ *$4; $5 combination ticket includes admission to Tucker House and Verdmont* ⊙ *Mon.–Sat. 10–4.*

⑱ **Bermudian Heritage Museum.** The history, trials, and accomplishments of black Bermudians are traced in this museum's exhibits. Photographs of early black Bermudians, including slaves, freedom fighters, and professionals line the walls. A model of the slave ship *Enterprise* is part of a display that describes how the ship, with its load of human "cargo," was blown off its course from Virginia to South Carolina. It landed in

Bermuda, where slavery had already been abolished. Technically, the 78 slaves, though American, were free in Bermuda. Local Friendly Societies—organizations of black Bermudians dedicated to the cause of freeing and supporting slaves—obtained an injunction to bring the slaves' case into court, and Society members escorted the slaves to their hearing in Hamilton, where many spoke in their own defense. All except one woman and her four children accepted the offer of freedom. Many Bermudians can trace their ancestry to those who arrived on the *Enterprise* in 1835.

Other rooms in the museum hold artifacts from early homes, including antique and reconstructed furniture made by black artisans. The museum building was constructed as a warehouse in 1844 and, by 1907, was home to one of the Friendly Societies. Today it is a Bermuda National Trust property. ✉ *Water and York Sts.* ☎ *441/297–4126* 💵 *$3* ⏲ *Tues.–Sat. 10–3.*

16 **Bridge House.** Named for a bridge that once crossed a small tidal creek nearby, this house was built sometime prior to 1700 and is a fine example of Bermudian architecture. It has been home to several of Bermuda's governors and is now a property of the Bermuda National Trust, which has restored and leased its rooms as private apartments, an art studio, and a shop.

22 **Featherbed Alley Printery.** In a quaint little cottage, this printing office houses a working press of the sort invented by Johannes Gutenberg in the 1450s. ✉ *Featherbed Alley* ☎ *441/297–0423* 💵 *$5, including admission to St. George's Historical Society Museum* ⏲ *Apr.–Nov., weekdays 10–4; Jan.–Mar., Wed. 11–4.*

12 **King's Square.** Now the hub and heartbeat of St. George's, King's Square is actually comparatively new. For 200 years after the town was settled the square was a marshy part of the harbor. It was filled in only in the 1800s. Prominently displayed in King's Square are cedar replicas of the stocks and pillory originally used to punish criminals. The grisly gizmos now serve as props for photos and for special activities staged here on Wednesday during low season. If you're greeted in the square by the town crier, whose resounding voice is almost enough to wake the dead and who is on hand in full colonial costume, you'll know a walking tour is starting. In summer, there are re-enactments of historical incidents, including the dunking of offenders by way of a dunking stool perched over a pool of water. Check with the Visitors Service Bureau for a schedule of events.

24 **Nea's Alley.** The 19th-century Irish poet Tom Moore lived on this street, then known as Cumberland Lane, during his brief tenure as registrar of the admiralty court. Moore, who was endowed with considerable charm, had an impact on the island that endures to this day. His legacy is somewhat scandalous: Moore was invited to stay in the home of Admiral Mitchell, the neighbor of Mr. William Tucker and his wife, Hester, who is the "Nea" to whom Moore pours out his heart in several poems. Moore is thought to have first seen Hester here in Cumberland Lane, which he describes in one of his odes as "the lime-covered alley that leads to thy home."

23 **The Old Rectory.** Built about 1690 by pirate George Dew, this home is said to be haunted by a mysterious woman who sometimes plays the harpsichord. The house takes its name from a later resident, Alexander Richardson, two-time rector of St. Peter's Church between 1755 and 1805. In addition to handsome gardens, the house has lovely examples of traditional Bermudian architectural features, such as cedar beams and a "welcoming arms" staircase. ✉ *Broad Alley, behind St. Peter's Church*

🖾 *441/236–6483* ⊕ *www.bnt.bm* 🖾 *Free, donations accepted* ⊗ *Nov.–Mar., Wed. 12–5.*

⑰ Old State House. A curious ritual takes place every April in King's Square. One peppercorn, regally placed upon a velvet pillow, is presented to the mayor of St. George's amid much pomp and circumstance. The peppercorn is the annual rent paid to the town by the Masonic Lodge St. George No. 200 of the Grand Lodge of Scotland. The fraternal organization has occupied the Old State House since Bermuda's Parliament vacated it when the capital moved from St. George's to Hamilton in 1815. The oldest house in Bermuda, it was built in 1620 in what Governor Nathaniel Butler believed was the Italian style. The limestone building used a mixture of turtle oil and lime as mortar and set the style for future Bermudian buildings. 🖾 *Princess St.* 🖾 *441/292–2480; 441/297–1206 Wed. only* 🖾 *Free* ⊗ *Wed. 10–4.*

★ ⊙ **⑬ Ordnance Island.** *Land Ho!*—a splendid Desmond Fountain statue of Sir George Somers—dominates Ordnance Island. The dunking stool is a replica of the one used to dunk gossips, nagging wives, and suspected witches. Demonstrations are sometimes given, although volunteers report that getting dunked is no fun, even in fun.

Also on the island is the *Deliverance II,* a replica of one of two ships— the other was the *Patience*—built by the survivors of the 1609 wreck of the *Sea Venture* to carry them to Jamestown, Virginia, their original destination. 🖾 *Across the harbor from King's Square* 🖾 *441/297–2750* 🖾 *$3* ⊗ *Mar.–Nov., daily 9–5.*

㉑ St. George's Historical Society Museum. Furnished to resemble its former incarnation as a private home, this typical Bermudian building from the early 1700s houses artifacts and documents pertaining to the island's earliest days. There's even a whale-blubber cutter. The cottage gardens behind the museum are beautiful, and there is no fee to visit them. 🖾 *Featherbed Alley* 🖾 *441/297–0423* 🖾 *$5, includes admission to Featherbed Alley Printery* ⊗ *Apr.–Nov., weekdays 10–4; Jan.–Mar., Wed. 11–4.*

★ **㉕ St. Peter's Church.** Because parts of St. Peter's Church date back to its construction in 1620, it holds the distinction of being the oldest continuously operating Anglican church in the Western Hemisphere. It was not the first church to stand on this site, however. It replaced a 1612 structure of posts and palmetto leaves that was destroyed in a storm. The present church was extended in 1713, and the galleries on either side were added in 1833. The oldest part of the church is the area around the 17th-century triple-tier pulpit. The dark-red cedar altar is the oldest piece of woodwork in Bermuda, carved under the supervision of Richard Moore, a shipwright and the colony's first governor. The baptismal font, brought to the island by the early settlers, is about 500 years old, and the late-18th-century bishop's throne is believed to have been salvaged from a wreck. 🖾 *Duke of York St.* 🖾 *441/297–8359* 🖾 *Free, donations accepted* ⊗ *Daily 10–4:30.*

> **need a break?** Sitting almost cheek-by-jowl with St. Peter's Church, **Temptations Cafe & Bakery** (🖾 31 Duke of York St. 🖾 441/297–1368) entices its customers with delectable pastries and sandwiches.

⑲ Somers Garden. After sailing to Jamestown and back in 1610, Sir George Somers, the British admiral charged with developing the Bermudian colony, fell ill and died. According to local lore, Somers told his nephew Matthew Somers to bury his heart in Bermuda, where it belonged. Matthew, who seldom paid much attention to his uncle's wishes, sailed for England soon afterward, sneaking Somers's body aboard in a cedar chest. Somers was

CloseUp

ISLAND WEDDINGS

WITH MOONLIT BEACHES, amazingly vibrant flowers, and an honest-to-goodness Lover's Lane, it's no wonder so many people want to exchange their vows in this romantic paradise. If you're looking for an unforgettably beautiful spot to tie the knot, a wedding in Bermuda could be a fairy tale come true.

There are more than 100 places of worship on the island and you can exchange your vows in most of them. Two of the prettiest churches, especially for a smallish wedding, are Christ Church (Church of Scotland/Presbyterian) in Warwick Parish and St. Paul's (Church of England/Anglican) in Paget Parish. If you prefer to marry in a natural setting, you can choose from a nearly endless number of lovely outdoor locations—many overlooking the ocean—including Astwood Cove and Sonesta Beach Resort. If you wish to bring your own minister to perform the ceremony, you need permission from the Department of Immigration. All civil weddings take place at the Marriage Room at the Registrar's office—a surprisingly attractive spot to tie the knot.

As you plan, you may even want to consider adding a traditional Bermuda note to the festivities. Bermudians serve two cakes at their weddings. The groom's cake is plain, often pound cake, wrapped in gold leaf to symbolize wealth. The multitiered bride's cake is a fruitcake for blessings of fertility and is wrapped in silver leaf, symbolizing purity. A cedar seedling traditionally adorns one of the cakes and is planted by the couple to mirror the strength and growth of their love. And it is said that the bride and groom who walk under a Bermuda Moongate—an archway made of limestone and coral usually found at the entrance to gardens—will be assured good luck. The happy couple then travel to their local honeymoon destination on a traditional horse-and-carriage ride.

If you want to have a full-service wedding, it's a good idea to contact a local wedding coordinator to handle the legalities and logistics and provide advice. **Bermuda Weddings and Special Events** (☎ 441/293–4033 ⊕ www.bermudaweddings.bm) organizes weddings and publishes "A Guide To Your Bermuda Wedding." The staff at **Bridal Suite** (☎ 441/292–2025 ⊕ www.bridalsuitebermudaweddings.com) can also assist you in planning a perfect wedding. At the **Wedding Salon** (☎ 441/292–5677 ⊕ www.bermudaweddingsalon.com), consultant Barbara Whitecross is available to help with your planning. **BermudaWeddings.com** is a good resource with information about and links to other local companies. Don't forget to request a "Notice of Intended Marriage" form from the **Registrar General's Office** (☎ 441/297–7706 or 441/297–7707). Notices must be published in the newspaper several weeks in advance of your wedding.

— Kim Dismont Robinson

eventually buried near his birthplace in Dorset. Nevertheless, many people on both sides of the Atlantic believed that Matthew had carried out his uncle's wish before departing the island. However, when the tomb in Bermuda was opened many years later, only a few bones, a pebble, and some bottle fragments were found, so no one knows whether Matthew Somers buried the heart here or not. Nonetheless, ceremonies were held at the empty grave in 1920, when the Prince of Wales christened this pleasant, tree-shrouded park Somers Garden. ⊠ *Bordered by Shinbone Alley, Blockade Alley, and Duke of Kent and Duke of York Sts.* ☎ *no phone* ☒ *Free* ☉ *Daily 9–4.*

 Town Hall. St. George's administrative offices are housed in this two-story building constructed in 1808. The hall is paneled and furnished with cedar, and a collection of mayoral photos is on display. ⊠ *King's Sq.* ☎ 441/297–1425 ☒ *Free* ☉ *Town Hall Mon.–Sat. 10–4.*

need a
break? Return to the 21st century for a while to check your e-mail, cup of coffee in hand, at the **Cyber Caffe Latte** (✉ 8 York St. ☎ 441/297–8196), near St. George's main bus stop. You can also pick up bagels, soup, sandwiches, and smoothies, and sit on the sunny patio or in the comfortable air-conditioned shop.

★ ㉖ **Tucker House.** Constructed of native limestone, Tucker House is typical of many early Bermudian houses. It was built in 1711 for a merchant who used the basement as storage space for his wares, and it was originally close to the shore, though landfill has since moved the water back. Henry Tucker, president of the Governor's Council, lived here with his family from 1775 to 1807. Today, the beautifully preserved home is maintained, owned, and lovingly preserved as a museum by the Bermuda National Trust. Tucker's grandson donated much of the silver and fine cedar and mahogany furniture, which dates primarily from the mid-18th and early 19th centuries.

The Tucker name has been important in Bermuda since the birth of the colony, and a number of interesting family portraits hang in the house. Henry Tucker's father and brother were both involved in the famed "Gunpowder Plot" of 1775. The Continental Congress had imposed a ban on exports to all British colonies not taking part in the revolt against England, but Bermuda depended upon the American colonies for grain, so a delegation of Bermudians traveled to Philadelphia offering salt in exchange for the resumption of grain shipments. Congress rejected the salt, but agreed to lift the ban if Bermuda sent gunpowder instead. A group of Bermudians, including the two Tuckers, then broke into the island's arsenal, stole the gunpowder, and shipped it to Boston. The ban was soon lifted.

A short flight of stairs leads down to the kitchen, originally a separate building, and to an enclosed kitchen garden. Through the courtyard is the Bermuda National Trust's archaeological exhibit, which contains some of the artifacts discovered in its excavations.

The house is at the corner of Barber's Alley, named for Joseph Haine Rainey, a freed slave from South Carolina who fled to Bermuda at the outbreak of the American Civil War and made his living here as a barber. After the war, Rainey returned home and, in 1870, became the first black man to be elected to the U.S. House of Representatives. ✉ *Water St.* ☎ *441/297–0545* ⊕ *www.bnt.bm* ✍ *$4; $5 combination ticket includes admission to Bermuda National Trust Museum in the Globe Hotel and Verdmont* ☉ *Mon.–Sat. 10–4.*

㉕ **Unfinished Church.** Considering how much attention and affection are lavished on St. Peter's these days, it's hard to believe that residents in the 19th century wanted to replace the old church with a new one. Work began on this church in 1874, but construction was halted when disagreements erupted between church members. The building sat, unfinished and crumbling, for over a century. The Bermuda National Trust leased this elegant and picturesque ruin in 1992 and has repaired and stabilized it for locals and visitors to enjoy. ✉ *Kent St.* ☎ *441/236–6483* ⊕ *www.bnt.bm* ✍ *Free* ☉ *Daily, dawn to dusk.*

THE WEST END & DOCKYARD

In contrast to Hamilton and St. George's, the West End is rather pastoral. With the notable exception of the Royal Naval Dockyard, many of the attractions here are natural: wildlife reserves, wooded areas, and beautiful harbors and bays.

The story of the Dockyard begins with the post–American Revolution period, when Britain found itself with neither an anchorage nor a major ship-repair yard in the western Atlantic. Around 1809, when Napoléon was surfacing as a serious threat and British ships became increasingly vulnerable to pirate attack, Britain began construction of a major stronghold in Bermuda. The work was done by slaves and English convicts toiling under appalling conditions and living on prison ships. Thousands of workers died before the project was completed. The Dockyard operated as a naval shipyard for nearly 150 years. It was closed in 1951, although the Royal Navy maintained a small presence there until 1976 and held title to the land until 1995.

The Bermudian government and development groups began to plan for civilian use of the Dockyard in 1980. Since then, thanks to $21 million in public funding and $42 million in private investment, the area has literally blossomed—grassy lawns, trees, and shrubs grow where there used to be vast stretches of concrete. Cruise ships dock at the terminal and private yachts float calmly in the marina. The handsome, century-old Clocktower Building, now called the Clocktower Mall, holds restaurants, galleries, and shops. In the Cooperage Building, there's an art gallery and a permanent art-and-crafts market. Every year new Dockyard projects and attractions open to great fanfare and enthusiasm from local residents. You can reach the Dockyard from Hamilton in 45 minutes by ferry or by bus.

a good tour

To get the most out of a visit to the West End, plan to combine sea and land transportation. If you've bought a bus pass, rather than tickets, it works on both ferries and buses and allows you to board and descend wherever you like. If you're on a scooter or bicycle, you can take your bike on the ferry, though it costs an extra adult fare to take a scooter, and scooter space on some ferries is limited.

You can walk around the Dockyard, but other West End sights are rather far apart, so plan to take a taxi, bus, or ferry to Somerset and elsewhere. Start your tour at the Royal Naval Dockyard. A morning visit to the **Bermuda Maritime Museum and Dolphin Quest** ㉗ ⏋ is a lovely way to begin your day and get acquainted with seafaring practices. The museum's collections are in a large stone fortress spread over 6 acres, and the dolphins are located in the fort's Keep area. Across from the museum entrance is the **Old Cooperage** ㉘, a barrel-maker's shop dating from 1831, now home to the Craft Market. Take in some Bermudian art next door at the **Bermuda Arts Centre at Dockyard** ㉙. Behind the Cooperage is the Victualling Yard. Ahead and to the right, opposite the boat haul-out, you'll see old military warehouses, which now house stores and other businesses, such as a pottery shop and glassblowing center. A few yards further is the beautifully renovated Clocktower Mall, a former military storehouse enjoying a new life as a shopping area. You can finish your tour here, or take the ferry to Somerset Island.

For an interesting change of pace, take the slow ferry (not the one heading directly to Hamilton) out of Dockyard. You'll pass by Boaz and Watford islands on your way to Somerset Island, fringed on both sides with beautiful secluded coves, inlets, and bays. Get off the ferry at Watford Bridge for **Somerset Village** ㉚, with its shops, restaurants, and pretty homes snuggled beside Mangrove Bay.

The next sights, reached via Somerset Road, are best visited by bus or scooter. About 2 mi east of Somerset Village, opposite Willowbank guest house, is the entrance to the open spaces and tiny 1616 chapel of the **Heydon Trust property** ㉛. Just around the bend on your left is **Fort**

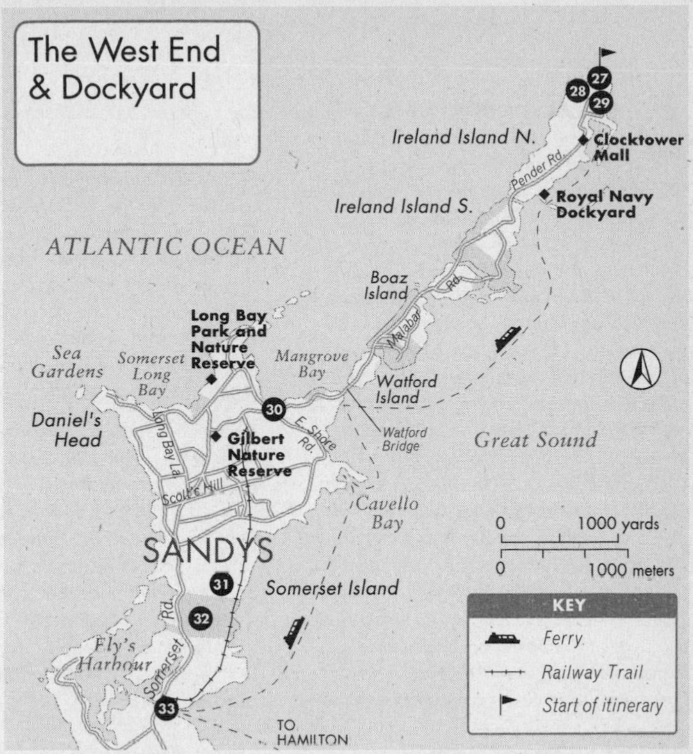

Scaur 32, a peaceful spot from which you can see sweeping views of the Great Sound.

Linking Somerset Island with the rest of Bermuda is **Somerset Bridge** 33, said to be the world's smallest drawbridge. Near the bridge is the Somerset ferry landing, where you can catch a ferry back to Hamilton. Across the bridge, Somerset Road becomes Middle Road, which leads into Southampton Parish.

TIMING Allow a full day for exploring this area. Check the bus and ferry schedules carefully. The ferry trip can take anywhere from half an hour to more than an hour, depending on which ferry you take. However, there are worse ways to spend an hour than boating on Bermuda's Great Sound. Buses 7 and 8 depart from Hamilton every 15 minutes and take either South Shore Road or Middle Road to the West End.

What to See

29 **Bermuda Arts Centre at Dockyard.** High-quality, innovative Bermuda artwork by local artists and artisans is displayed here in this compact member-run gallery. The exhibits change often and may include watercolors, oils, sculpture, and photography. Jewelry and fabric arts are also on display and for sale. Several artists have their studios on the premises and you can watch them at work. ✉ *Dockyard* ☎ *441/234–2809* ⊕ *www.artbermuda.bm* *Free, donations accepted* ⊙ *Daily 10–5.*

27 Fodor's Choice ★ **Bermuda Maritime Museum and Dolphin Quest.** Inside Bermuda's largest fort, built between 1837 and 1852, the Maritime Museum exhibits its collections in six old, stone munitions warehouses, which surround the parade grounds and the Keep pond. You enter the museum over a moat. From the entrance, you can wander into rooms filled with artifacts and

CloseUp

WITH CHILDREN?

BERMUDA IS A GREAT PLACE TO bring your family—or send your kids to with Grandma and Grandpa. When children need a break from the beach, there is plenty to see and do. And everyone will be worn out at the end of the day and ready for a long, restful night. **The Bermuda Aquarium, Museum & Zoo,** in Flatts Village, easily reached by buses 10 or 11, is one of the most child-friendly attractions on the island. The fishy creatures and land-roving animals are both educational and entertaining and there are activities for children of all ages. The same buses, plus the No. 1, take you close to the **Crystal Caves,** where children age 5 and older can explore underground spaces so unusual they look like sets from Star Wars or Lord of the Rings. Just west of Hamilton, kids can take a simulated deep-sea dive at the **Bermuda Underwater Exploration Institute (BUEI).** Here, old coins and household objects resurrected

from underwater oblivion are displayed as treasure.

Highly recommended for the overenergetic is a climb up the 185 steps to the top of **Gibb's Hill Lighthouse,** in Southampton, walkable from the No. 7 bus stop. It's the highest spot in Bermuda, so you can see for miles—and you can get very close to the huge lens that produces the beacon that can be seen for 40 mi. Then you can enjoy lunch or tea at the Lighthouse Tea Room.

Bermuda's forts offer plenty of space and stone walls over which to roam and romp, plus there are underground passageways and abandoned cannons to peer into. **Fort Scaur** and **Fort Hamilton** charge no admission. The grounds and battlements, and the exhibits and activities at **Fort St. Catherine,** just outside St. George's, and the **Maritime Museum,** in an old fort at Dockyard, are open to children at reduced rates.

relics from approximately 300 ships wrecked on the island's reefs. Elsewhere, you can examine dinghies, whaling tools, and photographs from the early 20th century. Then let all that information sink in as you stroll the restored ramparts with their commanding views of the Great Sound.

Atop the hill is the **Commissioner's House,** an unusual, cast-iron building constructed from 1823 to 1828 in England and shipped to Bermuda for the chief administrator of the Dockyard. When the office of commissioner was eliminated in 1837, the building became a barracks. The Royal Marines Light Infantry was housed there during World War I, and it was used for military intelligence during World War II. Today, the lower floors contain exhibits on the military history of Bermuda, including the activities the American and Canadian armed forces, as well as the British Royal Navy. Half a dozen goats wander around the house, keeping its lawn well-mowed.

But the Maritime Museum's most popular attraction, by far, is undoubtedly **Dolphin Quest** (☎ 441/234–4464 ⊕ www.dolphinquest. org), set within the fortress's historic Keep. Dolphin Quest is your chance to get close to one of the ocean's most amazing mammals. Several different programs designed for adults and/or children age five and older let you actually get into the water and touch, play with, and swim alongside the dolphins. There are also land-based activities. Admission to the Dolphin Quest area is free with museum admission, though the dolphin programs cost $135–$265. ⊠ *Maritime Museum, Dockyard* ☉ *Daily 9:30–5* ☎ *441/234–1418* ⊕ *www.bermudamall.com/marmuse* ☎ *$7.50.*

 Fort Scaur. The British chose the highest hill in Somerset for the site of this fort, built in the late 1860s and early 1870s to defend the flank of

THE BERMUDA RAILWAY

THE HISTORY OF THE BERMUDA RAILWAY is as brief as the track is short. The railway supplemented horse, buggy, and boat transportation on the island from 1931 to 1948. Bermuda's Public Works Department considered proposals for a railroad as early as 1899, and Parliament finally granted permission, in 1922, for a line to run from Somerset to St. George's. Laying tracks was a formidable undertaking, requiring the construction of long tunnels and swing bridges. By the time it was finished, the railway had cost investors $1 million. Mile for mile, it was the most expensive railroad ever built, and at a sluggish 2½ mi per year, was the slowest construction ever recorded.

"Old Rattle and Shake," as it was nicknamed, began to decline during World War II. Soldiers put the train to hard use, and it proved impossible to obtain the necessary maintenance equipment. At the end of the war the government acquired the distressed railway for $115,000. Automobiles arrived in Bermuda in 1946, and train service ended in 1948, when the government sold the railway, in its entirety, to British Guiana (now Guyana).

Today's secluded 18-mi recreational Bermuda Railway Trail runs the length of the island along the route of the old railway. Restricted to pedestrians, horseback riders, and cyclists (including scooters), the trail is a delightful way to see the island, away from the traffic and noise of main roads. The bits of the trail that pass through Southampton and Sandys parishes are among the most scenic and best maintained. Visitors Service Bureaus can give you brochures that include suggested Railway Trail walks. Note that many of the trails are isolated—so avoid setting out alone or in the dark.

the Dockyard. British troops were garrisoned here until World War I, and during World War II, American forces were stationed here. Today the stone walls are surrounded by 22 acres of pretty gardens. The view of the Great Sound from the parapet is unsurpassed. While you're up here, don't miss the opportunity to check out the Early Bermuda Weather Stone, the "perfect weather indicator." A sign posted nearby explains all. ⊠ *Somerset Rd., Ely's Harbour* 🖭 *Free* ☉ *Apr.–Oct., daily 9–4:30; Nov.–Mar., daily 9–4.*

③① Heydon Trust property. A reminder of what the island was like in its early days, this quiet, peaceful property of 41 acres has been maintained as undeveloped open space, except for a few citrus groves and flower gardens. Pathways dotted with park benches wend through the preserve, affording some wonderful views of the Great Sound. If you persevere along the main path, you'll reach the tiny, rustic **Heydon Chapel**, which dates from before 1620. Services, which include Gregorian chant, are still held in the chapel at 3 PM Monday through Saturday. ⊠ *Somerset Rd.* 🕾 *441/234–1831* 🖭 *Free* ☉ *Daily dawn–dusk.*

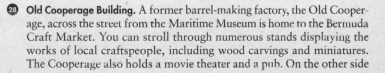

need a break? For a cool pick-me-up on a warm day, stop for a cone at **Nannini's Häagen-Dazs** (🕾 441/234–2474), with hard ice cream and frozen yogurt, plus nonfat soft-serve, from that giant of the ice cream trade. You'll find this chain tempting shoppers in the Clocktower Mall.

②⑧ Old Cooperage Building. A former barrel-making factory, the Old Cooperage, across the street from the Maritime Museum is home to the Bermuda Craft Market. You can stroll through numerous stands displaying the works of local craftspeople, including wood carvings and miniatures. The Cooperage also holds a movie theater and a pub. On the other side of the Cooperage is the **Victualling Yard,** a grassy open space sur-rounded by as-yet-unrestored military buildings. Cross the Victualling Yard to reach the Visitors Service Bureau, where knowledgeable guides provide you with information, and sell bus and ferry tickets and phone cards. The bureau is open from Sunday to Friday, 9 to 5. ✉ *Dockyard* 🕿 *Craft Market 441/234–1333; Visitors Service Bureau 441/234–3824* 🖾 *Free* ☉ *Craft Market daily 10–5.*

❸❸ **Somerset Bridge.** Reputed to have the smallest draw in the world, this bridge on Somerset Road opens a mere 18 inches, just wide enough to accommodate a sailboat mast. When you cross over Somerset Bridge heading west, you are, as Bermudians say, "up the country."

❸⓿ **Somerset Village.** A quiet retreat, this village only has one road running through it. Somerset Village looks much as it did in 1962 when it was featured in the film *A Touch of Mink,* starring Doris Day and Cary Grant—a town of quiet streets and charming old buildings skirting lovely Mangrove Bay. Its few shops are mostly branches of Hamilton stores, along with two banks.

ELSEWHERE IN THE PARISHES

Bermuda's other points of interest—and there are many—are scattered throughout the island's nine parishes. This section covers the length and breadth of the island, commenting on the major sights. Half the fun of exploring Bermuda, though, is wandering down forgotten lanes or dis-covering some little-known beach or cove. A motor scooter, or bicycle if you don't mind hills, is ideal for this kind of travel. You can also plan to take public transportation. Pick up ferry and bus maps and sched-ules at any Visitors Service Bureau. A guided taxi tour (about $90 for three hours) is the quickest way to see the upcountry sights in all the parishes, and it's safer than biking. Many taxi-tour drivers are experi-enced and knowledgeable guides who will take you through less-trav-eled backroads for a glimpse of real Bermudian life.

TIMING With roads as narrow and winding as Bermuda's it takes longer to tra-verse the island than you'd think. Pick a couple of close-by sights to visit rather than trying to explore them all in a day. The parishes *are* less con-gested than the towns, but the area to the east of Hamilton—especially the traffic circle where Crow Lane intersects with The Lane and Trim-ingham Road—is very busy during morning (7:30–9) and afternoon (4–5:30) rush hours.

ST. GEORGE'S PARISH

Starting from the town of St. George's, walk north on Duke of Kent Street, following signs to **Fort St. Catherine** ❸❹ ⌐. If you prefer not to walk, check at the Visitors Service Bureau to see if the minibus is operating from King's Square. From Fort St. Catherine, head down the hill and turn left on Barry Road. Just over a mile down this rugged shore road is **Gates Fort** ❸❺ which, in addition to its military and historical interest, is a good spot to watch boats passing through the Town Cut to St. George's. If you have a Wednesday morning free, consider taking a guided tour of the **Bermuda Biological Station for Research (BBSR)** ❸❻. To get there, take a bus or taxi across the Ferry Reach to St. David's Road. Near the end of St. David's Road, up Lighthouse Hill, is a small, quiet village and **St. David's Lighthouse** ❸❼.

HAMILTON & SMITH'S PARISHES

Hamilton and Smith's Parishes encircle the Harrington Sound. Starting on the northeastern end of the Sound, take a bus, taxi, or scooter onto Wilkinson Avenue to find the **Crystal Caves** ❸❽ ⌐. Guided tours into the caves pass stalactites, stalagmites, and other limestone formations. Off

North Shore Road, you'll find the **Bermuda Perfumery & Gardens** ❸❾, where you can walk through fragrant flower gardens and tour the factory. North Shore Road leads to Flatts Village, home of the **Bermuda Aquarium, Museum & Zoo** ❹⓿. Before leaving Flatts, stand on the bridge to watch the power of the water as it rushes through the narrows. Your next stop is **Verdmont** ❹❶, a historic home off Middle Road in Smith's Parish. If you have any energy left at the end of the day, head down Collector's Hill to South Shore Road, turn left, and in less than a mile you'll be at **Spittal Pond Nature Reserve** ❹❷.

DEVONSHIRE, PAGET, WARWICK & SOUTHAMPTON PARISHES
If you're interested in plants, start at the **Botanical Gardens** ❹❸ ▶. There, if your timing is right, you can catch a morning walking tour. With or without the tour, you can see the unusual trees and explore the various plant collections. Exiting through the north gate puts you on Berry Hill Road. From here you can take a bus or taxi (or ride your rented scooter, if you have one) to Waterville, headquarters of the **Bermuda National Trust** ❹❹. An hour is long enough to see the manicured gardens and historic furnishings. From there, walk or ride along The Lane turning right at the traffic circle onto Harbour Road, then left onto Lover's Lane, which will take you to **Paget Marsh** ❹❺, where you can see what Bermuda was like before settlement. Leaving the marsh, you're just around the corner from Middle Road, where you can catch the bus to historic **Christ Church** ❹❻ in Warwick and to **Gibb's Hill Lighthouse** ❹❼ in Southampton, for tea and breathtaking views.

What to See

👋 ❹⓿
Fodor'sChoice
★
Bermuda Aquarium, Museum & Zoo. The aquarium has always been a pleasant diversion, but thanks to an ambitious expansion project it has become awesome. The 145,000-gallon tank holding the North Rock Exhibit, in the main gallery, gives you a diver's view of Bermuda's famed living coral reefs and colorful marine life. The Islands exhibits give you a chance to see wildlife from Australasian and Caribbean islands. Other displays include a touch pool and a reptile walkway that gives you a close-up look at alligators and Galápagos tortoises. ✉ *Flatts Village, Smith's Parish* ☎ *441/293-2727* ⊕ *www.bamz.org* 💲 *$10* ⊙ *Daily 9–5 (last admission at 4:30), guided tours 1:10.*

❸❻ **Bermuda Biological Station for Research.** In 1903—long before environmental issues were in fashion—scientists began researching marine life at this mid-Atlantic scientific research facility, which welcomes scientists from around the world. Research programs deal with such issues as global environmental change, marine biology/ecology, and acid rain. You can take a guided tour of the grounds and laboratory on Wednesdays at 10 AM only, beginning in the main building. The Bermuda Biological Station for Research is also the leaving point for half-day eco-tours (every Thursday, weather permitting) to **Nonsuch Island,** a nature reserve with restricted access. It has been recreated as a living museum showing what Bermuda was like before human contact. Reservations are required for the Nonsuch Island tour, and lunch is included in the per-person rate. ✉ *17 Biological La., Ferry Reach, St. George's Parish* ☎ *441/297–1880* ⊕ *www.bbsr.edu* 💲 *Free, donations accepted; Nonsuch tour $75.*

❹❹ **Bermuda National Trust.** The nonprofit organization that oversees the restoration and preservation of many of the island's gardens, open spaces, and historic buildings has its offices in Waterville, a rambling 18th-century house built by the Trimingham family. The drawing and dining rooms are open to the public during business hours. ✉ *29 The Lane, Paget Parish* ☎ *441/236 6183* ⊕ *www.bnt.bm* 💲 *Free, donations accepted* ⊙ *Bermuda National Trust weekdays 9–5.*

Elsewhere in the Parishes

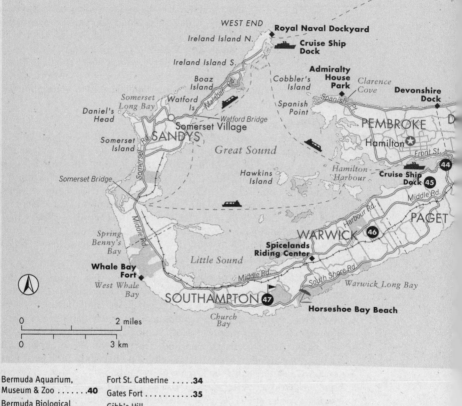

ATLANTIC OCEAN

WEST END
Royal Naval Dockyard
Ireland Island N.
Cruise Ship Dock
Ireland Island S.
Boaz Island
Cobbler's Island
Admiralty House Park
Clarence Cove
Devonshire Dock
Somerset Long Bay
Watford Is.
Spanish Point
Daniel's Head
Watford Bridge
Somerset Village
PEMBROKE
Somerset Island
SANDYS
Great Sound
Hamilton
Front St.
Somerset Bridge
Hawkins Island
Hamilton Harbour
Cruise Ship Dock 45
44
Middle Rd.
PAGET
Spring Benny's Bay
Harbour Rd.
WARWICK 46
Little Sound
Spicelands Riding Center
Whale Bay Fort
Middle Rd.
West Whale Bay
South Shore Rd.
Warwick Long Bay
SOUTHAMPTON 47
Horseshoe Bay Beach
Church Bay

0   2 miles
0   3 km

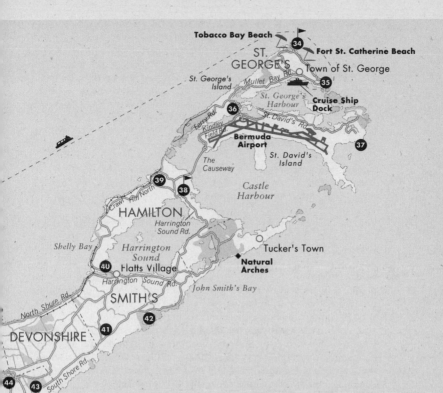

Tobacco Bay Beach

34

Fort St. Catherine Beach

ST.
GEORGE'S

Town of St. George

St. George's
Island

Mullet Bay Rd.

35

St. George's
Harbour

Cruise Ship
Dock

36

St. David's Rd.

BERMUDA
Airport

The
Causeway

St. David's
Island

37

Castle
Harbour

39

38

HAMILTON

Harrington
Sound Rd.

Shelly Bay

Harrington
Sound

Tucker's Town

4U

Flatts Village

Natural
Arches

Harrington Sound Rd.

John Smith's Bay

North Shore Rd.

SMITH'S

42

DEVONSHIRE

41

44

43

South Shore Rd.

ATLANTIC OCEAN

ET

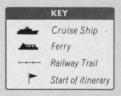

KEY	
	Cruise Ship
	Ferry
	Railway Trail
	Start of itinerary

39 **Bermuda Perfumery & Gardens.** In 1929 the Lili Perfume Factory began extracting natural fragrances from the island's flowers, and the enterprise eventually blossomed into the present perfumery and sightseeing attraction. You can take a guided tour of the factory, which is in a 200-year-old cottage with cedar beams, but the biggest draw is the self-guided garden and nature trail teeming with (depending on the season) oleander, frangipani, jasmine, orchids, and passionflowers. ⊠ *212 North Shore Rd., Hamilton Parish* ☎ *441/293–0627 or 800/527–8213* ⊕ *www. bermuda-perfumery.com* ☞ *Free* ☉ *Apr.–Oct., Mon.–Sat. 9:15–5, Sun. 10–4; Nov.–Mar., Mon.–Sat. 9:15–4:30.*

> **need a break?** **Bailey's Ice Cream Parlour & Food D'Lites** (⊠ Blue Hole Hill, Hamilton Parish ☎ 441/293–8605) has 40 varieties of freshly made natural ice cream, as well as shakes, sodas, yogurts, and sorbets.
>
> For something a bit stronger, cross the road for a rum swizzle and a "Swizzleburger" at the **Swizzle Inn** (⊠ Blue Hole Hill, Hamilton Parish ☎ 441/293–1845).

▶ **43** **Botanical Gardens.** A fragrant haven for the island's exotic subtropical plants, flowers, and trees, the 36-acre Botanical Gardens encompass a miniature forest, an aviary, a hibiscus garden with more than 150 species, and other plant collections, such as orchids and cacti. Follow your nose to the sensory garden filled with the scents of sweet geranium, lemon, lavender, and spices. Free 75-minute guided tours of the gardens are available several mornings a week. The pretty white house within the Gardens is **Camden** (☎ 441/236–5732), the official residence of Bermuda's premier. Camden is open for tours Tuesday and Friday noon–2, except when official functions are scheduled. Behind Camden is the old Arrowroot Factory, home to the **Masterworks Arts Centre** (☎ 441/236–2960 ⊕ www.masterworks.bm ☞ Free), open weekdays from 10 to 4 and on Saturday by appointment. As well as maintaining a gallery with changing exhibits of Bermuda-inspired art, there is a display of arrowroot processing. ⊠ *Point Finger Rd., Paget Parish* ☎ *441/ 236–4201* ☞ *Free* ☉ *Daily dawn–dusk.*

46 **Christ Church, Warwick.** This one-story stone church with its soaring spire was built in 1719 and is reputedly the oldest Presbyterian house of worship in any British colony or dominion. It's open for visits through the week. Sunday services are at 8 and 11. ⊠ *Middle Rd., Warwick Parish* ⊕ *www.christchurch.bm* ☉ *Mon.–Fri. 9:30–3:30, Sat. 9:30–12:30.*

☾ ▶ **38** **Crystal Caves.** In 1907 while playing ball, two boys made a startling discovery. When the ball disappeared down a hole, the boys burrowed after it and found themselves in a vast, fantastic cavern 120 feet underground. Catch a guided tour, offered throughout the day, and journey through geologic time as you walk the pontoon pathways past spectacular stalactite formations. ⊠ *8 Crystal Caves Rd., off Wilkinson Ave., Hamilton Parish* ☎ *441/293–0640* ☏ *441/293–1656* ☞ *$7.50* ☉ *May–Sept., daily 9:30–5:30; Oct.–Apr., daily 9:30–4:30.*

★ ☾ ▶ **34** **Fort St. Catherine.** This restored fortress is one of the most impressive on the island. It has enough cannons, tunnels, and ramparts to satisfy the most avid military historian—or scrambling child. The original fort was built around 1613, but it was remodeled and enlarged at least five times. In fact, work continued on it until late in the 19th century. As you travel through the tunnels, you'll come across some startlingly lifelike figures tucked into niches. Several dioramas depict the island's development, and an audiovisual presentation describes the building and

BERMUDIAN ARCHITECTURE

THE TYPICAL BERMUDIAN BUILDING *is built of limestone block, usually painted white or a pastel shade, with a prominent chimney, and a tiered, white-painted roof. This distinctive roof was not developed for aesthetic reasons. It's part of a system that allows Bermudians to collect rainwater and store it in large tanks beneath their houses. The special white roof paint contains a purifying agent. If your visit includes some rainy days, you may hear the expression, "Good day for the tank!" Bermuda has no fresh water, relying on rain for drinking, bathing, and cooking water, as well as golf-course and farmland irrigation, so residents are careful not to waste the precious liquid. The island has never run out of water, though the supply was stretched during World War II, when thousands of U.S. soldiers were stationed on the island.*

"Moongates" are another interesting, Bermudian structural feature, usually found in gardens and walkways around the island. These Chinese-inspired freestanding stone arches, popular since the late 18th century, are still often incorporated into new construction. Thought to bring luck, they're also favored as backdrops for wedding pictures.

Other architectural details you may notice are "welcoming arms" stairways, with banisters that seem to reach out to embrace you as you approach the first step, and "eyebrows" over window openings. Also look for "butteries": tiny, steep roofed cupboards, separate from the house, and originally built to keep dairy products cool in summer. If you wonder why, in this warm climate, so many houses have fireplaces in addition to air conditioners, visit in January, when the damp makes it warmer outside than in.

---

significance of the fort. There is also a small but elaborate display of replicas of the Crown Jewels of England. ⊠ *15 Coot Pond Rd., St. George's Parish* ☎ *441/297–1920* ☎ *$5* ☉ *Daily 10–4:30.*

㉟ Gates Fort. St. George's has always had the greatest concentration of fortifications on Bermuda. Gates Fort is a reconstruction of a small militia fort dating from the 1620s. Don't expect turrets, towers, and tunnels, however. There is little to see here apart from the sea. The fort and Gates Bay, which it overlooks, were named for Sir Thomas Gates, the first survivor of the *Sea Venture* to reach dry land. Upon doing so, he is said to have shouted, "This is Gates, his bay!" ⊠ *Cut Rd., St. George's Parish* ☎ *No phone* ☎ *Free* ☉ *Daily 10–4.*

Fodor'sChoice **Gibb's Hill Lighthouse.** The second cast-iron lighthouse ever built soars
★ above Southampton Parish. Designed in London and opened in 1846,
☝㊼ the tower stands 117 feet high and 362 feet above the sea. The light was originally produced by a concentrated burner of four large, circular wicks. Today the beam from the 1,000-watt bulb can be seen by ships 40 mi out to sea and by planes 120 mi away at 10,000 feet. The haul up the 185 spiral stairs is a long one, but you can stop to catch your breath at platforms along the way, where photographs and drawings of the lighthouse divert your attention. At the top you can stroll the balcony for a spectacular view of Bermuda. ⊠ *Lighthouse Rd., Southampton* ☎ *441/238–0524* ☎ *$2.50* ☉ *Daily 9–4:30.*

need a break? At Gibb's Hill Lighthouse, in the lighthouse keeper's cottage, the **Lighthouse Tea Room** (⊠ Lighthouse Rd., Southampton Parish ☎ 441/238–8679) is a charming place to relax over breakfast, lunch, or afternoon tea, while taking in the breathtaking island vistas.

45 Fodor'sChoice ★ **Paget Marsh.** This small, easily walkable, slice of nature, just minutes from bustling Hamilton, is a trip back in time—to Bermuda as it was when the first humans found it. As you follow the boardwalk through the shady mangrove, grassy savannah, and forested areas, interpretive signs describe the native and endemic flora and fauna that surround you. Listen for the cries of the native and migratory birds who visit this natural wetland, jointly owned and preserved by the Bermuda National Trust and the Bermuda Audubon Society. ✉ *Lover's Lane, Paget Parish* ☎ *No phone* 🌐 *www.bnt.bm* 🎫 *Free* ⏲ *Sunrise to sunset.*

37 **St. David's Lighthouse.** Built in 1879 of Bermuda stone and occupying the highest point on Bermuda's eastern end, the lighthouse rises 208 feet above the sea. Although only about half the height of Gibbs Hill Lighthouse in Southampton Parish, it nevertheless has spectacular views. From the balcony you can see St. David's and St. George's, Castle Harbour, and the reef-fringed south shore. The lighthouse is not always open. Check with the **Park Ranger's Office** (☎ 441/236–5902) for hours. ✉ *St. George's Parish.*

need a break?

Right on the water near St. David's Lighthouse, the casual **Black Horse Tavern** (✉ 101 St. David's Rd., St. George's Parish ☎ 441/297–1991) serves delicious sandwiches, shark hash, and curried conch stew. It's closed Monday.

★ 42 **Spittal Pond Nature Reserve.** A showpiece of the Bermuda National Trust, this nature park has 60 acres for carefree roaming, although you're asked to keep to the walkways. More than 25 species of waterfowl winter here between November and May. On a high bluff overlooking the ocean, Spanish Rock stands out as an oddity. Early settlers found this rock crudely carved with the date 1543 and other markings that were unclear. It's now believed that a Portuguese ship was wrecked on the island in 1543 and that her sailors built a new ship on which they departed. The carvings are thought to be the initials RP (for *Rex Portugaline*, King of Portugal) and the cross to be a badge of the Portuguese Order of Christ. The rock was removed to prevent further damage by erosion, and the site is marked by a bronze casting of the original carving. A plaster-of-paris cast of the Spanish Rock is also on display at the Bermuda Historical Society Museum, in Hamilton. ✉ *South Shore Rd., Smith's Parish* ☎ *no phone* 🌐 *www.bnt.bm* 🎫 *Free* ⏲ *Daily dawn–dusk.*

★ 41 **Verdmont.** Now owned by the Bermuda National Trust, Verdmont was opened as a museum in 1956. Though it was used as a home until the mid-20th century, the house has had virtually no structural changes since it was built in about 1710. Its former owners never even added electricity. Verdmont holds a notable collection of historic furnishings. Some are imported from England—such as the early-19th-century piano—but most of the furniture is 18th-century cedar, crafted by Bermudian cabinetmakers. The nursery and attic recall how children lived and played in days gone by. A china coffee service, said to have been a gift from Napoléon to President Madison, is also on display. The president never received it, since the ship bearing it across the Atlantic was seized by a Bermudian privateer and brought to Bermuda. ✉ *Collector's Hill, Smith's Parish* ☎ *441/236–7369* 🌐 *www.bnt.bm* 🎫 *$3; $5 combination ticket with Bermuda National Trust Museum in the Globe Hotel and Tucker House* ⏲ *Tues.–Sat. 10–4.*

WHERE TO EAT

FODOR'S CHOICE

Aggie's Garden & Waterside Café, *in Hamilton*

Ascots, *in Pembroke Parish*

Black Horse Tavern, *in St. George's Parish*

Horizons, *in Paget Parish*

Newport Room, *in Southampton Parish*

Seahorse Grill, *in Paget Parish*

Tom Moore's Tavern, *in Hamilton Parish*

Waterloo House, *in Hamilton*

Waterlot Inn, *in Southampton Parish*

HIGHLY RECOMMENDED

Aqua, *in Devonshire Parish*

Barracuda Grill, *in Hamilton*

Café Lido, *in Paget Parish*

Harbourfront, *in Hamilton*

Harley's, *in Hamilton*

House of India, *in Hamilton*

La Coquille, *in Hamilton*

Palms, *in Paget Parish*

Rib Room, *in Southampton Parish*

Ristorante Primavera and Omakase Sushi Bar, *in Hamilton*

Revised by
Judith Wadson

WHAT'S INCREDIBLE ABOUT the Bermuda restaurant scene isn't so much the number or high quality of excellent restaurants—that the island's dining options would match its lodging in that respect is no surprise—but the sheer variety of ingredients and cuisines represented on menus, considering that Bermuda is such a tiny, secluded place. The island is host to a medley of global cuisines—British, French, Italian, Portuguese, American, Caribbean, Indian, Chinese, Japanese, and Thai—palatable reminders of Bermuda's history of colonization. Many superior, well-funded independent and resort restaurants attract a constant and steady stream of internationally acclaimed chefs, assuring that the latest techniques and trends, such as California-style, health-conscious cooking with organic ingredients, are menu regulars. At the same time, virtually all restaurant menus list traditional Bermudian dishes and drinks, so you have the opportunity to taste local specialties at almost any meal.

One of the more recent trends to take Bermuda by a storm (no pun intended) are Asian specialties. Sushi bars have cropped up all over the island, and some restaurateurs have even tacked them into a corner or onto the second floor of their traditional Continental restaurants, such as at Primavera Restaurant and Omasake Sushi Bar. Asian ingredients have crept their way into island specialties—it's not unusual to find, say, a local fish grilled in a lemongrass reduction.

As you might surmise, methods are not all that's imported. Roughly 80% of Bermuda's food is flown or shipped in, most of it from the United States. This explains why restaurant prices are often higher here than on the mainland. Nevertheless, there are a number of delicious local ingredients that you can look for. At the top of the list is the extraordinary seafood, like lobster (September through March), crab, oysters, mussels, clams, red snapper, rockfish, tuna, and wahoo. Additionally, many chefs work with local growers to serve fresh, seasonal fruits and vegetables, such as potatoes, carrots, leeks, tomatoes, corn, broccoli, and Bermuda onions (one of the island's earliest exports); and in the dessert department, strawberries, cherries, bananas, and loquats. Imports notwithstanding, Bermudian cuisine really begins and ends with local ingredients and traditional preparations, and therein lies the island's culinary identity.

HAMILTON & ENVIRONS

Bermudian

$–$$$ ✕ **The Pickled Onion.** Laughter and music reverberate off the walls and high ceilings of this former whiskey warehouse, now a lively restaurant serving creative, contemporary Bermudian cuisine. The local tuna is flame-seared and dressed with avocado, tomato, and cilantro salsa. If you are lusting for Angus beef, this is the place for melt-in-your-mouth tenderloin or prime rib grilled to perfection. Try it with the sauce of your dreams—whisky-peppercorn, port reduction, crumbled Gorgonzola, or herbed garlic butter. For dessert, go straight for Melanie's Bermuda banana bread with brûléed bananas. (Melanie, by the way, is the wife of owner Phillip Barnett.) The veranda, overlooking Front Street and the harbor, is the most popular dining area. Live pop, jazz, and blues from April to November make the Onion a great nightlife destination, too. ⊠ 53 Front St., Hamilton ☎ 441/295–2263 ▭ AE, MC, V.

$–$$ ✕ **Monty's.** Fluffy omelettes make a good start to the day at this cozy café just west of Hamilton. The lunch menu lists fresh, filling sandwiches—try the grilled chicken and avocado on a roll accompanied by romaine lettuce, tomato and red-onion slices, and honey-mustard dressing. You might start dinner with mango wrapped in smoked salmon, Portuguese

Reservations

Reservations are always a good idea. We mention them only when they're essential or not accepted. Book as far ahead as you can and re-confirm when you arrive, especially in high season. Many restaurants close—or curtail hours, or days of service—in the off season, so call ahead before setting out for lunch or dinner.

Dress

Bermudians on the whole are a dressy lot, and dinner attire is no exception. Even when not required, a jacket for men is rarely out of place in upscale restaurants. In our restaurant reviews, we mention dress only when men are required to wear either a jacket or a jacket and tie.

Prices

Much harder to swallow than the average spoonful of Bermuda fish chowder are the prices of dining out. Bermuda has never sought a reputation for affordability, and restaurants are no exception. A few greasy spoons serve up standard North American fare (and a few local favorites) at a decent price, but by and large you should prepare for a bit of sticker shock. Don't be surprised if dinner for two with wine at one of the very top places—the Newport Room or La Coquille, for example—puts a $200–$300 dent in your pocket. And a 15% service charge is almost always added to the bill "for your convenience."

3

WHAT IT COSTS In U.S. Dollars					
	$$$$	$$$	$$	$	¢
AT DINNER	over $40	$31–$40	$21–$30	$10–$20	under $10

Prices are per person for a main course at dinner. The final tab usually includes a 15% service charge.

red-bean soup, or Bermuda fish chowder. For your main course, consider the catch of the day simply grilled, or cooked in a champagne sauce; bangers and mash (sausages and mashed potatoes); or curried chicken. You may have to be patient, though, as the service can be slow. ⊠ 75 *Pitts Bay Rd., near Woodburne Ave., Hamilton* ☎ 441/295–5759 🖰 *AE, MC, V.*

British

$–$$ ✕ **Hog Penny Pub.** Veterans of London pub crawls may feel nostalgic at this dark, wood-filled watering hole off Front Street. Those die-hard (and probably rare) aficionados of old-style British cooking will adore the Yorkshire pudding, shepherd's pie, steak-and-kidney pie, fish-and-chips, and bangers and mash. There's even a small sampling of curries. And you can wash it all down with British ale from the tap. Live, foot-tapping music is scheduled nightly from May through August and on weekends the rest of the year. ⊠ *Burnaby Hill, Hamilton* ☎ 441/292–2534 🖰 *AE, DC, MC, V.*

¢–$ ✕ **Docksider.** Locals come to mingle at this sprawling Front Street sports bar. If you find things a little hectic at the main bar, try the wine bar in back—it's quieter and more intimate. Or you can go out to the porch to watch passersby while sipping on a Dark 'n' Stormy (Gosling's black rum combined with ginger beer). The menu lists standard pub fare, which can

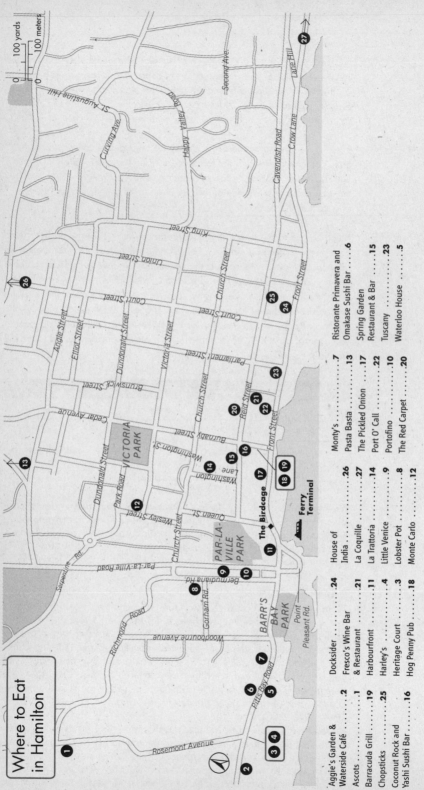

Where to Eat in Hamilton

Aggie's Garden & Waterside Café **2**
Ascots **1**
Barracuda Grill **19**
Chopsticks **25**
Coconut Rock and Yashi Sushi Bar **16**

Docksider **24**
Fresco's Wine Bar & Restaurant **21**
Harbourfront **11**
Harley's **4**
Heritage Court **3**
Hog Penny Pub **18**

House of India **26**
La Coquille **27**
La Trattoria **14**
Little Venice **9**
Lobster Pot **8**
Monte Carlo **12**

Monty's **7**
Pasta Basta **13**
The Pickled Onion **17**
Port O' Call **22**
Portofino **10**
The Red Carpet **20**

Ristorante Primavera and Omakase Sushi Bar **6**
Spring Garden Restaurant & Bar **15**
Tuscany **23**
Waterloo House **5**

CloseUp

QUICK EATS

IF YOU ARE LOOKING FOR a simple lunch before a great view of Hamilton Harbour, drop in at **Cafe on the Terrace** (☎ 441/296–5265), on the second floor of A. S. Cooper & Son for a tasty sandwich-and-salad combo priced at about $9. It's not a huge place, so come early or you might not get a table.

Tucked away in the Emporium building, next to the Bank of Butterfield is **Kathy's Kaffee** (☎ 441/295–5203), serving robust breakfasts and satisfying lunches for reasonable prices. A morning croissant with bacon, cheese, and avocado or an omelette with a good cup of coffee is a great way to begin the day. Healthy vegetarian choices at lunch include Greek or Asian salad, and pita bread filled with falafel and greens. Protein shakes provide you with the energy you need for power shopping in the surrounding shops. If meat is your fancy, try one of the burgers, topped with bacon or cheese. And if you've never

had a low-fat ostrich or buffalo burger, this is your chance to try one.

Always busy, and seemingly open all the live-long day, **Kentucky Fried Chicken** (☎ 441/296–4532) is a novelty on Bermuda—the island's only fast-food chain. The restaurant is on Queen Street between Front and Reid. Be prepared to wait in line at peak times.

For some good people-watching, head to **Paradiso Café** (☎ 411/295–3263), in Washington Mall, and take a seat at a table or banquette by the window overlooking Reid Street. The salads and wraps are just mediocre, but the pastries are worth every calorie. Paradiso also serves excellent, authentic espresso.

Cheap and cheerful **Take Five** (☎ 441/295–4903), above the shops at Washington Mall, is the perfect place to go for a good burger. There are other kinds of sandwiches, too, and the service is fast and cheerful.

taste like a gourmet meal after a couple of drinks. Go for the English beef pie, fish-and-chips, or a fish sandwich. After dark, live rock or jazz music starts up and people start dancing in the nightclub in the back. If you're up for something more mellow, watch or play a game in the pool room. ⊠ 121 Front St., Hamilton ☎ 441/296–3333 ▣ MC, V.

Caribbean
$–$$ ✕ **Spring Garden Restaurant & Bar.** If you've never had Barbadian food, come to Spring Garden, where there's a palm tree growing inside and up through the cedar ceiling, and try panfried flying fish—a delicacy in Barbados. Another good choice is the broiled mahimahi served in creole sauce, with peas and rice. During lobster season, an additional menu appears, featuring steamed, broiled, or curried lobster ($35 for the complete lobster dinner). For dessert, try the coconut-cream pie or the raspberry-mango cheese cake. ⊠ 19 Reid St., Hamilton ☎ 441/295–7416 ▣ AE, MC, V ☼ Closed Sun. Nov.–Apr. No lunch Sun. May–Oct.

Chinese
$–$$ ✕ **Chopsticks.** Perhaps more Pan-Asian than strictly Chinese, Chopsticks mixes it up with a menu of Szechuan, Hunan, and Cantonese, and Thai favorites. Top Chinese choices include beef with vegetables in ginger sauce, and sweet-and-spicy chicken. For Thai tastes, try the beef with onion, scallions, and basil in hot chili sauce, or the shrimp panang (in coconut-curry sauce). Special diets are easily accommodated, and takeout is available, too. ⊠ 88 Reid St., Hamilton ☎ 441/292–0791 ▣ AE, MC, V.

Contemporary
★ $$$–$$$$ ✕ **Barracuda Grill.** The tastefully decorated dining room—mahogany-framed chairs and banquettes, soft-gold lights over the tables—is reminiscent of sophisticated big-city restaurants on the mainland. And the

food that comes to the table is created by a culinary team that is dedicated to preparing consistently excellent food. The island-style fish chowder and the steak-and-tomato salad with blue cheese and roasted-garlic in balsamic vinaigrette are two good ways to start out your meal. Moving on, you might try the roasted salmon with carmelized onion, smoked bacon, and white-bean cassoulet; the classically prepared rack of Australian lamb; or the rigatoni Bolognese. If you save room for dessert, opt for the chocolate-banana bread pudding or perhaps the chocolate fondue for two. ⊠ *5 Burnaby Hill, Hamilton* ☎ *441/292–1609* ▤ *AE, MC, V.*

★ $$–$$$$ ╳ **Harbourfront.** Few Bermuda restaurants have menus as long and wide-ranging as this busy spot, where sushi is served alongside Continental and Mediterranean specialties. For lunch, you might have a good burger, a salad, or a couple of sushi rolls. For dinner, you can start with calamari or carpaccio, followed by lobster, rack of lamb, or any of the excellent pastas. Sushi devotees can order their miso soup, tempura, and sushi platters at the small sushi bar or at the tables. If you dine on the porch, you can watch the action on Front Street and in the harbor. ⊠ *21 Front St., Hamilton* ☎ *441/295–4207* ▤ *AE, MC, V* ☉ *Closed Sun. Nov.–Mar.*

$$–$$$ ╳ **Ascots.** In an elegant former mansion just outside downtown Hamilton, Ascots gives you a wonderful excuse for leaving the city. When the weather permits, meals are served on the covered terrace, with its stone fountain, or on the front veranda, as well as indoors. You can assemble at the handsome cedar bar before and after meals. The high standards of owners Angelo Armano and Edmund Smith—the chef and manager, respectively—result in creative and seasonal menu offerings that incorporate fresh ingredients from local farmers and fishermen. You might find grilled grouper on panfried potatoes with spinach-and-crab rolls, or pan-seared lamb chops with vegetable risotto. ⊠ *Royal Palms Hotel, 24 Rosemont Ave., Pembroke Parish* ☎ *441/295–9644* ▤ *AE, MC, V.*
Fodor's Choice
★

★ $$–$$$ ╳ **Harley's.** Serene water views and gracious service (a Fairmont tradition) combine with top-notch Continental and Bermudian cuisine to make Harley's one of the best restaurants in Hamilton. Dry, aged beef is always cooked to perfection. Try the slow-cooked prime rib or the grilled porterhouse, along with Harley's Mash—potatoes with caramelized onion, butternut squash, and black trumpet mushrooms. As for fish, Harley's chefs prepare a wonderful Bermudian specialty: almond-crusted and banana-glazed baked rockfish, which might be accompanied by a pumpkin risotto and sweet pepper sauce. If you prefer something vegetarian, try the hand-rolled cannelloni filled with ricotta cheese and grilled vegetables with a blackened-tomato coulis. ⊠ *Fairmont Hamilton Princess, 76 Pitts Bay Rd., Hamilton* ☎ *441/295–3000* ▤ *AE, DC, MC, V.*

$$–$$$ ╳ **Heritage Court.** Classic and conservative, with a refined afternoon tea service and piano music throughout the day, the Heritage Court, beside the lobby in the Fairmont Hamilton Princess, is a calm, relaxing spot for any meal. Clinking china can be heard at breakfast and tea times, while lunch and dinner bring businesspeople, hotel guests, couples, and families for reliable Bermudian-Continental fare and like-clockwork service. The Bermuda fish chowder, classic Caesar salad, and grilled tuna glazed with *mirin* (a sweet Japanese rice wine) are faultless. Some evenings a jazz band livens things up. ⊠ *Fairmont Hamilton Princess, 76 Pitts Bay Rd., Hamilton* ☎ *441/295–3000* ▤ *AE, MC, V.*

$$–$$$ ╳ **The Red Carpet.** This tiny restaurant in the old Armoury is popular at lunch, especially among local politicians and businesspeople. But at dinner, the dining room is usually uncrowded, and the pace relaxes so

LOCAL SPECIALTIES

BERMUDIAN CUISINE *may seem elusive—after all, what could constitute "local" tastes in a place where most ingredients are imported? And yet many restaurants highlight local dishes amid their global offerings. As you will soon discover, Bermudian food is defined by a unique blend of ingredients and style of preparation that incorporates influences as diverse and rich as the island's history and heritage.*

Fish, naturally, is a key component of many Bermudian meals, eaten at any time of day. Bermuda's own special version of fish chowder is a staple, served in homes, diners, and high-end restaurants alike. The chowder is traditionally accompanied by a splash of sherry peppers (ripe and very hot bird peppers marinated in sherry with herbs and spices) and black rum (rum darkened by molasses and a special barrel aging process). Native fish, often called Bermuda fish, include tuna; mahimahi; rockfish, a delicate, sweet, white fish; and wahoo, a dense game fish, often cut into steaks and grilled. A delicious local preparation involves panfrying the fish, then topping it with almonds and a fried banana. Bermuda spiny lobster, seasonally available from September through March, is about the same size as your average Maine lobster and incredibly succulent.

A popular Bermudian appetizer is shark hash: minced shark meat sautéed with spices, usually served on toast. Codfish cakes are made of salted cod mashed with cooked potatoes and fresh thyme and parsley, then shaped into a patty and panfried. These days it's possible to enjoy them topped with a zesty fruit salsa and a side of mesclun salad instead of the old-fashioned way: between the two ends of a white bun, slathered with mayonnaise.

The island's traditional weekend brunch is a huge plate of boiled or steamed salt cod with boiled potatoes, onions, and sliced bananas, all topped with a hard-boiled egg or tomato sauce, and, sometimes, avocado slices. The Paraquet, on South Shore Road in Paget, and Paw-Paws, in Warwick, both serve excellent, full-blown codfish brunches.

Cassava pie—a savory blend of cassava, eggs, sugar, and either pork or chicken—is a rich, flavorful dish formerly reserved solely for Christmas dinner. Today restaurants frequently offer cassava pie as a special side dish. More common is mussel pie, made of shelled mussels, potatoes, and onions, baked and seasoned with thyme, parsley, and curry.

Vegetarians won't find a huge selection on menus, but most restaurants have at least two or three meatless dishes, and chefs can sometimes create a dish impromptu using fresh Bermuda carrots, onions, potatoes, and green beans.

As for Bermudian desserts, bananas baked in rum and brown sugar are to die for. Loquat or banana crumble is sweet and rich, and fresh strawberries and cherries in season are a joy.

that diners can take their time with the deliciously prepared food. Among the culinary highlights are the grilled lamb chops with rosemary, grilled fresh Bermuda fish with fried banana and almonds, and the seafood kettle (mussels, shrimp, fish, scallops, and lobster tail in a creamy white-wine-and-curry sauce). ⊠ *Armoury Bldg., Reid St., Hamilton* ☎ 441/292–6195 ☱ *AE, MC, V* ☉ *Closed Sun.*

★ **$$–$$$** ✕ **Ristorante Primavera and Omakase Sushi Bar.** High-backed, elegant banquettes and crisp, white tablecloths set the scene for delicious Italian or Japanese meals delivered with superlative service. Those hankering for authentic Italian classics will love the beef carpaccio with Parmesan and pesto over arugula, and the *vongole al vino bianco* (baby clams sautéed with white wine, garlic, and parsley). Other excellent pastas here include the *penne al gorgonzola e noci* (penne sautéed with Gorgonzola and walnuts) and the *ravioli neri* (black ravioli) filled with lobster meat and served

CloseUp

KID-FRIENDLY EATERIES

SINCE DINING IN BERMUDA CAN be an expensive and lengthy affair, adults with children in tow appreciate a restaurant with a kid-friendly menu and speedy service. For an advance look at menus and prices from a number of different restaurants, check the useful "Menu Pages" in the Bermuda Telephone Directory. Bermuda has no fast-food chains, except for a lone Kentucky Fried Chicken in Hamilton, but children have no trouble finding familiar foods in welcoming settings at the more casual restaurants on the island.

La Trattoria (☎ 441/295–1877), a lively Italian restaurant on Washington Lane in Hamilton, makes a kid's favorite food: pizza, with all kinds of yummy toppings. Tried-and-true pastas, like spaghetti with meatballs and fettucine Alfredo, plus colorful salads, assure that all tastes, even adult ones, can be accommodated. At lunch time, it's best to go before 1 PM to be seated promptly. *Rosa's Cantina* (☎ 441/295–1912), on Front Street, is where to get Tex-Mex tacos and burritos. The bright decorations impress most kids, too. If you're in Bermuda on a Wednesday evening, April through October, you can take children to Hamilton's *Harbour Nights* street festival for a standing-up dinner of fish sandwiches, fish patties, wraps, sweets, and the like, sold from booths and kiosks along Front Street.

The Specialty Inn (☎ 441/236–3133), on the south shore in Smith's Parish has burgers, sandwiches, pizza, and even sushi, and it's open for breakfast, lunch, and dinner. Over in Dockyard, the *Frog & Onion Pub* (☎ 441/234–2900) has a varied menu with children's portions and reasonable prices. Kids who'll experiment may like to try one of the meat pies. Otherwise, the finger-friendly fish-and-chips rarely fails. Dripping candelabras, and flags and crests, may tempt little ones to explore.

in a light, pink sauce. The sushi bar, Omakase, is upstairs but you may order from downstairs as well. Delicacies include the Bermuda maki roll stuffed with crab meat, avocado, and cucumber. Several vegetarian rolls, stuffed with asparagus or shiitake, are also on the menu. ⊠ *69 Pitts Bay Rd., Hamilton* ☎ *441/295–2167* ☐ *AE, MC, V* ⊙ *No lunch weekends.*

$ ✕ **Coconut Rock and Yashi Sushi Bar.** Whether you're in the mood for shrimp tempura and sashimi served in a quiet room with black-lacquer tables and paper lanterns, or whether you would rather have chicken chimichanga, fried tiger shrimp, and grilled sirloin steak surrounded by loud music videos on multiple screens—or if you want a little of both—these adjoining restaurants can satisfy. ⊠ *Williams House (downstairs), Reid St., Hamilton* ☎ *441/292–1043* ☐ *AE, MC, V* ⊙ *No lunch Sun.*

¢–$ ✕ **Aggie's Garden & Waterside Café.** The charm of this tiny restaurant
Fodor'sChoice is its location beside the water, just a few hundred yards from Hamil-
★ ton. You go down a brick stairway, whose walls are covered with ferns, to a harborside garden planted with herbs and flowers. The open kitchen—where cooking classes are taught at night—is on the harbor level of an old Bermuda home. The seating is mostly in the garden, with former church pews, and umbrellas over the tables. The house and garden are quite an escape from the surrounding office blocks, and businesspeople often come here for lunch. Some patrons even moor their boats alongside the dock and skip the stairs altogether. The creative, seasonal menu lists soups, sandwiches, and salads made with locally grown produce, as well as grilled local fish, free-range chicken, and homemade pizza with organic toppings. The daily sweets, such as the ginger or oatmeal-nut cookies and the fresh fruit tarts, are perfect with a cup of fair-trade tea or coffee. ⊠ *Falconer House, 108 Pitts Bay Rd., Hamilton* ☎ *441/296–7346* 🖶 *441/296–3299* ☐ *No credit cards* ⊙ *No dinner.*

French

$$$-$$$$ ✕ **Waterloo House.** This restaurant and small Relais & Châteaux hotel
FodorsChoice in a former private house on Hamilton Harbour serves traditional
★ Continental specialties, such as lamb and veal, plus a number of Bermu-
dian dishes, including just-off-the-boat local fish. The menu changes
every day, and you can't go wrong with any choice. Fish can be grilled
or panfried upon request. Anton Mosimann of Horizons is the restau-
rant's consultant chef. You can dine either on the waterside patio (in
good weather) or in the more formal dining room, with its deep-rasp-
berry walls, rich chintzes, and attractive lighting. Jacket and tie are re-
quired after 6 PM. ✉ *100 Pitts Bay Rd., Hamilton* ☎ *441/295–4480*
⌂ *Jacket and tie* ⊟ *AE, MC, V.*

★ **$$-$$$** ✕ **La Coquille.** When you dine at a table beside the enormous open win-
dows at La Coquille, you might feel as though you were floating on the
harbor yourself. Nearly every seat in the house has beautiful views of
the water, a pleasant distraction from the worthy Provençal specialties
by Chef Serge Bottelli, previously of Café Lido. Businesspeople and BUEI
visitors alike enjoy the delicious seafood. Every type of shellfish is avail-
able, and local fish are grilled or panfried and served with vegetables
or pasta. The chicken stuffed with sun-dried tomatoes is an excellent
alternative to seafood. The very long wine list includes bottles from France,
Australia, California, Chile, Italy, and Spain. ✉ *Bermuda Underwater
Exploration Institute (BUEI), 40 Crow La., Hamilton* ☎ *441/292–
6122* ⊟ *AE, MC, V.*

Indian

★ **$** ✕ **House of India.** Take a taxi to this out-of-the-way restaurant on the less-
safe north side of Hamilton. The superb traditional Indian food, with
specialties from across the subcontinent, is well worth the ride. Start with
vegetable *samosas* (small deep-fried turnovers), which are sure to whet
your palette. For your second course, you really can't go wrong with any
entrée you choose—meat, fish, or vegetarian. Lamb in cashew sauce is
quite popular. All the *nan* (a flat, doughy bread) is freshly made in the
tandoor, and the *lassi* (sweetened yogurt) drinks, particularly the mango,
are delicious and refreshing. A filling weekday lunch buffet is worth every
penny of the cost ($16). You can also opt for take-out. ✉ *57 North St.,
Hamilton* ☎ *441/295–6450* ⊟ *MC, V* ☉ *No lunch weekends.*

Italian

$$-$$$ ✕ **Little Venice.** Head for this trattoria if you want to be entertained by
waiters who may break into song at any time. Little Venice is expen-
sive, but it has plenty of character and flavorful, reliable Italian food.
A stand-by starter is the antipasto plate with calamari, mozzarella, and
salami, although the salads topped with Gorgonzola croutons are hard
to resist. Good choices for a main course include the thinly sliced grilled
veal, duck with smoked bacon, and linguine with shellfish and calamari
in tomato sauce. ✉ *32 Bermudiana Rd., Hamilton* ☎ *441/295–3503*
⌂ *Reservations essential* ⊟ *AE, MC, V.*

$-$$ ✕ **La Trattoria.** Tucked away in a Hamilton alley, this no-nonsense trattoria has red-and-white tablecloths and a familiar mom-and-pop feel. Any
of the pastas, such as lasagna, manicotti, and spaghetti with mixed
seafood, can be served in smaller portions as appetizers. Fish fillets are
generally panfried with olive oil, garlic, and herbs. La Trattoria's pizzas
are cooked in Bermuda's only brick wood-burning pizza oven. About 20
inventive topping combinations (such as arugula and prosciutto) are
listed on the menu, but the chef will mix and match any topping you like.
✉ *Washington La., Hamilton* ☎ *441/295–1877* ⊟ *AE, MC, V.*

$-$$ ✕ **Portofino.** This popular Italian indoor-outdoor restaurant is often
busy and noisy. Creative pizzas include Cesare's Special (Cesare is the

owner), with anchovies, capers, garlic, and red bell pepper; and the Caprese, with shrimp, scallops, mussels, calamari, and lobster meat. A complete selection of pasta, risotto, fish, and meat dishes are also on the menu. The scampi grilled with a touch of olive oil are very tasty. Be sure to reserve in advance to avoid waiting for a table. ⊠ *Bermudiana Rd., off Front St., Hamilton* ☎ *441/292–2375 or 441/295–6090* ▤ *AE, MC, V* ⊙ *No lunch weekends.*

$–$$ ✕ **Tuscany.** The balcony of this owner-operated spot overlooks Front Street and has a great view of Hamilton Harbour—when no cruise ships are moored alongside. Traffic noises may be offputting, but you can dine inside for quietude. A fresco of the Tuscan countryside decorates the otherwise white-washed walls of the spacious dining room, which is crowned with a Bermuda beam-and-slate ceiling. Some dishes are classic Tuscan, such as the *quattro stagioni* (four seasons) pizza, while others have a bit of the Bermudian thrown in, like the rockfish with fried bananas and pine nuts. Other choices include veal sautéed in white wine, with fresh tomatoes, olives, capers, and spinach; and the crèpe marinara, filled with baby shrimp, scallops, and fish, baked and served with lobster sauce. ⊠ *Front St., off Bermuda House La., Hamilton* ☎ *441/292–4507* ▤ *AE, MC, V.*

¢–$ ✕ **Pasta Basta.** This local haunt is hard to find, so be sure to bring your map if walking from Front Street. Its colorful tables and chairs, and the photos of Italian scenery and food, make it an upbeat place to enjoy the food, which is always tasty. The ever-changing menu of simple northern-Italian dishes keeps things interesting. Try the fettuccine Alfredo, classic or spinach lasagna, *orecchiette* ("little ears" or tiny disk-shape pasta) with pesto, or any of the daily specials. No liquor is served, and smoking is not allowed. ⊠ *1 Elliot St. W, Hamilton* ☎ *441/295–9785* ▤ *No credit cards.*

Mediterranean

$$–$$$ ✕ **Fresco's Wine Bar & Restaurant.** Fresco's is known for its homemade pasta, seafood, and vegetarian specialties—dishes that might be best categorized as Mediterranean cuisine, often with a French and Caribbean flair. Consider the *tarte Provençal* (roasted vegetables and caramelized onions in a freshly baked pastry crust), panfried yellowtail snapper with zucchini-lime couscous and sweet red-pepper reduction, or the lobster medallions roasted with vanilla. At lunch, ask for a table in the courtyard, with its fountain, palms, and flowers—it's just like being in Europe. Before or after dinner, you can swirl a glass of *rosso* beneath the vaulted ceiling of the wine bar. ⊠ *Chancery La., off Front St., Hamilton* ☎ *441/295–5058* ⌔ *Reservations essential* ▤ *AE, MC, V* ⊙ *No lunch weekends.*

$$–$$$ ✕ **Monte Carlo.** Bright, with trompe l'oeil murals, country-style wood chairs, and exposed Bermuda-cedar beams in the ceiling, this conveniently situated restaurant behind City Hall attracts businesspeople from surrounding offices. Its owners are Italian, and cuisine from northern Italy—white-bean soup, pumpkin gnocchi, angel-hair pasta with porcini—predominates, although the south of France is also well-represented. Consider a savory crepe, the giant mushroom-scallop ravioli with lobster sauce, or the totally original seafood ragout, which is topped with mango, avocado, and tomato salsa and dressed with cilantro vinaigrette. No matter what you order, save room for a homemade pastry from the dessert trolley. ⊠ *3 Victoria St., Hamilton* ☎ *441/295–5453* ▤ *AE, MC, V.*

Seafood

$$–$$$ ✕ **Port O' Call.** Resembling the interior of a yacht, Port O' Call is a popular yet intimate restaurant. It's also one of the few ground-level din-

WHAT'S MISSING HERE?

F YOU THINK SOMETHING may be missing from the horizon of Bermuda eateries, you are quite right. No big golden double arches rise up anywhere on the island, no red-head, pig-tail, freckle-face girl smiles a promise of "old-fashioned hamburgers." That's right, apart from a lone Kentucky Fried Chicken, which snuck in sometime during 1970s, you won't find any fast-food chains on the island.

After the KFC appeared, the Bermudian government systematically barred other fast-food chains from establishing their own restaurants on the island. When Bermuda's premier Sir John Swan (who served from 1982 to 1995) saw his plans for independence from Britain rejected in a referendum, he resigned from his post and instead promptly applied for permission to open a McDonald's.

Swan's successor, premier David Saul, was ready to approve the proposition, but a fervor of opposition among Bermuda's citizenry caused him to resign, too. The majority of Bermuda's residents strongly believed that allowing American franchises onto the island would dilute Bermuda's distinctive foreign (and rather upscale) appeal, eventually leading to the island's resembling Anyplace, USA.

Parliament voted against the proposition, and after several appeals, the highest court—the London-based Privy Council—made the final decision that no new fast-food franchises would be permitted on the island. Bermuda governor Thorold Masefield signed the law in 1997.

---

ing spots on Front Street, with an outdoor dining area like a European sidewalk café. Fresh local fish—such as wahoo, tuna, grouper, and snapper—is cooked perfectly, and the preparations are creative. Consider the pan-roasted snapper or the sesame-crusted tuna. ⊠ *87 Front St., Hamilton* ☎ *441/295–5373* ⊟ *AE, MC, V* ⊘ *No lunch weekends.*

$$ ✕ **Lobster Pot.** Bermudians swear by the Lobster Pot, with its maritime-theme dining room filled with brass nautical gear, lobster traps, and sun-bleached rope. Local conviction comes from the cooking, no doubt, which turns out excellent versions of island standards, including fresh local lobster (September through March), and yellowtail or rockfish with bananas and almonds. You might also want to consider the delicious Lobster Pot snails in their buttery garlic-curry sauce. ⊠ *Bermudiana Rd., Hamilton* ☎ *441/292–6898* ⊟ *AE, MC, V* ⊘ *Closed Sun.*

ST. GEORGE'S

British

$$–$$$ ✕ **Carriage House.** Hearty British fare is the daily bread at the Carriage House, an attractive slice of the restored Somers Wharf area. Try to secure a table outside on the patio or inside by a window so you can watch the action on the harbor. This is the place to tuck into roast prime rib, cut to order tableside, or roast leg of lamb with rosemary. But don't overlook the fresh Bermuda fish, like panfried wahoo in lemon-butter sauce. Sundays the Carriage House lays out a generous buffet brunch that includes champagne and a pianist playing background music. Afternoon tea with all the trimmings is served daily except Sunday. On Friday and Saturday nights, a jazz combo entertains. ⊠ *Somers Wharf, St. George's* ☎ *441/297–1270* ⊟ *AE, DC, MC, V.*

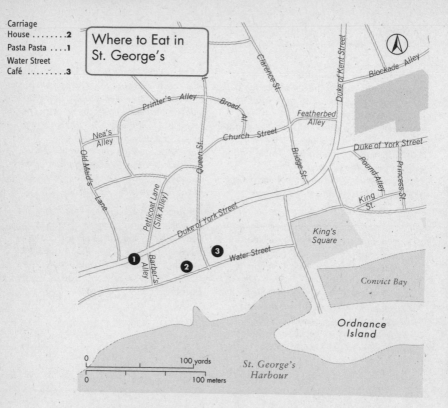

Where to Eat in
St. George's

Contemporary

$–$$ ✕ **Water Street Café.** With a waterside terrace on the harbor, Water Street
is one of the most pleasant and romantic restaurants in the East End. The
young Bermudian owners, Chris Malpas and James Perry, have a wealth
of experience between them—Mr. Malpas graduated from the Culinary
Institute of America, and Mr. Perry has cooked in Europe and Asia—
and the two conspire to treat diners to a decidedly different menu. You
might find cripsy artichoke and parmesan-crusted chicken on the seasonal menu, plus a fresh Bermuda fish on the daily-changing black-
board. For dessert, anything made with chocolate is definitely worth the
calories. ✉ *36 Water St., St. George's* ☎ *441/297–1307* ▭ *MC, V.*

Italian

¢–$ ✕ **Pasta Pasta.** A brightly painted interior, a lively (if slightly institutional)
atmosphere, and plentiful portions of home-style northern Italian cook-
ing quickly turn first-time customers into repeat diners. The pizza as well
as the pastas, such as penne with chicken-and-pepper sauce, are sound
choices. No liquor is served, and smoking is not allowed. ✉ *York St., St.
George's* ☎*441/297–2927* ✍*Reservations not accepted* ▭*No credit cards.*

ELSEWHERE IN THE PARISHES

The Central Parishes

Contemporary

$$$$ ✕ **Horizons.** The dining room at Horizons cottage colony is one of
Fodor's Choice Bermuda's most elegant, and reservations can be difficult to secure even
★ weeks in advance. Chef Anton Mosimann's delicate, healthful, fusion
cuisine has brought the world's rich, famous, and trim to his table on

DIVINE PICNIC SPOTS

SURE, BERMUDA IS FULL OF *pleasant restaurants with forks, knives, and tablecloths, but the island also has some gorgeous, quiet corners for those times when you'd rather dine closer to nature.* **Clearwater Beach** *in St. David's is one of Bermuda's nicest picnic spots, with tables near to and on the beach. The large half-moon strand with calm waters has been a local favorite, especially for families with children, since the 1995 closing of the U.S. naval base in St. George's Parish. You can pick up picnic supplies at the grocery store about ¼ mi away or order lunch to go from one of St. David's casual eateries, such as the Black Horse Tavern or Dennis's Hideaway.*

With verdant open spaces sprinkled with shady poinciana trees, the **Botanical Gardens,** *on Middle Road in Paget, make a peaceful inland setting for a picnic. The gardens have a few picnic tables and plenty of benches, plus spacious lawns where you can spread a blanket. Bring your own supplies as there is no on-site café.*

Just west of popular Warwick Long Bay, tiny, tranquil **Jobson Cove** *beach is backed by the dramatic cliffs and greenery of South Shore Park. There are no tables and no snack bars, so the cove is usually uncrowded at lunch time, perfect for a romantic, solitary picnic on the sand.*

Adjacent to a Bermuda Audubon Society nature reserve, **Somerset Long Bay Park** *in Sandys has a semicircular beach, fluffy spruce trees, and shallow water. It is also a terrific place for birding as it borders on an Audubon Society sanctuary. You'll find tables under the trees near the beach, and a grocery store less than a ½ mi away. With these and other lovely picnic spots to discover, you won't miss your proper place settings one bit!*

countless occasions. Dinner is a five-course, prix-fixe (around $45) affair with a menu that changes nightly but may include vegetable terrine with basil oil and tomato coulis, and roasted snapper over sun-dried tomato polenta. The staff is, naturally, impeccably trained, swift, and discreet. You can linger over coffee on the terrace and listen to the sounds of the local tree frogs, or if entertainment has been scheduled, enjoy live jazz or blues and perhaps take a swing around the dance floor. ⊠ *Horizons & Cottages, South Rd., Paget Parish* ☎ *441/236–0048* ⌂ *Reservations essential* ⚲ *Jacket and tie* ▭ *AE, MC, V.*

★ **$$$–$$$$** ✕ **Aqua.** Everything about Aqua is wonderfully romantic. Set on the island's southern coast, it overlooks a lovely beach and the endless Atlantic Ocean. You can dine at one of the many tables on the large, covered deck or enjoy the view set back a bit in the dining room. The colors inside emulate the turquoise and deep-blue hues of the ocean. Blue glassware complements the white tablecloths and the white wood beams and slate flooring of the porch. The oft-changing menu is created according to the seasonal, fresh ingredients that are available. For a starter, the sugar-cured beef carpaccio on roasted peppers with cashews and parsnip chips is beyond compare. Seafood addicts should go for the panfried scallops on arugula. The choices of delectable entrées make a decision difficult; however, the tandoori-spiced rack of lamb with citrus yogurt on cumin flat bread is a winner, as is the panfried snapper on soba noodles with pickled-ginger sauce. Aqua is sometimes closed for lunch in winter. ⊠ *Ariel Sands Hotel, 34 South Shore Rd., Devonshire Parish* ☎ *441/236–2332* ▭ *AE, MC, V.*

★ **$$$** ✕ **Palms.** Low-key and romantic, this is the perfect place to escape the world. Dining can be outside by the pool overlooking the ocean or in the plant-filled garden dining room with its wall of French doors that open to the outside. You are in good hands with veteran restaurateur

Llew Harvey. The menu is not extensive, but the dishes listed are all creative and flavorful. Popular appetizers include the goat cheese, leek, and apple tart with saffron sauce, and the fresh vegetable-and-shrimp spring roll with a savory Asian-style sauce. When it's available, go for the signature rockfish entrée, cooked in a sumptuous blend of coconut curry and served with stir-fried vegetables. Another good entrée is the classic duck á l'orange. Desserts are worth every calorie—for best, it's a tie between the rum cake with rum-and-raisin ice cream and the crème brûlée of the day. Palms is sometime closed for lunch in winter. ⊠ *Surf Side Beach Club, South Shore Rd., Paget Parish* ☎ *441/236–7100* ⊟ *AE, MC, V.*

$$$–$$$$ ✕ **Norwood Room.** Don't be put off by the fact that this Stonington Beach Hotel restaurant is run by students of the Hospitality and Culinary Institute of Bermuda: under the supervision of their mentors, they produce both superb food and service. The oversize training kitchen uses local ingredients and European culinary techniques to create a range of fresh tastes. Have a preprandial cocktail at the sunken bar overlooking the swimming pool. Then, go for the cold fruit soup (piña colada, strawberry, or watermelon), followed by mahimahi on spinach and roasted garlic or grilled beef tenderloin with red bell pepper pesto. ⊠ *Stonington Beach Hotel, South Shore Rd., Paget Parish* ☎ *441/236–5416* ⋔ *Jacket and tie* ⊟ *AE, MC, V.*

$$–$$$ ✕ **Seahorse Grill.** A chic, enduring restaurant with a minimalist, white-
Fodor'sChoice brick and wood-beam interior, Seahorse is a perennial favorite of local
★ hipsters and professionals. The ever-changing menu showcases locally grown produce and fresh Bermuda fish prepared in a light, contemporary style with a nod to island tastes. On the menu, ingredients are described in detail, with even their geographic origins named. If it's listed, try the baked Caesar salad and anchovy tempura for an appetizer, and the seafood paella for a main course. The service can be a bit slow, so come prepared to linger between courses. ⊠ *Elbow Beach Hotel, 60 South Shore Rd., Paget Parish* ☎ *441/236–3535* ⊟ *AE, MC, V.*

Continental

$$$ ✕ **Fourways Inn.** Fourways has risen to preeminence as much for its lovely 18th-century surroundings as for its reliable cuisine. The elegant interior, with mahogany banisters, burgundy carpeting, impressionist prints, and silver and crystal table settings, evokes the image of a fine French manor. Traditional Continental dishes, such as veal scallopine and roast duck, are beautifully presented and delicious. ⊠ *1 Middle Rd., Paget Parish* ☎ *441/236–6517* ⋔ *Jacket required* ⊟ *AE, MC, V.*

Italian

★ **$$–$$$** ✕ **Café Lido.** On the beachfront terrace at the Elbow Beach Hotel, with waves breaking just below, Café Lido is often invoked as one of the island's most romantic settings. At this writing, the restaurant is closed for renovations due to damage from Hurricane Fabian. The specialties are seafood casserole and pasta. You might try the fusilli with pink sauce and fresh garden vegetables, or the house lasagna. The ever-changing dessert menu might include crème brûlée or Italian gelato. ⊠ *Elbow Beach Hotel, off Shore Rd., Paget Parish* ☎ *441/236–9884* ⟜ *Reservations essential* ⊟ *AE, MC, V.*

The Western Parishes

Bermudian

$–$$ ✕ **Freeport Gardens.** If it's large amounts of locally caught fish you want, this is the place—try the fish platter or the combination seafood platter with scallops, shrimp, and wahoo or snapper. The fish-and-chips and the fish sandwiches are unforgettable. Most are deep-fried, but they can be grilled upon request. If you don't fancy fruits of the sea, choose from a range of pizzas, hamburgers, and sandwiches. For dessert you might be offered freshly baked apple or lemon-meringue pie. ⊠ *Pender Rd., Dockyard* ☎ *441/234–1692* ▭ *AE, MC, V.*

British

$$ ✕ **Somerset Country Squire.** Overlooking Mangrove Bay, this typically English tavern is all dark wood and good cheer, with a great deal of malt and hops in between. Much of the food isn't good enough to warrant a special trip across the island, but some of it is: the Bermuda fish chowder, the panfried mahimahi, and the steak-and-kidney pie are all good choices. ⊠ *Mangrove Bay, Somerset* ☎ *441/234–0105* ▭ *AE, MC, V.*

$–$$ ✕ **Frog & Onion Pub.** With its vaulted limestone ceilings and thick walls, the former Royal Naval Dockyard warehouse is a fitting place for this nautically decorated pub and its large poolroom. The food caters to every taste, running the gamut from hearty English pub fare to European dishes to a selection of fresh local fish plates. Pub favorites are bangers and mash, the Argus Bank fish sandwich, panfried local rockfish or tuna, and the Frog & Onion burger, which is topped with fried onions and bacon. A children's menu is available. ⊠ *The Cooperage, Dockyard* ☎ *441/234–2900* ▭ *MC, V.*

$–$$ ✕ **Henry VIII.** As popular with locals as it is with vacationers from nearby Southampton resorts, the lively Henry VIII effects an Old English look that stops just short of "wench" waitresses and Tudor styling. You'll find a mix of English and Bermudian menu favorites, including steak-and-kidney pie, rack of lamb, and fish chowder. Save room for the sticky toffee pudding. Sometimes a strolling singer serenades diners. After dinner you can move along to the bar for a round of calypso. The outdoor tables overlook compelling views of the southern coast. ⊠ *56 South Shore Rd., Southampton Parish* ☎ *441/238–1977* ▭ *AE, MC, V.*

¢ ✕ **Lighthouse Tea Room.** At the base of Gibbs Hill Lighthouse, in the old home of the former lighthouse keeper, this adorable little teahouse serves a selection of properly brewed teas and British pastries, such as scones with clotted cream. It's the perfect place to rest after the climb up and down the 185 spiraling steps of the lighthouse. You'll find expertly blended black teas and unusual herbal teas, such as dandelion and juniper berry, served iced as well as hot in summer. A lunch menu lists homemade soups and sandwiches, plus smoked trout and pork pie with chutney. For dessert, you might find fresh banana cake or gingerbread with lemon sauce. Breakfast (sausage, eggs, and crumpets, anyone?) is also served. Dinner is available weekends only, with a weekly-changing menu. Owner Heidi Cowen, who does all the baking, grew up in the old dwelling. Her grandfather was the last lighthouse keeper before self-maintaining electronic lights were introduced in the late 1960s. ⊠ *Lighthouse Rd., Southampton Parish* ☎ *441/238–8679* ▭ *AE, MC, V* ☼ *No dinner weekdays.*

Contemporary

$$$$ ✕ **Waterlot Inn.** This graceful, two-story manor house, which dates
Fodor'sChoice from 1670 and functioned as a bed-and-breakfast in the 1900s, now
★ holds one of Bermuda's most elegant and elaborate restaurants. The service is impeccable, with waiters that have just enough island exuberance to take the edge off their European-style training. The Bermudian-Continental menu changes every season but always offers an excellent fish chowder. The seafood ravioli is another stellar choice of appetizer. Grilled fish-of-the-day over a plate of local, colorful vegeta-

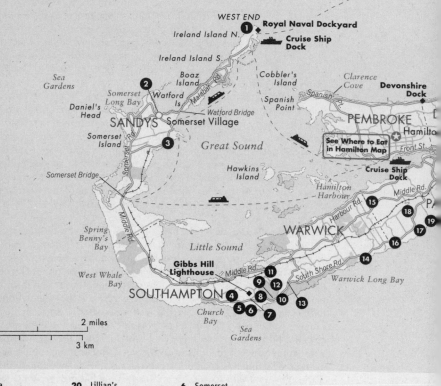

Where to Eat in the Parishes

ATLANTIC OCEAN

WEST END
Royal Naval Dockyard **1**
Ireland Island N.
Cruise Ship Dock
Ireland Island S.
Boaz Island
Cobbler's Island
Clarence Cove
Devonshire Dock
Sea Gardens
Somerset Long Bay
Watford Is
Watford Bridge
Spanish Point
Spanish Pt.
PEMBROKE
Hamilton
Daniel's Head
Maidban
SANDYS
Somerset Village
Great Sound
See Where to Eat in Hamilton Map
Front St.
Somerset Island
3
Hawkins Island
Cruise Ship Dock
Somerset Bridge
Hamilton Harbour
Spring Benny's Bay
Little Sound
Harbour Rd.
Middle Rd.
WARWICK
15
18 **19**
17
Gibbs Hill Lighthouse
Middle Rd.
16
14
West Whale Bay
11
9 **12**
South Shore Rd.
Warwick Long Bay
SOUTHAMPTON
4
8
10 **13**
Church Bay
5 **6** **7**
Sea Gardens
2 (Somerset Country Squire)

0 — 2 miles
0 — 3 km

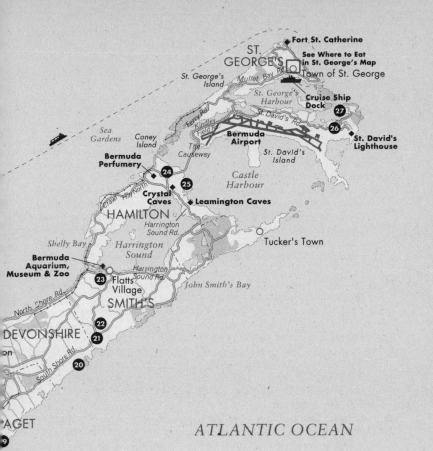

Fort St. Catherine

ST. GEORGE'S

See Where to Eat
in St. George's Map

Town of St. George

St. George's
Island

Mullet Bay Rd.

St. George's
Harbour

St. David's Rd.

Cruise Ship
Dock

27

26

St. David's
Lighthouse

Sea
Gardens

Coney
Island

Bermuda
Airport

Ferry Rd.

Kindley
Field Rd.

The
Causeway

Bermuda
Perfumery

St. David's
Island

Castle
Harbour

24

25

Crawl Hill North

Crystal
Caves

Leamington Caves

HAMILTON

Harrington
Sound Rd.

Harrington
Sound

Tucker's Town

Shelly Bay

Bermuda
Aquarium,
Museum & Zoo

23

Flatts
Village

Harrington
Sound Rd.

John Smith's Bay

North Shore Rd.

SMITH'S

22

DEVONSHIRE

21

on

20

South Shore Rd.

AGET

9

ATLANTIC OCEAN

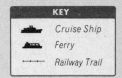

KEY	
	Cruise Ship
	Ferry
	Railway Trail

bles makes a perfect main course. Decadent desserts, like profiteroles in sweet vanilla cream, will cap off an extremely satisfying meal. ⊠ *Fairmont Southampton Hotel, Middle Rd., Southampton Parish* ☎ *441/238–0510* ⋔ *Jacket required* ⊟ *AE, DC, MC, V* ⊙ *Closed Jan.–mid-Mar. No lunch.*

$$–$$$$ ✕ **Coconuts.** Nestled between high cliff rocks and a pristine private beach on the southern coast, this outdoor restaurant is one of the best places to nab that table overlooking the ocean. The view is made even more dramatic at night by floodlights. The menu changes often, but you can always be sure of being served fresh, local produce and fish prepared with a mix of contemporary Bermudian and international culinary styles. Savor the Bermuda fish chowder or perhaps the Reefs Caesar salad with crispy bacon. Fish and meat entrées have a sophisticated twist for the discerning gourmet, and there is always a selection of vegetarian dishes, too. A fixed price of about $60 (including 15% gratuity) includes four courses at dinner. A simpler, less-expensive lunch menu includes daily specials, burgers, sandwiches, and salads. ⊠ *The Reefs, South Shore Rd., Southampton Parish* ☎ *441/238–0222* ⌀ *Reservations essential* ⊟ *AE, MC, V* ⊙ *Closed Nov.–Apr.*

$$–$$$ ✕ **Wickets Trattoria.** Prints of cricket games and players decorate the walls of this casual restaurant. Simple but satisfying Italian and American fare, and prompt service, make Wickets a good spot for families. Big omelettes with all kinds of fillings are whipped up at breakfast. Lunch and dinner menus offer more pleasing classics: salads, burgers, sandwiches, pastas, and pizza. You can also get good fish-and-chips, chicken cacciatore, and grilled steak. Sweet endings that should not be missed are tiramisu and the chocolate-crunch cheesecake. ⊠ *The Fairmont Southampton, South Shore Rd., Southampton Parish* ☎ *441/238–8000* ⊟ *AE, DC, MC, V* ⊙ *Closed Jan.*

$$ ✕ **Lillian's.** True culinary ambidexterity is at work here: two teams of chefs work on the same premises to deliver both northern-Italian cuisine and sushi. On the Italian side, the Gorgonzola whip with roasted snails is unforgettable, the osso buco is incredibly tender, and the homemade pasta is always a sure bet. Tucked into a quiet corner of the spacious restaurant, the sushi bar is tiny, and reservations to sit here are essential. The fresh and innovative sushi, such as the Mt. Fuji roll with lobster and spiced scallops, attracts knowing sushi aficionados. You can order sushi at the tables, too, even alongside a plate of pasta. ⊠ *Sonesta Beach Resort, South Shore Rd., Southampton Parish* ☎ *441/238–8122* ⊟ *AE, MC, V* ⊙ *No lunch.*

$$ ✕ **Ocean Echo.** Compelling views of the island's southern coast and outlying reefs combine with innovative Southwestern American cuisine to provide you with an experience that all of your senses can enjoy. The chef seems to be continually in high gear at Ocean Echo—the menu changes almost daily and, though not long, always promises creative dishes with complex flavors and dramatic presentations. Tasty starters include the blue-corn–crusted calamari and the grilled-cactus salad. For your main course, you might go for the red snapper with jalapeños, smoked sirloin steak, or the tortillas with vegetables and goat cheese. ⊠ *The Reefs, South Shore Rd., Southampton Parish* ☎ *441/238–0222* ⌀ *Reservations essential* ⊟ *AE, MC, V* ⊙ *Closed Nov.–Apr.*

Eclectic

$$ ✕ **Paw-Paws.** This bistro serves a rather dazzling array of Bermudian, Caribbean, European, and North American dishes, including Bermuda codfish cakes and a fabulous mixed-grill entrée: filet mignon surrounded by sautéed shrimp and scallops, and fried calamari. You can take a seat on the patio overlooking the continual stream of traffic along South Shore

Road or in the cozy dining room with colorful murals of Italian garden scenes. Paw-Paws has a small staff, so service can be slow when it's busy. ⊠ *87 South Shore Rd., Warwick Parish* ☎ *441/236–7459* ☰ *MC, V.*

French

$$$–$$$$
Fodor'sChoice
★

✕ **Newport Room.** Glistening teak and models of victorious America's Cup yachts give this fine restaurant a nautical theme. Newport Room has been adored by the island's elite and repeat visitors for years. Each dish is beautifully presented, and the service is exceptional. The menu changes each season and the chef works with as much local produce as possible. Appetizers of Scottish smoked salmon, carved tableside, or Hudson Valley foie gras with a port sauce will send the tastebuds soaring. But it's the entrées that really shine. You might have pan-seared Arctic char and bay scallops in a lobster-vanilla sauce, or black Angus beef tenderloin with tomato tart, foie-gras mousse, and Madeira jus. For dessert, try the soufflé of the day or the ginger-and-lime crème brûlée with pineapple spears and red-currant frozen yogurt. ⊠ *Fairmont Southampton, 101 South Shore Rd., Southampton Parish* ☎ *441/ 239–6964* ⋔ *Jacket required* ☰ *AE, DC, MC, V* ⊘ *Closed Jan. No lunch.*

Italian

$$

✕ **Tio Pepe.** You needn't spend much money for a quick meal at this Italian restaurant with a Mexican name. Plus, the easygoing atmosphere makes it an ideal stop for bathers returning from a day at nearby Horseshoe Bay Beach—just grab a seat at one of the plastic tables on the porch and get ready to chow down. The pizza is worth every bite, as they are freshly made with superb sauces, and there's an extensive list of comforting, classic Italian dishes, including lasagna and spaghetti. ⊠ *South Shore Rd., Southampton Parish* ☎ *441/238–1897 or 441/238–0572* ⋒ *Reservations essential* ☰ *AE, MC, V.*

Seafood

$$$$

✕ **Whaler Inn.** From your table overlooking the crashing surf, you can sometimes see fishing boats offshore, catching the seafood for this restaurant's next meals. The Whaler Inn is one of the top seafood restaurants on the island. To start, try the Bermuda fish chowder or the lobster, crab, and shrimp salad. The grilled Bermuda seafood triangle of tuna and swordfish fillets, and shrimp on sugarcane brochette, each with a different sauce, gives the palate plenty to savor. If you prefer landside fare, then go for the grilled pork chop with pumpkin-and-potato mash, or the chicken breast stuffed with goat cheese and sun-dried tomatoes and accompanied by corn risotto and spiced pineapple coulis. Desserts, such as the coconut-and-chocolate-brownie sundae, are stupendous and unforgettable. The restaurant closes for one month in winter, usually January. ⊠ *The Fairmont Southampton, South Shore Rd., Southampton Parish* ☎ *441/238–0076* ☰ *AE, DC, MC, V* ⊘ *No lunch Nov.–Mar.*

Steak

★ $$$–$$$$

✕ **Rib Room.** Hands down, this is the best place on the island for barbecued ribs and char-grilled steaks and chops. The dining room, overlooking the Fairmont Southampton golf course, is an easy place to relax, and the service runs like a Swiss clock. Start off with a classic Caesar salad, or indulge in potato skins loaded with cheese, green onions, crispy bacon, and cucumber-dill sauce. The house specialty, prime rib, is perfection in the genre and served in its juices with traditional Yorkshire pudding and creamed horseradish. The grilled garlic-rosemary lamb chops, herbed roasted chicken, and Bermuda

CloseUp

WHERE TO TAKE TEA

WHEN AFTERNOON ARRIVES, Bermuda, like Britain, pauses for tea. You can join residents in this tradition at several hotels (where afternoon tea is often complimentary to guests) and a few restaurants. Usually, tea is served between 3 and 5 PM, but tea time means anything from an urn or thermos and cookies sitting on a sideboard to the more authentic presentation of brewed-to-order tea in a porcelain or silver teapot, served with cream and sugar on a tray, and accompanied by finger sandwiches and scones with clotted cream and jam.

A very proper English high tea is served at **Waterloo House** (⊠ 100 Pitts Bay Rd., Hamilton ☎ 441/295–4480). In summer, tea-takers sip from their cups in the coolness of the ocean breeze on the harborside terrace. A pot of tea costs $7 for non-hotel guests. Tea at **Elbow Beach**

Hotel (⊠ 60 South Shore Rd., Paget Parish ☎ 441/236–3535), served in the lobby, costs $20 and includes everything from cucumber and egg-and-tomato sandwiches to pound cake and French pastries. Imported and special tea blends come with panoramic views at the hilltop **Lighthouse Tea Room** (⊠ Lighthouse Rd., Southampton Parish ☎ 441/238–8679), which also serves breakfast and lunch. A pot of tea costs $8. The **Fairmont Hamilton Princess** (⊠ 76 Pitts Bay Rd., Hamilton ☎ 441/295–3000 or 800/441–1414)serves a fabulous afternoon tea in its Heritage Court, adjacent to the lobby and Japanese Koi pond. Fine Eastern teas are brought to your Italian-linen covered table in shining silver teapots and poured into delicate porcelain cups. The cost is $11 for tea, and miniature sandwiches and cakes.

---

fish chowder are crowd-pleasers, too. ⊠ *Fairmont Southampton, 101 South Shore Rd., Southampton Parish* ☎ *441/238–8000* ⊟ *AE, MC, V* ☺ *No lunch.*

The Eastern Parishes

Bermudian

$$–$$$ ✕ **Dennis's Hideaway.** Little more than a pink ramshackle structure with a scattering of homemade picnic tables, Dennis's may be decidedly grubby, but it serves good, basic local seafood. For 35 years, starting in 1968, eccentric owner Dennis Lamb could usually be found stirring his stews and arguing with local patrons about the state of the world. Since his death in 2003, his son, Graham—also known as Sea Egg—has taken the helm. Order the "fish dinner with the works"—a feast of shark hash on toast, conch fritters, mussel stew, conch stew, fish chowder, fried fish, conch steak, shark steak, shrimp, and scallops for around $35. The chef may even throw in some bread-and-butter pudding for good measure. Only the most determined diners can partake, though, as hours are erratic and the place is way off the beaten path. ⊠ *Cashew City Rd., St. George's Parish* ☎ *441/ 297–0044* ⌂ *Reservations essential* ⊟ *No credit cards.*

$ ✕ **Black Horse Tavern.** This is a great place for island originals: fish **Fodor'sChoice** chowder and curried conch stew with rice are favorites, as are the ★ straightforward renderings of amberjack, rockfish, shark, tuna, wahoo, and Bermuda lobster. Just about everything is deep-fried, so if that doesn't suit, then request it be cooked the way you like. Be sure to go on a sunny day and sit outside, overlooking the bay. Inside, there are plenty of tables, but it feels somewhat institutional with its bare tables and tile floors. ⊠ *101 St. David's Rd., St. George's Parish* ☎ *441/ 297–1991* ⊟ *AE, MC, V* ☺ *Closed Mon.*

Contemporary

$$$–$$$$
Fodor'sChoice
★

✕ **Tom Moore's Tavern.** In a house that dates from 1652, Tom Moore's Tavern has a colorful past, thanks to the Irish poet for which it is named. Tom Moore visited friends here frequently in 1804 and caused a scandal by writing odes to a local woman who was already married. Today, fireplaces, casement windows, and shipbuilders' cedar joinery capture a sense of history that in no way interferes with the fresh, light, and innovative cuisine. Broiled scampi, Bermuda lobster (in season), and sautéed-then-broiled Bermuda fish with pine nuts stand out. The soufflés are always excellent, as is the chef's pastry. Both change daily. Eat in one of five cozy rooms; by special arrangement, groups may dine alfresco on a terrace that overlooks Walsingham Bay. ⊠ *Walsingham La., Bailey's Bay, Hamilton Parish* ☎ *441/293–8020* ⋔ *Jacket and tie* ⊟ *AE, MC, V* ☺ *Closed Jan.–mid-Feb. No lunch.*

$$–$$$

✕ **North Rock Brewing Company.** The copper and mahogany tones of the handcrafted beers and ales are reflected in the warm interior of this bar and restaurant, Bermuda's only brewpub. Seating surrounds the glass-enclosed brewery where David Littlejohn, who runs North Rock with his wife, Heather, tinkers with the gleaming copper kettles. Sit in the dining room or outside on the breezy patio for fish-and-chips, codfish cakes, or prime rib. ⊠ *10 South Rd., Smith's Parish* ☎ *441/236–6633* ⊟ *AE, MC, V.*

$$–$$$

✕ **Swizzle Inn.** People come here as much to drink as to eat. In fact, Swizzle Inn created one of Bermuda's most hallowed (and lethal) drinks— the rum swizzle (amber and black rum, triple sec, orange and pineapple juices, and bitters). Grab a spot in the shadowy bar—plastered with business cards from all over the world—to sip one of these delightful concoctions, or sit on the porch or upstairs balcony and watch the traffic go by. Be sure to take a taxi or bus if you've had a few too many swizzles, though. If you get hungry, try a "Swizzleburger" (basically a bacon cheeseburger), shepherd's pie, liver and onions, or a delicious Bermuda fish sandwich. The nightly special might be pad thai or fresh fish cooked in the style of your choosing. ⊠ *Blue Hole Hill, Bailey's Bay, Hamilton Parish* ☎ *441/293–1854* ⊟ *AE, MC, V.*

Italian

$$–$$$

✕ **Rustico Restaurant & Pizzeria.** Owned by Odilio Angeli, the same Italian restaurateur who runs the top-notch Ristorante Primavera in Hamilton, at Rustico you can eat and drink in the quaint village of Flatts, across from the Bermuda Museum, Aquarium & Zoo. In fact, the kitchen takes advantage of the seafood for sale right off fishermen's boats each day, hence Bermudian favorites are on the menu along with Italian specialties. The wine list is surprisingly comprehensive. Families will appreciate the children's menu and the prompt service. ⊠ *8 North Shore Rd., Flatts Village, Smith's Parish* ☎ *441/295–5212* ⊟ *AE, MC, V.*

$–$$

✕ **Specialty Inn.** A favorite with locals and families, this south-shore restaurant is cheerful and clean, with lower prices. Always packed at dinner, you may have to wait a few minutes for a table, but it is worth the wait. The no-frills food is Bermudian with Italian and Portuguese accents. A sushi bar seats only about four people at a time, but you can order sushi at any of the tables. You will find fish chowder or red-bean soup on the menu, along with chicken cacciatore and pizza (vegetarian or pepperoni). ⊠ *Collectors Hill, Smith's Parish* ☎ *441/236–3133* ⊟ *MC, V.*

WHERE TO STAY

4

FODOR'S CHOICE

The Fairmont Hamilton Princess, *in Hamilton*

Grotto Bay Beach Resort, *in Hamilton Parish*

Horizons & Cottages, *in Paget Parish*

Oxford House, *in Hamilton*

The Reefs, *in Southampton Parish*

Salt Kettle House, *in Hamilton*

Waterloo House, *in Hamilton*

HIGHLY RECOMMENDED

Ariel Sands, *in Devonshire Parish*

Aunt Nea's Inn at Hillcrest, *in St. George's*

Cambridge Beaches, *in Sandys Parish*

Elbow Beach Hotel, *in Paget Parish*

The Fairmont Southampton, *in Southampton*

Little Pomander Guest House, *in Paget Parish*

Pink Beach Club & Cottages, *in Smith's Parish*

Pompano Beach Club, *in Southampton Parish*

Royal Heights Guest House, *in Southampton Parish*

Royal Palms Hotel, *in Pembroke Parish*

Revised by
Sandra Davis-
Taylor

PICTURE A BEACHFRONT COTTAGE COLONY— freestanding cottages painted in solid pastels (usually pink), with white trim and gleaming white tiered roofs, clustered around a main building that houses a restaurant, a bar, a lounge, and an activities desk. Many island properties, especially the cottage colonies, are sprawling affairs on expansive, manicured grounds, with little walkways and steps connecting the cottages and main building. Although there are a few large hotels, happily, there are no high-rises and no neon signs on Bermuda. Actually, most of Bermuda's lodging properties are guest houses, identifiable only by small, inconspicuous signs or plaques.

The greatest concentration of lodgings is along the south shore, in Paget, Warwick, and Southampton parishes, which have the best beaches. Hotels near Front Street in Hamilton, and the many Hamilton Harbour properties (which are a 5- to 10-minute ferry ride from the capital), put you close to a slew of shops and restaurants. Fortunately, Bermuda is so small that, no matter where you stay, you won't have to travel far to see and do everything you want.

The island's nightlife is concentrated in resort and cottage colony bars and lounges, so hotel properties vie for patrons from all over the island, not just their own guests. Most bring in live entertainment—anything from jazz to classical—at least one night a week in high season. Barbecues and dinner dances are also popular. Afternoon tea is served daily, in keeping with British tradition, and a rum-swizzle party is usually held on Monday night. Although guest houses and apartments do not have regularly scheduled entertainment, informal gatherings are not uncommon.

Bermuda was not traditionally a family destination, but that has changed. Most hotels, guest houses, and cottage colonies welcome families with children. Some hotels—including Elbow Beach Hotel, Grotto Bay Beach Resort, the Fairmont Southampton, and Willowbank—have supervised programs for children, which are part of attractive packages. Many hotels can also arrange for baby-sitters.

Resort Hotels

★ **$$$$** 🏨 **Elbow Beach Hotel.** You would never guess from its pristine appearance that this lovely seaside resort is one of the oldest on the island—it opened in 1908. After traversing the long driveway, you come to a halt under an expansive porte cochere. Inside, you walk across shining marble floors that extend to tall, wood-paneled walls. Enormous, breezy rooms invite you to relax completely before views of the ocean or gardens through floor-to-ceiling windows. Furnishings and marble bathrooms reflect the high standards of the Mandarin Oriental Hotel Group. Of the rooms that have ocean views (88%), more than half have balconies. Nine deluxe suites overlooking the pool area are scheduled to open for summer 2004. Two separate, quiet, beachfront cottages contain six luxurious "royal suites." The resort's Café Lido, perched above the ocean, is a flurry of children and beachgoers at lunch. At night the restaurant becomes one of the most romantic in Bermuda, with candlelight, white tablecloths, and superb Mediterranean cuisine. The Deep, an on-site nightclub, hosts top island DJs. ⊠ *60 South Shore Rd., Paget Parish PG 04* ⌂ *Box HM 455, Hamilton HM BX* 🕾 *441/236–3535; 800/223–7434 in the U.S. and Canada* 🖷 *441/236–8043* ⊕ *www.elbowbeach.com* ✈ *169 rooms, 75 suites* ⌂ *3 restaurants, room service, in-room data ports, in-room safes, minibars, cable TV, some in-room VCRs, putting green, 5 tennis courts, pool, gym, hair salon, outdoor hot tub, massage, private beach, croquet, 4 bars, nightclub, shops, children's programs (ages 4–11), concierge, business services, no-smoking rooms* ▭ *AE, DC, MC, V.*

$$$$
Fodor'sChoice
★

▣ **The Fairmont Hamilton Princess.** While Bermudians take this enormous landmark for granted, visitors have been known to stand for some time in awe of the hotel's vast pinkness. The Princess bills itself as the only urban resort in Bermuda, and indeed, it is steps away from the shops and liveliness of Front Street, on the edge of Hamilton Harbour. Opened in 1885, the hotel was named in honor of Princess Louise, Queen Victoria's daughter, who visited the island in 1883, and it is credited with launching Bermuda's tourist industry. On the mezzanine you can view the Heritage Wall: pictures of politicians, members of British royalty, and writers—Mark Twain is one notable—who have stayed in the hotel. Classy, contemporary rooms and suites have elegant hard-wood furnishings and marble bathrooms. Not all rooms have balconies, and some have showers without tubs, so be sure to make a special request if either is important to you. In the main and oldest wing of the hotel is the Fairmont Gold, an exclusive boutique hotel within the larger hotel, with the most luxurious rooms in the building, plus a gorgeous lounge in the former ballroom. Downstairs, Harley's Restaurant serves international cuisine at tables overlooking the harbor. The Heritage Court, adjacent to the lobby and Japanese Koi pond, provides Bermuda's most posh afternoon tea service, with British silver tea sets and fine Belgian china. The Princess does not have a beach, but a private ferry makes regular runs across the harbor to the Fairmont Southampton, where you can enjoy a beach and a golf course. ⊠ *76 Pitts Bay Rd., Hamilton HM 08* ☍ *Box HM 837, Hamilton HM CS* ☎ *441/295–3000 or 800/441–1414* ☒ *441/295–1914* ⊕ *www.fairmont.com* ⟿ *413 rooms, 60 suites* ☍ *2 restaurants, room service, in-room data ports, in-room safes, minibars, cable TV, putting green, 2 pools, gym, hair salon, sauna, 2 bars, lobby lounge, shops, baby-sitting, dry cleaning, laundry service, concierge, Internet, business services, convention center, no-smoking rooms* ▭ *AE, DC, MC, V.*

★ $$$$

▣ **The Fairmont Southampton.** Six stories high and nearly a quarter-mile long, the modern (built in 1972) Fairmont Southampton is the island's most complete full-service resort. Top floor suites were completely rebuilt in the wake of Hurricane Fabian, which struck in September 2003. Crowning a hilltop near Gibbs Hill Lighthouse, the hotel overlooks its own private south-shore beach. Rooms have light-color wood furniture and marble bathrooms. Avoid rooms on the first three floors of the west and north wings, as they overlook a rooftop. The on-property Waterlot Inn serves Bermudian-European cuisine in a 17th-century building on the dock, while the Whaler Inn is a seafood restaurant perched above the surf. Men must don jackets to dine in the Newport Room, a superior French restaurant off of the main lobby. The Willow Stream Spa (the largest in Bermuda) has 15 treatment rooms, three lounges, two hot tubs overlooking the ocean, and an indoor heated pool with waterfalls. ⊠ *101 South Shore Rd., Southampton Parish SN02* ☍ *Box HM 1379, Hamilton HM FX* ☎ *441/238–8000 or 800/441–1414* ☒ *441/238–8968* ⊕ *www.fairmont.com* ⟿ *594 rooms, 24 suites* ☍ *5 restaurants, room service, in-room data ports, in-room safes, minibars, cable TV, driving range, putting green, 18-hole golf course, 11 tennis courts, 2 pools, hair salon, health club, spa, beach, dive shop, jet skiing, croquet, volleyball, 4 bars, lobby lounge, video game room, shops, children's programs (ages 4–16), dry cleaning, laundry service, concierge, Internet, business services, convention center, no-smoking rooms* ▭ *AE, DC, MC, V.*

$$$

▣ **Sonesta Beach Resort.** Set on a low promontory fringed by coral reefs, this six-story modern building has a stunning ocean view and direct access to three superb beaches. At this writing, the hotel is closed for renovations to rooms damaged by Hurricane Fabian in 2003; it is due to

Bermuda is a land of cottage colonies, cliff-top apartments, and beachfront resort hotels. Hidden along small parish roads, however, you can also find family-run, flower-filled guest houses and simple, inexpensive efficiencies. The lodgings we list are the cream of the crop in each price category.

Facilities & Services

Considering Bermuda hotel rates, it might come as a surprise that perks like 24-hour room service and same-day laundry service are rare. Fortunately, however, personalized attention, exceptionally comfortable rooms, and trim, scenic surroundings are not. The number and quality of facilities vary greatly according to the size and rates of the property. Resort hotels are the best equipped, with restaurants, pools, beach clubs, gyms, and sometimes golf courses. Cottage colonies also typically have a clubhouse with a restaurant and bar, plus a pool or private beach, and perhaps a golf course. Each cottage has a kitchen, so you can cook your own meals, and housekeeping services are provided. Small hotels usually have a pool, and some have a restaurant or guest-only dining room, but few have fitness facilities or in-room extras like minibars. Efficiencies or housekeeping apartments almost always come with a kitchen or kitchenette. Some properties have pools, but you may have to take the bus or a scooter to get to the beach. Even the smallest property can arrange sailing, snorkeling, scuba, and deep-sea fishing excursions, as well as sightseeing.

Unless otherwise noted, rooms in all lodgings listed are equipped with private bathrooms and air-conditioning. In each review, we list the facilities that are available, but we don't specify whether they cost extra; when pricing accommodations, always ask what's included and what entails an additional charge. Most lodgings offer a choice of meal plans, several with "dine-around" privileges at other island restaurants. Under a Full American Plan (FAP), breakfast, lunch, and dinner are included in the hotel rate. A Modified American Plan (MAP) covers breakfast and dinner. A Breakfast Plan (BP) includes a full, cooked-to-order breakfast, although a Continental Plan (CP) means pastries, juice, and coffee. Unless otherwise noted, the rates quoted below are based on the European Plan (EP), which includes no meals at all.

Reservations

It's a good idea to reserve at least two months in advance for stays between May and September. Most hotels require a two-night deposit two to three weeks prior to arrival. Note that some hotels close for 2 to 4 weeks in January or February.

Prices

Rates at Bermuda's luxury resorts are comparable to those at posh hotels in New York, London, and Paris. A 7.25% government occupancy tax is tacked on to all hotel bills, and a service charge is levied. Some hotels calculate a service charge as 10% of the bill, whereas others charge a per diem amount. Virtually every hotel on the island offers at least one vacation package—frequently some kind of honeymoon special—and many of these are extraordinarily good deals.

You can shave about 40% off your hotel bill by visiting Bermuda in low or shoulder seasons. Because temperatures rarely dip below 60°F in the winter, the low season (November through March) is ideal for tennis, golf, and shopping, although the water is a bit chilly for swimming. The trick to finding low rates is trying to pin down a hotel's low-season dates. Some hotels begin high-season rates on April 1, others April 15, and a few kick in as late as May 1. So it's best to call and ask about low- and shoulder-season rates.

WHAT IT COSTS In U.S. Dollars				
	$$$$	$$$	$$	$	¢
FOR 2 PEOPLE	over $400	$300–$400	$200–$300	$110–$200	under $110

Prices are for two people in a standard double room in high season, excluding 7.25% tax and 10% service charge.

reopen May 1, 2004. An activities director coordinates bingo games, theme parties, movies, water sports, children's programs, teen activities, and other diversions. South Side Scuba Watersports has a rental outlet here, and dive and snorkel boats leave the resort daily from April through November and on request the rest of the year. A shuttle takes you to the hotel's beach at Cross Bay, but beach-lovers should reserve a Bay Wing Beachfront Junior Suite that opens onto a private sandy beach. All rooms on the 33-acre property have balconies, but island-view rooms in the main building have just that—land views only. The Sonesta also has a popular health and beauty spa, and special spa packages are available. A shuttle transports guests to South Shore Road, where you can catch a bus to Hamilton. ⊠ *6 Sonesta Dr., off South Shore Rd., Southampton Parish SN 02* ⊕ *Box HM 1070, Hamilton HM EX* ☎ *441/238–8122; 800/766–3782 in the U.S.* 🖷 *441/238–8463* ⊕ *www. sonesta.com* ↩ *365 rooms, 34 suites* ⚭ *3 restaurants, in-room safes, minibars, 6 tennis courts, 2 pools, gym, hot tub, massage, spa, steam room, beach, 2 bars, shops, children's programs (ages 4–10), playground, concierge* ▤ *AE, DC, MC, V.*

$$–$$$
Fodor's Choice
★
🏨 **Grotto Bay Beach Resort.** A collection of lodges, undulating gardens, and walkways spread over 21 acres makes up this resort. The grounds slope down to a beautiful enclosed bay and a private beach. Here there is an aquarium, where you can feed the fish, and a few feet away are two illuminated, underground caverns: Prospero's Cave shelters a placid lagoon, and the Cathedral Cave bears oddly shaped limestone formations that you may view from a path. In the main lodge on the hill, you'll find the reception, lounge, and dining areas, all decorated in the Bermuda tradition: wood floors, potted palms, and a pastel palette bathed in natural lighting. The 14 three-story guest lodges have large, bright rooms with ocean views and either balconies or patios. Families love Grotto Bay's excellent supervised children's programs, which include activities like kitemaking and cave exploration. Sightseeing, scuba diving, and snorkeling cruises depart from the on-site deepwater dock. The optional all-inclusive package is one of the better deals in Bermuda. ⊠ *11 Blue Hole Hill, Bailey's Bay, Hamilton Parish CR 04* ☎ *441/293–8333 or 800/582–3190* 🖷 *441/293–2306* ⊕ *www.grottobay.com* ↩ *198 rooms, 3 suites* ⚭ *2 restaurants, room service, in-room data ports, cable TV with movies, 4 tennis courts, pool, gym, beach, dive shop, boating, shuffleboard, 2 bars, children's programs (ages 4–12), baby-sitting, playground, concierge, business services, meeting room, no-smoking rooms* ▤ *AE, MC, V.*

Small Hotels

★ $$$$ ▣ **Pompano Beach Club.** Expect a friendly, personal welcome at this family-run hotel, which was a fishing club (the island's first) until 1956. Pompano is flanked by the Port Royal Golf Course, attractive woodland, and the south shore, the views of which are spectacular from here, especially at sunset. The pink-and-white, crescent-shape main building houses the dining room (with alfresco tables), a small pub, a cozy lounge, and a fitness center, all with sea views. Terraced up a hillside are the rooms and one-bedroom suites, all with balconies or patios and ocean views. The "superior" rooms are larger than the suites and have ocean views from the bedroom. Suites have an ocean view through the living-room windows. More spacious and only a few dollars extra are the "deluxe" rooms. A heated swimming pool and a children's wading pool are on a spacious cliff-side patio high above the ocean. The beach has been enlarged over the years to almost four times its original size, but the real boon is a low-tide stroll 250 yards into waist-high crystal-clear waters. ⊠ *36 Pompano Beach Rd., Southampton Parish SB 03* ☎ *441/234–0222; 800/343–4155 in the U.S.* 🖷 *441/234–1694* ⊕ *www. pompano.bm* ⇆ *36 rooms, 20 suites* ⌂ *Restaurant, in-room safes, refrigerators, cable TV, golf privileges, 4 tennis courts, pool, wading pool, gym, 2 outdoor hot tubs, beach, windsurfing, snorkeling, boating, bar, baby-sitting, laundry service, concierge, Internet* ▭ *AE, MC, V.*

$$$$
Fodor'sChoice
★   ▣ **The Reefs.** Hugging the cliffs that wind around Christian Bay, this long arm of connected, pink apartments and a few separate cottages fronts unparalleled south-shore views. The Reefs is a popular wedding and honeymoon getaway, but it also welcomes families back year after year. Room rates include breakfast, afternoon tea, and dinner, and special packages include airport transfers, and bus and ferry passes. The clubhouse, in a traditional pink Bermuda cottage, has a formal restaurant and bar where local entertainers play nightly. But be sure to try Coconuts, a more casual restaurant on the waterfront. Suites near the beach and overlooking the pool each have a Jacuzzi tub, large walk-in shower for two, and complete entertainment system, including flat-screen TV. For seclusion and tranquillity (no TV, even), the cliff-side rooms perched above wave-washed boulders at the far end of the resort are best. Most rooms are modestly sized but all have ocean views and balconies. Tiled floors, neutral suede-like fabrics, and rattan predominate. ⊠ *56 South Rd., Southampton Parish SN 02* ☎ *441/238–0222; 800/742–2008 in the U.S. and Canada* 🖷 *441/ 238–8372* ⊕ *www.thereefs.com* ⇆ *41 rooms, 4 suites, 8 junior suites, 8 cottage suites* ⌂ *3 restaurants, in-room data ports, in-room safes, minibars, 2 tennis courts, pool, gym, beach, 2 bars, lounge, piano, baby-sitting, dry-cleaning, laundry service, no-smoking rooms; no TV in some rooms* ▭ *AE, MC, V* ⏐❍⏐ *MAP.*

$$$–$$$$ ▣ **Harmony Club.** This sprawling pink-and-white 1930s villa is Bermuda's only all-inclusive hotel. Mature Bermuda cedars, manicured lawns, and well-tended flower beds weave around the building and pool area. Past the long, white-pillared porte cochere is a spacious reception area, lounge, and small room off to the side containing a computer with Internet access. Rooms are spacious and bright, with either white-tile or hard-wood flooring and simple wood and wicker furniture. Most rooms have a patio or balcony. The base rate covers everything, including meals and alcohol. The hotel is adult-oriented and does not accept children. South-shore beaches are about five minutes away via complimentary shuttle. In high season a host of activities from informal barbecues to formal dances with Bermuda's top bands keeps things lively. ⊠ *109 South Shore Rd., Paget Parish PG 03* ✆ *Box PG 299, Paget PG BX* ☎ *441/236–3500; 888/427–6664 in the U.S.* 🖷 *441/236–2624*

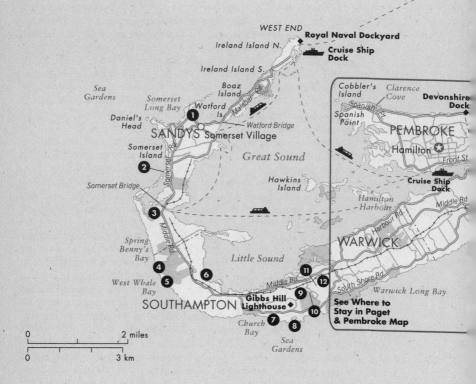

See Where to Stay in Paget & Pembroke Map

Where to Stay in the East & West Ends

ATLANTIC OCEAN

WEST END · **Royal Naval Dockyard**

Ireland Island N. · **Cruise Ship Dock**

Ireland Island S.

Boaz Island

Sea Gardens

Somerset Long Bay

Watford Is.

Daniel's Head

Somerset Village

SANDYS · Watford Bridge

Somerset Island

Somerset Bridge

Great Sound

Hawkins Island

Spring Benny's Bay

Little Sound

Cobbler's Island · Clarence Cove · **Devonshire Dock**

Spanish Point · PEMBROKE · Hamilton · Front St

Hamilton Harbour

Cruise Ship Dock

Middle Rd

Harbour Rd

WARWICK

West Whale Bay

SOUTHAMPTON

Gibbs Hill Lighthouse

Church Bay

Sea Gardens

Warwick Long Bay

South Shore Rd

Middle Rd

See Where to Stay in Paget & Pembroke Map

0 — 2 miles
0 — 3 km

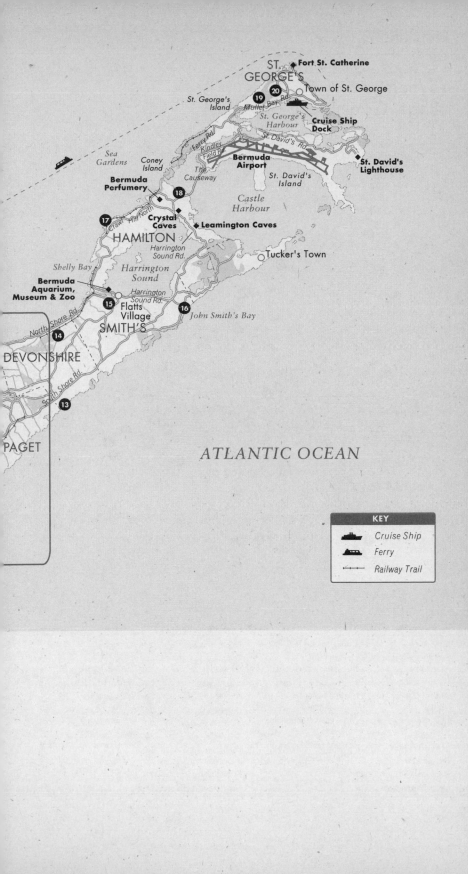

Where to Stay in Paget & Pembroke

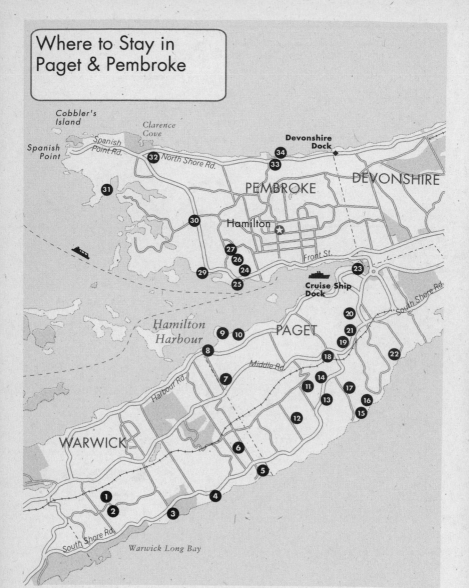

BERMUDA'S BEST SPA RESORTS

AS BEFITTING THEIR LOVELY *island location, the best of Bermuda's hotel spas are spectacular in appearance, with white columns, marble floors, flowing linens, and burbling fountains. Waterfalls tumble into hot and cold plunge pools, whirlpools, and foot pools. Quiet, cool, private massage rooms are the domain of internationally trained therapists. Mud baths, body wraps, facials, and reflexology—these are the logical extensions to your active Bermudian vacation.*

Day-long and multi-day spa packages typically incorporate wellness programs that include healthy meals, fitness classes, and talks about nutrition and stress management. You need not worry about your taste buds suffering, however. Spa menus are chef-designed with the utmost care so that they are palate pleasing as well as low in fat and high in vitamins.

For when you want to move, resort health clubs have state-of-the-art exercise machines, plus saunas, steam rooms, Vichy showers, and hydrotherapy tubs. And each venue has a myriad of activities from which to choose. You might hit balls with a Davis Cup champ, find a squash partner, or sign up for a snorkeling tour.

A favorite among Bermuda's society ladies, the day spa at the secluded **Ariel Sands** *offers head-to-toe pampering in a lovely beachside-retreat setting. The signature facial employs French-made Yon-Ka exfoliating and hydrating products to cleanse pores, restore elasticity, and soothe your skin with all-natural, aromatic masks and lotions. The deep-tissue massage is another much-requested treatment. Skilled therapists using pressure and heat to alleviate pain from chronic and acute conditions. Another method, the hot-and-cold stone massage, combines heated basalt stones, frozen marble stones, traditional massage, and aromatherapy to ease muscle tension, improve circulation, and invigorate the body.*

Sunlight dapples the indoor swimming pools at the **Cambridge Beaches Ocean Spa,** *inside a traditional, two-story Bermudian cottage with pink-stucco walls*

and a ridged roof. The glass dome that covers the pools is opened in warm weather, allowing salt-tinged ocean breezes to drift into the villa. The treatments offered here are hard to find outside Europe. Facials using Guinot of Paris products incorporate gentle stimulation of skin tissue with rollers that cause a tingling sensation. Using a clay mask, the therapist dissolves impurities and toxins, leaving the tissue feeling rejuvenated. Body-toning treatments use electrical stimuli to firm and tone the skin and help rid the body of cellulite. These treatments can be combined with body wraps using seaweed, plant extracts, and other natural ingredients. The classic day-spa package might start with a consultation and body-fat analysis, followed by exercise, a sauna session, and a massage. A half-day program for men includes a massage, facial, and hair treatment. Both full-day and half-day packages include lunch on a bayside terrace.

The Fairmont Southampton's *Willow Stream Spa, opened in 2003, is the largest and most luxurious spa on the island. Besides a complete health club, including personal trainers, there is a garden-enclosed indoor pool, a sundeck overlooking the ocean, two Jacuzzis, three lounges, steam rooms, inhalation rooms, and 15 treatment rooms. Specially designed, lengthy treatments combine baths, wraps, and massage conducted with the utmost skill. Spice-, orange-, and lavender-scented lotions, salts, and stones induce island dreams, and scrubs and body polishes leave you feeling silky-smooth. Rose-hip oil is the key ingredient in the 90-minute rejuvenation treatment, which begins with gentle exfoliation, followed by a thorough massage, and relaxing body wrap.*

Spa treatment prices range from $30 for a 20-minute localized body rub to $270 for a 120-minute aromatherapy bath, body wrap, and massage.

— By Sandra Davis-Taylor

⊕ *www.harmonyclub.com* ⇦ *68 rooms* ♨ *Dining room, in-room safes, refrigerators, cable TV, putting green, 2 tennis courts, pool, hot tub, sauna, bar, dry-cleaning, laundry service, concierge, Internet, no-smoking rooms; no kids under age 18* ⊟ *AE, DC, MC, V* ⋈ *FAP.*

$$$–$$$$ ▦ **Stonington Beach Hotel.** This training ground for students of the Hospitality & Culinary Institute of Bermuda has one of the friendliest and hardest-working staffs on the island. On the south-shore campus of Bermuda College, Stonington has access to the largest multimedia meeting space on the island, as well as the college gym and sports field. You can even attend a lecture. The spa and sports facilities at the Elbow Beach Hotel are also open to guests. At this writing, Stonington is closed for renovations to its rooms and lobby until April 2004. Rooms are in two-story terraced lodges facing one of the island's best beaches, after which the hotel is named. A cottage near the ocean has a one-bedroom and a three-bedroom apartment, both with kitchens. The spacious lobby in the main building has a fireplace and ocean views. There's also a library with well-stocked shelves and a large-screen TV. At the Norwood Room restaurant, creative international dishes are served by a helpful, gracious staff of eager-to-please students. ⊠ *8 College Dr., Paget Parish PG 04* ⊕ *Box HM 523, Hamilton HM CX* ☎ *441/236–5416; 800/447–7462 in the U.S. and Canada* 🖷 *441/236–0371* ⊕ *www.stoningtonbeach.com* ⇦ *64 rooms, 2 cottages* ♨ *Restaurant, in-room safes, refrigerators, cable TV, golf privileges, 2 tennis courts, pool, beach, snorkeling, bar, library, laundry service, business services, meeting room, no-smoking rooms* ⊟ *AE, DC, MC, V.*

$$$–$$$$ ▦ **Waterloo House.** This waterside Relais & Châteaux retreat has a long
Fodor'sChoice history. The house was built circa 1815 and named in honor of the de-
★ feat of Napoléon. Facing the harbor, its spacious Poinciana Terrace is used for outdoor dining and entertainment—perhaps piano, jazz, or calypso on any given night. The lounge has a large fireplace and is filled with beautiful flower arrangements. Most rooms are in the main house, and a few are in the two-story stone buildings beside the pool and patio. Antique and Victorian-style furnishings—well-padded sofas, delicate mahogany end tables—fill the rooms, all of which have water views. Bathrooms are large and luxurious, with marble counters and whirlpool baths. The very popular meal-plan options include dining privileges at sister properties Horizons & Cottages and the Coral Beach & Tennis Club. You can also play golf at Horizons and sign up for watersports at the Coral Beach & Tennis Club; transportation between all three properties is provided. The Waterloo's own Wellington Room won a *Wine Spectator* magazine award in 2003 (the fifth year in a row) for having one of the world's outstanding restaurant wine lists. For a breezy dining experience, join a picnic lunch aboard the hotel's small boat. ⊠ *100 Pitts Bay Rd., Hamilton HM 11* ⊕ *Box HM 333, Hamilton HM BX* ☎ *441/295– 4480; 800/468–4100 in the U.S.* 🖷 *441/295–2585* ⊕ *www.waterloohouse. com* ⇦ *28 rooms, 6 suites* ♨ *Restaurant, in-room safes, in-room hot tubs, refrigerators, cable TV, golf privileges, pool, dock, boating, 2 bars, baby-sitting, dry cleaning, laundry service, concierge, Internet, business services, meeting room, no-smoking rooms* ⊟ *AE, MC, V.*

★ **$$–$$$** ▦ **Royal Palms Hotel.** The brother-and-sister team of Richard Smith and Susan Weare have transformed this grand home into a hotel with exceptionally high standards. The main house, built around 1903, and three other buildings are set amid lush grounds with tall palms and trees bearing avocados, grapefruit, oranges, peaches, guava, and bananas. Canopied swinging chairs are excellent spots for contemplating the greenery. Hamilton is a five-minute walk away, but you'll need to take a cab or bus to get to the beach. All rooms, suites, and cottages are individually decorated by Susan. Whether yours has carpeting or polished wood floors with Oriental rugs, it is certain to be tasteful. In the morning, you are invited to pick up pastries, tea, coffee, and juice at the complimentary Continental breakfast buffet. Ascots restaurant, popular among locals, has one of the island's most imaginative menus. In summer, lunch and dinner are served on the main-house terrace. ✉ *24 Rosemont Ave., Pembroke Parish HM 06* 🕭 *Box HM 499, Hamilton HM CX* 🕾 *441/292–1854; 800/678–0783 in the U.S.; 800/799–0824 in Canada* 🖶 *441/292–1946* 🌐 *www.royalpalms.bm* 🖘 *27 rooms* 🕭 *Restaurant, in-room data ports, in-room safes, cable TV, pool, bar, lounge, baby-sitting, dry cleaning, laundry facilities, laundry service, Internet, no-smoking rooms* 🖃 *AE, MC, V* 🍽 *CP.*

$$–$$$ 🏨 **Surf Side Beach Club.** Each of the terraced condominium-style apartments of this small resort overlooks the south-shore beach below. Cliffs curve behind the apartments, enclosing the resort in a quiet, private crescent. Some of the apartments are in buildings close to the water, others are high on the hill, overlooking the pool, which in turn overlooks the ocean. Each apartment has a porch, most have fully equipped kitchens, and the largest suites have open fireplaces. All are decorated with lightwood furnishings, island-motif fabrics, and tile floors or wall-to-wall carpeting. The room rate includes Continental breakfast and dinner for two daily. The poolside Palms restaurant has an à la carte menu designed by one of the island's most talented chefs. Special diets are particularly well accommodated. ✉ *90 South Shore Rd., Warwick Parish WK 7* 🕭 *Box WK 101, Warwick WK BX* 🕾 *441/236–7100 or 800/553–9990* 🖶 *441/236–9765* 🌐 *www.surfside.bm* 🖘 *10 apartments, 23 studios, 3 suites, 2 penthouse units* 🕭 *Restaurant, in-room safes, some in-room hot tubs, some kitchens, minibars, microwaves, refrigerators, cable TV, golf privileges, pool, hair salon, massage, sauna, spa, beach, snorkeling, bar, baby-sitting, laundry facilities, laundry service, Internet* 🖃 *AE, MC, V* 🍽 *MAP.*

$$–$$$ 🏨 **Wharf Executive Suites Hotel.** The first hotel to be built in Bermuda since the Stonington Beach Hotel was completed in 1980, the Wharf opened to much anticipation (especially from business travelers) in July 2002. Fifteen spacious executive rooms and one-bedroom suites are completely equipped for the business traveler, down to the ergonomic desk chair, fax machine, printer, two-line speaker phone, and high-speed Internet connection. All rooms have balconies and wall-size windows overlooking Hamilton Harbour. Suites have full kitchens—perfect for extended stays. Adjacent to Darrell's Wharf on Harbour Road, the hotel is a seven-minute ferry ride from Hamilton. Continental breakfast is included in the rate, and dine-around options are available. ✉ *1 Harbour Rd., Paget Parish PG 01* 🕾 *441/232–5700* 🖶 *441/232–4008* 🌐 *www.wharfexecutivesuites.com* 🖘 *15 suites* 🕭 *In-room data ports, in-room fax, in-room safes, kitchens, microwaves, refrigerators, cable TV with movies, golf privileges, pool, dry cleaning, laundry facilities, laundry service, Internet, business services, no-smoking rooms* 🖃 *AE, MC, V* 🍽 *CP.*

$$–$$$ 🏨 **Willowbank.** This former estate, located on six acres of landscaped gardens overlooking Ely's Harbour, was converted to a family-style hotel by a Christian trust. Morning devotions are held in a lounge and grace is said before meals, which are announced by an ancient ship's bell and served family style. But there is no proselytizing. Willowbank is simply a serene and restful alternative to the glitzy resorts, with wonderful views and marvelous beaches nonetheless. The two large lounges are the focal point for quiet conversations and afternoon tea. Guests also meet for fellowship in the library and the Loaves and Fishes dining room. You may have liquor in your room, but there is no bar. The guest rooms, many with ocean or harbor views, are in one-story white cottages. They are large and simply furnished but have neither phones nor TVs. There is a free summer children's program including crafts and trips around the island. No service charge is added to the bill, but most guests tip on their own. ⊠ *126 Somerset Rd., Sandys Parish MA 06* ⬡ *Box MA 296, Sandys MA BX* ☎ *441/234–1616 or 800/752–8493* 🖷 *441/234–3373* ⊕ *www.willowbank.bm* ⮑ *64 rooms* ⟳ *Restaurant, in-room safes, 2 tennis courts, golf privileges, pool, gym, beach, snorkeling* ☰ *MC, V* ⊚| *MAP.*

$$ 🏨 **Rosedon.** As you approach this hotel, the first thing you notice is its majestic garden and spacious veranda, behind which rises the bright, blue-shuttered, white manor house, built in 1906. Inside, traditional rooms have 12-foot ceilings, and antique and reproduction furniture. A modern two-story building behind the main house has deluxe rooms, some with four-poster beds, love seats, and whirlpool baths. All rooms have either balconies or patios from which you can enjoy the thick, exotic garden setting. Rosedon has no restaurant, but breakfast and light meals can be ordered and brought to your room or to your umbrella-shaded table by the pool. Afternoon tea is offered in the large lounge in the main house, where films are shown nightly. The hotel has no beach, but guests have access to the Stonington Beach Hotel facilities; transportation is free. ⊠ *61 Pitts Bay Rd., Hamilton HM 06* ⬡ *Box HM 290, Hamilton HM AX* ☎ *441/295–1640; 800/742–5008 in the U.S. and Canada* 🖷 *441/295–5904* ⊕ *www.rosedonbermuda.com* ⮑ *47 rooms* ⟳ *Room service, in-room safes, refrigerators, cable TV, pool, bar, baby-sitting, laundry service, concierge, Internet, no-smoking rooms* ☰ *AE, MC, V.*

$–$$ 🏨 **Hamiltonian Hotel & Island Club.** High on Langton Hill overlooking Pembroke Parish and the city of Hamilton, this generic hotel offers stunning ocean views from all of its 32 suites. The rooms are decorated in summery pastel shades and have tiled hallways and living rooms, and carpeted bedrooms. All have sofa beds, a balcony, and TV (no cable). Suites have a refrigerator, a microwave, a toaster, and a coffeemaker. Centrally located in a tropical garden setting on the outskirts of Hamilton, the hotel is a two-minute walk to a bus stop that will take you to the city center in about five minutes. A large outdoor pool and sun deck have great sea views. There's a golf course nearby. ⊠ *Langton Hill, Pembroke Parish* ⬡ *Box HM 1738, Hamilton HM GX* ☎ *441/295–5608; 401/848–7870 in the U.S.* 🖷 *441/295–7481* ⮑ *32 suites* ⟳ *In-room safes, some refrigerators, 3 tennis courts, pool* ☰ *AE, MC, V.*

Cottage Colonies

★ **$$$$** 🏨 **Ariel Sands.** Spreading out behind a sandy Cox's Bay beach in Devonshire Parish is a statue of Ariel, the sprite in Shakespeare's *The Tempest.* She is the namesake of this informal cottage colony owned by the family of actor Michael Douglas. The snorkeling is superb here, and there are two ocean-fed pools and a heated freshwater pool. The Bermudian cottage–style clubhouse has a comfortable dining room and a lounge called the Michael Douglas Bar, with photographs of the actor on the walls. Locals come here to enjoy the quiet atmosphere and sip cocktails. On the sloping grounds are 12 cottages with 2 to 8 guest rooms in each. All rooms have unobstructed ocean views and are decorated with English-floral and plaid cottons, and Tommy Bahama furniture down to the pineapple-finial four-poster beds. The Aqua Restaurant, with a divine alfresco seaside setting, is a hot spot with island residents and visitors alike. The well-reputed Nirvana spa indulges your every whim with blissful and unusual massages and facial treatments. ⊠ *34 South Shore Rd., Devonshire Parish DV 07* ⬡ *Box HM 334, Hamilton HM BX* ☎ *441/236–1010; 800/468–6610 in the U.S.* 🖷 *441/236–0087* ⊕ *www.*

PRETTY IN PINK: THE COTTAGE COLONIES

LONG BEFORE Bermuda's tourism heyday, when only British aristocrats, Hollywood stars, and blue bloods from America's East Coast could afford to come to the island and disappear for a while, Bermuda's would-be hoteliers were sowing the seeds of one of the island's most important future economy bases. The beautiful people, with their well-lined pockets, were transforming Bermuda into a chic getaway destination, and this exclusive clientele would want seclusion, colonial sophistication, and traditional Bermudian hospitality. And so the cottage colony was born: a purpose-built resort that left no comfort unexplored, no luxury ignored—a plush home-away-from-home for those who could afford it.

Since Cambridge Beaches, the first cottage colony, was built at the turn of the 20th century, six more official colonies have sprung up, many still frequented by a glamorous set. Jumping on the bandwagon has been a cornucopia of efficiencies and housekeeping apartments selling themselves under the tried-and-tested banner of "cottages" or "cottage suites." The result is confusing. Today it's hard to find anyone who really knows what a cottage colony is, but perhaps it's distinguishing what they are not that sparks the true debate.

The Bermuda Department of Tourism recognizes nine properties as cottage colonies: Ariel Sands, Cambridge Beaches, Coral Beach & Tennis Club, Fourways Inn, Horizons & Cottages, Mid Ocean Club, Pink Beach Club & Cottages, the St. George's Club, and Willowbank. (Coral Beach and Mid Ocean are private clubs for members or friends of members only.) Despite the tourism department's demarcation, you might well be baffled by the island's numerous lodgings that have the word cottages in their names or descriptions, and that's before realizing that there are even more cottages (often private homes) that have been converted into lodgings, and which might not have the word cottage in their title.

Confused? So are many locals. "Just what is a cottage colony, anyway?" is a common refrain on the island, even among Bermuda tourism officials. The definitive line over what does and does not qualify to earn the title continues to blur, but generally speaking it describes a purpose-built beachfront collection of Bermudian cottages, separated from a main building that often houses the front desk, restaurants, bars, and lounge areas. Often, twisting walkways connect the cottages to the main building and lead down to the beach, over to the tennis courts, and elsewhere on the property. Many of the cottages are pink (Bermuda's trademark color) or other pastel shades, and most have either stunning water views or lush, tropical garden settings. Traditionally, the cottages have Bermudian white stair-step roofs, terraces or balconies, cedar-beamed ceilings and furniture, and British country-style fabrics and ornaments. Newer cottage complexes, however, may have much larger cottages of more modern design, divided into suites, or they may have attached apartments. Some may not even have kitchens—a staple of the traditional cottages.

Whatever a cottage colony is, it certainly isn't basic or budget. Bermuda's home-grown accommodations are some of the island's most exceptional—and expensive—and while many offer a unique holiday experience, they won't suit everyone. The emphasis is on peace and quiet, and they offer this admirably. Entertainment, children's programs, and other activities are not emphasized, so they may not be ideal for those seeking a lively, fun-packed vacation.

While the concept and reality of cottage colonies continues to evolve, the unabashed romance of these magical oases is alive and well. The pursuit of authentic Bermudian living, with a distinct British colonial tradition, still remains to transport guests into gracious lifestyle rather than simply a hotel room.

— Vivienne Sheath

arielsands.com ⊊ *47 rooms, 3 suites, 2 cottages* ۏ *Restaurant, in-room data ports, in-room safes, refrigerators, cable TV, putting green, 3 tennis courts, pool, 2 saltwater pools, gym, spa, beach, snorkeling, volleyball, 2 bars, concierge, business services, meeting room, no-smoking rooms* ⊟ *AE, MC, V* ⚏ *BP.*

★ **$$$$** ⊞ **Cambridge Beaches.** Bermuda's original cottage colony, Cambridge Beaches rests placidly on a beautiful, 25-acre peninsula edged with private coves and five pink-sand beaches. It has continued to attract international royalty and celebrities since it opened at the turn of the 20th century. The varying sizes, styles, and locations of the cottages and rooms make for a wide range of prices. Pegem, on the high end, is a 300-year-old, two-bedroom Bermuda cottage with marble bathrooms, a Jacuzzi, a cedar-beam ceiling, a den, a sunporch, and English antiques. The suites on the hill, built in 2001, have sunken living rooms and beach views from the bedrooms; and their bathrooms have whirlpool tubs, separate showers, double sinks, and separate rooms for toilet and bidet. Less-expensive rooms overlook lawns and gardens instead of the ocean, but you can sit on the terrace of the Tamarisk restaurant for splendid views of Mangrove Bay. The resort's health and beauty spa offers an exquisite French facial, plus various massages and body treatments. Chauffeured shopping trips to Hamilton are scheduled three times per week in high season. The colony's marina has Windsurfers, Boston Whalers, sailboats, canoes, kayaks, and snorkeling equipment. ⊠ *30 King's Point Rd., Sandys Parish MA 02* ☎ *441/234–0331; 800/468–7300 in the U.S.* ⎙ *441/234–3352* ⊕ *www.cambridgebeaches.com* ⊊ *66 rooms, 25 suites, 2 2-bedroom cottages* ۏ *2 restaurants, room service, in-room data ports, in-room safes, some in-room hot tubs, minibars, some microwaves, refrigerators, cable TV with movies, putting green, golf privileges, 3 tennis courts, pool, saltwater pool, gym, hair salon, hot tub, outdoor hot tub, sauna, spa, steam room, beach, dive shop, dock, snorkeling, boating, marina, croquet, 2 bars, lounge, shops, baby-sitting, dry cleaning, laundry facilities, laundry service, concierge, Internet, business services, no-smoking rooms* ⊟ *MC, V.*

$$$–$$$$ ⊞ **Horizons & Cottages.** Oriental rugs, polished wood floors, cathedral
Fodor'sChoice ceilings, and open fireplaces are elegant reminders of the 18th century,
★ when the main house in this Relais & Châteaux resort was a private home. Guest cottages are spread out across terraced lawns. Most have a large common room with a fireplace, a library, and board games, and all have terraces. Each cottage has a distinct personality. Some have white wicker furnishings, others have traditional European-style furnishings, such as four-poster beds. Most cottages also have a kitchen, where a cook prepares breakfast before bringing it to your room. Horizons, the outstanding restaurant, serves beautifully presented meals on pink-dressed tables in the formal dining room and on two terraces. You may sign up for dine-around arrangements with sister properties Waterloo House and the Coral Beach & Tennis Club. The colony has no beach of its own—though there is a 9-hole golf course—but guests may use the beach and facilities at the Coral Beach & Tennis Club. ⊠ *33 South Shore Rd., Paget Parish PG 04* ⎙ *Box PG 198, Paget PG BX* ☎ *441/ 236–0048; 800/468–0022 in the U.S.* ⎙ *441/236–1981* ⊕ *www. horizonscottages.com* ⊊ *45 rooms, 3 suites* ۏ *2 restaurants, in-room data ports, in-room safes, some kitchens, some refrigerators, cable TV, 9-hole golf course, golf privileges, putting green, 2 tennis courts, pro shop, pool, gym, hair salon, sauna, steam room, croquet, bar, baby-sitting, dry cleaning, laundry facilities, laundry service, Internet, business services* ⊟ *No credit cards* ⚏ *BP.*

★ **$$$–$$$$** ⊞ **Pink Beach Club & Cottages.** This secluded colony, opened in 1947, is Bermuda's largest and a favorite with celebrities. The location is ideal:

it's on the south shore, a five-minute ride from two of the island's best golf courses, 10 minutes from the airport, and 15 minutes from Hamilton. The main house, where you'll find the reception desk and restaurant, looks like a private club, with dark-wood paneling, a large fireplace, and beam ceilings. Paved paths wend their way through 16½ acres of gardens, leading to two pretty beaches and 25 pink cottages. Single-room suites are expansive, with king-size beds, pull-out couches, and sitting areas. One- and two-bedroom suites have separate living rooms, and some have two bathrooms. All have sliding glass doors that open onto a balcony or terrace. Most have ocean views. At this writing, the hotel is due to close for renovations to rooms damaged by Hurricane Fabian in 2003; hotel is scheduled to reopen in March 2004. The Bermudiana, the formal restaurant, serves fresh, local specialties. Casual poolside dining with nightly entertainment is an alternative. ✉ *1016 South Shore Rd., Tucker's Town, Smith's Parish HS 01* ☎ *Box HM 1017, Hamilton HM DX* ☎ *441/293–1666; 800/355–6161 in the U.S. and Canada* 🖷 *441/293–8935* ⊕ *www.pinkbeach.com* ☞ *91 suites* ♻ *2 restaurants, room service, in-room data ports, in-room safes, refrigerators, cable TV, golf privileges, 2 tennis courts, pro shop, pool, gym, hair salon, massage, beach, snorkeling, bar, baby-sitting, dry-cleaning, laundry facilities, laundry service, Internet, no-smoking rooms* ▭ *AE, MC, V* ⑩ *BP.*

$$–$$$ ▣ **St. George's Club.** Within walking distance of King's Square in St. George's, this hotel and time-share resort in a residential neighborhood adjoins a golf course designed by Robert Trent Jones. The sleek, three-story main building contains the lobby, business center, a convenience store where you can buy anything from champagne to sunblock, and two restaurants: Tillie's, serving Caribbean food, and Blackbeard's Hideout, a summer-only pub. Bright, contemporary cottages are spread over 18 acres and around a pool. Each one- and two-bedroom unit is huge and sunny, with a fully equipped kitchen, but otherwise they are individually decorated. ✉ *6 Rose Hill, St. George's Parish, GE O5* ☎ *Box GE 92, St. George's GE BX* ☎ *441/297–1200* 🖷 *441/297–8003* ⊕ *www.stgeorgeclub.com* ☞ *71 cottages* ♻ *Restaurant, in-room safes, kitchens, microwaves, refrigerators, cable TV, 18-hole golf course, putting green, 3 tennis courts, 3 pools, massage, bar, shop, baby-sitting, dry cleaning, laundry facilities, laundry service, Internet, no-smoking rooms* ▭ *AE, MC, V.*

$$ ▣ **Fourways Inn.** This small luxury inn and cottage colony lies a bit inland from Hamilton Harbour, in Paget Parish near the Warwick border. The main building, dating from 1727, is the former family home of the owners of Harvey's Bristol Creme. Five separate cottages are set in a profusion of greenery and flowers around a pool. The rooms and suites have marble floors and bathrooms, large closets paneled with full-length mirrors, and either a balcony or terrace. Perks include bathrobes and slippers. You receive a complimentary fruit basket on arrival, and homemade pastries and the morning paper are delivered daily to your door. Fourways' fine restaurant has a wine list with 650 selections (there are 8,000 bottles in the wine cellar), so you are sure to find the perfect accompaniment to your meal. The hotel is about a five-minute walk from the ferry landing and a five-minute bus ride to south-shore beaches. ✉ *1 Middle Rd., Paget Parish PG 01* ☎ *Box PG 294, Paget PG BX* ☎ *441/236–6517; 800/962–7654 in the U.S.* 🖷 *441/236–5528* ⊕ *www.fourwaysinn.com* ☞ *6 rooms, 4 suites* ♻ *Restaurant, kitchenettes, minibars, microwaves, refrigerators, cable TV, golf privileges, pool, bar, piano bar, baby-sitting, dry cleaning, laundry service, Internet, business services, meeting rooms, no-smoking rooms* ▭ *AE, MC, V* ⑩ *CP.*

Housekeeping Cottages & Apartments

$$$ ☒ **Grape Bay Cottages.** Beach Crest and Beach Home are two almost-identical cottages overlooking the soft sands of Grape Bay Beach. Each two-bedroom cottage has an open fireplace, hardwood floors, a full-size kitchen, a king-size bed, and a pull-out couch. You can't step directly from door to beach, but the stroll down takes little more than two minutes. The area is very quiet and secluded, ideal for beach-lovers who like to cook for themselves, and do serious sand-and-surf time. The cottages are a bit costly for one couple, but for two couples sharing expenses this is an eminently affordable choice. Beach Home is next door to the beach house of the American consulate. A grocery store and cycle shop are nearby. ☒ *Grape Bay Dr., Paget Parish* ☐ *Box HM 1851, Hamilton HM HX* ☎ *441/296–0563; 800/637–4116 in the U.S.* ☐ *441/ 296–0563* ✎ *grapebaycottages@northrock.bm* ➬ *2 cottages* ☐ *Kitchens, microwaves, refrigerators, beach, snorkeling, laundry facilities; no room TVs* ☐ *AE, MC, V.*

$$–$$$ ☒ **Marley Beach Cottages.** Scenes from the films *Chapter Two, The Deep,* and *Bermuda Grace* were filmed here, and it's easy to see why: the setting is breathtaking. Near Astwood Park on the south shore, the resort sits high on a cliff overlooking a private beach, stunning coastline, and dramatic reefs. A long path leads down to the sand and the sea. (If you plan to stay here, pack light. There are steep steps all over the property.) Each cottage contains a suite and a studio apartment that can be rented separately or together. Some rooms could stand to be upgraded, but all are large and sunny, with superb ocean views, private porches or patios, and fully equipped kitchens. The Heaven's Above and Seasong executive suites are especially big, and each has a fireplace. You can have groceries delivered, and there is daily housekeeping service. If you're a pet lover, the resort's namesake—Marley, a pretty tabby cat—might keep you company. ☒ *South Shore Rd., Warwick Parish* ☐ *Box PG 278, Paget PG BX* ☎ *441/236–1143 Ext. 42; 800/637–4116 in the U.S.* ☐ *441/ 236–1984* ⊕ *www.netlinkbermuda.com/marley* ➬ *6 studios, 4 suites, 3 executive suites* ☐ *In-room safes, kitchens, microwaves, refrigerators, cable TV, pool, hot tub, beach, snorkeling, fishing, baby-sitting, laundry facilities* ☐ *AE, MC, V.*

$$–$$$ ☒ **Munro Beach Cottages.** Seclusion and privacy are the key words at this small group of cottages spread over 5 acres at Whitney Bay on the western end of the south shore. A beautiful palm-fringed beach is the view from the duplex cottages hidden away behind one of Bermuda's (and maybe the world's) most picturesque golf courses, Port Royal. What these cottages lack in facilities (there is no club room or restaurant) they make up for in tranquillity and views of stunning sunsets. All standard units have a king-size bed or two twin beds and a double sofa bed and can accommodate up to four people. Although the furnishings are a bit dated, the kitchens are fully equipped. Barbecues are available and daily housekeeping services are included. The resort is a 20-minute walk across the golf course to the nearest South Shore Road bus stop, so you may want to rent a motor scooter or bicycle while you are here. ☒ *2 Port Royal Golf Course Rd., Southampton Parish SN BX* ☐ *Box SN 99, Southampton SN BX* ☎ *441/234–1175* ☐ *441/234–3528* ⊕ *www.munrobeach. com* ➬ *9 cottages* ☐ *In-room safes, kitchens, golf privileges, beach, snorkeling, fishing, baby-sitting* ☐ *AE, DC, MC, V.*

$$ ☒ **Clear View Suites & Villas.** Each light-pink villa in this complex has breathtaking views over the north shore. Within the villas are one- to four-bedroom suites, each with a kitchenette and separate living and dining areas. The furnishings are traditional English style—overstuffed chairs and couches, with carefully chosen fabrics. Shelly Bay Marketplace is within walking distance, but if you don't want to cook, Clear View's delightful cliff-top Landfall Restaurant, designed with a mix of British colonial and Bermudian architecture, offers hearty breakfast, lunch, dinner, and Sunday brunch. Walkers love being near one of the most attractive coastal stretches of the Bermuda Railway Trail. Special packages, like the Educational Focus and Learn & Leisure, combine lodging and guided field trips to museum and landmarks. Housekeeping service is included. ⊠ *Sandy La., Hamilton CR 02* ☎ *441/293–0484; 800/468–9600 in the U.S.* ᗺ *441/293–0267* ⊕ *www.bermuda-online.org/clearview. htm* ⇨ *12 apartments ᗢ Restaurant, in-room safes, kitchenettes, cable TV, tennis court, pool, baby-sitting, laundry facilities, Internet, meeting rooms* ⊟ *AE, DC, MC, V.*

$$ ▦ **Ocean Terrace.** Panoramic views of the island and ocean surround these three one-bedroom apartments, perched on one of Bermuda's highest points. Each contemporary, coral-color unit has a queen-size bed, sofa, full kitchen, and veranda. Extra roll-out beds are available upon request. A five-minute walk to the bottom of the hill brings you to Horseshoe Bay and South Shore Road, where a bus goes into Hamilton (a 30-minute ride) or toward Dockyard. A small, poolside terrace is dotted with tables, chairs, and sun loungers. ⊠ *2 Scenic Heights La., Southampton Parish SN03* ᗺ *Box SN 501, Southampton SN BX* ☎ *441/238–0019; 800/637–4116 in the U.S.* ᗺ *441/238–4673* ⇨ *4 apartments ᗢ Kitchens, cable TV, pool, laundry facilities* ⊟ *AE, MC, V.*

$–$$ ▦ **Dawkins Manor.** This enormous pink house, built in the 1950s, is in rural Paget, with an idyllic garden all around it. The hostess and staff are friendly and informal, and you are sure to get a taste of real Bermuda life here. There are eight modern different-size apartments, from simple rooms to a two-bedroom suite. Six of the apartments have kitchens with coffeemakers, and some have private patios. The cheerful furnishings are of sturdy wood, some with floral upholstery. Units without kitchens have king-size beds, a refrigerator, and a hot-pot for drinks. South-shore beaches and restaurants are easily accessible by bus; Hamilton is just 10 minutes away. ⊠ *29 St. Michaels's Rd., Box PG 34, Paget Parish PG BX* ☎ *441/236–7419 or 800/637–4116* ᗺ *441/236–7088* ⊕ *www. bermuda-charm.com* ⇨ *6 apartments ᗢ Some kitchens, microwaves, refrigerators, pool, lounge, laundry facilities* ⊟ *AE, MC, V.*

$–$$ ▦ **Greenbank Cottages.** On a quiet lane less than a minute's walk from the Salt Kettle ferry landing, these single-story cottages nestle among tall trees next to Hamilton Harbour. They're small and family-oriented rather than grand, but they come with the attention and excellent service of the Ashton family. The lounge in the 200-year-old main house has hardwood floors, a TV, and a grand piano. Four units (two with kitchens) are in the main house. Continental breakfast is delivered to the rooms without kitchens. The rest of the units are self-contained, with kitchens, private entrances, and shaded verandas. The waterside cottages, especially Salt Winds, have lovely harbor views. Rooms themselves are simply furnished, with queen-size beds, flouncy bedskirts, and sofa beds. There is a private dock for deepwater swimming, and the beaches are less than 10 minutes away by taxi or scooter. One of the island's best water-sports operators—Salt Kettle Yacht Charters—is on the property. ⊠ *17 Salt Kettle Rd., Paget Parish PG 01* ᗺ *Box PG 201, Paget PG BX* ☎ *441/236–3615; 800/637–4116 in the U.S.* ᗺ *441/236–2427* ⊕ *www.greenbankbermuda.com* ⇨ *3 rooms, 8 apartments ᗢ Some kitchens, some microwaves, some refrigerators, swimming, dock; no phone in some rooms, no room TVs* ⊟ *AE, MC, V* ❍ *CP, EP.*

$–$$ ▦ **Paraquet Guest Apartments.** Elbow Beach, one of the prettiest beaches on the island, is just a five-minute walk from the Paraquet (pronounced "parakeet") apartments. You can also walk to the grocery store and cook your own meals in the kitchenettes. If you'd rather not bother, or if you choose a room with just a refrigerator and coffeemaker, you can have breakfast and lunch at Paraquet's casual restaurant. The home-style dishes (burgers, fish-and-chips) are well-liked by locals, too. For special evenings out, the fine restaurants at Horizons & Cottages and the Stonington Beach Hotel are within walking distance, and Hamilton is a five-minute moped ride away. Nine efficiencies are in a row near the courtyard, with the one- and two-bedroom units in separate cottages. Rooms are contemporary, spacious, and sunny, with tile or carpeted floors and simple, but up-to-date furnishings. All rooms have inland views and a private patio. Most of the apartments have showers only, so be sure to request a full bath if you want a tub. Use of in-room telephones costs $2.50 extra per day. ⌧ *72 South Rd., Paget Parish PG 04* ✆ *Box PG 173, Paget PG BX* ☎ *441/236–5842* ☒ *441/236–1665* ⊕ *www.paraquetapartments. com* ⮡ *12 rooms* ⚐ *Restaurant, some kitchenettes, refrigerators* ⊟ *No credit cards.*

$–$$ ⊞ **Rosemont.** Looking like an upscale motel, Rosemont is composed of a long two-story building with garden suites, and another three-story building with poolside suites. The family-owned property was the first to corner Bermuda's self-catering niche, and it's not hard to see why. It's surrounded by trees in a quiet residential area, with excellent views of Hamilton Harbour and the Great Sound. The apartment-style suites have a bedroom, sitting area, kitchen, full bathroom, and balcony or patio. Each has its own entrance. Furnishings are simple, with plain wooden headboards and chairs; some rooms have upholstered sofas and recliners. The penthouse suite—a two-bedroom unit that can be converted into three rooms—has panoramic views, balconies, and whirlpools. ✆ *Box HM 37, Hamilton HM AX* ☎ *441/292–1055* ☒ *441/295–3913* ⊕ *www. rosemont.bm* ⮡ *47 apartments* ⚐ *In-room data ports, in-room safes, some in-room hot tubs, kitchens, cable TV, golf privileges, pool, shuffleboard, baby-sitting, playground, laundry facilities* ⊟ *AE, MC, V.*

$ ⊞ **Astwood Cove.** With access to the nearby south-shore beaches and a good smattering of restaurants within a 2-mi radius, these gleaming white apartments are a boon for beach-loving budget travelers. As a guest you can help yourself to the fruits of the terraced orchards around which the apartments are set. Standard and superior studios and suites have either a full kitchen or a microwave and refrigerator. The poolside rooms are a favorite with families, and the upstairs suites are an excellent value, with views over Astwood Park and glimpses of the sea. Wicker, rattan, and hardwood furnishings fill the bright rooms. Bathrooms have showers only, and there are no TVs apart from the communal one in the barbecue pavilion, where you can cook food on the gas grills. ⌧ *49 South Rd., Warwick Parish WK 07* ☎ *441/236–0984* ☒ *441/236–1164* ⊕ *www.astwoodcove.com* ⮡ *20 apartments* ⚐ *Kitchenettes, microwaves, refrigerators, pool, sauna, baby-sitting, laundry facilities; no room TVs* ⊟ *MC, V.*

$ ⊞ **Barnsdale Guest Apartments.** Budget travelers who want to be near south-shore beaches and the Hamilton ferry should consider the small apartments in this two-story, terra-cotta house. On the bus route in a residential neighborhood and close to a grocery store, the apartments are set in a garden with an orchard of loquat, banana, and peach trees—all of whose fruits you are encouraged to sample. Stay a week and you'll benefit: Barnsdale treats guests to every seventh night free. All apartments are neat and clean efficiencies, each with a private entrance. Rooms are simply decorated and annually spruced up and sleep up to four guests—although the kitchen area can seem awfully close to the sleeping area. An outdoor barbecue gives you a chance to enjoy those balmy Bermuda nights, and diving trips and tours can be arranged. ⌧ *2 Barnes Valley, Box DV 628,*

KID-FRIENDLY LODGING

FAMILIES WITH CHILDREN FIND Bermuda's resorts, cottage colonies, and housekeeping apartments the most comfortable and convenient lodgings on the island. Many hotels have pools, beaches, and family-friendly restaurants, and many allow children under a certain age to stay in their parents' room at no extra charge.

But there are a few select hotels, among them the Fairmont Southampton, Elbow Beach Hotel, Grotto Bay Beach Resort, and Willowbank, that go the extra mile for kids. These hotels offer summer children's programs, which may include participation in sand castle competitions, treasure hunts, face painting, arts and crafts, kite making, trips to the aquarium or botanical gardens, or a ferry ride around the harbor. Activities on the premises are generally free, although there is an additional charge for off-property excursions. Most programs are divided into two groups, one for preteens and teenagers, the other for younger children. The age ranges vary from hotel to hotel.

Grotto Bay in particular has facilities that seem designed for families with small children. The enclosed bay, fish feeding aquarium, two underground caves with supervised exploring, and the "kiddies" pool beside the larger pool put parents at ease when their children hit the water. Paddleboats and rafts are available at the dock house. Four tennis courts are on the premises and the spacious two-room suites are popular among families.

Two smaller properties (with smaller price tags) are also excellent choices for families with children: Salt Kettle House has homelike cottages with fully equipped kitchens, and a hearty breakfast is included in the rates; and Clairfont Apartments offers one-bedrooms close to the south-shore beaches and a playground.

Devonshire Parish DV BX ☎ 441/236–0164 or 800/637–4116 🖷 441/236–4709 ⊕www.bermuda.com/barnsdale ⬅7 apartments ⭘Fans, kitchenettes, pool; no room TVs ▤ AE, MC, V.

$ ▦ **Brightside Guest Apartments.** You can see pretty Flatts Inlet from the verandas of this pretty, white, blue-shuttered, Spanish-style hotel. The apartments in the main building are small, with basic, rather outdated furnishings, but they are within walking distance of Flatts Village and the Bermuda Aquarium, Museum & Zoo. The two cottages are in a quiet spot amid the gardens behind the main hotel. On the other side of the property is a pool and a patio with tables and chairs. Brightside is 15 minutes by bus from Hamilton and 25 minutes by bus from St. George's. ⊠ 38 North Shore Rd., Flatts Village, Smith's Parish FL BX ⬦ Box FL 319, Flatts FL 07 ☎ 441/292–8410 🖷 441/295–6968 ⊕ www.bermuda.com/brightside ⬅9 apartments, 2 cottages ⭘ Kitchens or kitchenettes, microwaves, refrigerators, cable TV, pool ▤ No credit cards.

$ ▦ **Clairfont Apartments.** On a hill close to the south-shore beaches, the Clairfont Apartments offer quietude and lovely views across the valley to the water. You can choose between a studio or a one-bedroom—all with fully equipped kitchens. The four sunny upstairs units have balconies, and the downstairs apartments have patios, leading onto a communal lawn. A good playground is a five-minute walk away. The property welcomes a lot of families with children during the summer months. Inexpensive monthly off-season rates start from $1,000. Early booking is recommended. ⊠ 6 Warwickshire Rd., Warwick Parish WK 02 ⬦ Box WK 85, Warwick WK 02 ☎441/238–0149 or 800/637–4116 🖷 111/238 3503 ⬅8 apartments ⭘ Kitchens, pool, baby-sitting ▤ AE, MC, V.

$ ▦ **Garden House.** Hospitable owner and manager Rosanne Galloway will make sure you feel at home at her beautiful harborside property near Somerset Bridge. Here you can choose between a studio or a one-

or two-bedroom cottage with separate living room and kitchen. All the units have patios that lead out to well-tended gardens. A stroll to the end of the lawn will lead you to Elys Harbour, where you can swim as long as you don't mind diving into deep water right off the shore. Children under 12 stay free. ⊠ *4 Middle Rd., Sandys Parish SB 01* ☏ *441/ 234–1435* 🖷 *441/234–3006* ⇆ *3 apartments, 2 cottages* ⚲ *Kitchens or kitchenettes, no-smoking rooms* ⊟ *AE, MC, V* ⊘ *Closed Dec.–Feb.*

$ ▥ **Marula Apartments.** Next to Mills Creek *and* overlooking the ocean, with expansive grounds all around, these apartments seem quite removed from the hustle and bustle of Hamilton, especially when you are lounging by the pool listening to the waves. But in fact, the city is just five minutes away by bus. The five apartments and the two-bedroom cottage are all very basic but comfortable and roomy, with kitchenettes (microwaves are available on request), bedrooms, and separate living rooms. You can wander over to Admiralty House Park for a walk and to Clarence Cove for a swim. ⊠ *17 Mariners La., Pembroke Parish HM 02* ⚲ *Box HM 576, Hamilton HM CX* ☏ *441/295–2893* 🖷 *441/292– 3985* ⇆ *5 apartments, 1 cottage* ⚲ *Fans, kitchenettes, refrigerators, cable TV* ⊟ *AE, MC, V.*

$ ▥ **Mazarine by the Sea.** These small efficiencies are in a former home on the water's edge 1 mi from Hamilton. Five of the seven units have ocean views. Each has a well-maintained kitchenette, bedroom, and small patio or balcony overlooking gardens or sea. There is no beach, but you can go deepwater swimming and snorkeling in the ocean just off the doorstep, or swim in the pool. A grocery store and bus stops are a short walk away. ⊠ *91 North Shore Rd., Pembroke Parish* ⚲ *Box HM 91, Hamilton HM AX* ☏ *441/292–1659* 🖷 *441/292–6891* ⇆ *7 apartments* ⚲ *Kitchenettes, pool, snorkeling, fishing* ⊟ *AE, MC, V.*

$ ▥ **Robin's Nest.** Three of the four apartments in this little valley property open onto tranquil, intimate gardens. The fourth is elevated, with sea views from its rooftop terrace. All the apartments are spacious and modern, with full kitchens. The small number of rooms means you are more than likely to enjoy the good-size pool and patio all to yourself. A short bus ride can take you to Hamilton, Admiralty Park, or to north-shore snorkeling sites. ⊠ *10 Vale Close, Pembroke, HM 04* ☏ *441/292– 4347* ⇆ *4 apartments* ⚲ *Kitchens, cable TV, pool* ⊟ *No credit cards.*

$ ▥ **Sandpiper Apartments.** Spacious, simple, and cheerfully decorated, these apartments are ideal for families wanting quiet, inexpensive lodging near south-shore beaches and bus routes. The 14 whitewashed units include five one-bedroom apartments with full kitchens and nine studios with kitchenettes. Each has either a balcony or patio. Most can accommodate up to four people. Tile floors and bold floral-print curtains and bedspreads predominate. The apartments, pool, and hot tub are encircled by lawns and shrubs, and there's a smattering of blue-and-white shade umbrellas. You can walk to South Shore Road, where a bus can take you to Hamilton in about 20 minutes. Paw-Paws restaurant is within walking distance, and you can use the nearby beach and bar at Surf Side Beach Club. ⊠ *Off South Shore Rd., Warwick Parish* ⚲ *Box HM 685, Hamilton HM CX* ☏ *441/236–7093* 🖷 *441/236–3898* ⇆ *14 apartments* ⚲ *Kitchens or kitchenettes, microwaves, cable TV, pool, hot tub, laundry facilities* ⊟ *AE, MC, V.*

$ ▥ **Sky Top Cottages.** Aptly named, this hilltop property has spectacular views of the island's southern coastline and the azure ocean beyond. Runners and walkers will appreciate the proximity to Elbow Beach, one of Bermuda's best stretches of sand for a run. Neat, sloping lawns, carefully tended gardens, and paved walkways edge around the studios and one-bedroom apartments. Owners John and Andrea Flood decorate each unit in a different style, with carefully coordinated colors and prints.

Studios have shower baths, and one-bedrooms have full baths. The very private one-bedroom Frangipani apartment has an eat-in kitchen, a king-size bed, and a sofa bed. Barbecue grills are available. ⊠ *65 South Shore Rd., Paget Parish PG 03* ⬠ *Box PG 227, Paget PG BX* ☏ *441/ 236–7984* 🖶 *441/232–0446* 📞 *11 apartments* ⚅ *Kitchenettes, cable TV, volleyball* ⊟ *MC, V.*

$ 🖳 **Syl-Den.** Warwick Long Bay is just a 5- to 10-minute walk from these blue-painted apartments set back against a hillside off of South Shore Road. Most of the spacious rooms have tiled floors and are simply furnished. Three have a private patio or garden, and there is also a small communal sun terrace. It takes about 25 minutes to reach Hamilton by bus. ⊠ *8 Warwickshire Estate, Warwick Parish WK 02* ☏ *441/238– 1834* 🖶 *441/238–3205* ⊕ *www.bermudareservation.net* 📞 *12 apartments* ⚅ *Kitchenettes, cable TV, pool* ⊟ *AE, MC, V.*

¢–$ 🖳 **Valley Cottages & Apartments.** These pretty, informal Bermuda cottages and apartments are perfect for beach-lovers, with one of the island's top stretches of sand—Elbow Beach—a short walk away. Choose from self-contained studio apartments or a larger one-bedroom cottage that can house up to four guests. Room are set in three attractive and traditional pink buildings. Palm trees and lush greenery surround the property. Most apartments have an accompanying patio or garden area. A peaceful terrace and secluded spa pool are perfect for tanning and relaxing. You'll also have the use of the tennis courts at the Harmony Club. ⊠ *Valley Rd., Paget Parish PG BX* ⬠ *Box PG 173, Paget PG BX* ☏ *441/236–0628; 800/637–4116 in the U.S.* 🖶 *441/236–3895* ⊕ *www.netlinkbermuda.com/ valley* 📞 *9 apartments* ⚅ *Kitchens or kitchenettes, cable TV, pool, outdoor hot tub* ⊟ *AE, MC, V.*

¢ 🖳 **Burch's Guest Apartments.** This smart-looking whitewashed house with red shutters and panoramic views is situated right in the middle of the island, in a residential area. Hamilton is a five-minute bus ride away, and there is a small grocery store within walking distance. Apartments are simply furnished; the most spacious of the five is at the front of the building and has the best views of the ocean. Three beds make it ideal for families with small children. The four smaller units have twin beds. Studios 6 and 7 have sea glimpses. There is a small garden with a pool at the back of the building. ⊠ *110 North Shore Rd., Devonshire Parish FL 03* ☏ *441/292–5746 or 800/637–4116* 🖶 *441/295–3794* 📞 *5 apartments* ⚅ *Kitchenettes, cable TV, pool* ⊟ *No credit cards.*

¢ 🖳 **Serendipity.** These two studio apartments tucked away in a residential area in Paget are part of the family residence of Albert and Judy Corday, and those staying here have use of the owners' large family pool and benefit from a flat rate with no tax (an exemption applies to properties accommodating five or fewer people). Both ground-floor apartments are clean and pleasantly decorated. They have fully equipped kitchenettes, bathrooms with showers only, TVs (no cable), and small private patios. One apartment has a queen-size bed with a love-seat sofa bed; the other has two single beds. There is no view, but a 15-minute walk will take you to Elbow Beach. Two grocery stores and a take-out restaurant are within a few minutes walking distance. A bus stop is just outside the front gate. Housekeeping services can be arranged. ⊠ *6 Rural Dr., Paget Parish PG 06* ☏ *441/236–1192* 🖶 *441/232–0010* 📞 *2 apartments* ⚅ *Kitchenettes, pool; no-smoking* ⊟ *No credit cards.*

¢ 🖳 **Sound View Cottage.** This Bermudian cottage with three housekeeping apartments is set in an elevated residential area overlooking the Great Sound. Rooms have bright, soft furnishings and full kitchens. The cottage also has a pool, patio, and barbecue, and is very convenient to the south-shore beaches. Enviable views of both the south shore and the Great Sound extend on either side of the property. Furthermore, the personal attention bestowed upon you by hosts Barbara and Eldon Raynor has brought them many repeat visitors and local hospitality awards. ⊠ *9 Bowe La., Southampton Parish SN 04* ☎ *441/238–0064* ↝ *3 apartments* ⚭ *Kitchens, pool* ☷ *No credit cards.*

Bed & Breakfasts

★ **$–$$** ▦ **Aunt Nea's Inn at Hillcrest.** Fine furniture and attention to detail have transformed this charming 18th-century house into an enchanting inn. Each of the Jasmine rooms and suites (some with whirlpools) have gorgeous, old-fashioned bed frames, from wicker sleigh beds to solid-oak four-posters with canopies. The three Palm suites have wrought-iron, Corsican-designed beds, a living room with open fireplace, heavy Chinese rosewood chairs inlaid with mother-of-pearl, and access to the public balcony. The self-catering one- and two-bedroom suites and cottages across from the main house are ideal for families. For breakfast, choose from a spread of fresh-baked muffins and other pastries, then join other guests at a large communal table. Your enthusiastic hosts are Delaey Robinson, parliamentarian and tourism advisor to the government, and Andrea Dismont. Aunt Nea's is within putting distance of St. George's golf course and a five-minute scooter ride from Tobacco Bay Beach and the other secluded coves. ⊠ *1 Nea's Alley, St. George's GE 05* ⑅ *Box GE 96, St. George's GE BX* ☎ *441/297–1630* ᖴ *441/297–1908* ⊕ *www.auntneas.com* ↝ *12 rooms, 6 suites* ⚭ *Some in-room hot tubs, some kitchenettes, refrigerators, cable TV, golf privileges, croquet; no smoking* ☷ *AE, MC, V* ⦿ *CP.*

$–$$ ▦ **Edgehill Manor.** Atop a high hill surrounded by gardens and shrubs, this great colonial-style house, built around the turn of the 20th century, has terrific views of downtown Hamilton and, in the distance, the sparkling harbor. Hamilton is a 10-minute walk away, and the south-shore beaches are less than 15 minutes away by motor scooter or bus. French country–style furniture and lots of bright florals fill the guest rooms and common rooms. The bathrooms were renovated in 2003, with new fixtures and white tiling. Ground-floor rooms have private terraces, and everywhere there are large windows that let in plenty of Bermuda sunshine. A large poolside room with its own kitchen is perfect for families. The staff is welcoming and attentive. In the morning you can feast on home-baked croissants, scones, muffins, and coffee cake in the cheery family-style breakfast room. ⊠ *36 Rosemont Ave., Hamilton HM EX* ⑅ *Box HM 1048, Hamilton HM EX* ☎ *441/295–7124* ᖴ *441/295–3850* ⊕ *www.bermuda.com/edgehill* ↝ *9 rooms* ⚭ *In-room safes, some kitchens, some refrigerators, some microwaves, cable TV, pool; no smoking* ☷ *No credit cards* ⦿ *CP.*

$ ▦ **Greene's Guest House.** On part of the Bermuda Railway Trail in the quiet western end of Southampton Parish, this family-run guest house is a tranquil retreat with beautiful views of the Great Sound. Rooms have modern furnishings and facilities, and some have water views. A large swimming pool at the back of the house overlooks Jennings Bay and the ocean. Greene's is a two-minute walk from bus stops on Middle Road, and it's a five-minute bus ride from the south-shore beaches. You can also take the bus to Port Royal Golf Course and motor scooter rental shops, nearby, and to Hamilton, 30 minutes away. The Golf Academy, where you can practice your swing at a 40-station driving range, is a short walk away. Dinner can be arranged. ⊠ *Jennings Bay, Southampton Parish SN BX* ⑅ *Box SN 395, Southampton SN BX* ☎ *441/238–0834; 800/637–4116 in the U.S.* ᖴ *441/238–8980* ↝ *6 rooms* ⚭ *Dining room, refrigerators, cable TV, in-room VCRs, pool, lounge; no smoking* ☷ *No credit cards* ⦿ *BP.*

4

Apartment & Villa Rentals

If you want a home base that's roomy enough for a family, consider renting a private house or apartment. Furnished rentals can save you money, especially if you're traveling with a group. **BermudaGetaway** (⊕ www.bermudagetaway.com) lists a selection of high-standard properties but does not accept reservations. For that, you can contact the property owner directly. **Bermuda Accommodations** (☎ 416/232–2243 🖷 416/232–9138 ⊕ www.bermudarentals.com) maintains an up-to-the-minute listing of available properties all over the island *and* makes reservations. The Web site has photos and good descriptions of what you can expect to find. **Coldwell Banker JW Bermuda Realty** (🏠 Box HM 1886, Hamilton HM HX ☎ 441/292–1793 🖷 441/292–7918 ⊕ www.bermudarealty.com/frmvacation.htm) requires you to register with the company before an agent will help you find a property that exactly meets your requirements. You can also make reservations with **Villas International** (✉ 4340 Redwood Hwy., Suite D309, San Rafael, CA 94903 ☎ 415/499–9490 or 800/221–2260 🖷 415/499–9491 ⊕ www.villasintl.com).

Bed & Breakfasts

B&Bs in Bermuda range from grand, converted Victorians to a couple of rooms with shared bath in a small home. Breakfasts, too, run the gamut, though light Continental breakfasts with fresh fruit are more common than hearty bacon-and-eggs meals. Sometimes there is a pool on the property, but to get to the beach, you usually have to travel by bus or scooter. **Bermuda Accommodations** (☎ 416/232–2243 🖷 416/232–9138 ⊕ www.bermudarentals.com) lists and takes reservations for rooms available in B&Bs.

Home Exchanges

If you would like to exchange your home for someone else's, join a home-exchange organization, which will send you its updated listings of available exchanges for a year and will include your own listing in at least one of them. It's up to you to make specific arrangements. **HomeLink International** (🏠 Box 47747, Tampa, FL 33647 ☎ 813/975–9825 or 800/638–3841 🖷 813/910–8144 ⊕ www.homelink.org) charges $110 yearly for a listing, on-line access, and catalog, or $70 without the catalog. **Intervac U.S.** (✉ 30 Corte San Fernando, Tiburon, CA 94920 ☎ 800/756–4663 🖷 415/435–7440 ⊕ www.intervacus.com) charges $105 yearly for a listing, on-line access, and a catalog, or $50 without the catalog.

★ $ 🖫 **Little Pomander Guest House.** In a quiet residential area on Hamilton Harbour, the Little Pomander is a find if you're seeking affordable accommodation near the capital. The rooms, in a charming waterside cottage, are decorated with plump, pastel comforters, and coordinated fabrics. Often guests congregate at sunset on the waterside lawn to enjoy views of Hamilton Harbour and stay to cook dinner on the barbecue grill. For a $10 fee you can play tennis across the road at the Pomander Tennis Club. A Continental breakfast of sticky buns, muffins, coffee, and tea is served in a sunny room. ✉ *16 Pomander Rd., Paget Parish PG 02* 🏠 *Box HM 384, Hamilton HM BX* ☎ *441/236–7635* 🖷 *441/236–8332* ↝ *5 rooms* ♻ *Microwaves, refrigerators, cable TV; no smoking* ⊟ *AE, MC, V* ¶◯¶ *CP.*

$ 🏨 **Oxford House.** White pillars and flower pots welcome you through
Fodor'sChoice the entrance of this elegant, pale-pink, two-story town house, just a five-
★ minute walk from the capital's shops, ferries, and buses. The inn is family-owned and -operated, and each room is individually decorated with
pretty matching fabrics, and antique and reproduction furniture. Polished cedar-wood floors, a fireplace, and handsome Chippendale chairs
lend warmth and class to the breakfast room, where you can sample
scones, English muffins, fresh fruit, boiled eggs, and cereal each morning. There are coffeemakers in the rooms as well. A small bookcase in
the upstairs hall is filled with paperbacks that you're welcome to bor-
row. ⊠ *20 Woodbourne Ave., Hamilton* ⊕ *Box HM 374, Hamilton
HM BX* ☎ *441/295–0503; 800/548–7758 in the U.S.; 800/272–2306
in Canada* 🖷 *441/295–0250* ⊕ *www.oxfordhouse.bm* ⇴ *12 rooms*
⚒ *Dining room, cable TV, laundry service* ☰ *AE, MC, V* ⍾ *CP.*

★ **$** 🏨 **Royal Heights Guest House.** At the top of a nearly vertical driveway,
this modern B&B has views of Gibbs Hill Lighthouse and a fantastic
panorama of the Great Sound. Breathtaking sunsets can be seen from
the spacious, carpeted living room and from the pool area. The rooms
are large, each with a private entrance, big windows, and a terrace. While
all rooms benefit from great views, Nos. 3 and 6 are popular because
they overlook the Great Sound. The matching drapes and quilted spreads
in good-quality fabrics give rooms a cozy domestic feel, and there is ample
closet space. Room No. 5, with its double bed and daybed, is good for
families. For breakfast, pastries, muffins, fruit, and sometimes eggs are
served. The Fairmont Southampton golf course and some of the island's finest dining are within walking distance. ⊠ *4 Crown Hill,
Southampton Parish SN 03* ⊕ *Box SN 144, Southampton SN BX*
☎ *441/238–0043* 🖷 *441/238–8445* ⇴ *7 rooms* ⚒ *Some microwaves,
refrigerators, cable TV, saltwater pool* ☰ *AE, MC, V* ⍾ *CP.*

¢–$ 🏨 **Loughlands Guest House & Cottage.** This stately white mansion has seen
grander days, but it retains the charm and character of a home built in
1920. Lladro figurines grace the mantelpiece in the formal parlor, antique grandfather clocks stand in corners, and handsome breakfronts
display Wedgwood china and Baccarat and Waterford crystal. The
rooms are somewhat worn, but most have large, comfortable chairs and
cotton bedspreads. Singles, doubles, triples, and quads are available in
both the main house and a large cottage beside it. The houses stands
amid spacious grounds above South Shore Road, less than a five-minute
walk from Elbow Beach. Breakfast includes cereals, croissants, Danishes,
prunes, and fruit juice. ⊠ *79 South Rd., Paget Parish PG 03* ☎ *441/
236–1253* ⇴ *18 rooms with bath, 6 with shared bath* ⚒ *Tennis court,
pool; no room phones, no room TVs* ☰ *No credit cards* ⍾ *CP.*

¢ 🏨 **Salt Kettle House.** Behind a screen of palm trees on a bay adjoining
Fodor'sChoice Hamilton Harbour, only a quick walk from the Hamilton ferry, this small,
★ secluded guest house is a gem for the budget traveler looking for the
best of British hospitality. Just left of the entrance is a cozy lounge with
a fireplace where guests gather for cocktails and conversation. A hearty
English breakfast is served family style in the dining room, which has
water views. The main house has two guest rooms, and an adjoining
apartment has a bedroom, bathroom, living room, and kitchen. Four
waterside cottages have shaded patios and lounge chairs, bedrooms, sitting rooms, and kitchens. Guest rooms are small but bright and well
kept, with plain, mostly white-painted wood furniture. The owner,
Hazel Lowe, loves to chat with guests and make sightseeing and dining
recommendations. She can refer you to a nearby cove for swimming.
⊠ *10 Salt Kettle Rd., Hamilton PG 01* ☎ *441/236–0407* 🖷 *441/236–
8639* ⇴ *3 rooms, 4 cottages* ⚒ *Lounge; no room phones, no TV in some
rooms, no smoking* ☰ *No credit cards* ⍾ *BP.*

NIGHTLIFE & THE ARTS

5

FODOR'S CHOICE
The Deep, *in Paget Parish*
Hubie's Bar, *in Hamilton*
Jasmine, *in Southampton Parish*

HIGHLY RECOMMENDED

NIGHTLIFE Clayhouse Inn, *in Devonshire Parish*
Club 40, *in Hamilton*
Harley's, *in Hamilton*
Michael Douglas Bar, *in Devonshire Parish*
The Oasis, *in Hamilton*

THE ARTS Bermuda Conservatory of Music, *in Hamilton*
Bermuda Musical & Dramatic Society, *in Devonshire Parish*
Bermuda Philharmonic Society, *in Hamilton*
National Dance Theatre of Bermuda, *in Hamilton*

FOR A RUNDOWN OF WHAT'S HAPPENING in Bermuda while you're there, pick up a copy of the "Bermuda Calendar of Events" brochure at any visitor service bureau. The free monthly *Preview Bermuda* magazine and www.previewbermuda.com list upcoming island events. *The Bermudian* ($5), a monthly magazine, has a calendar of events, as does *RG* magazine, which is included free in the *Royal Gazette* newspaper on or around the first of the month. *This Week in Bermuda,* another free magazine, describes arts and nightlife venues. Some hotels carry a TV station that broadcasts information about cultural events and nightlife on the island. Radio VSB, FM 1450, gives a lineup of events daily at 11:15 AM. You can also dial ☎ 974 for recorded information on cultural events. Because the arts scene in Bermuda is so casual, many events and performers operate on a seasonal or part-time basis. If you see a bulletin board, inspect it for posters advertising upcoming events.

NIGHTLIFE

Because Bermuda has no casinos and only a few nightclubs, you'll find most of the action in hotel bars, pubs, lounges (mostly in Hamilton); at beach parties; and on evening boat excursions.

Don't overlook the work of local musicians: Bermuda has a long tradition of producing superb jazz artists and hosts an annual jazz festival in the fall. One of the best places to catch a jam session is at Hubie's Bar on Friday night; it's a typical smoky jazz bar, with an obscure entrance in a somewhat dicey area of town. However, everyone knows where Hubie's is, so a cab can easily get you there—and it's the kind of club where you'll see the common man rubbing shoulders with members of Parliament.

As a general rule, men tend to dress smart-casual for clubs. This means you may not want to wear your T-shirts, jeans, or running shoes. For women the dress code is casual-chic, or just plain casual. Pubs and clubs begin to fill up around 9:30 or 10.

Bars & Lounges

Most bars serve light pub fare in addition to a mean rum swizzle or a Dark and Stormy, two local rum-based drinks. Too lazy to call a cab and too prettied up to ride your moped? Some of the island's nightlife takes place at hotel bars—maybe even yours. Non-hotel guests are always welcome too.

Hamilton

The Beach (✉ 103 Front St. ☎ 441/292–0219) is your place if you're looking for a reasonably priced drink without the pretensions of upscale bars. For the locals, it's the spot to hang out either straight from work or when everywhere else has closed. It attracts a mixed crowd, has seating outside, and is open until 3 AM daily.

Blue Juice (✉ Bermuda House La., off Front St. ☎ 441/292–4507), one of the trendiest bars in Bermuda, attracts the younger set and has an open-air courtyard area with a video screen, as well as an indoor bar. When it rains, a canvas roof is pulled out over the terrace. Appetizers are served at lunch and dinner, and the bar stays open until 3 AM daily. It's very popular, so you may have to wait for a seat.

Consider **Casey's** (✉ Queen St., across from the Little Theatre ☎ 441/292–9994), a narrow room with a jukebox and a few tables, if you like to toss 'em back in a hard-core bar. It's by no means fancy or touristy, and it really packs them in, especially on Friday night. Casey's is open from 10 to 10 every day except Sunday.

With a trendy Bermudian restaurant on one level and an even trendier sushi bar called Yashi in the back, **Coconut Rock** (✉ 20 Reid St. ☎ 441/292–1043) is filled with music and Hamilton's young and beautiful. Yet it's interesting and fun, and open daily for lunch and dinner (Sunday dinner only). Don't confuse this place with Coconuts, the upscale restaurant at the Reefs resort in Southampton.

Docksider (✉ Front St. ☎ 441/296–3333) attracts a mixed crowd of visitors and locals with 15 big-screen TVs. If the activity at the long cedar bar is too noisy, opt for the wine bar, which is quieter and more intimate, or the poolroom. A nightclub ($10 cover) in the back room plays dance, pop, and Soca music (a fast, steel pan–based music whose name is derived from "the *so*ul of *ca*lypso"). Docksider is open until 1 AM Sunday through Thursday and 2 AM on Friday and Saturday.

Flanagan's Irish Pub & Restaurant (✉ 69 Front St. ☎ 441/295–8299), on the second floor of the Emporium Building, is a favorite for folks who like to dance and talk over drinks. Lots of exotic, fun drinks, like frozen mudslides, are on offer. Local music groups entertain Wednesday through Saturday nights after 10 PM. Otherwise a giant TV screen flickers with sporting events. It's open daily from 11 AM to 1 AM.

Fresco's Wine Bar & Restaurant (✉ 2 Chancery La. ☎ 441/295–5058) has the largest selection of wine by the glass in Bermuda, plus desserts to die for. Sip your wine on the enclosed patio or at the upstairs bar. Dinner is served at the bar until 10:30 PM.

★ **Harley's** (✉ Fairmont Hamilton Princess, 76 Pitts Bay Rd., Hamilton ☎ 441/295–3000) is the life of the island on Friday nights, May through October, when management sets up an outdoor buffet, offers special drink prices, and schedules live bands.

Small, cozy **Hog Penny** (✉ 5 Burnaby Hill ☎ 441/292–2534) was the inspiration for the Bull & Finch Pub (the "Cheers" bar) in Boston. With dark-wood paneling and pub fare like steak-and-kidney pie, and bangers and mash, the Hog Penny probably will remind you more of an English country pub than a Boston hangout. Live bands play most nights in summer (just Friday and Saturday in winter), when the floor is cleared for dancing. It's open daily until 1 AM, and it can be very busy.

M. R. Onions (✉ 11 Par-la-Ville Rd. ☎ 441/292–5012) likes to market itself as a sports bar—you can watch any number of sports events on several wide-screen TVs and also access the Internet ($10 for the first hour and $5 thereafter)—but it's also a restaurant in its own right.

The Pickled Onion (✉ 53 Front St. ☎ 441/295–2263) is a restaurant and bar that caters to a well-heeled crowd of locals and visitors. Live music— usually jazz and pop—plays nightly from about 10:30 PM to 1 AM in the high season and irregularly off-season.

Poinciana Terrace (✉ Waterloo House, 100 Pitts Bay Rd., Hamilton ☎ 441/295–4480), on the water's edge, is the perfect spot for a glass of wine and conversation to the tune of light, island music, and with a backdrop of bobbing sailboats on Hamilton Harbour.

Casual, friendly **Robin Hood** (✉ Richmond Rd. ☎ 441/295–3314) is popular at night for pub fare, pizza, and beer served on the patio under the stars. Sports can be watched almost anytime on the TV screens.

Outside Hamilton

As the name indicates, **After Hours** (✉ 117 South Rd., past intersection with Middle Rd., Paget Parish ☎ 441/236–8563) is late-night spot. It opens at midnight and serves good curries, hamburgers, and sandwiches until 4 AM.

At this writing **Café Lido** (⊠ Elbow Beach Hotel, 60 South Shore Rd., Paget Parish ☎ 441/236–9884) is closed for renovations due to damage from Hurricane Fabian. It is due to reopen in early 2004. The bar area overlooks the blue waters just beyond the south shore's beautiful Elbow Beach.

The Clubhouse (⊠ The Reefs, 56 South Rd., Southampton Parish ☎ 441/238–0222) is an elegant restaurant and cocktail lounge with a long bar, sofas, and tiny tables. Nightly piano or Calypso music brings in couples and friends for quiet talks. It's an especially good spot to stop if you're staying east of Warwick.

The serious, dark-wood **English Pub** (⊠ Cambridge Beaches, 30 King's Point Rd., Sandys Parish ☎ 441/234–0331) at the island's oldest cottage colony has live music nightly in summer and a lovely outdoor terrace. You'll mostly mingle with hotel guests at this secluded West End resort.

Frog & Onion Pub (⊠ Cooperage Building, Sandys Parish ☎ 441/234–2900) serves a splendid variety of down-to-earth pub fare in a dark-wood, barnlike setting. If you're spending the day at Dockyard, it's a great place to recharge your batteries.

Henry VIII (⊠ South Shore Rd., Southampton Parish ☎ 441/238–1977) is a popular, snazzy restaurant and bar with rich oak paneling, polished brass, and a good program of local or visiting entertainment almost every night. If you're looking for a quiet chat in the late evening, you may find the volume of music off-putting. A competent menu of English and Bermudian fare is offered until 10 PM. The bar is below Gibbs Hill Lighthouse, just down the carriage way from the Fairmont Southampton.

Fodor's Choice   **Jasmine** (⊠ Fairmont Southampton, 101 South Shore Rd., Southampton Parish ☎ 441/238–8000) draws the smartly dressed set to its lounge
★   and dance floor. Definitely check out the Joe Wylie Trio in season. Sandwiches, salads, and other light fare are served until 1 AM.

★   The **Michael Douglas Bar** (⊠ Ariel Sands Beach Resort, 34 South Shore Rd., Devonshire Parish ☎ 441/236–1010), in the resort's clubhouse, is decorated with publicity photos of the actor and his family. Pull up a stool or relax on a couch beside the giant central fireplace.

The Loyalty Inn (⊠ Somerset Rd., Sandys Parish ☎ 441/234–4502) aims to please the whole family with a small restaurant area, live music, and a children's play area on site.

Swizzle Inn (⊠ 3 Blue Hole Hill, off North Rd., Bailey's Bay, Hamilton Parish ☎ 441/293–1854) has a dartboard; a jukebox that plays soft and hard rock; and business cards from all over the world tacked on the walls, ceilings, and doors. "Swizzle Inn, swagger out" is the motto.

The **Veranda Bar** (⊠ Elbow Beach Hotel, 60 South Shore Rd., Paget Parish ☎ 441/236–3535) is a cozy lounge with an outdoor patio and separate cigar room. Live bands play nightly in summer.

The yachting crowd gathers at **Wharf Tavern** (⊠ Somers Wharf, St. George's ☎ 441/297–1515) for rum swizzles, moderately priced pub fare, and nautical talk.

The Wine Cellar Bar (⊠ Fairmont Southampton, 101 South Shore Rd., Southampton Parish ☎ 441/238–8000) is an upper-class pub (you may not get in with shorts on) next to the hotel pool, with billiard tables, big-screen TVs, pitchers of draft beer, and appetizers until 2 AM. DJs or bands rock the house every night except Monday from 9 PM to 3 AM. Take your pick between country music on Tuesday, jazz on Wednesday, reggae and calypso on Thursday, karaoke on Friday, Top 40 on Saturday, and golden oldies on Sunday.

Music & Dance Clubs

Given that the island is 500 mi from the United States, and much farther from anywhere else, it makes sense that in Bermuda the music scene is pretty much dominated by local bands, playing the hotel-and-pub circuit. Music is generally Afro-Caribbean–inspired, with reggae, calypso, and steel-drum bands at the forefront. The island's longtime superstar Gene Steede—a guitarist, singer, and comedian who has been described as Tony Bennett, Harry Belafonte, and Johnny Carson rolled into one—can usually be found, with his band, at the airport arrivals hall greeting visitors with bouncy island music. Other popular acts to seek out are the Coca-Cola Steel Band, the calypso-playing Bermuda Strollers, the rock-and-roll Sharx and the Kennel Boys, and Tropical Heat, with a reggae-calypso-Soca-Latin sound. Outside performers are billed occasionally, particularly during the Bermuda Festival in January and February. Jazz is a big deal in Bermuda, too, which culminates in the annual Bermuda Jazz Festival in September or October.

Hamilton

The **Bermuda Folk Club** (⊠ Old Colony Club, Trott Rd. ☎ 441/296–6362) hosts monthly get-togethers, which usually take place at 8:30 on the first Saturday of the month. Note that musicians might perform any number of musical styles besides folk. Drinks are often served at happy-hour prices, and the cover is $6 but can rise to more than $20 for off-island acts. It's worth calling for nights other than first Saturdays, too, as unpublicized gigs and events sometimes pop up.

★ **Club 40** (⊠ 119 Front St. ☎ 441/292–9340) is a hoppin' nightclub with live bands or DJs playing the best Latin and Top 40 hits from the '70s to the present day. It's open Tuesday through Saturday, 10 PM to 2 AM (there's a $10 cover after 11). On Thursday nights from 6:30 to 8:30, you can take Latin dance classes for $10, including a drink.

Escape Venue (⊠ Par-la-Ville Rd., below M. R. Onions ☎ 441/292–7978) attracts young trendy things who are serious about disco. It tends to be open Thursday, Friday, and Saturday nights until about 3 AM, but you should call to make sure.

FodorśChoice **Hubie's Bar** (⊠ 10 Angle St., off Court St. ☎ 441/293–9287) books the
★ best jazz bands on the island for weekly sessions on Friday from 7 to 10 PM. Other kinds of live music or poetry readings might be on the schedule other nights—whatever it is, it's bound to be good here. There's a $5 cover. The area is a bit dodgy, so it's best to take a cab to and from the bar at night.

★ **The Oasis** (⊠ Emporium Building, Front St. ☎ 441/292–4978 or 441/292–3379) is a hot dance spot for rock and disco. In summer, there's dancing nightly from 9 PM to 3 AM. One of Bermuda's top bands, the Kennel Boys, plays from Wednesday to Saturday, beginning at midnight. The cover charge is $10.

Outside Hamilton

FodorśChoice At **The Deep** (⊠Elbow Beach Hotel, 60 South Shore Rd., Paget Parish ☎441/
★ 232–6969) you can dance the night away and sip drinks at tables overlooking the dance floor. The island's top DJs and bands make appearances here. The music and the comprehensive champagne, wine, and cocktail menu bring the fashionable people of Bermuda's social register.

★ The **Clayhouse Inn** (⊠ North Shore Rd., Devonshire Parish ☎ 441/292–3193) is the place to be. Expect a rowdy show starring limbo dancers, the Bermuda Strollers, and the Coca-Cola Steel Band. Shows are Monday through Thursday at 10:15. About $25 covers the entry fee (unless a major player is booked), plus two drinks.

Club Azure (⊠ 511 South Side St., St. David's, St. George's Parish ☎ 441/297–3070) is where the hip people go on a night out in the island's east end. It's busiest on weekends and is open until the early hours—sometimes with thematic dance nights and performers. Be prepared to boogie.

THE ARTS

Bermuda's arts scene is concentrated in Hamilton's numerous art galleries (*See* Art Galleries *in* Chapter 8), a handful of performance venues, and a few artist gathering spots, like Rock Island Coffee Cafe. For dramatic and musical performances, the City Hall Theatre and the Ruth Seaton James Auditorium host the country's best, including Bermuda Festival events.

Venues & Societies

The **Bermuda Society of Arts** (⊠ City Hall, 17 Church St. ☎ 441/292–3824 🖷 441/296–0699) has outstanding gallery space in City Hall, and it's a good place to meet local painters and see some of their work.

City Hall Theatre (⊠ City Hall, 17 Church St. ☎ 441/295–1727) is the major venue for top-quality cultural events each year.

Rock Island Coffee Cafe (⊠ 48 Reid St. ☎ 441/296–5241) is a good place to stop and ask what's going on. Not only is it the unofficial watering hole for Bermuda's eclectic group of artists—it also doubles as an informal art space.

Dance

The **Bermuda Civic Ballet** (🖅 Box HM 661, Hamilton HMCX ☎ 441/293–4147) performs classical ballet at various venues during the academic year. Internationally known artists sometimes appear as guests.

The **Bermuda School of Russian Ballet** (🖅 Box HM 661, Hamilton HM CX ☎ 441/293–4147 or 441/295–8621) has been around for half a century and presents unique ballet and modern dance performances. Show times and venues vary, so call for details.

The **Jackson School of Performing Arts** (⊠ Arcade Building, Burnaby St., Hamilton ☎ 441/292–5815 or 441/292–2927) presents innovative gymnastics and dance performances throughout the year.

★ The **National Dance Theatre of Bermuda** (🖅 Box 1759, Hamilton HM HX ☎ 441/239–4091) began in 1980 and has enjoyed much success in Bermuda and abroad. The company presents classical, modern, and jazz performances throughout the academic year.

United Dance Productions (⊠ Alexandrina Hall, 75 Court St., Hamilton ☎ 441/295–9933 or 441/295–0397), under the artistic direction of Suzette Harvey, has been around for more than a decade. UDP has a reputation for producing some of the island's most funky and creative dance shows in modern, African, hip-hop, ballet, jazz, and tap dance. Show times and venues vary, so call for details.

Film

Liberty Theatre (⊠ Union and Victoria Sts., Hamilton ☎ 441/291–2035) is a 270-seat cinema with four daily show times, including a matinee. The area immediately outside the theater is safe during the day, but you should not linger in this neighborhood after dark.

GOMBEY DANCERS

The Gombey dancer is one of the island's most enduring and uniquely Bermudian cultural icons. The Gombey (pronounced gum-bay) tradition here dates from at least the mid-18th century when enslaved Africans and Native Americans covertly practiced a unique form of dance, also incorporating West Indian, British, and biblical influences. Nowadays, Gombeys mainly perform on major holidays. The Gombey name originates from a West African word which means, literally, "rustic drum." The masked, exclusively male dancers move to the accompaniment of Congolese-style drums and the shrill, whistle-blown commands of the troupe's captain. The dancers' colorful costumes include tall headdresses decorated with peacock feathers, and capes covered with intricate embroidery, ribbons, and tiny mirrors. It's traditional to toss money at the dancers' feet. Performance times and locations vary, but check out the No. 1 Shed on Front Street on Tuesdays around 3, or consult the Visitors Bureau.

The **Little Theatre** (✉ Queen St., Hamilton ☎ 441/292–2135) is a 173-seat theater across the street from Casey's Bar. There are usually three show times per evening.

Neptune Cinema (✉ The Cooperage, Dockyard ☎ 441/291–2035) is a 118-seat cinema that typically shows feature films twice nightly, with matinees Friday, Saturday, and Sunday.

Southside Cinema (✉ 1 Kindley Field Rd., St. David's, St. George's Parish ☎ 441/297–2821), the island's largest theater, is on the former U.S. military base near the airport. Show times are usually at 7:30 PM. Advanced tickets are available at **Unlimited Supplies** (✉ 2 Woodlands Rd., Hamilton ☎ 441/295–9229).

Kids love Movie Day at the Youth Branch of the **Bermuda National Library** (✉ 74 Church St., Hamilton ☎ 441/295–0487).

Music

★ The **Bermuda Conservatory of Music** (✉ Colony Club, Trott Rd., Hamilton ☎ 441/296–5100) was formed when the country's two leading music schools merged in 1997. Concerts are presented periodically during the academic year at various venues.

★ The **Bermuda Philharmonic Society** (✉ Box HM 552, Hamilton HM CX ☎ 441/291–6690 🖶 441/295–3770) presents several programs throughout the year featuring both the full orchestra and various soloists. Students of the Menuhin Foundation, established in Bermuda by the late violin virtuoso Yehudi Menuhin, and visiting musicians sometimes perform with the orchestra.

The **Gilbert & Sullivan Society of Bermuda** (✉ Box HM 3098, Hamilton HM NX ☎ 441/295–3218 🖶 441/295–6812), devoted to performing the works of the famous libretto- and playwriting duo, began in 1972 under the name Warwick Players. The society puts on a musical each year, usually in October. In addition to Gilbert and Sullivan operettas, the group occasionally stages Broadway shows.

Readings & Talks

There are two major open-mike poetry hot spots in Bermuda. Both start with hip-hop and jazz music played on turntables by DJ Beatnik. **Flow Sunday,** founded in 1997 by poet Andra Simons, was the first island event

VERY FINE ARTS FESTIVALS

Bermuda Festival. In January and February, the Bermuda Festival brings internationally renowned artists to the island. The two-month program includes theater, as well as classical and jazz concerts. Most shows take place in City Hall, with additional lunchtime and cocktail-hour concerts at various venues. ☎ 441/292–8572 Dec.–Feb.; 441/295–1291 Mar.–Nov. 🖷 441/295–7403 Dec.–Feb.; 441/295–7403 Mar.–Nov. ⊕ www.bermudafestival.com.

Festival Fringe. Held at the same time as the annual Bermuda Festival, the Fringe was designed to complement the more formal Bermuda Festival performances with smaller, avant-garde ones by local and visiting artists. Bermuda Department of Tourism: ☎ 441/292–0023 in Bermuda; 800/223–6106 in the U.S.

Bermuda International Film Festival. This top-notch festival is a celebration of independent films from all over the world. Screening lasts a full week during late April or early May at the cinemas in Hamilton. Tickets are sold for individual films as well as for workshops and seminars on topics that include screenwriting, camera techniques, and the marketing of independent films. Festival parties are also popular as Hamilton mimics—for a few days at least—the glamour of Sundance, minus the stretch limos. ☎ 441/293–3456 ⊕ www.bermudafilmfest.com.

Bermuda Jazz Festival. This festival kicks off each fall at Dockyard, usually during a long weekend in September. Local and internationally known jazz artists pump out the tunes, and tickets go fast. Shop around for hotel-and-festival combination packages. ☎ 441/292–0023 for information; 441/295–4839 for tickets.

in which poets and musicians were allowed a no-holds-barred forum for artistic expression. Flow is held on alternate Sunday nights, sometimes at Rock Island Coffee Cafe. Contact Simons (☎ 441/296–6457) for the venue. The mission statement of open-mike poetry session **Neno Letu** is "Bring the Word." Founded in 1999, the group meets alternate Wednesdays at **Hubie's Bar** (⊠ 10 Angle St., Hamilton ☎ 441/293–9287).

The **Bermuda National Gallery** (⊠ City Hall, 17 Church St., Hamilton ☎ 441/295–9428) often hosts a series of lunchtime lectures on art and film. You can stop by or call the gallery for a schedule.

Theater

★ The **Bermuda Musical & Dramatic Society** (✉ Box DV 631, Devonshire DV BX ☎ 441/292–0848 or 441/295–5584) has some good amateur actors on its roster. Formed in 1944, this active theater society stages performances year-round at their Daylesford headquarters, one block north of City Hall. The Christmas pantomime is always a sellout, as are most other performances. Visit or call the box office at Daylesford, on Dundonald Street, for reservations and information. Tickets are about $10.

Bermuda is the only place outside the United States where Harvard University's **Hasty Pudding Theatricals** performs. For almost 30 years this satirical troupe has entertained the island during Bermuda College Weeks (March–April). Produced by the Bermuda Musical & Dramatic Society, each of these Bermuda-based shows incorporates political and social issues of the past year. They're all staged at the **City Hall Theatre** (⊠ City Hall, 17 Church St. ☎ 441/295–1727). Tickets are about $20.

BEACHES, SPORTS & THE OUTDOORS

6

FODOR'S CHOICE

"Don't Stop the Carnival Party" Cruise, *from Hamilton to Hawkin's Island*

Blue Water Divers Ltd. scuba diving trips

Church Bay, *in Southampton Parish*

Elbow Beach, *in Paget Parish*

Horseshoe Bay Beach, *in Southampton Parish*

Wildcat Adventure Tours, *departing from Hamilton and St. George's*

HIGHLY RECOMMENDED

Atlantic Spray Charters reef-fishing trips

Bermuda Barefoot Cruises charter tours

Cup Match, *in St. George's or Somerset*

Elbow Beach, *in Paget Parish*

The Railway Trail, *from Paget Parish to Somerset*

Restless Native Tours snorkeling trips

Revised by
Sarah Titterton

LONG BEFORE YOUR PLANE TOUCHES DOWN in Bermuda, the island's greatest asset becomes breathtakingly obvious—the crystal-clear, aquamarine water that frames the tiny, hook-shape atoll. So clear are Bermuda's waters that, in 1994, the government nixed a plan by local scuba-diving groups to create a unique dive site by sinking an abandoned American warplane in 30 feet of water off the island's East End, fairly close to the end of the airport's runway. The government feared that the plane would be easily visible from above—to arriving passengers—and could cause undue distress. It is the incredible clarity of the water that makes Bermuda one of the world's greatest places for exploratory scuba diving and snorkeling, especially among the age-old shipwrecks off the island. The presence of these sunken ships is actually one of Bermuda's ironies—as translucent as the water is, it wasn't quite clear enough to make Bermuda's treacherous reefs visible to the hundreds of ship captains who have smashed their vessels on them through the centuries.

Thanks to Bermuda's position near the Gulf Stream, the water stays warm year-round. In summer the ocean is usually above 80°F, and it's even warmer in the shallows between the reefs and shore. In winter the water temperature only occasionally drops below 70°F, but it seems cooler because the air temperature is usually in the mid-60s. There's less call for water sports December through March, not because of a drop in water temperature, but because of windy conditions. The wind causes rough water, which in turn creates problems for fishing and diving boats, and underwater visibility is often clouded by sand and debris.

In high season, mid-April through mid-October, fishing, diving, and yacht charters fill up quickly. Three major water-sports outfitters on the island, Blue Hole Water Sports, Somerset Bridge Watersports, and Windjammer Watersports, provide most of the rentals. Most boats carry fewer than 20 passengers, so it's advisable to sign up as soon as you arrive on the island. The shoulder seasons are March through mid-April and mid-October through November. During the off season, December through February, many operators close to make repairs and perform routine maintenance. Though a few operators stay open on a limited basis, most will only schedule an outing when there are enough people to fill a boat.

Bermudians take their on-shore sports seriously, too. The daily newspaper's sports section is full of local coverage. Cricket and soccer, the two national sports, grab most of the headlines, but road running, golf, field hockey, rugby, and a host of other island activities also get their share of space. Bermudian star soccer players, such as former Manchester City striker Shaun Goater, have delighted crowds in British and U.S. leagues through the years, and Bermudian sailors hold their own in world competition, as do runners, equestrians, and swimmers. Tennis is a big deal here, too—with 70 courts packed into these 21.6 square mi, it's hard to believe there's room left for horseback riding, cycling, running, and playing squash.

Beaches

Bermuda's south-shore beaches are more scenic than those on the north side, with fine, pinkish sand, and coral bluffs topped with summer flowers. The water at south-shore beaches does get a little rougher when the winds are from the south and southwest, but mainly the pale-blue waves break at the barrier reefs offshore and roll gently upon the sandy shoreline. You can join locals in the popular pastime of body surfing, or pick up a body board for as little as $20 from many shops in town. Most Bermudian beaches are relatively small compared with ocean beaches in the United

States, ranging from about 15 yards to half a mile or so in length. In winter, when the weather is more severe, beaches may erode—even disappear—only to be replenished as the wind subsides in spring.

The Public Transportation Board publishes "Bermuda's Guide to Beaches and Transportation," available free in all Visitors Service Bureaus and most hotels. A combination map and bus-and-ferry schedule, the guide shows the locations of the beaches and how to reach them. The Bermuda telephone directory, available in hotels, also has maps and public transportation schedules, plus a calendar of events.

Few Bermudian beaches offer shade, but some have palm trees and thatched shelters. The sun can be intense, so bring a hat and plenty of sunscreen. You can rent umbrellas at some beaches, but food and drink are rare, so pack snacks and lots of water.

North-Shore Beaches

Shelly Bay Beach. As at Somerset Long Bay, the water at this beach near Flatts is well protected from strong southerly winds. In addition, a sandy bottom and shallow water make this a good place to take small children. Shelly Bay also has shade trees, a rarity at Bermudian beaches. A playground behind the beach attracts hordes of youngsters on weekends and during school holidays. A drawback can be the traffic noise from nearby North Shore Road. ⊠ *North Shore Rd., Hamilton Parish* Ⓣ *Bus 10 or 11 from Hamilton.*

Somerset Long Bay. Popular with Somerset locals, this beach is on the quiet northwestern end of the island, far from the bustle of Hamilton and major tourist hubs. In keeping with the area's rural atmosphere, the beach is low-key. Undeveloped parkland shields the beach from the light traffic on Cambridge Road. The main beach is long by Bermudian standards—nearly ¼ mi from end to end. Although exposed to northerly storm winds, the bay water is normally calm and shallow—ideal for children. The bottom, however, is rocky and uneven, so it's a good idea to put on water shoes before wading. ⊠ *Cambridge Rd., Sandys Parish* Ⓣ *Bus 7 or 8 to Dockyard or Somerset from Hamilton.*

Tobacco Bay Beach. The most popular beach near St. George's—about 15 minutes northwest of the town on foot—this small north-shore strand is huddled in a coral cove. Its beach house has a snack bar, equipment rentals, toilets, showers, and changing rooms. From the bus stop in the town of St. George's, it's a 10-minute hike, or you can flag down one of St. George's Minibus Service vans and ask to for a lift here ($2 per person). In high season it becomes very busy, especially midweek when the cruise ships are docked. ⊠ *Coot Pond Rd., St. George's Parish* ☎ *441/297–8199* Ⓣ *Bus 1, 3, 10, or 11 from Hamilton.*

South-Shore Beaches

Chaplin and Stonehole Bays. In a secluded area east of Horseshoe Bay Beach, these tiny adjacent beaches almost disappear at high tide. An unusual high coral wall reaches across the beach to the water, perforated by a 10-foot-high, arrowhead-shape hole. Like Horseshoe Bay, the beach fronts South Shore Park. ⊠ *Off South Rd., Southampton Parish* Ⓣ *Bus 7 from Hamilton.*

★ **Elbow Beach.** Swimming and body surfing are great at this beach, which lies adjacent to the prime strand of sand reserved for guests of the Elbow Beach Hotel. As pleasant as the setting is, however, it can get very noisy and crowded on summer weekends. A nearby lunch wagon sells fast food and cold soft drinks. ⊠ *Off South Rd., Paget Parish* Ⓣ *Bus 2 or 7 from Hamilton.*

Beaches
& Golf Courses

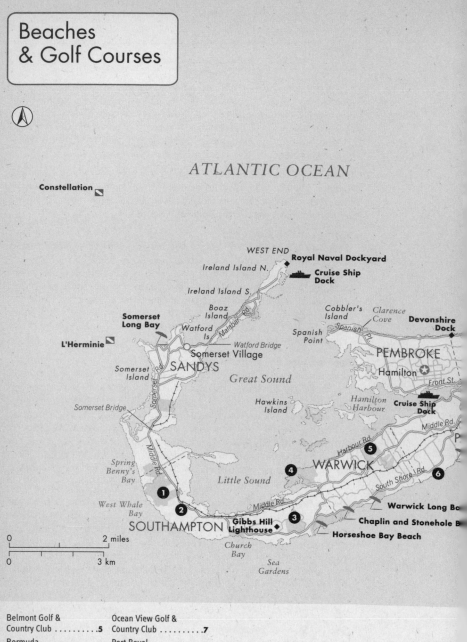

ATLANTIC OCEAN

Constellation

WEST END

Royal Naval Dockyard

Ireland Island N.

Cruise Ship
Dock

Ireland Island S.

Cobbler's
Island

Clarence
Cove

Devonshire
Dock

Somerset
Long Bay

Boaz
Island

Spanish
Point

Spanish

PEMBROKE

L'Herminie

Watford
Is

Watford Bridge

Somerset Village

Hamilton

Somerset
Island

SANDYS

Great Sound

Front St.

Maidban Rd.

Cruise Ship
Dock

Somerset Bridge

Hawkins
Island

Hamilton
Harbour

Middle Rd.

Spring
Benny's
Bay

Little Sound

Harbour Rd.

5

WARWICK

P

West Whale
Bay

4

South Shore Rd.

6

1

Middle Rd.

2

Middle Rd.

SOUTHAMPTON

3

Gibbs Hill
Lighthouse

Warwick Long Bo

Chaplin and Stonehole B

Horseshoe Bay Beach

Church
Bay

Sea
Gardens

0   2 miles

0   3 km

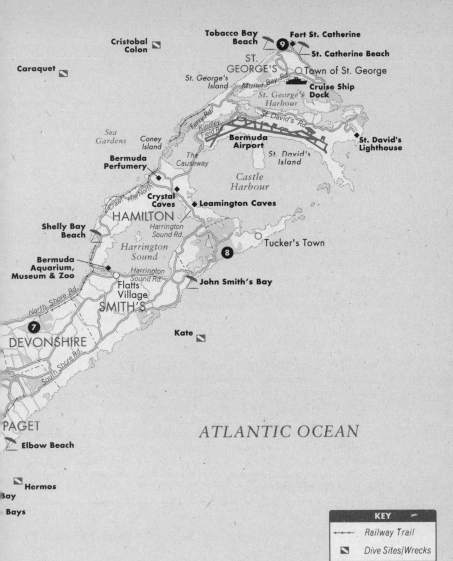

Caraquet

Cristobal
Colon

Tobacco Bay
Beach

Fort St. Catherine

9

St. Catherine Beach

ST.
GEORGE'S

St. George's
Island

Town of St. George

Mullet Bay Rd.

St. George's
Harbour

Cruise Ship
Dock

Ferry Rd.

St. David's Rd.

Sea
Gardens

Coney
Island

Kindley
Field Rd.

Bermuda
Airport

St. David's
Lighthouse

The
Causeway

St. David's
Island

Bermuda
Perfumery

Castle
Harbour

Crystal
Caves

Leamington Caves

HAMILTON

Harrington
Sound Rd.

Shelly Bay
Beach

Harrington
Sound

8

Tucker's Town

Bermuda
Aquarium,
Museum & Zoo

Harrington
Sound Rd.

Crawl Hill North

North Shore Rd.

Flatts
Village

John Smith's Bay

SMITH'S

7

Kate

DEVONSHIRE

South Shore Rd.

PAGET

ATLANTIC OCEAN

Elbow Beach

Hermos

Bay

Bays

KEY	
━━━	Railway Trail
◪	Dive Sites/Wrecks

Fodor's Choice
★

Horseshoe Bay Beach. Horseshoe Bay has everything you would expect of a Bermudian beach: clear water, a ⅓-mi crescent of pink sand, a vibrant social scene, and the uncluttered backdrop of South Shore Park—hence it's one of the island's most popular beaches. Outdoor concerts and events, like crab-racing and the Annual Kite Competition on Good Friday, take place in the high and shoulder seasons. Rental facilities, a snack bar, rest rooms, and, of course, lifeguards (in summer) add to the beach's appeal. In fact, it can become uncomfortably crowded here on summer weekends. Parents should keep a close eye on children in the water, as the undertow can be strong, especially on the main beach. A better place for children is ☺ **Horseshoe Baby Beach,** which you can reach from a path leading off the main beach (ask at the snack bar). Sheltered from the ocean by a ring of rocks, this cove is shallow and almost perfectly calm. And in summer toddlers can find lots of playmates. ✉ *Off South Rd., Southampton Parish* ☎ *441/238-2651* Ⓣ *Bus 7 from Hamilton.*

John Smith's Bay. Backed by the odd residence and South Shore Road, this beach consists of a pretty strand of long, flat open sand. The presence of a lifeguard in summer makes it an ideal place to bring children. The only public beach in Smith's Parish, John Smith's Bay is also popular with locals. Groups of young folks like to gather in the park area surrounding the beach for parties, especially on weekends and holidays, so if you're not in the mood for a festive bunch with loud radios, this may not be the place for you. ✉ *South Shore Rd., Smith's Parish* Ⓣ *Bus 1 from Hamilton.*

Warwick Long Bay. Unlike the covelike bay beaches, Warwick Long Bay has about a ½-mi stretch of sand—the longest of any beach here. Its backdrop is a combination of very steep cliffs and low grass- and brush-covered hills. The beach is exposed to some strong southerly winds, but the waves are usually moderate because the inner reef is close to shore. A 20-foot coral outcrop less than 200 feet offshore looks like a sculpted boulder balancing on the water's surface. South Shore Park, which surrounds the bay, is often empty, a fact that only heightens the beach's appealing isolation and serenity. ✉ *Off South Rd., Southampton Parish* Ⓣ *Bus 7 from Hamilton.*

Bicycling

The best and sometimes the only way to explore Bermuda's nooks and crannies—its little hidden coves and 18th-century tribe roads—is by bicycle or motor scooter. Arriving at the small shore roads and hill trails, however, means first navigating Bermuda's rather treacherous main roads. They are narrow, with no shoulders, and often crowded with traffic (especially near Hamilton during rush hours). Fortunately, there is another, safer option for biking in Bermuda: the Railway Trail, a dedicated cycle path blissfully free of cars.

Despite the traffic, bicycle racing is a popular sport in Bermuda, and club groups regularly whir around the island on evening and weekend training rides. Be prepared for some tough climbs—the roads running north–south across the island are particularly steep and winding—and the wind can sap even the strongest rider's strength, especially along South Shore Road in Warwick and Southampton parishes. Island roads are no place for novice riders, however. Helmets are strongly recommended, and parents should think twice before allowing preteen children to bike.

The "Bermuda Handy Reference Map," available free at Visitors Service Bureaus, depicts bike routes, but not as clearly as the highly detailed "Bermuda Islands" map, available at the Bermuda Book Store in Hamil-

SHOCKING PINK!

THE SANDS OF THE WORLD'S BEACHES come in many hues, from basaltic black to gleaming quartz white, with a rainbow of red, green, yellow, and brown thrown in—and yes, even pink. Pink sand is considered choice by many beach connoisseurs, and Bermuda's south shore has plenty of it. You'll find the rosy tint of the island's sand most intense in the bright sun of midday, but in the gentler light of early morning and late afternoon the hue can appear darker, tending toward mauve.

In only a few regions where tropical coral reefs flourish offshore do pink-sand beaches form. What makes the sand pink is an amalgam of calcium-rich shells and fragments of invertebrate sea creatures, from minute, single-cell protozoa to spiny sea urchins. Chiefly responsible are foraminifera ("foram" for short), a type of protozoan that lives in great profusion in reef environments. The microscopic red Homotrema rubrum (red foram) variety is numerous both on the reefs and in the ocean sediments that surround Bermuda, and their persistent red pigment remains even in the microscopic "skeletons" these animals leave behind when they die. The red gets mixed in with other (predominantly white) reef debris—broken clam and snail shells, fragments of coral— and, when washed ashore, forms the island's signature pink sand.

The most visited pink-sand beaches are Warwick Long Bay Beach and Horseshoe Bay Beach in Southampton. But just about any beach you visit on the south shore will have the famous sand in abundance.

ton. Neither of these guides are indispensable, as bike-rental shops and hotel clerks can recommend bike routes, but serious cyclists may find them worth examining.

★ **The Railway Trail.** Running intermittently the length of the old Bermuda Railway, this trail is scenic, paved, and restricted to pedestrian and bicycle traffic. You can ask the staff at any bike-rental shop for advice on where to access the trail. One especially lovely route starts at Somerset Bridge and ends 2½ mi (4 km) later near the Somerset Country Squire pub. You can take your bike onto the ferry for a pleasant ride from Hamilton or St. George's to the Somerset Bridge stop. From there, bike to the bridge on the main road, turn right, and ride uphill for about 50 yards until you reach the sign announcing the Railway Trail. Turning onto the trail, you find yourself along a course with spectacular views of the Great Sound. Along the way, you pass old Fort Scaur, several schools, and the large, pink Somerset Cricket Club. Toward the end of the trail segment, you find yourself on Beacon Hill Road opposite the bus depot. Here you can turn around and head back to Somerset Bridge, or, for refreshment, turn left and ride to the main road (you'll see Somerset Police Station), and make a sharp right turn to find Mangrove Bay beach and the Somerset Country Squire pub and restaurant. Because the Railway Trail is somewhat isolated and not lighted, you should avoid it after dark.

Tribe Road 3. Tribe roads are small, often unpaved side roads, some of which date back to the earliest settlement of Bermuda. They make for good exploring, though many are quite short and come up to dead ends. Beginning at Oleander Cycles in Southampton, Tribe Road 3 climbs steeply up on the hillside just below Gibbs Hill Lighthouse, with views of the south shore below. And it eventually leads to a point where you can see the north shore as well.

South Shore Road. This main island road passes absolutely gorgeous ocean views. South Shore Road is well-paved and, for the most part, wider than Middle Road, North Shore Road, and Harbour Road, with relatively few hills. However, it is one of Bermuda's windiest and most heavily traveled thoroughfares.

Bike Rentals

In Bermuda, bicycles are called pedal or push bikes to distinguish them from the more common, motorized two-wheelers, which are called bikes, too. Some of the cycle liveries around the island rent both, so make sure to specify whether you want a pedal or motor bike. If you are sure you want to bicycle while you're in Bermuda, try to reserve rental bikes a few days in advance. Rates are around $25 a day, though the longer you rent, the more economical your daily rate. You may be charged an additional $15 for a repair waiver and for a refundable deposit.

Eve's Cycle Livery. In three convenient locations around the island, Eve's rents standard-size mountain bikes, as well as motor scooters, including your mandatory helmet. The staff readily supplies advice on where to ride, and there is no charge for a repair waiver. ⊠ *110 Middle Rd., near South Shore Rd., Paget Parish* ☎ *441/236–6247* ⊠ *441/236–6996* ⊠ *Water St., St. George's* ☎ *441/236–0839* ⊠ *Reid St., Hamilton* ☎ *441/236–4491.*

Oleander Cycles. Known primarily for its selection of motor bikes, Oleander Cycles also rents mountain bikes, though none for kids. A repair waiver is charged. ⊠ *Middle Rd., west of the fire station, Southampton Parish* ☎ *441/234–0629* ⊠ *Middle Rd., at Valley Rd., Paget Parish* ☎ *441/236–2453* ⊕ *www.bermuda.com/oleander.*

Wheels Cycles. If you're staying in one of Bermuda's large resorts, chances are there's a Wheels Cycles right in the hotel. And even if you're not in a resort you may find a location nearby. The store has 13 branches all over the island. You can rent mountain bikes for children and adults. ⊠ *Front St., near the docks, Hamilton* ☎ *441/292–2245* ⊠ *441/296–6423* ⊕ *www.bermuda.com/wheels* ⊠ *Dundonald St., Hamilton* ⊠ *Fairmont Hamilton Princess* ⊠ *Devil's Hole* ⊠ *Fairmont Southampton* ⊠ *Flatts Village* ⊠ *Horizons & Cottages* ⊠ *Coral Beach* ⊠ *Sonesta Beach Resort* ⊠ *Stonington Beach Hotel* ⊠ *Surf Side Beach Club.*

Bike Tours

Fantasea Cruises. This comprehensive outfitter offers a 1½-hour bike tour along the Railway Trail, starting with a short boat cruise to the trail and ending with a cool-off swim. Depending on the day, the tour will start from either Albuoy's Point, Dockyard, or the Waterlot Inn at the Fairmont Southampton. The tour is $50 per person and includes equipment and drinks. ⊠ *Albuoy's Point, Hamilton* ☎ *441/236–1300 or 441/295–0460* ⊕ *www.fantasea.bm.*

Bird-watching

Forty species of warblers have been spotted in Bermuda, especially in the casuarina trees along the south shore and West End. Other omnipresent species include kiskadee, swifts, cuckoos, flycatchers, swallows, thrushes, kingbirds, and orioles. Bird conservation is a big deal in Bermuda. You'll see bluebird boxes on every island golf course, which act as safe nesting sites for this jeopardized species, threatened by development and the invasive sparrow.

The largest variety of birds can be spotted during fall migration, when thousands of birds pass overhead, stop for a rest on their way south, or spend the winter on the island. You might spot the rare American avocet or the curlew sandpiper. In spring, look for brightly colored Central and South American birds migrating north. The white-tail tropicbird, a beautiful white bird with black markings and a 12- to 17-inch-long tail (locals call it a "longtail"), is one of the first to arrive. Summer is the quietest season for bird-watching in Bermuda. Late migrants, like the barn swallow and chimney swift pass by, and if you check the ponds you may see the occasional shorebird.

Bermuda Audubon Society. The society has issued an excellent book called *A Birdwatching Guide to Bermuda*, by president Andrew Dobson, published by the Arlequin Press. In it are maps, illustrations, and descriptions of birds and their habitats. Several birding events are organized throughout the year, including the Christmas Bird Count—Bermuda averages 74 species per count, although 200 species have been recorded in total. The Web site has a bird-watching checklist. ✆ *Box HM 1328, Hamilton HM FX* ☎ *441/292–1920* ⊕ *www.audubon.bm.*

Bermuda Biological Institute. Birders may be interested in David Wingate's efforts to repopulate the native cahow bird (Bermuda petrel) population via artificial burrows and other means on Nonsuch Island. Tours of the island are arranged by the institute and cost $75 for 3 to 4 hours. ✉ *17 Biological La., Ferry Reach, St. George's Parish* ☎ *441/297–1880.*

Seymour's Pond Nature Reserve. Seymour's Pond is smaller than Warwick and Spittal ponds, but it has the advantage of being a bit farther inland, and therefore better protected. Twenty-eight species of duck are recorded in Bermuda and you quite likely to see many of them here. ✉ *Middle Rd., Southampton Parish, near Barnes Corner* Ⓣ *Bus 7 or 8 from Hamilton or Dockyard.*

Spittal Pond Nature Reserve. Stretching placidly within a 60-acre nature reserve, Spittal Pond is an excellent place to view wildlife, especially birds. As long as the water level is not too high, some 30 species of shorebird can be present on the margins of the pond. On a good day in September you might see more than 100 birds. Semipalmated sandpipers are perhaps the most abundant. In winter herons and egrets roost serenely in the shallow water. You can tour the reserve yourself, or take a scheduled tour with a park ranger, usually on Fridays. ✉ *South Rd., Smith's Parish* ☎ *441/236–4201* 🎫 *Free* Ⓣ *Bus 1 from Hamilton or St. George's.*

Warwick Pond. In a well-kept inland nature preserve, Bermuda's only natural fresh-water pond is prime bird territory. Shorebirds and herons gather around its edges in fall and winter. A note of warning: in the heat of summer, the stagnant water lets off a rather putrid smell. ✉ *Middle Rd., Warwick Parish, near the Ettrick Animal Hospital* Ⓣ *Bus 8 from Hamilton or Dockyard.*

Boating, Sailing & Yachting

You can either rent your own boat or charter one with a skipper. Rental boats, which are 18 feet at most, range from sailboats (typically tiny Sunfish) to motorboats (usually 13-foot Boston Whalers), in addition to kayaks and pedal boats. Some of these vessels are ideal for exploring the coves and harbors of the sounds, or, in the case of motorboats, dropping anchor and snorkeling around the shorelines, which teem with various coral and colorful fish. In the Great Sound, several small islands, such as Hawkins Island and Darrell's Island, have tiny secluded beaches and coves that are usually empty during the week. If the wind is blowing in the right direction, the islands are about half an hour's sail from Hamilton Harbour or Salt Kettle. The beaches are wonderful places to picnic, although some are privately owned and aren't open to visitors. Check with the boat-rental operator before planning an island trip. The trade winds pass well to the south of Bermuda, so the island does not have predictable air currents. To the casual sailor, wind changes can be troublesome. Mangrove Bay, often protected, is the ideal place for novice sailors and pedal boaters. The average summer breeze is 7 to 10 knots, often out of the south or southwest.

Boat Rentals

Rates for small powerboats start at about $65 for two hours and go up to $185 for a full day. Gas is extra. Sailboat rentals begin at $60 for four hours and go up to $170 for a full day. A credit card number is usually required.

Blue Hole Water Sports. Powerboat rentals cost $75 for two hours and $120 for four hours, including snorkeling gear and a cooler. A maximum of four people can fit in the powerboats, which are straightforward to operate. Blue Hole staff offers instructions on how to navigate for first-time users. ⊠ *Grotto Bay Beach Hotel & Tennis Club, 11 Blue Hole Hill, Hamilton Parish* ☎ *441/293–2915 or 441/293–8333 Ext. 37* ⊕ *www.blueholewater.bm.*

Pompano Beach Club Watersports Centre. If you want a taste of open water in summer, head for the western shore, where this center will equip you right and send you on your way. Several kinds of boats are available, including SunKat cruisers ($35 per hour), E-Scotter boats ($30 per hour), Sunfish sailboats ($20 per hour), and paddleboats ($15 per hour). Pompano also rents rafts and rubber tubes. ⊠ *36 Pompano Beach Rd., Southampton Parish* ☎ *441/234–0222.*

Somerset Bridge Watersports. This West End outfitter rents 13- and 15-foot Boston Whalers. Rates are $65 for two hours, $100 for four hours, $140 for six hours, or $165 for eight hours. ⊠ *Somerset Bridge, Sandys Parish* ☎ *441/234–0914 or 441/234–3145* ⊕ *www.bermuda-watersports.com.*

Windjammer Watersports. You can sail off from Bermuda's northwestern tip, at the Dockyard, if you get your rentals from Windjammer. The Great Sound opens up before you and the island curves around to your right, while the Atlantic fans out to your left. Setting off from the Dockyard also permits you a one-of-a-kind vantage point—you'll see ships of all shapes and sizes entering or leaving Bermuda via the channel between the Dockyard and the tip of Pembroke Parish across the water. Windjammer rents 17-foot-long motorboats for $35 for the first hour, plus $20 for each additional hour. Fishing and snorkeling gear are also available. ⊠ *Dockyard Marina* ☎ *441/234–3082* ⊠ *Cambridge Beaches, Sandys Parish* ☎ *441/234–0250.*

Charter Boats

More than 20 large power cruisers and sailing vessels, piloted by local skippers, are available for charter. Primarily 30 to 60 feet long, charter sailboats can carry up to 30 passengers, sometimes overnight. Meals and drinks can be included on request, and a few skippers offer dinner cruises for the romantically inclined. Rates generally range from $300 to $450 for a three-hour cruise, or $650 to $1,500 for a full-day cruise, with additional per-person charges for large groups. Where you go and what you do—exploring, swimming, snorkeling, cruising—is up to you and your skipper. Generally, however, cruises travel to and around the islands of the Great Sound. Several charter skippers advertise year-round operations, but the off-season schedule can be haphazard. Skippers devote periods of the off-season to maintenance and repairs or close altogether if bookings lag. Be sure to book well in advance; in the high season do so before you arrive on the island.

Adventure Enterprises. A 36-foot motorized trimaran, the *Argo II,* can carry up to 34 people and rents for $250 per hour, while a smaller nautica rib, the *Argo I,* can carry up to 12 and rents for $175 per hour. ✉ *Ordnance Island, St. George's* ☎ *441/297–1459.*

★ **Bermuda Barefoot Cruises.** Skipper Doug Jones will accommodate your every need. He has two 32-foot boats, the *Minnow* and the *Veebyes,* available strictly by private charter, and he will pick you up and take you anywhere you like. It's like hiring a limousine for a tour of a city, instead of taking a bus. Rates vary depending on the length of the sail. ☎ *441/236–3498* ⊕ *www.bermudabarefootcruises.com.*

Restless Native Tours. Homemade cookies on every sail are the famous trademark of this family-owned and -operated charter company. A fresh batch is baked on board and washed down with lemonade or rum swizzles. Restless Native is also unique in its educational approach to chartering—they offer a crash course on Bermuda's fish and a guided snorkeling trip. The 50- by 30-foot boat is excellent for dinner charters, evening cocktail cruises, birthday parties, and weddings. The owners can pick you up at any wharf on the island. ☎ *441/234–8149 or 441/234–1434.*

Rising Sun Cruises. The *Rising Sun* is a beautiful, 40-passenger catamaran with a full bar. Besides offering sailing, swimming, and snorkeling trips, the accommodating crew can arrange for you to spend part of the day on Jet Skis, in kayaks, or with a parasailing outfitter. Rates start at $500 for the first hour and go up to $1,050 for five hours. ✉ *Town Square, St. George's* ☎ *441/232–5789* ⊕ *www.charterbermuda.com.*

Tam-Marina. Founded in 1969, Tam-Marina has a reputation for lively dinner and cocktail cruises on a fleet of elegant, white ships. Sightseeing and snorkeling tours, which last 2 to 4 hours and cost $30 to $50 per person, are offered on the glass-bottom *Coral Princess. Lady Erica* and *Lady Tamara* frequently can be seen accommodating private parties on the Great Sound. ✉ *61 Harbour Rd., Paget Parish* ☎☎ *441/236–0127* ⊕ *www.ladyboats.com.*

Wind Sail Charters. You can rent a 41-, 51-, or 60-foot Morgan yacht, including snorkeling equipment, from Wind Sail. Captain Mike or his daughter, Captain Melissa, will sail to your location and take you for a spin. The rates for six people are $350 to $500, depending on the boat, for three hours. Lunch catering is available for an extra charge. ☎ *441/234–8547* ☎ *441/238–1614* ⊕ *www.bermudawindsailcharters.com.*

Boat Tours

Bermuda Island Cruises. Island tours and cocktail cruises are scheduled regularly year-round. A glass-bottom boat tour of the Sea Gardens costs $35 per person and lasts two hours. The tours leave year-round from the ferry terminal in Hamilton. Departures are Monday through Wednesday, Friday, and Saturday at 10 AM and 1:30 PM; Thursday at 2 PM; and Sunday at 1:30 PM. A six-hour sightseeing cruise costs $65 to $75 per person. The boat leaves Hamilton at 8:15 AM, cruises to Dockyard to gather more passengers at 9, then travels to St. George's and Hawkins Island.

A three-hour Calypso Cruise runs Tuesday and Thursday afternoons, with rum swizzles, live entertainment, and a Hawkins Island swim. The cost of the cruise is $52 for adults. It leaves Albuoy's Point in Hamilton at 2 PM. Not exactly a tour per se, the "Don't Stop the Carnival Party" Cruise carries giddy partyers and entertainers to Hawkin's Island for $79 per person. With music, gombey dancers, a limbo competition, a buffet of Bermudian barbecue, and an open bar, this roughly two-hour cruise is

Fodor'sChoice ★

definitely worth the money. The 200-passenger boat leaves Albuoy's Point in Hamilton at 7 PM daily except Thursday and Sunday. ⊠ *Albuoy's Point, Hamilton* ☎ *441/292–8652* 🖷 *441/292–5193* ⊕ *www.bicbda.com.*

Coral Sea Cruises. The glassbottom, double-deck *Coral Sea* holds 40 to 100 passengers and departs from Hamilton or St. George's on one-hour morning, afternoon, or twilight tours of the coral reefs. Tours cost $25 to $40 per person. Charter lunch, dinner, and sunset-cocktail cruises are also available. ⊠ *Town Square, St. George's* ☎ *441/235–2425* ⊕ *www. charterbermuda.com.*

Rising Sun Cruises. Sailing, swimming, and snorkeling trips aboard the 40-passenger catamaran, *Rising Sun,* cost $40 to $60. Rum swizzles, wine, and sodas are served on board. The sunset tour is perfect for romantics. ⊠ *Town Square, St. George's* ☎ *441/232–5789* ⊕ *www. charterbermuda.com.*

Fodor'sChoice   **Wildcat Adventure Tours.** You can cruise around the entire country in less
★   than two hours aboard the *Wildcat,* a bright-yellow, 50-foot catamaran with two 800-horsepower engines. The fun-loving tour guides point out hotels, famous houses, and historical landmarks; and they are not averse to diverting from the chartered course—the crew has been known to stop to watch lobster divers in action. Tours cost $55 and leave from the flagpole on Front Street in Hamilton at 10 AM and 2 PM every day except Wednesday, when the tours leave from St. George's. This is a high-speed and, at times, rough ride, so consider opting out if you are pregnant or have a physical disability. ⊠ *Front and Burnaby Sts., Hamilton* ☎ *441/293–7433.*

Races & Events

Bermuda has a worldwide reputation as a yacht-racing center. The sight of the racing fleet, with brightly colored spinnakers flying, is striking even if it's difficult to follow the intricacies of the race. The racing season runs from March to November. Most races are held on weekends in the Great Sound, and several classes of boats usually compete. You can watch from Spanish Point and along the Somerset shoreline. Anyone who wants to get a real sense of the action should be on board a boat near the race course. The Gold Cup race is held in October, and International Race Week is held at the end of April. In June in alternating years, Bermuda serves as the finish point for oceangoing yachts in three major races starting off from the United States.

Bermuda Ocean Race. This race, from Annapolis, Maryland, takes place every other year in June. For information, contact **St. George's Dinghy & Sports Club** (☎ 441/297–1612).

Colorcraft Gold Cup International Match Race Tournament. This is the event of choice if you're more interested in racing than gawking at the expensive yachts. Managed by the **Royal Bermuda Yacht Club** (☎ 441/295–2214), the October tournament hosts many of the world's top sailors—some of whom are America's Cup skippers—and includes the elite among Bermudians in a lucrative chase for thousands in prize money.

Marion (MA)-to-Bermuda Cruising Yacht Race. Only slightly smaller in scale than the Newport-to-Bermuda, this race is held in odd-numbered years. Contact the **Royal Hamilton Amateur Dinghy Club** (☎ 441/ 236–2250 ⊕ www.rhadc.bm) for information on where to watch it.

Newport (RI)-to-Bermuda Ocean Yacht Race. Powerhouse yachtsmen flock to this event in June. After the race the **Royal Bermuda Yacht Club** (☎441/ 295–2214) throws a party open to the public that is always extremely well attended.

FOR LOVE OF CRICKET

The Oval and Lords are names of English cricket grounds that evoke memories of Britain long ago, a time of cucumber sandwiches and tea poured from china pots—but the cricket scene in Bermuda is very definitely Caribbean. The thwack of leather on willow is the same, but overcast skies and frequent breaks as the ground staff move quickly to put the rain covers in place are not for these players. The fans, gathered on grassy knolls and open terraces, are also far removed from those back in England where the game originated. Polite clapping and hearty hurrahs are not to be heard here. Instead the air is filled with chanting and the structures reverberate to the sound of music. Allegiances are clearly defined though few miles separate the opposing factions—mothers, fathers, sons, and daughters all cheering on their favorites. As the match comes to a conclusion, the setting sun falls low behind the clubhouse and players and fans mingle as one to await the dawn of another day of runs, catches, and cries of "Howzat."

Non-Mariners Race. Though not as prestigious as the rest, this annual race, which takes place in early August during Cup Match weekend (the annual cricket holiday), is one of the highlights of the year. Held out of the **Sandys Boat Club** (☎ 441/234–2248 or 441/234–4137) at Mangrove Bay, the goal of this race is simple: to see whose boat (constructed on the beach minutes before) can make it out of the harbor without sinking. Easy to watch as the boats never get very far from land, this race sets the stage for an afternoon of music, barbecue, and merry-making. Legend has it that someone even tried to float an old bus one year. A good viewpoint from which to watch the race is the Somerset Country Squire pub (☎ 441/234–0105).

Bowling

Southside Family Bowl. Rates are generally $2.50 per person per game from 11 AM to 3 PM, $3 from 3 PM to 8 PM, and $3.50 from 8 PM on. Shoes are $1 to rent all the time. Southside is crowded on weekends and Tuesday nights, when the league plays, so lane reservations are recommended. You can bring food and drinks with you—a Pizza House restaurant is nearby—but no alcohol. ⊠ *On Southside Road in St. David's* ☎ 441/293–5906 ☉ *Mon. and Wed.–Sat. 11 AM–11 PM, Tues. 3 PM–11 PM, Sun. 3 PM–10 PM.*

Warwick Lanes. Adults pay $4 per game, plus $1.25 for shoes, and there is a small restaurant inside, as well as vending machines. The place can fill up, so it's best to reserve a lane. ⊠ *Middle Rd., near St. Mary's* ☎ 441/236–5290 or 441/236–4125 🖨 441/236–1179 ☉ *Mon.–Sat. 6 PM–11 PM, Sun. 3 PM–11 PM.*

Cricket

★ Cricket is the big team sport in summer, and **Cup Match** in late July or early August is *the* summer sporting event, played over two days. The event celebrates the emancipation of slaves in Bermuda with the top players from around the island competing in two teams: the East End team and the West End team. Although the match is taken very seriously, the event itself is a real festival, complete with plenty of Bermudian food and music. Bermuda's only venue for legal gambling, the Crown & Anchor tent is pitched at the field each year. Thousands of picnickers and partyers show up during the two-day match. Although the players wear only white, fans wear colors to support their team—blue on blue rep resents the East End and blue on red represents the West End. A $10 entry fee is charged per day. The regular cricket season runs from April through September. Contact the **Bermuda Cricket Board of Control** (⊠ 48 Cedar Ave., Hamilton ☎ 441/292–8958 🖶 441/292–8959 ⊕ www. bermuda.cricket.org) for information about the match and other events throughout the year.

Fishing

Fishing in Bermuda falls into three basic categories: shore or shallow-water fishing, inshore reef fishing, and offshore deep-sea fishing. No license is required, although some restrictions apply, particularly regarding the fish you can keep (for instance, only Bermudians with commercial fishing licenses are allowed to take lobsters). There's also a prohibition against spearguns.

Reef & Offshore Fishing

Three major reef bands lie at various distances from the island. The first is anywhere from ½ mi to 5 mi offshore. The second, the Challenger Bank, is about 12 mi offshore. The third, the Argus Bank, is about 30 mi offshore. As a rule, the farther out you go, the larger the fish—and the more expensive the charter.

Most charter fishing captains go to the reefs and deep water to the southwest and northwest of the island, where the fishing is best. Catches over the reefs include snapper, amberjack, grouper, and barracuda. Of the most sought-after deepwater fish—marlin, tuna, wahoo, and dolphinfish—wahoo is the most common, dolphinfish the least. Trolling is the usual method of deepwater fishing, and charter-boat operators offer various tackle setups, with test-line weights ranging from 20 pounds to 130 pounds. The boats, which range from 31 feet to 55 feet long, are fitted with gear and electronics to track fish, including depth sounders, global-positioning systems, loran systems, video fish finders, radar, and computer scanners.

Half-day and full-day charters are offered by most operators, but full-day trips offer the best chance for a big catch because the boat has time to reach waters that are less often fished. Rates are about $600 per boat for half a day (four hours), $850 per day (eight hours). Many captains encourage clients to participate in the catch-and-release program to maintain an abundant supply of fish, but successful anglers may keep fish if they like. For more information about chartering a fishing boat, you can request or pick up a copy of "What to Do: Information and Prices" at the Bermuda Department of Tourism.

Game Fishing Competition. Anglers can take part in this competition, organized by the Bermuda Department of Tourism, year-round. Catches of any of 26 game varieties can be registered with the department, and prizes are awarded. ⊠ *Bermuda Department of Tourism, Global House, 43 Church St., Hamilton* ☎ *441/292–0023* ⊕ *www.bermudatourism.com.*

Bermuda Sport Fishing Association. Information on local tournaments and advice about charter-fishing companies is readily available from this association. ⊠ *Creek View House, 8 Tulo La., Pembroke Parish* ☎ *441/ 295–2370.*

St. George's Game Fishing Association. With half-day and all-day charters available from Messaround Charters at the Game Fishing Association, it's easy to get to some of the prime offshore fishing grounds. ⟲ *Box 107GE, St. George's* ☎ *441/297–8093 or 441/234–8953* 🖶 *441/297–1455* ⊕ *www.fishandfun.bm.*

★ **Atlantic Spray Charters.** Half-day and full-day charters are available on Atlantic's 40-foot *Tenacious*. Rates are $640 for the six-hour half day, and $1,000 for the ten-hour full day, including all the equipment you need, sodas and water, and, most importantly, the knowledge you need to catch the big fish. ⊠ *St. George's* ☎ *441/235–9444* ⊕ *www.atlanticspraycharters.bm.*

Shore Fishing

The principal catches for shore fishers are pompano, bonefish, and snapper. Excellent sport for saltwater fly-fishing is the wily and strong bonefish, which hovers in coves, harbors, and bays. Among the more popular spots for bonefish are West Whale Bay and Spring Benny's Bay, which have large expanses of clear, shallow water protected by reefs close to shore. Good fishing holes are plentiful along the south shore, too. Fishing in the Great Sound and St. George's Harbour can be rewarding, but enclosed Harrington Sound is less promising. Ask at local tackle shops about the latest hot spots and the best baits. You can also make rental arrangements through your hotel or contact Windjammer Water Sports.

Windjammer Watersports. Rods and reels rent for about $15 to $20 a day ($20 to $30 deposit or credit card required), including bait and a tackle box. ⊠ *Dockyard Marina* ☎ *441/234–3082* ⊠ *Cambridge Beaches, Sandys Parish* ☎ *441/234–0250.*

Golf

For descriptions of and information about Bermuda's eight golf courses, see Chapter 7.

Helmet Diving

A different, less technical type of diving popular in Bermuda is helmet diving, offered between April and mid-November. Although helmet-diving cruises last three hours or more, the actual time underwater is about 25 minutes, during which time underwater explorers walk along the sandy bottom in about 10 to 12 feet of water (depending on the tide), wearing helmets that receive air through hoses leading to the surface. Underwater portraits are available for an extra charge. A morning or afternoon tour costs about $50 for adults and includes wet suits when the water temperature is below 80°F. Note that not all outfitters permit children to helmet dive.

Adventure Enterprises. Two-hour helmet diving tours cost about $50 per person, including hot coffee for everyone. ⊠ *Ordnance Island, St. George's* ☎ *441/297–1459.*

Bermuda Bell Diving. Trips are scheduled daily at 10 AM and 2 PM, and cost $60 per person. It's recommended that you make reservations one month ahead of time, although they are willing to accommodate you on short notice if there is room on the boat. ⊠ *Flatts Village, Smith's Parish* ☎ *441/292–4434* 🖷 *441/295–7235* ⊕ *www.belldive.bm.*

Greg Hartley's Under Sea Adventure. The Hartleys schedule two diving trips per day, usually at 10 AM and 1:30 PM, six days per week, in high season. Dives cost around $60 per person. Non-divers are not allowed to snorkel or swim in the same area as the divers, the theory being that fish that are used to helmet divers and approach them for food may endanger themselves by becoming used to snorkelers, swimmers, and eventually fishermen. ⊠ *Watford Bridge, Sandys Parish* ☎ *441/234–2861* 🖷 *441/234–3000* ⊕ *www.hartleybermuda.com.*

Kayaks

Good sea-kayaking areas can be found in protected coves and the open ocean. Calm Mangrove Bay in Somerset is an especially popular spot. Hourly rental rates begin at about $15 for a single-seat kayak and about $20 for a double-seater. For a full day, plan to spend about $80 for a single and $85 for a double.

Blue Hole Water Sports. You can rent single- and double-seat kayaks and head out on your own or take a tour with an experienced guide. On the nature tour (about $35 per person), you paddle through Walsingham and Ferry Point parks. Rental rates are $20 for a single and $25 for a double for the first hour, and $15 each additional hour. ⊠ *Grotto Bay Beach Hotel & Tennis Club, 11 Blue Hole Hill, Hamilton Parish* ☎ *441/ 293–2915 or 441/293–8333 Ext. 37* ⊕ *www.blueholewater.bm.*

Kayak Bermuda. Three-hour tours depart from St. George's and cost $60 per person. You take a boat to Castle Harbour, then transfer to a kayak. Your guide will point out landmarks and identify Bermuda birds and wildlife. Your tour ends with a chance to do a little swimming and snorkeling. ⊠ *Town Square, St. George's* ☎ *441/505–2925* ⊕ *www. charterbermuda.com.*

Somerset Bridge Watersports. Although they don't offer tours, staff can advise you on where to kayak in Ely's Harbour and the Great Sound. Rentals cost $15 per hour for single-seat kayaks and $20 per hour for double kayaks, but the rates drop to $25 and $40, respectively, for two hours, then $40 and $50 for four hours. ⊠ *Somerset Bridge, Sandys Parish* ☎ *441/234–0914* ⊕ *www.bermuda-watersports.com.*

Windjammer Watersports. You can rent kayaks from Windjammer's Cambridge Beaches location. Rentals are $15 for a single and $20 for a double for the first hour, and $10 for each additional hour. They do not offer tours but can advise you on where to go. ⊠ *Cambridge Beaches, Sandys Parish* ☎ *441/234–3082.*

Horseback Riding

Because most of the land on Bermuda is residential, opportunities for riding through the countryside are few. The chief exception is South Shore Park, between South Shore Road and the Warwick beaches. Sandy trails, most of which are open only to walkers or riders, wind through stands of dune grass and oleander and over coral bluffs.

Spicelands Riding Centre. Guides lead riders on trails along the dunes above the south-shore beaches at 7 AM, 10 AM, and 11:30 AM daily. These one-hour jaunts cost $50 per person, with a maximum of 10 people in each group (and no one under age 12). In winter you can ride along the beach. Afternoon rides are also offered on weekdays. Spicelands gives private lessons in its riding ring for $30 per half hour. Beginners are required to take a series of at least three lessons. On Saturday, children ages 12 and under can take 15-minute pony rides for $10. ⊠ *Middle Rd., Warwick Parish* ☎ *441/238–8212 or 441/238–8246.*

Equestrian Events

Events are held at the National Equestrian Centre most weekends from October to May. One highlight is the FEI Competition in dressage and show jumping in March and April, an intense event for young riders. The Annual Exhibition, still called the Agricultural Exhibition by locals, is a three-day event held at the Botanical Gardens in Pembroke near the end of April. Harness pony racing is held on weekends between

October and March, with an atmosphere more friendly than competitive. Ponies are harnessed to sulkies (small, two-wheeled frames with an unsprung seat) and race against each other around the ⅕-mi track.

Bermuda Equestrian Federation. Contact the federation for information on shows and races. You may be referred to one of its affiliates, such as the Bermuda Horse & Pony Association (☎ 441/232–2162), the Horse & Pony Driving Club (☎ 441/293–4964), or the Bermuda Dressage Group (☎ 441/297–4203). ✉ *Box DV 583, Devonshire DV BX* ☎ *441/234–0485.*

Saddle Club of Bermuda. The Saddle Club hosts the two-day Malabar show in May, traditionally the closing show of the equestrian season. ☎ *441/236–4093.*

Jet-Skiing

If riding a moped on terra firma isn't enough for you, consider mounting a Jet Ski. In Bermuda you can ride these high-speed aqua-cycles only in the company of a guide.

Somerset Bridge Watersports. You can arrange to take a "speed tour" at the western end of the island, in the Great Sound, Ely's Harbour, Mangrove Bay, and above the visible Sea Gardens coral formations. Groups are kept small—no more than six Jet Skis per guide. The 1¼-hour tours cost $90 for a single-seater, $115 for a double-seater, and $135 for a triple-seater. ✉ *Somerset Bridge, Sandys Parish* ☎ *441/234–0914* ⊕ *www. bermuda-watersports.com.*

Windjammer Watersports. Tours last 1¼ hours and cost $105 for a single-seater, $125 for a double-seater, and $140 for a triple-seater. The tours do not follow a set course or speed. Depending on weather and traffic conditions, you might feed fish or visit a shipwreck. ✉ *Dockyard Marina, Sandys Parish* ☎ *441/234–0250* ✉ *Cambridge Beaches, Sandys Parish* ☎ *441/234–3082.*

Parasailing

Parasailing outfitters operate in the Great Sound and in Castle Harbour from May through October. The cost is about $45 per person for an eight-minute flight. Want to sail through the sky with your significant other under a single parachute? Two-person trips costs around $80.

Kite Ski Bermuda. Up to four people can sit in the Kite Ski chair as it soars more than 300 feet above Harrington Sound. (Kite Ski also offers a variety of watersports such as knee-boarding, tubing, banana-boating, and kite-boarding.) Parasailing is $60 per person. ✉ *13 Harrington Sound Rd., Smith's Parish* ☎ *441/293–1968.*

Skyrider Bermuda. Skyrider tours over the Great Sound depart every hour on the hour and cost $50 ($15 if you just want to ride in the boat). ✉ *Dockyard Marina, Sandys Parish* ☎ *441/234–3019.*

Rugby

Bermuda's rugby season runs from September to April The **World Rugby Classic** (☎ 441/291–1517 ⊕ www.worldrugby.bm), in November, brings erstwhile top players, now retired, to the island for a week of top play and parties. Tickets cost about $12. The Classic can provide information about other matches as well.

Running & Walking

Top runners flock to the island in January for the Bermuda International Race Weekend, which includes a marathon and 10-km races. Many of the difficulties that cyclists face in Bermuda—hills, traffic, and wind—also confront runners. Be careful of traffic when walking or running along Bermuda's narrow roads—most don't have shoulders.

The Railway Trail. Runners who like firm pavement are happiest and safest along this former train route, one of the most peaceful stretches of road in Bermuda. *See* Bicycling.

South-Shore Beaches. If you like running on sand, head for the south shore. The trails through South Shore Park are relatively firm. A large number of serious runners can be seen on Horseshoe Bay Beach and Elbow Beach early in the morning and after 5 PM. Another beach for running is ½-mi Warwick Long Bay, the island's longest uninterrupted stretch of sand. The sand is softer here, however, than at Horseshoe and Elbow, so it's difficult to get a good footing, particularly at high tide. By using South Shore Park trails to skirt coral bluffs, you can create a route that connects several beaches. Note that the trails can be winding and uneven in some places.

Races

Bermuda International Marathon, Half Marathon and 10K Race. Part of International Race Weekend, held in mid-January, these races attract world-class distance runners from several countries, but it's open to everyone. ☞ *Race Committee, Box DV 397, Devonshire DV BX* ☎ *441/236–6086.*

Bermuda Marathon Derby. It may be second to International Race Weekend in worldwide appeal, but the Marathon Derby captures the imagination of the island like no other race. Held on Bermuda Day, a public holiday, the race brings thousands of locals and visitors, who line the edges of the 13.3-mi course. The race, which begins in Somerset and finishes near the Government Tennis Stadium, is open to residents only.

Bermuda Triathlons. These three-sport events are held about once a month from April to October. The events combine a swim, a cycling leg, and a run. ☞ *Bermuda Triathlon Association, 48 Par-la-Ville Rd., Suite 547, Hamilton HM 11* ☎ *441/293–2765.*

Mid-Atlantic Athletic Club Fun Runs. These 2-mi sprints are held Tuesday evening April through October. Runs begin at 6 PM near the Berry Hill Road entrance to the Botanical Gardens. There is no fee. ☞ *Box HM 1745, Hamilton HM BX* ☎ *441/293–8103* 🖷 *441/293–4089.*

Scuba Diving

Bermuda has all the ingredients for classic scuba diving—reefs, wrecks, underwater caves, a variety of coral and marine life, and clear, warm water. Although you can dive year-round (you will have to bring your own gear in winter, when dive shops are closed), the best months are May through October, when the water is calmest and warmest. No prior certification is necessary. Novices can learn the basics and dive in water up to 25 feet deep on the same day. Three-hour resort courses ($95 to $110) teach the basics in a pool, on the beach, or off a dive boat and culminate in a reef or wreck dive.

The easiest day trips involve exploring the south-shore reefs that lie inshore. These reefs may be the most dramatic in Bermuda. The oceanside drop-off exceeds 60 feet in some places, and the coral is so honeycombed with caves, ledges, and holes that opportunities for discovery are pretty much infinite. Despite concerns about dying coral and dwindling fish populations, most of Bermuda's reefs are still in good health. No one eager to swim with multicolored schools of fish or the occasional barracuda will be disappointed. In the interest of preservation, however, the removal of coral is illegal and subject to hefty fines.

Dive shops around Bermuda prominently display a map of the outlying reef system and its wreck sites. Only 38 of the wrecks from the past three centuries are marked. They are the larger wrecks that are still in good condition. The nautical carnage includes some 300 wreck sites in all—an astonishing number—many of which are well preserved. As a general rule, the more recent the wreck or the more deeply submerged it is, the better its condition. Most of the well-preserved wrecks are to the north and east, and dive depths range between 25 feet and 80 feet. Several wrecks off the western end of the island are in relatively shallow water, 30 feet or less, making them accessible to novice divers and even snorkelers.

Fodor'sChoice
★ **Blue Water Divers Ltd.** The major operator for wrecks on the western side of the island, Blue Water Divers offers lessons, tours, and rentals. The lesson-and-dive package for first-time divers, including equipment, costs $99. From the Elbow Beach Hotel location, you can ride a diver-propulsion vehicle (DPV), which is like an underwater scooter, past a wreck and through caves and canyons. A one-tank dive for experienced divers costs $60, while a two-tank dive is $85. With two tanks you can explore two or more wrecks in one four-hour outing. For all necessary equipment—mask, fins, snorkel, scuba apparatus, and wet suit (if needed)—plan to spend about $40 more. Night dives are available, too. ⊠ *Elbow Beach Hotel, Paget Parish* ☎ *441/232–2909* 🖶 *441/234–3561* ⊠ *Robinson's Marina, Somerset Bridge, Sandys Parish* ☎ *441/234–1034* 🖶 *441/234–3561* ⊕ *www.divebermuda.com.*

Fantasea. You can explore the shallow reefs and shipwrecks with Fantasea guides. A single-tank afternoon dive costs $65, while a double-tank morning dive to two sites costs $85. Fantasea also offers a 3½-hour lesson-and-dive combination for $100. ⊠ *Sonesta Beach Resort, Southampton Parish* ☎ *441/238–1833* 🖶 *441/236–0394.*

Nautilus Diving Ltd. Nautilus Diving has locations on the south shore and Hamilton Harbour. A lesson-and-dive package costs $115 including equipment, the same as a single-tank dive. A double-tank dive costs $135. Group rates and multiple dives cost less. ⊠ *Fairmont Hamilton Princess Hotel* ☎ *441/295–9485* ⊠ *Fairmont Southampton Hotel* ☎ *441/238–2332.*

Scuba Look. For East End diving among wrecks and coral reefs, head for this outfitter in the Grotto Bay Beach Hotel. A range of dive tours is offered, as well as PADI (Professional Association of Diving Instructors) certification courses. ⊠ *Grotto Bay Beach Hotel, 11 Blue Hole Hill, Hamilton Parish* ☎ *441/293–7319* 🖶 *441/295–2421* ⊕ *www.scubalookbermuda.com.*

Snorkeling

The clarity of the water, the stunning array of coral reefs, and the shallow resting places of several wrecks make snorkeling in the waters around Bermuda—both inshore and offshore—particularly worthwhile. You can snorkel year-round, although a wet suit is advisable for anyone planning to spend a long time in the water in winter, when the water temperature can dip into the 60s. The water also tends to be rougher in winter, often restricting snorkeling to the protected areas of Harrington Sound and Castle Harbour. Underwater caves, grottoes, coral formations, and schools of small fish are the highlights of these areas.

Some of the best snorkeling sites are accessible only by boat. As the number of wrecks attests, navigating around Bermuda's reef-strewn waters is no simple task, especially for inexperienced boaters. If you rent a boat yourself, stick to the protected waters of the sounds, harbors, and bays, and be sure to ask for an ocean-navigation chart. These point out shallow waters, rocks, and hidden reefs.

For trips to the reefs, let someone else do the navigating—a charter-boat skipper or one of the snorkeling-cruise operators. Some of the best reefs for snorkeling, complete with shallow-water wrecks, are to the west, but where the tour guide or skipper goes often depends on the tide, weather, and water conditions. For snorkelers who demand privacy and freedom of movement, a boat charter (complete with captain) is the only answer, but the cost is considerable—$650 a day for a party of 18. By comparison, half a day of snorkeling on a regularly scheduled cruise generally costs $45 to $65, including equipment and instruction.

Fodor'sChoice
★ **Church Bay.** When Bermudians are asked to name a favorite snorkeling spot, they invariably rank Church Bay in Southampton (at the western end of the south-shore beaches) at or near the top of the list. A small cove cut out of the coral cliffs, the bay is full of nooks and crannies, and the reefs are relatively close to shore. Snorkelers should exercise caution here (as you should everywhere along the south shore), as the water can be rough. A small stall often sells snorkeling equipment, underwater cameras, and fish food.

John Smith's Bay. This popular snorkeling spot off the south shore of Smith's Parish has several reefs close to the shore as well as the added safety of a lifeguard overseeing the beach.

Tobacco Bay. This beautiful bay is tucked in a cove near historic Fort St. Catherine's beach, where shipwreck survivors first landed on Bermuda. Tobacco Bay offers wonderful snorkeling, and there is a snack bar near the shore.

West Whale Bay. Tiny West Whale Bay, off the western shore near the Port Royal Golf Course in Southampton, is quiet and typically uncrowded.

Snorkeling Equipment Rentals
Snorkeling equipment and sometimes underwater cameras are available for rent at most major hotels and at several marinas. The Grotto Bay Beach Hotel & Tennis Club, Sonesta Beach Resort, and Fairmont Southampton have dive operators on-site. A deposit or credit card number is usually required when renting equipment.

Horseshoe Bay Beach. A mask, snorkel, and flipper set rents for $16 per day here, or $10 per day for just the mask and snorkel. ⊠ *Off South Shore Rd., Southampton Parish* ☎ *441/238–2651.*

Pompano Beach Club Watersports Centre. Equipment at Pompano rents for $8 per day, or $4 per hour, for a mask, snorkel, and flippers. Each piece is also available separately. ⊠ *36 Pompano Beach Rd., Southampton Parish* ☎ *441/234–0222.*

Windjammer Watersports. You can rent mask, snorkel, and flippers here for $20 per 24-hour period. Two of three pieces cost just $10. ⊠ *Dockyard Marina, Sandys Parish* ☎ *441/234–0250.*

Snorkeling Cruises

Snorkeling cruises, offered from April to November, are a less expensive albeit less personal way to experience the underwater world. Some boats carry up to 40 passengers to snorkeling sites but focus mostly on their music and bars (complimentary beverages are usually served on the trip back from the reefs). Smaller boats, which limit capacity to 10 to 16 passengers, offer more personal attention and focus more on the beautiful snorkeling areas themselves. Guides on such tours often relate interesting historical and ecological information about the island. To make sure you choose a boat that's right for you, ask for details before booking. Most companies can easily arrange private charters for groups.

Hayward's Snorkeling & Glass Bottom Boat Cruises. Groups of about 35 people board Hayward's 54-foot glass-bottom *Explorer* for 3¾-hour snorkeling trips. Access into and out of the water from the boat is easy. Special excursions are arranged during the spring migration of the humpback whales. ⊠ *Adjacent to Hamilton Ferry Terminal* ☎ *441/236–9894* 🖃 *$50* ⊙ *Daily 9:45 AM and 1:30 PM.*

Jessie James Cruises. Half-day trips aboard the 40-passenger luxury Chris Craft *Rambler* cost $50, including gear and instruction. ⊠ *47 Front St., Hamilton* ☎ *441/296–5801* ⊕ *www.jessiejames.bm.*

★ **Restless Native Tours.** Captain Kirk Ward has regularly scheduled sailing and snorkeling trips to the outer reefs on a 50- by 30-foot catamaran. With a crash course in Bermuda's marine life, plus fresh cookies on board, it's hard to resist this popular outfitter. The tours depart from wharfs all over the island. ☎ *441/234–8149 or 441/234–1434.*

Soccer

Football (soccer) season runs from September through April in Bermuda. You can watch local teams in various age divisions battle it out on fields around the island. For details, contact the **Bermuda Football Association** (⊠ Cedar Ave., Hamilton ☎ 441/295–2199).

Squash

Bermuda Squash & Racquets Association. The club makes its four courts available to nonmembers between 11 AM and 11 PM by reservation, and a staff member may be able to hook you up with a suitable partner. A $10 per person fee (plus $5 to $7 court fees, depending on the time of day) buys 40 minutes of play, and you can borrow rackets and balls. Temporary memberships are available, if you plan to play a lot. ⊠ *111 Middle Rd., Devonshire Parish* ☎ *441/292–6881* ⊕ *www.bermudasquash.com.*

Coral Beach & Tennis Club. You must be introduced by a member to play on the two courts here. ⊠ *South Shore Rd., Paget Parish* ☎ *441/236–2233.*

Swimming

Beaches and hotel pools are your best bets for swimming, as there are no public swimming pools on the island.

Bermuda Amateur Swimming Association (BASA). Contact BASA to inquire about swim classes and competitions. Although there is no longer a National Swim Team, Bermuda's competitive swimming is still alive and well, with international swimmers and Olympians flying down several times a year to compete. ⊠ *Canal Rd., Pembroke Parish* ☎ *441/292–1713.*

Aquamania Swimming. Group and private lessons are offered in pools all over the Island. It's best to call or e-mail well in advance as Aquamania instructors are usually in very high demand. ☎ 441/234–3484.

Tennis

Bermuda has one tennis court for every 600 residents, a ratio that even the most tennis-crazed countries would find difficult to match. Many are private, but the public has access to more than 70 courts in 20 locations island-wide. Courts are inexpensive and seldom full. Hourly rates for nonguests are about $10 to $16. You might want to consider bringing along a few fresh cans of balls, because balls in Bermuda cost $6 to $7 per can—two to three times the rate in the United States. Among the surfaces used in Bermuda are Har-Tru, clay, cork, and hard composites, of which the relatively slow Plexipave composite is the most prevalent. Despite Bermuda's British roots, the island has no grass court.

Wind, heat (in summer), and humidity are the most distinct characteristics of Bermudian tennis. From October through March, when daytime temperatures rarely exceed 80°F, play is comfortable throughout the day. But in summer, the heat radiating from the court (especially hard courts) can make play uncomfortable between 11 and 3, so some clubs take a midday break. Most tennis facilities offer lessons, ranging from $25 to $30 for 30 minutes of instruction, and racket rentals for $4 to $6 per hour or per play.

Coral Beach & Tennis Club. Introduction by a member is required to play at this exclusive club, which is the site of the annual XL Capital Bermuda Open tournament in April. Coral Beach has eight clay courts, three of which are floodlit. It's open daily from 8 AM to 8 PM. Resident pro Derek Singleton is the man to talk to about scheduling lessons, which run $45 for a half hour. Tennis whites are required. ⊠ *Off South Shore Rd., Paget Parish* ☎ *441/236–6495 or 441/236–2233.*

Elbow Beach Hotel. This facility is fortunate to have as its Director of Tennis David Lambert, who is also president of the Bermuda Lawn Tennis Association. There are five Plexipave courts on hand, two with lights, and hours of play are 8 AM to 6 PM daily. Courts cost $16 per hour. Lessons and match play can be arranged for hotel guests or other visitors at $30 per half hour. ⊠ *Off South Shore Rd., Paget Parish* ☎ *441/236–3535.*

The Fairmont Southampton. Despite their position at the water's edge, the Plexipave hard courts here are reasonably shielded from the wind, although the breeze can be swirling and difficult. Six courts are at hand with fees ranging from $12 to $16 per hour on any of the three courts that have lighting. Hours of service are daily from 8 AM to 6 PM, until 8 PM in summer. Lessons from pro Mark Cordeiro are available at $40 per half hour or $75 per hour. ⊠ *South Shore Rd., Southampton Parish* ☎ *441/238–1005.*

Government Tennis Stadium. These are the busiest of Bermuda's tennis courts, their inland location ideal for combating strong winds. Of the eight all-weather courts available, five are Plexi-Cushion and three are Har-Tru. Three courts in the main stadium have floodlights. Hours are from 8 AM to 10 PM on weekdays and from 8 AM to 6 PM on weekends. Rates are $8 per hour during the day and $16 per hour at night. Tennis attire is required, and lessons are available from Eugene Woods starting at $30 per half hour and $50 per full hour. ⊠ *2 Marsh Folly, Pembroke Parish* ☎ *441/292–0105.*

Grotto Bay Beach Hotel & Tennis Club. A little more than a stone's throw from the Bermuda International Airport, Grotto Bay has four Plexipave cork-based courts, two lighted, with an hourly rate of $12. It's open daily, 7 to 7, with a midday break. Lessons are $25 per half hour and $45 per full hour. Tennis attire is required. ✉ *North Shore Rd., Hamilton Parish* ☎ *441/293–8333 Ext. 1914.*

Pomander Gate Tennis Club. There are five hard courts available (four with lighting) at this scenic club located off Hamilton Harbour. Temporary membership is available for $30 per couple per week. Hours of play are 7 AM to 11 PM on weekdays, until 10 PM on weekends. ✉ *Pomander Rd., Paget Parish* ☎ *441/236–5400.*

Port Royal Golf Course. Port Royal has four hard courts, two of which are floodlit. A host of pros are on hand to offer instruction to juniors and seniors—one is Starfield Smith who runs lessons for $20 per half hour and $35 per hour. Rates for court play are $10 per hour in the day and $14 per hour at night until 10 PM. Arrangements can be made through the golf club from 10 AM. ✉ *Off Middle Rd., Southampton Parish* ☎ *441/238–9430.*

Sonesta Beach Resort. The Sonesta offers players one of the more spectacular settings on the island, but the courts are exposed to summer winds from the south and southwest. The hotel has six clay courts, two lighted for night play. Rates are $10 per hour (free for guests), with lessons also available from the resident pro Cal Simons at $22.50 per half hour and $45 per hour between 9 AM and 6 PM. ✉ *Off South Shore Rd., Southampton Parish* ☎ *441/238–8122.*

Tennis Tournaments

Bermuda Lawn Tennis Association. Established in 1964, the association hosts all the important tennis events on the island. Ask for an events calendar. ✐ *Box HM 341, Hamilton HM BX* ☎ *441/296–0834* 🖷 *441/295–3056* ⊕ *www.blta.bm.*

XL Capital Bermuda Open. In April, the clay courts at the Coral Beach & Tennis Club host this ATP Tour, a USTA-sanctioned event of the world's top professionals. Big names, such as Patrick Rafter and Todd Eldridge, have played in this event, as well as several of Bermuda's own tennis stars, such as James Collieson. In November there is back-to-back tournament activity at the club, too. The action begins with the Bermuda Lawn Tennis Club Invitational followed by the Coral Beach Club Invitational.

Water Polo

Bermuda Water Polo Association. Established in fall 2002, the Bermuda Water Polo Association practices three times per week at the Bermuda Amateur Swimming Association pool. Anyone age 16 and up is welcome to join in the activity. For more information, contact Marc Fullerton, the founder of the association and a former high school and collegiate player in the United States and Canada. *Bermuda Amateur Swimming Association* ✉ *Canal Rd., Pembroke Parish* ☎ *441/292–1713.*

Waterskiing

Kite Ski. Unless you know a local with a boat, Kite Ski is your best option for waterskiing on the island. They offer lessons for first-timers, as well as knee-boarding, tubing, and even kiteboard lessons. Kite Ski also does watersport-theme corporate and birthday parties. While you are waiting your turn to ski, you can paddle around Harrington Sound in a kayak. ✉ *13 Harrington Sound Rd., Smith's Parish* ☎ *441/293–1968.*

Windsurfing

Elbow Beach, Somerset Long Bay, Shelly Bay, and Harrington Sound are the favorite haunts of Bermuda board sailors. For novices, the often calm waters of Mangrove Bay and Castle Harbour are best. The open bays on the north shore are popular among wave enthusiasts when the northerly storm winds blow. Only experts should consider windsurfing on the south shore. Wind, waves, and reefs make it so dangerous that rental companies are prohibited from renting boards there.

Even the most avid board sailors should rent sailboards rather than bring their own. Transporting a board around Bermuda is a logistical nightmare. There are no rental cars, and few taxi drivers are willing to see their car roofs scratched in the interest of sport. Rentals cost $25 to $35 an hour and $60 to $90 a day. Some shops negotiate special long-term rates.

Blue Hole Water Sports. Lessons and rentals are both available from Blue Hole. Rentals cost $30 for the first hour and $15 for each additional hour. ✉ *Grotto Bay Beach Hotel & Tennis Club, 11 Blue Hole Hill, Hamilton Parish* ☎ *441/293–2915* ⊕ *www.blueholewater.bm.*

Pompano Beach Club Watersports Centre. Pompano rents windsurfing equipment for $15 per hour. ✉ *36 Pompano Beach Rd., Southampton Parish* ☎ *441/234–0222.*

Windjammer Watersports. Windsurfing is a Windjammer specialty (at the Cambridge Beaches location only), and they have probably the best instructors on the island. Lessons cost $75 for 1½ hours. Equipment rentals cost $35 for the first hour, and $15 for each additional hour. ✉ *Cambridge Beaches, Sandys Parish* ☎ *441/234–0250.*

Yoga

Bermuda caught the yoga bug from its North American neighbors in the late '90s, although it's a slow-moving fad here. Many hotels, such as the Fairmont Southampton, offer free classes for hotel guests.

Integral Yoga Centre. Open one-hour classes cost $10 and are held Tuesday and Thursday at 12:10. Classes lasting 1½ hours cost $15 and are held Tuesday and Saturday at 9:30. The center also offers weekend health retreats. ✉ *Dallas Bldg., 8 Victoria St., Hamilton* ☎ *441/295–3355.*

GOLF

7

Updated by
Liz Jones

GOLF COURSES MAKE UP CLOSE TO 17% of Bermuda's 21.6 square mi of land. Swinging the club here is about as popular as going to the beach. Naturally, the scenery on the golf courses is spectacular—blue-green waves, semitropical flora, birds gliding on ocean breezes—and, although the courses tend to be short, they are remarkably challenging.

Of the eight courses on Bermuda, four are championship courses: Belmont Hills, the Mid Ocean Club, Port Royal, and Tucker's Point, and all are beautifully well kept. However, you should not expect the soft, manicured fairways and greens typical of U.S. golf courses. Just as courses in Scotland have their own character, those in Bermuda are distinguished by plenty of sand, firm fairways and greens, relatively short par fours, and wind—*especially* wind.

Because the island's freshwater supply is limited, irrigation is minimal and the ground around the green tends to be quite hard. That said, Tucker's Point and Belmont Hills, two courses completed in 2002 and 2003, respectively, do irrigate year-round and both seed their greens with TifEagle, a state-of-the-art, drought-resistant Bermuda grass that promotes fast and true putting.

Most Bermudian greens are seeded with some type of Bermuda grass and then overseeded with rye, which means that you putt on Bermuda grass in warmer months (March through November) and on rye when the weather cools and the Bermuda grass dies out. Greens are reseeded anytime from late September to early November, depending on the weather. Some courses use temporary greens for two to four weeks. Others keep the greens in play while reseeding and resurfacing. Greens in Bermuda tend to make for slower play than do the bent-grass greens prevalent in the United States, and putts tend to break less. Also, Bermudian greens are generally elevated and protected by sand traps rather than thick grass. Most traps are filled with soft, fine limestone sand and pulverized pieces of pink shell.

Another characteristic of Bermudian courses is the preponderance of rolling, hummocky fairways, making a flat lie the exception rather than the rule. Little effort has been made to flatten the fairways, because much of the ground beneath the island's surface is honeycombed with caves. Bulldozer and backhoe operators are understandably uneasy about doing extensive landscaping.

Keep in mind that all courses in Bermuda have dress codes: usually long pants for men, and collared shirts for both men and women. Restrictions may vary, however, so ask about the dress code when you call to make your tee-time reservation.

The ratings of Bermuda's golf courses, devised and administered by the United States Golf Association (USGA), "represent the expected score of an expert amateur golfer based upon yardage and other obstacles." For example, a par-72 course with a rating of 68 means that a scratch golfer would hit a four-under-par round, and ordinary hackers would probably score a little better, too. Ratings are given for the blue tees (championship), white tees (men's), and red tees (women's). Tee times are available by calling any of the courses directly. "Sunset" tee times (at lower greens fees) start at 3:30 PM in summer and at 1:30 PM in winter.

Lessons, available at all courses, usually cost $40 to $60 for a half hour, and club rentals cost $25 to $40. Caddies are a thing of the past, except at the Mid Ocean Club.

GOLF TOURNAMENTS

WITH EIGHT COURSES, *not counting the 9-hole course at Horizons & Cottages, Bermuda's golf competitions are many and varied and offer something for all categories of player. Overseas entrants are actively encouraged, but you will face stiff competition from the savvy islanders who are used to playing these challenging courses. The last day for entry to most competitions is about a month prior to the event.*

Golf season is almost year-round. The Bermuda Golf Association Calendar begins in early March with the Men's Amateur Match Play Championship at the Mid Ocean Club. With a handicap limit of 12, the tournament offers singles match play at scratch in flights. At the same time and venue is the Bermuda Ladies Amateur Match Play Championship. The Bermuda

Senior Amateur Championships are staged in early May for men and women at Riddell's Bay. A month later, the Bermuda Men's Amateur Stroke Play Championship is held over 72 holes for men and 54 for women at Port Royal. The Mixed Foursomes Championship is held in mid-September also at Port Royal, although the highlight of the year, the Bermuda Open (for men), takes place in mid-October at the same course. The end of the year sees the Four Ball Stroke Play Amateur Championship for men and women in early November at Port Royal. And December brings the main overseas competition, the Goodwill Tournament.

*For more information and entries contact the **Bermuda Golf Association** (✉ Box HM 433, Hamilton HM BX, Bermuda ☎ 441/ 238–0983).*

GOLF COURSES & CLUBS

🏌 **Belmont Hills Golf Club**
18 holes. 5,759 yards. Par 70. Rating: blue tees, 68.4; white tees, 66.8; red tees, 67.9.

Belmont Hills, opened in June 2003, was designed by California architect Algie Pulley and built on the site of the former Belmont Golf & Country Club. "Hills" was added to the name in honor of its new, steep contours. You are likely to be distracted by panoramic views of the Great Sound and Hamilton Harbour as you play, especially on the 9th, 17th, and 18th holes. A waterfall connects two, large man-made lakes that border the 2nd, 7th, and 8th holes. By far the most challenging are the final four holes: the 463-yard, par-four 15th; the 385-yard, par-four 16th; the 167-yard, par-three 17th; and the 412-yard, par-four 18th. (These are reputedly the hardest finishing four on the island.) Despite tough landscaping, you'll find greens sprigged with ultra-smooth TifEagle grass and fairways prettily defined by strategically planted palm trees. An automated irrigation system keeps the entire course in lush condition year-round. The owners have plans to build forty private residential homes and apartments over the next few years.

Highlight hole: Water winds round the scenic 7th hole, a par three.

Clubhouse: The clubhouse is slated to open in mid-2004 on the site of the former Belmont Hotel. Close to the 9th hole, it promises lovely views of the Great Sound and Hamilton Harbour, plus an airy lounge, a full restaurant (with al fresco seating), a bar, and a pro shop. ✉ *97 Middle Rd., Warwick Parish* ☎ 441/236–6400 🖷 441/236–6867 ⊕ *www.belmonthills.com* 💳 *Greens fees $75 weekdays, $95 weekends.*

Bermuda Golf Academy

When all you want to do is practice, head for the Bermuda Golf Academy's 320-yard driving range, which is floodlit at night until 10 (weekdays) or 10:30 (weekends). Of the 40 practice bays, 25 are covered. Eight target greens are placed 75 to 230 yards from the tees, and you can practice swinging out of a bunker. Golf lessons are available for $70 per hour.

A top-notch driving range notwithstanding, many golfers come to the academy with the little ones in tow solely to play on the 18-hole miniature golf course—the only one on the island. Pagodas, blue waterways, and a waterfall make the course seem like a tiny Wonderland. Negotiating the 16th hole means shooting a ball over a drawbridge. The mini-course is floodlit at night and takes about 45 minutes to complete. Inside the clubhouse is **Alegria Restaurant** (☎ 441/238–1831), under separate ownership. ✉ *10 Industrial Park Rd., off Middle Rd., Southampton Parish* ☎ *441/238–8800* ✆ *Driving range $4, $5 after 5* PM. *Miniature golf $7.50 weekdays, $8.50 weekends and holidays.*

♨ Fairmont Southampton Golf Club
18 holes. 2,737 yards. Par 54. Rating: none.

Unfurling on the hillside beneath the Fairmont Southampton Hotel, this golf course is known for its steep terrain, giving players who opt to walk (for sunset tee times only) an excellent work-out. The vertical drop on the first two holes alone is at least 200 feet, and the rise on the 4th hole makes 178 yards play like 220. The course is a good warm-up for Bermuda's full-length courses, offering a legitimate test of wind and bunker play with a minimum of obstructions and hazards. Ocean views are a constant feature of the front nine holes. There's no clubhouse, but a pro shop has the best selection of high-quality golf wear on the island, including designs by Bobby Jones, Descente, Ashworth, Thail, and Izod. You can pause at the 10th hole for snacks and sodas from the Golf Hut, or dine in any of the hotel restaurants. In summer, the Rib Room, close to the golf course, is particularly popular.

Highlight hole: The green of the 174-yard 16th hole sits in a cup ringed by pink oleander bushes. The Gibbs Hill Lighthouse, less than a mile away, dominates the backdrop. ✉ *Fairmont Southampton, South Rd., Southampton Parish* ☎ *441/239–6952* 🖷 *441/238–8479* ⊕ *www.fairmont.com* ✆ *Greens fees $66 per person with mandatory cart, $25 for sunset tee time without cart. Shoe rentals $8. Club rentals $25.*

♨ Horizons & Cottages Golf Course
9 holes. 756 yards. Par 3. Rating: none.

Part of the Horizons & Cottages colony, this Mashie, or irons only, course is ideal for beginners and players who are pressed for time, since it takes an average of 45 minutes to complete. No golf carts are available—understandable, given the longest hole (the 4th) is just 120 yards and the shortest (the 7th), a mere 51 yards. Hit a hole in one and your name will be added to the plaque in the Pub, which, dating to 1710, is the oldest part of the main building. Guests of the hotel are given preference for reservation times.

Highlight Hole: The 9th hole is the tightest and, with its elevated view of the South Shore, the most scenic. ✉ *33 South Rd., Paget Parish* ☎ *441/236–0048* 🖷 *441/236–1981* ⊕ *www.horizonscottages.com* ✆ *Greens fees: $20 weekdays, $25 weekends. Club rentals: $2.50 for set of three.*

A PROFITABLE PARTNERSHIP

L AND CRABS. They may be cute, sideways-walking creatures, but every Bermuda golf course manager knows they are a terror on the greens and fairways. Back in the '50s, '60s, and '70s, course managers relied heavily on pesticides to control the rampant population of land crabs, whose instinct to burrow left courses spotted with little caves and craters. Of course, pesticides did nothing to aid the efforts of local conservationists. Their aim was to restore Bermuda's open spaces to the natural beauty and abundance settlers found when they arrived on the island in 1609. The pesticides, which included DDT until the late '60s, were unabashedly detrimental to the bird population.

It was in the mid-1970s when Dr. David Wingate, then the president of the Bermuda Audubon Society, re-introduced the yellow-crowned night heron in Bermuda, bringing in several pairs from the Tampa Bay Nature Reserve. Natural shellfish predators, the herons had only to taste of few morsels of land crab, and they were well on their way to becoming the golf managers' best friends. Today, golfers will pause mid-swing to gaze at the pretty birds, which can be seen crab-hunting through just-mown fairways or roosting in the mangroves. And thick clouds of pesticide are no longer so common on Bermuda courses, which means you can see more than just herons when you are out hitting the balls. Eastern bluebirds walk daintily about the fairways. With nesting boxes built just for them on all courses, they are very much inclined to return the favor by pecking the courses clean of crickets, roaches, worms, and caterpillars. Migrating birds stop to rest in Bermuda in spring and fall, and one in particular, a white pelican from Canada, likes to return to the water at the Mid Ocean Club's 9th hole around Christmas time.

🏌 Mid Ocean Club

Fodor's Choice ★ 18 holes. 6,512 yards. Par 71. Rating: blue tees, 72; white tees, 70.1; red tees, 72.7.

It isn't Bermuda's oldest course—that honor belongs to Riddell's Bay—and other Bermudian courses are equally difficult, but the elite Mid Ocean Club is generally regarded as one of the world's top 50 courses. Something about it draws celebrities and politicians, like members Michael Douglas and Catherine Zeta-Jones, New York City Mayor Michael Bloomberg, and Ross Perot. Michael Jordon and tennis champion Patrick Rafter have also shot at Mid Ocean. Quite simply, the course has charisma, embodying everything that is golf in Bermuda—tees on coral cliffs above the ocean, rolling fairways lined with palm trees, doglegs around water, and windswept views. It's rich in history, too. At the dogleg 5th hole, for example, Babe Ruth is said to have splashed a dozen balls in Mangrove Lake in a futile effort to drive the green. The course rewards long, straight tee shots and deft play around the green while penalizing—often cruelly—anything less. The 5th and 9th holes, for example, require that tee shots (from the blue tees) carry 180 yards or more over water. And whereas length is not a factor on two fairly short par fives, the 471-yard 2nd and the 487-yard 11th, accuracy is. Tight doglegs ensure that any wayward tee shot ends up in trees, shrubbery, or the rough.

Highlight hole: The 433-yard 5th is a par-four dogleg around Mangrove Lake. The elevated tee overlooks a hillside of flowering shrubbery and the lake, making the fairway seem impossibly far away. Big hitters can take a shortcut over the lake (although the green is unreachable, as the Babe's heroic but unsuccessful efforts attest), but anyone who hits the fairway has scored a major victory. To the left of the green, a steep embankment leads into a bunker that is among the hardest in Bermuda from which to recover.

Clubhouse: Overlooking the 18th hole and fronted by the south shore, the Mid Ocean's peach-and-white clubhouse is classically Bermudian down to the interior cedar trim. Several of its rooms commemorate famous American and British 20th-century politicians who played the course—there's the Churchill Bar, the Eisenhower Dining Room, and the MacMillan Television Room. Breakfast, lunch, and dinner are served everyday, and fresh local fish is always on the menu. You'll also find a well-stocked pro shop. ⊠ *Mid Ocean Dr., off South Shore Rd., Tucker's Town* ☎ *441/293–0330* 🖷 *441/293–8837* ⊕ *www.themidoceanclubbermuda.com* 🗺 *Greens fees $200. Nonmembers must be introduced by a club member; nonmember starting times available Mon., Wed., and Fri., until noon, except holidays. Caddies $30–$35 per bag (tip not included). Cart rental $45.*

🏌 Ocean View Golf & Country Club
9 holes. 2,940 yards. Par 35. Rating: blue tees, 67.3 white tees.

One of Bermuda's busiest courses, Ocean View is known for a tough 9 holes before a magnificent backdrop of blue ocean beyond the island's north shore. It can be played as an 18-hole, 5,658-yard course by resetting the tees. The first hole is a tough par five with a long, tight fairway flanked by a 40-ft coral wall on one side and the shore on the other. An elevated green marks the par-four 6th hole; while the 9th has water guarding the front of the green, so shooting with accuracy is the key. Ocean View also has a 260-yard driving range, but drives are tricky when the wind is at your back, which is often.

Highlight hole: The green on the 187-yard, par-three 9th hole is cut out of a coral hillside that's beautifully landscaped with attractive plants. This is a demanding tee shot, and club selection can be tricky, particularly when strong winds are blowing from the north or west.

Clubhouse: Ocean View's Clubhouse houses the very popular bar and restaurant appropriately named **The Last Tee** (☎ 441/295–9069), where repartee is as much part of the scene as fresh seafood. A Bermuda codfish breakfast is served every Sunday from 7 AM to noon. Open every day, the bar really gets hopping during Friday night happy hour (5 to 7 PM). Summer barbecues are held on the terrace overlooking the North Shore. ⊠ *2 Barker's Hill, off North Shore Rd., Devonshire Parish* ☎ *441/295–9092* 🖷 *441/295–9097* 🗺 *Greens fee $58. Five-day three-course package (Ocean View, St. George's, and Port Royal) $240. Cart rental $13 per person for 9 holes, $26 for 18 holes; hand cart $8. Club rentals $25.*

🏌 Port Royal Golf Course
Fodor's Choice
★ *18 holes. 6,561 yards. Par 71. Rating: blue tees, 71.1; white tees, 68.5; red tees, 71.7.*

Jack Nicklaus ranked the Port Royal Golf Course among the world's best public courses. A favorite with Bermudians, too, the course is well laid out, and the greens fees are modest. By Bermudian standards, Port Royal is also relatively flat. Although there are some hills (on the back nine in particular), the course has few of the blind shots and hillside lies that prevail elsewhere, and the holes that do have gradients tend to run either directly uphill or downhill. In other respects, however, Port Royal is classically Bermudian, with close-cropped fairways, numerous elevated tees and greens, and holes raked by the wind, especially the 8th and the 16th. The 16th hole, one of Bermuda's most famous, is often pictured in magazines. The green sits on a treeless promontory overlooking the blue waters and pink-white sands of Whale Bay, a popular boating and fishing area. When the wind is blowing hard onshore, as it frequently does, you may need a driver to reach the green, which is 176 yards away.

Highlight hole: Like the much-photographed 16th hole, the 387-yard, par-four 15th skirts the cliffs along Whale Bay. The remains of Whale Bay Battery, a 19th-century fortification, lie between the fairway and the bay. Only golf balls hooked wildly from the tee have any chance of a direct hit on the fort. The wind can be brutal on this hole.

Clubhouse: With its pink walls and white roof and shutters, the Port Royal clubhouse has all the charm of a traditional Bermudian house. After a round of golf and an uphill walk to the clubhouse from the 18th hole, you may be ready for **Greg's Steakhouse** (☎ 441/234–6092). Bermuda cedar beams run the length of the dining room, and there is a patio which partially overlooks the south shore. Steaks, rack of lamb, fresh Bermuda fish, and pasta are always on the menu. The bar, open from 11 PM to 1 AM every day except Monday, has two 32-inch TVs usually broadcasting sports games. On Friday evenings, there's live entertainment and a happy hour from 6 to 8 PM. The pro shop stocks clothing and equipment; clubs not in stock can be specially ordered. ⊠ *Off Middle Rd., Southampton Parish* ☎ *441/234–0974 or 441/234–0975; 441/234–4653 for automated tee-time reservations up to 7 days in advance* 🖶 *441/234–3562* 🖾 *Greens fees: $130, $55 for sunset tee times. Cart rental $26 per person. Club rentals $30. Shoe rentals $15.*

🏌 ★ ## Riddell's Bay Golf & Country Club
18 holes. 5,800 yards. Par 70. Rating: blue tees, 68.5; white tees, 66.9.

Built in 1922, the Riddell's Bay course is Bermuda's oldest. In design it approximates a Florida course—relatively flat, with wide, palm-lined fairways. Black mangroves add to the scenery and come into play on the 7th, 11th, 12th, 13th, and 15th holes. You don't need to be a power hitter to score well here, although the first four holes, including a 274-yard par four and a 427-yard *uphill* par four might suggest otherwise. Despite the course's position on a narrow peninsula between Riddell's Bay and the Great Sound, water comes into play only on holes 8 through 11. With the twin threats of wind and water, these are the most typically Bermudian holes on the course, and accuracy off the tee is important. This is especially true of the par-four 8th, a 360-yard right dogleg around the water. With a tailwind, big hitters might try for the green, but playing around the dogleg on this relatively short hole is the more prudent choice. A few tees are fronted with stone walls—an old-fashioned touch that harks back to the old courses of Great Britain. Riddell's Bay is private and opens to the public only on weekdays. You may have better luck booking a tee time if you ask your hotel concierge to make the reservation.

Highlight hole: The tees on the 340-yard, par-four 10th are set on a grass-top quay on the harbor's edge. The fairway narrows severely after about 200 yards, and a drive hit down the right side leaves you no chance to reach the green in two. One pond guards the left side of a sloped and elevated green. The hole is rated only the sixth most difficult on the course, but the need for pinpoint accuracy probably makes it the hardest to par.

Clubhouse: The Riddell's Bay clubhouse, built in the 19th century, has locker rooms, a well-stocked pro shop, a Bermuda cedar bar, and dining rooms offering breakfast and lunch. Salads, sandwiches, burgers, and the Riddell's Bay fishcake are on the menu daily. ⊠ *Riddell's Bay Rd., Warwick Parish* ☎ *441/238–1060* 🖶 *441/238–8785* 🖾 *Greens fees $110 weekdays only. Cart rental (mandatory): $50. Club rentals start at $30.*

CloseUp

SECRETS FROM A GOLF PRO

MOST GOLF COURSES ELSEWHERE are designed with the wind in mind—long downwind holes and short upwind holes. Not so on Bermuda, where the wind is anything but consistent or predictable. Quirky air currents make play on a Bermudian course different every day. Some days a 350-yard par four may be drivable. On other days a solidly hit drive may fall short on a 160-yard par three. Regardless, the wind puts a premium on being able to hit the ball straight and grossly exaggerates any slice or hook.

The hard ground of most Bermudian courses means you must adjust your strategy used on lush, well-watered greens. For success in the short game, therefore, you need to run the ball to the hole, rather than relying on high, arcing chips, which require plenty of club face under the ball. It's also helpful to know that Bermudian greens are normally elevated and protected by sand traps rather than thick grass.

So, how should golfers prepare for a Bermuda trip? Answer: anticipate the wind and practice hitting lower shots. Punching the ball or playing it farther back in the stance may be helpful. Working on chip-and-run shots, especially from close-cropped lies, should also help. You can also save yourself some strokes by practicing iron shots from awkward hillside lies. On the greens, a long, firm putting stroke may keep you from the bugaboo that haunts many first-time visitors—gently stroked putts dying short of the hole. As Allan Wilkinson, the former professional at the Princess Golf Club, has said, "In Bermuda, ya gotta slam 'em into the back of the cup."

🏌 Tucker's Point Golf Club

★ *18 holes. 6,361 yards. Par 70. Rating: blue tees, 78.5; white tees, 68.5; red tees, 68.9.*

This gorgeous course, part of the Tucker's Point Club luxury resort and residential complex, opened in 2002 on the site of the former Castle Harbour Golf Club. The course, with 20 bunkers and TifEagle greens, was designed by Roger Rulewick, former senior designer for Robert Trent Jones. A one-acre lake by the 9th hole is used for irrigating the fairways and greens year-round and makes Tucker's Point one of only two fully irrigated private courses in Bermuda. The 4th hole, a par three, has the largest green on the course—watch for tricky undulations. Checking the yardage here is a good idea since this hole has multiple tees ranging 150 to 190 yards away from the hole. The 7th hole is a good driving hole; try to favor the left side to avoid the large bunkers on the right. Wind direction can affect your shot on the 14th hole, where a pear-shape green has three tiers flanked by bunkers to the left and right. You can warm up at the 240-yard driving range and the 10,000-square-foot practice putting green. Construction on the hotel is scheduled for completion in 2005. Nonmembers can reserve through resort hotels and cottage colonies on the island or be introduced by members.

Highlight holes: The 13th and 17th holes are positioned back to back in opposing westerly and easterly directions, respectively. The par-four 17th is arguably the most picturesque in Bermuda, with sweeping views of Tucker's Town and Castle Island. On the other hand, number 13 looks over the entire north coast and west end of the island. Try for an accurate drive to the narrow landing area, which is protected by a large fairway bunker.

Clubhouse: The Tucker's Point clubhouse sits atop a hillside overlooking the starting and finishing holes. Besides a pro shop and spacious, elegant locker rooms, it has a fully equipped fitness center. You can relax with a cocktail or dine al fresco on the second-floor veranda before panoramic views of Castle Harbour and Tucker's Town. ✉ *9 Paynters Rd., St. George's Parish* ☎ *441/298–6970* 🖷 *441/293–5159* 🌐 *www.tuckerspoint. com* ✉ *Greens fees $202 weekdays, $227 weekends with cart.*

🏌 **St. George's Golf Club**
18 holes. 4,043 yards. Par 62. Rating: blue tees, 62.8; white tees, 61.4; red tees, 62.8.

Short but brutal, St. George's course dominates a secluded headland at the island's northeastern end. No course in Bermuda is more exposed to wind, and no course has smaller greens. Some are as little as 25 feet across. To make matters trickier, the grass is hard and slick from the wind and salty air. Wind—especially from the north—can turn these short holes into club-selection nightmares. But don't let high scores here ruin your enjoyment of some of the finest views on the island. Many of the holes, particularly the 8th, 9th, 14th, and 15th, have incredibly lovely ocean vistas. The course's shortness and its relative emptiness midweek make it a good choice for couples or groups of varying ability.

Highlight hole: Pause to admire the view from the par-four 14th hole before you tee off. From the elevated tee area, the 326-yard hole curls around Coot Pond, an ocean-fed cove, to the green on a small, treeless peninsula. Beyond the neighboring 15th hole is old Fort St. Catherine, and beyond it the sea. With a tailwind, it's tempting to hit for the green from the tee, but Coot Pond leaves no room for error.

Clubhouse: Next to the 18th hole you'll find the clubhouse with locker rooms, pro shop, and **Mulligan's St. George's Golf Club Restaurant** (☎ 441/297–1836). The two dining rooms, bar area, and patio have a fine view of the North Shore and the ramparts of St. Catherine's Fort. Besides sandwiches, burgers, and salads, you can order the classic St. David's fish cake: a salt-codfish-and-mashed-potato concoction flavored with parsley and thyme. Dinner is served Friday until 8:30 PM. ✉ *1 Park Rd., St. George's Parish* ☎ *441/297–8067; 441/295–5600 tee times and information* 🖷 *441/297–2273* ✉ *Greens fees $60, $35 for sunset tee times. Cart rental $26 per person, hand cart $10.*

SHOPPING

8

FODOR'S CHOICE

A. S. Cooper Man, *in Hamilton*

Bermuda Arts Centre, *at the Royal Naval Dockyard*

Calypso, *in Hamilton*

Dockyard Glassworks and Bermuda Rum Cake Company, *at the Royal Naval Dockyard*

Trimingham's, *in Hamilton*

Windjammer Gallery, *in Hamilton*

HIGHLY RECOMMENDED

Astwood Dickinson, *in Hamilton*

Bermuda Society of the Arts, *in Hamilton*

The Bounty, *in St. George's*

Cow Polly, *in St. George's*

The Dive Shop, *in Hamilton*

Gosling's Black Seal Gift Shop, *in Hamilton*

Island Shop, *in Hamilton*

Sail On and Shades of Bermuda, *in Hamilton*

Stefanel, *in Hamilton*

Treats, *in Hamilton*

Walker Christopher, *in Hamilton*

IF YOU'RE ACCUSTOMED TO SHOPPING in Neiman Marcus, Saks Fifth Avenue, and Bergdorf Goodman, the prices in Bermuda's elegant shops won't come as a surprise. Designer clothing and accessories, from Max-Mara to Louis Vuitton, tend to be sold at prices comparable to those in the United States, but without the sales tax. Crystal, china, watches, and jewelry are often less expensive here and sometimes even on par with American outlet-store prices. Perfume and cosmetics are often sold at discount prices, and there are bargains to be had on woolens and cashemeres in early spring, when stores' winter stocks must go. The island's unforgiving humidity and lack of storage space means sales are frequent and really meant to sweep stock off the shelves.

Art galleries in Bermuda attract serious shoppers and collectors. The island's thriving population of artists and artisans—many of whom are internationally recognized—produces well-reputed work, from paintings, photographs, and sculpture to miniature furniture, hand-blown glass, and dolls. During your gallery visits, look for Bruce Stuart's abstract paintings, Graeme Outerbridge's vivid photographs of Bermudian architecture and scenery, and Chelsey Trott's slim wood and bronze sculptures.

Bermuda-made specialty comestibles include rum and rum-based liqueurs, and delicious local honey, which you can find in most grocery stores. Condiments from Outerbridge Peppers Ltd. add zip to soups, stews, drinks, and chowders. The original line has been expanded to include Bloody Mary mix, pepper jellies, and barbecue sauce.

The duty-free shop at the airport sells liquor, perfume, cigarettes, rum cakes, and other items. You can also order duty-free liquor at some of the liquor stores in town, and the management will make arrangements to deliver your purchase to your hotel or cruise ship. If you choose to shop in town rather than at the airport, it is best to buy the liquor at least 24 hours before your departure, or by 9:30 AM on the day of an afternoon departure, in order to allow enough time for delivery. With liquor, it pays to shop around, because prices vary. Grocery stores usually charge more than liquor stores. U.S. citizens age 21 and older who have been out of the country for 48 hours are allowed to bring home 1 liter of duty-free liquor. For more information, *see* Customs & Duties *in* Smart Travel Tips.

Shopping Districts

Hamilton has the greatest concentration of shops in Bermuda, and Front Street is its pièce de résistance. Lined with small, pastel-color buildings, this most fashionable of Bermuda's streets houses sedate department stores and snazzy boutiques, with several small arcades and shopping alleys leading off it. A smart canopy shades the entrance to the 55 Front Street Group, which houses several upmarket boutiques. Modern Butterfield Place has galleries and boutiques selling, among other things, Louis Vuitton leather goods. The Emporium, a renovated building with an atrium, has a range of shops, from antiques to souvenirs.

In St. George's, Water Street, Duke of York Street, Hunters Wharf, Penno's Wharf, and Somers Wharf are the sites of numerous renovated buildings that house branches of Front Street stores, as well as studios of local artisans. Historic King's Square offers little more than a couple of T-shirt and souvenir shops.

In the West End, Somerset Village has a few shops, but they hardly merit a special shopping trip. However, the Clocktower Mall, in a historic building at the Royal Naval Dockyard, has a few more shopping opportunities, including branches of Front Street shops and specialty boutiques. The Dockyard is also home to the Craft Market, the Bermuda Arts Centre, and Bermuda Clayworks.

Department Stores

Bermuda's three leading department stores are A. S. Cooper & Son, Trimingham's, and H. A. & E. Smith's, the main branches of which are on Front Street in Hamilton. The third or fourth generations of the families that founded them now run these elegant, venerable institutions; and you stand a good chance of being waited on by a Cooper, a Trimingham, or a Smith. In addition, many of the salespeople have worked at the stores for two or three decades. They tend to be unobtrusive but polite and helpful when you need them. The department stores in particular advertise planned sales or discount days in the local newspaper.

A. S. Cooper & Son. With branches in all major hotels, Cooper & Son is best known for its extensive inventory of crystal and china, with pieces and sets by Waterford, Swarovski, Wedgwood, Royal Doulton, Lladro, and Villeroy & Boch, many sold at 15% to 20% less than U.S. prices. A five-piece place setting of the Wedgwood Countryware pattern costs $64.20 (add about 15% for U.S. shipping, with duty, freight, and insurance). The store's private-label collection of clothing can be found in the well-stocked men's, women's, and children's departments. The gift department on the Front Street level carries a large selection of tasteful Bermudian gifts and souvenirs. ⊠ *59 Front St., Hamilton* ☎ *441/ 295-3961* ⊕ *www.coopersbermuda.com* ⊠ *Clocktower Centre, Dockyard* ⊠ *22 Water St., St. George's.*

Gibbons Co. One of Bermuda's oldest stores (still run by the Gibbons family) is also a fairly casual department store that stocks a wide range of men's, women's, and children's clothing, with brands such as Calvin Klein, Nine West, and DKNY. There's a substantial lingerie section, as well as quality handbags, purses, and scarves. Gibbons also has a sizable household department and is the exclusive supplier of Denby tableware, which sells at a much lower price than in Canada or the United States. The on-site Penniston-Brown perfume shop stocks many French, Italian, and American lines. ⊠ *21 Reid St., Hamilton* ☎ *441/295-0022.*

H. A. & E. Smith's. Founded in 1889 by Henry Archibald and Edith Smith, this is arguably the best men's store in Bermuda. Men's Burberry raincoats are priced from $555 to $665, and Johnston of Elgin cashmeres sell from $315. Men's 100% cashmere topcoats sell for $425, and Italian silk ties go for $26 and up. Linen Bermuda shorts sell at $46.

Burberry handbags (this is the only place in Bermuda they're sold) start at $160 for cloth bags and run up to $530 for certain leather bags. William Lockie cashmere turtleneck sweaters for women are priced from $278, while women's Burberry raincoats range from $575 to $695. The women's shoe department offers a broad choice of fine Italian styles, both classic and contemporary.

The Front Street–level china department carries a large selection of patterns from Royal Doulton and Rosenthal, with prices at 25% less than those in the United States. The store will also ship Rosenthal china anywhere in the United States with no delivery charge or added duty. Crystal of all types is also sold. Perfume sells at duty-free prices. As with many of the island's older buildings, the store has a confusing layout that makes it easy to get lost, though that may be what you're looking to do. Regardless, the staff is especially genteel and can help orient you. ⊠ *35 Front St., Hamilton* ☎ *441/295-2288* ⊠ *18 York St., St. George.*

Clothing, china, and jewelry in Bermuda are sold at prices similar to those abroad, but since there is no sales tax, you can get good deals, especially on high-end goods. If you see something you like, go ahead and buy it—comparison shopping isn't fruitful on Bermuda, as prices are typically fixed island-wide. In all but a few stores, shoppers leaving the fitting rooms are expected to return unwanted items to the store floor. The island's bounty of craft markets and artists' studios offers a multitude of inexpensive souvenirs, from Bermuda honey to hand-painted pillows. Buyers and sellers don't really bargain, although a vendor may offer a discount if you buy something in bulk.

8

Business Hours

Shops are generally open Monday to Saturday from 9 to 5 and closed on Sunday, although some supermarkets are open from 1 to 5 on Sunday. From April to October, some of the smaller Front Street shops stay open late and on Sunday. The shops in the Clocktower Mall at the Royal Naval Dockyard are usually open from Monday to Saturday 9:30 to 6 (11 to 5 in winter) and Sunday 11 to 5. Some extend their hours around Christmas. Almost all stores close for public holidays. Many of Bermuda's more exclusive shops have branches in the larger resort hotels.

Key Destinations

The three main department stores, Trimingham's, H. A. & E. Smith's, and A. S. Coopers & Son are excellent one-stop shopping destinations, but you may have more fun exploring the boutiques on Front Street and streets branching off it. For crafts, head to the Royal Naval Dockyard, where you'll find artisan's studios and a permanent craft market. The town of St. George's has a bit of everything, including lots of small, unique boutiques, where you might find the perfect island outfit or a Bermuda cedar model of a famous ship.

Smart Souvenirs

Small rum cakes from the Bermuda Rum Cake Company in the Dockyard make popular gifts and cost $9 duty free. Men may want to pick up a pair of real Bermuda shorts, which come in an array of bright colors, such as hot pink or royal blue. They sell for about $30 in department stores. The Outerbridge line of sherry peppers and other sauces is available at grocery stores and souvenir shops. Locals use them to flavor fish chowder, among other dishes. A Bermudian cook book makes a good accompaniment. An original photograph or painting is a meaningful, if expensive, souvenir. A coffee-table book of Bermudian art is another option.

Watch Out

It is illegal to take shipwreck artifacts out of the country without special permit. Likewise, visitors who want to export a Bermuda cedar carving or item of furniture that is more than 50 years old must apply for a permit at **Bermuda Customs** (⊠ 40 Front St., Hamilton ☎ 441/295–4816). A few stores in Bermuda sell Cuban cigars, but you may not bring them back to the United States.

Marks & Spencer. A franchise of the large British chain, Marks and Sparks (as it's called by everyone in Bermuda and England) is usually filled with locals attracted by its moderate prices for men's, women's, and children's clothing. Summer wear, including swimsuits, cotton jerseys, and polo shirts, is a good buy, as is underwear. The chain's signature line of food and treats, plus wine from all over the world, is at the back of the store. ⊠ *18 Reid St., Hamilton* ☎ *441/295–0031.*

Fodor'sChoice **Trimingham's.** Bermuda's largest department store has been a Hamilton
★ fixture since 1842. It's the home of Daks Bermuda shorts ($47.50) and Trimingham's own line of sportswear. Collections by Liz Claiborne, Tommy Hilfiger, and Calvin Klein, among other designers, are generally sold at prices comparable to those in the United States. You may find a great deal in the area behind the formal dresses. Women's clothing in this section is always on sale and up to 75% off original prices. The china department includes tableware by Mikasa, Lenex, and Spode, and is sold for 25% to 40% less than in the United States. The store has an impressive display of perfumes and cosmetics, and it's Bermuda's exclusive distributor of Christian Dior, Estée Lauder, and Yves St-Laurent. You'll also find a potpourri of fine leather, jewelry, children's fashions, and gift items. Trimingham branches—10 in all—can be found all over, including at Somers Wharf in St. George's, South Shore Road in Paget, and in Somerset Village. ⊠ *37 Front St., Hamilton* ☎ *441/295– 1183* ⊕ *www.triminghams.com.*

Specialty Stores

Antiques

The Bermuda Railway Museum. An extensive collection of historical artifacts from Bermuda's short-lived railway is in the museum. Plus, the museum shop sells photos, maps, books, prints, antiques, jewelry, coins, stamps, and china. If you take the bus here, get off at the first stop after the Bermuda Aquarium. The shop is open Tuesday to Friday from 10 to 4 or by appointment with Rose Hollis. ⊠ *37 North Shore Rd., Hamilton Parish* ☎ *441/293–1774.*

Second-Hand Rose. First-class second-hand English china, silverware, paintings, and knick-knacks fill this store. ⊠ *Hunter's Wharf, St. George's* ☎ *441/297–3353.*

Thistle Gallery. Antique British furniture, porcelain, china, glassware, and silver are laid out for sale in this large cottage store. ⊠ *7 Park Rd., Hamilton* ☎ *441/292–3839.*

Art Galleries

Art House Gallery. Watercolors, oils, and color lithographs by Bermudian artist Joan Forbes are displayed in this gallery. To be sure it is open, call ahead and make an appointment. ⊠ *80 South Shore Rd., Paget Parish* ☎ *441/236–6746.*

Fodor'sChoice **Bermuda Arts Centre at Dockyard.** Sleek and modern, with well-designed
★ displays of local art, this gallery is housed in one of the stone buildings of the former Royal Naval Dockyard. The walls are adorned with paintings and photographs, and glass display cases contain exquisitely crafted quilts as well as costume dolls, jewelry, and wood sculpture. Exhibits change frequently. Several artists' studios inside the gallery are open to the public. The center is open daily from 10 to 5. ⊠ *Museum Row, Dockyard* ☎ *441/234–2809.*

Bermuda Memories. Artist Jill Amos Raine displays her watercolors depicting Bermuda's houses, scenery, and wharfs in this small studio on the town square. ⊠ *7 King's Sq., St. George's* ☎ *441/297–8104.*

★ **Bermuda Society of the Arts.** Many highly creative society members sell their work at the perennial members' shows and during a revolving series of special group exhibits. You will find watercolor, oil, and acrylic paintings and pastel and charcoal drawings, as well as occasional photographs, collages, and sculptures. ✉ *Church St., West Wing, City Hall, Hamilton* ☎ *441/292–3824.*

Birdsey Studio. Renowned artist Alfred Birdsey died in 1996. Thanks to Jo Birdsey Linberg, his daughter, Birdsey's studio remains open and new works continue to be displayed at the studio, which is usually open weekdays 10:30 to 1, and by appointment. Watercolors cost from $50 and lithographs from $15. ✉ *Rosecote, 5 Stowe Hill, Paget Parish* ☎ *441/236–6658.*

Bridge House Gallery. Housed in part of a Bermuda home that dates from 1700, this gallery is of historical and architectural interest in its own right. During the 18th century the two-story white building was the home of Bermuda's governors. Today it's maintained by the Bermuda National Trust. Original works by local artists, inexpensive prints, and souvenirs are for sale. ✉ *1 Bridge St., St. George's* ☎ *441/297–8211.*

Carole Holding Print & Craft Shops. Commercial artist Carole Holding mass-produces watercolors of Bermuda's scenes and flowers; many of the same works are sold as signed prints and limited editions. Crafts, both imported and by local artists, are also available. Prices range from $15 for small prints to more than $3,000 for her framed original watercolors. ✉ *King's Sq., St. George's* ☎ *441/297–1373* ✉ *Fairmont Southampton* ☎ *441/238–7310* ✉ *81 Front St., Hamilton* ☎ *441/296–3431 or 800/880–8570.*

Clearview Art Gallery. The Clearview is owned by Otto Trott, a Bermudian artist known for his beautiful oil paintings of landscapes and local characters. His work can be found at other galleries, but often his best pictures are in his own gallery. Small watercolors are priced at $50, oils from about $200 to $2,000. Mr. Trott also gives painting lessons. ✉ *Crawl Hill, Hamilton Parish* ☎ *441/293–4057.*

Desmond Fountain Gallery. Mr. Fountain's sculptures may be seen at key locations around Bermuda, including the Bermuda Art Society galleries in City Hall, but his namesake shop is the place to go to purchase his work, in addition to selections by other local artists. ✉ *The Emporium, 69 Front St., Hamilton* ☎ *441/296–3518.*

Kafu Hair Salon. Proving that art can happen anywhere, artist and hairdresser Glen Wilks displays contemporary work, including paintings and sculpture, by local avant-garde artists at his salon. ✉ *8 Parliament St., near Victoria, Hamilton* ☎ *441/295–5238* 🖷 *441/295–1580.*

Masterworks Foundation Gallery. The Masterworks Foundation, formed in 1987, exhibits art by well-known Canadian, British, French, and American artists, including Georgia O'Keeffe and Winslow Homer, whose works were inspired by Bermuda. The Bermudiana Collection contains more than 400 works in watercolor, oil, pencil, charcoal, and other mediums. The Bermuda National Gallery locations at City Hall, Camden House, Government House, and Waterloo House all display selected pieces from this collection. ✉ *97 Front St., Hamilton* ☎ *441/236–2950* ✉ *Botanical Gardens.*

Michael Swan Galleries. Swan uses pastels to capture Bermuda's houses in a very special way. His depiction of the local architecture, in galleries and exhibitions all over the world, has made him one of the island's favorite artists. His two galleries also stock a good selection of designer collectibles and jewelry from around the world. ✉ *Walker Arcade, 12 Reid St., Hamilton* ☎ *441/296–5650* ✉ *Clocktower Mall, Dockyard* ☎ *441/234–3128.*

Omax Ceramics Studio. Christine Wellman shows her pastel ceramic tiles, mugs, vases, and crockery at her home studio in Southampton. An appointment is required. She may even agree to pick you up at your location and take you on a tour to the various vendors who sell her pieces. ⊠ *Southampton Parish* ☎ *441/292–8478.*

Picturesque. If you like photography, check out photographer Roland Skinner's two shops. His shots of Bermuda beach scenes and wildlife sell at $95 to $800. ⊠ *129 Front St. E, Hamilton* ☎ *441/292–1452* ⊠ *Clocktower Mall, Dockyard* ☎ *441/234–3342.*

Regal Art Gallery. Brightly colored paintings and prints by Robert Basset adorn the walls of this cheerful gallery and frame shop. ⊠ *86 Reid St., Hamilton* ☎ *441/295–7441.*

Fodor'sChoice ★ **Windjammer Gallery.** Individual and group shows in oil, acrylic, and watercolor are held regularly in this charming, four-room cottage, and work is exported to collectors worldwide. The knowledgeable staff can help with your selection and shipping arrangements. Benches in the pretty garden provide a restful spot to mull over a potential purchase. ⊠ *King and Reid Sts., Hamilton* ☎ *441/292–7861.*

Beauty & Perfume

Bermuda Perfumery Gardens. This highly promoted perfumery is on all taxi-tour itineraries. Free, regularly scheduled, guided tours of the facilities include a walk through the ornamental gardens and an exhibit on the distillation of flowers into perfume. At the Calabash gift shop you can purchase the factory's Lili line of fragrances as well as imported soaps and an assortment of fragrances. ⊠ *212 North Shore Rd., Bailey's Bay, Hamilton Parish* ☎ *441/293–0627.*

Peniston-Brown's Perfume Shop. In addition to being the exclusive agent for Guerlain products, Peniston-Brown's stocks an extensive selection of French, American, and Italian perfumes, as well as soaps, bath salts, and bubble bath. The Eau de Toilette Tempest Bermuda, a fragrance made from Bermudian flowers, is a popular gift costing $20 for 50 ml or $30 for 100 ml. ⊠ *23 W. Front St., Hamilton* ☎ *441/295–0570* ⊠ *6 Water St., St. George's* ☎ *441/297–1525* ⊠ *Gibbons Co., 21 Reid St., Hamilton* ☎ *441/295–5535.*

Scentsations. Perfumes by Ralph Lauren, Chanel, and other popular designers are sold at this accessible store. ⊠ *Washington Mall, Reid St., Hamilton* ☎ *441/296–8726.*

Sunshine Co. Although this shop caters mostly to professionals, it is open to the public on weekdays. The fantastic selection of OPI nail polish sells at $5 a bottle. OPI lipstick, other nail polish brands, manicure tools, blow dryers, and curling irons are also available. ⊠ *Dallas Building, 6 Park Rd., Hamilton* ☎ *441/295–6077.*

Bookstores

Bermuda Book Store. Owner Hannah Willmott keeps this bright little bookstore stocked with best-sellers, children's books, and special Bermuda titles (including some out-of-print books). ⊠ *Queen St., Hamilton* ☎ *441/295–3698.*

The Book Cellar. In a small space underneath the Tucker House, this shop crams in a surprisingly large selection of books about Bermuda and an interesting assortment of novels beyond the contemporary best-sellers. Coffee-table books and children's books are plentiful. Owner Jill White and her well-read staff will be happy to help you search for an obscure title. ⊠ *Water St., St. George's* ☎ *441/297–0448.*

The Bookcase. Three rooms full of floor-to-ceiling bookshelves hold a variety of British and American titles for all ages. ⊠ *International Centre, 26 Bermudiana Rd., Hamilton* ☎ *441/292–9078.*

The Bookmart. The island's largest bookstore carries plenty of contemporary titles and classics, plus a complete selection of books on Bermuda. Paperbacks and children's books are in abundance. This is also the place to come for greeting cards, balloons, and little gift items. ⊠ *Phoenix Centre, 3 Reid St., Hamilton* ☎ *441/295-3838.*

Buds, Beans & Books. Grab a fresh cup of coffee, a bouquet of flowers, or the latest best-seller at this books-and-more store. Snacks, sunglasses, and sunblock are among the other sundries. ⊠ *Front St. and Par-la-Ville Rd., Hamilton* ☎ *441/292-7658.*

Metaphysical Bookshop. This incense-scented store sells books on meditation, alternative medicine, numerology, and yoga. Owner Kelvin Richardson also offers a bountiful supply of wind chimes, cards, candles, and other gift items. ⊠ *77 Reid St., Hamilton* ☎ *441/295-5683.*

Washington Mall Magazine. Come here for Bermuda's best selection of magazines, including hard-to-find periodicals. You can also find novels, children's books, and publications about the island. ⊠ *Washington Mall, Reid St., Hamilton* ☎ *441/292-7420.*

Cigars

Chatham House. In business since 1895, this shop looks like an old-time country store. Thick, gray, lusty cigar smoke fills the air, and a life-size Indian Princess greets you as you walk in. You'll find top-quality cigars from Cuba (Romeo y Julieta, Bolivar, Partagas, Punch), Briar and Meerschaum pipes, Dunhill lighters, and Swiss Army knives. ⊠ *63 Front St., Hamilton* ☎ *441/292-8422.*

Clothing & Accessories

CHILDREN'S CLOTHING **Bears Repeating.** Stuffed with new and second-hand clothing for babies and children, this large consignment store is hard to navigate. Strollers and furniture are also on sale. ⊠ *129 Front St., Hamilton* ☎ *441/232-2474.*

IANA. Fine, Italian-designed and -made clothing for girls and boys newborn to age 16 are sold here at prices matching the quality of goods. ⊠ *Walker Arcade, 12 Reid St., Hamilton* ☎ *441/292-0002.*

Pirate's Port Boys. Casual wear for boys is crowded into this small store and sold at very reasonable prices. **Pirate's Port Girls** (⊠ Washington Mall, Reid St., Hamilton) has trendy, inexpensive clothes for toddlers to teens. ⊠ *Bermudiana Arcade Queen St., Hamilton* ☎ *441/292-1080.*

MEN'S CLOTHING **Archie Brown.** Sportswear, swimwear, and casual clothing is Archie Brown's focus. One room is devoted to Levi's, and another is devoted to Nautica. A Scottish cashmere and tartan outlet at the back has a good selection of sweaters, kilts, mohair rugs, and ties. Taylor's, the Archie Brown store in St. George's, is dedicated entirely to Scottish-made knits. ⊠ *51 Front St., Hamilton* ☎ *441/295-2928* ⊠ *Taylor's* ⊠ *Water St., St. George's* ☎ *441/297-1626.*

Aston & Gunn. An upmarket store owned by the island's English Sports Shop group, this handsome store carries European-designed men's clothing and accessories. Armani, Hugo Boss, Iceberg, and Van Gil are well represented. Aston & Gunn cotton dress shirts start at $100. ⊠ *2 Reid St., Hamilton* ☎ *441/295-4866.*

Fodor'sChoice ★ **A. S. Cooper Man.** This branch of the classy department store is first-rate, with a staff that is reserved and courteous, but very helpful when needed. The store is the exclusive supplier of Polo Ralph Lauren. ⊠ *29 Front St., Hamilton* ☎ *441/295-3961.*

The Edge. You will find trendy, casual clothing for men at this nice shop including brand names such as Quick Reflex and DKNY. ⊠ *Washington Mall, Reid St., Hamilton* ☎ *441/295-4715.*

English Sports Shop. This shop specializes in British knitwear. The store's own line of cotton sweaters is priced at $30, although cashmere sweaters start from $200. Upstairs is a good supply of men's business and formal wear, and children's clothes. Women's clothing and accessories are

CloseUp
BERMUDA SHORTS IN THE OFFICE

YOU MAY HAVE HEARD OF Bermuda's peculiar business fashion, and you may even have seen pictures of businessmen in shorts and long socks, but nothing can quite prepare you for the first sighting. First-time visitors have been spotted sniggering in shop doorways after discovering the bottom half of a blazer-and-tie-clad executive on his cell phone. After all, where else in the world could he walk into a boardroom wearing bright-pink shorts without so much as a batting an eyelid? Only in Bermuda. These unique, all-purpose garments, however flamboyantly dyed, are worn with complete seriousness and pride. Bermudians would go so far as to say it is the rest of the world that is peculiar, and they have a point—particularly in the steaming humidity of the summer months, when full-length trousers are unthinkable to any self-respecting local.

What is surprising is how the original khaki cutoffs evolved into formal attire. They were introduced to Bermuda in the early 1900s by the British military, who adopted the belted, baggy, cotton-twill version to survive the sweltering outposts of the Empire. By the 1920s Bermudian pragmatism and innovation were at play as locals started chopping off their trousers at the knees to stay cool. Tailors seized on the trend and started manufacturing a smarter pair of shorts, and men were soon discovering the benefits of a breeze around the knees.

But for an island that has a love affair with rules there was always going to be a right and a wrong way to wear this new uniform. Bermudas had to be worn with knee-high socks, and a jacket and tie were the only acceptable way of dressing them up for business. But it didn't stop there. Obsession with detail prevailed, fueled by gentlemen who were disturbed at the unseemly shortness of other men's shorts. A law was passed to ensure propriety, and the bizarre result was patrolling policemen, armed with tape measures and warning tickets, scouring the capital for men showing too much leg. Officially, shorts could be no more than 6 inches above the knee,

while 2 to 4 was preferable.

Other rigid but unwritten rules made it unheard of to wear them in hotel dining rooms after 6 PM or in churches on Sunday mornings, and even to this day they are out of bounds in the Supreme Court, although in 2000, legislation was changed to allow them to be worn, even by ministers, in the House of Assembly. Viewed as conservative and respectable men's wear for almost any occasion, they can be seen paired with tuxedo jackets and are even acceptable (provided they are black) at funerals.

If you're planning on joining in the local tradition, however, play by the rules. Don't expect to be allowed in a restaurant with a pair of check-patterned American interpretations. Real Bermudas are characterized by their fabric and styling— linen or wool blends and a 3-inch hem. The official shorts season is from May to November. Take your cue from the local policemen, who trade in their full-length navy blues at the start of summer.

But if Bermuda shorts are practical, smart dress for men, where does that leave the island's women during the sticky summer months? Wearing brightly colored cotton dresses and skirts, it would seem. Shorts are not considered ideal business wear for women and are only really acceptable on the beach and while shopping (but again, not if they're skimpy). In a country where pink is a man's color and men's bare legs are all but mandatory for six months of the year, perhaps the men feel the need to stamp their masculine pride on their pants. Whatever the motives, men have truly claimed Bermudas as their own and look set to be showing leg well into the 21st century.

—Vivienne Sheath

on the ground level. Another branch is in the Fairmont Southampton. ✉ *49 Front St., Hamilton* ☎ *441/295–2672* ✉ *Water St., St. George's* ☎ *441/297–0142.*

Flatt's Mens Wear and Big Men's Shop. Owner Mick Adderley runs the only shop on the island specializing in big-and-tall sizes for men. ✉ *13 North Shore Rd., Flatt's Village* ☎ *441/292–0360.*

The Sports Source. Popular with locals, the Sports Source offers men's and youth urban wear and hip-hop gear. The labels are trendy, but the prices are reasonable. ✉ *Washington Mall, Reid St., Hamilton* ☎ *441/ 292–9442.*

MEN'S & WOMEN'S CLOTHING

Davison's of Bermuda. Davison's offers exactly what you would expect of an island clothing store—light, comfortable cotton shirts, pants, and shorts for adults and children. Sherry peppers, aprons, teddy bears, and a collection of stuffed trolls are among the gift items. There's a branch in the Fairmont Southampton, too. ✉ *73 Front St., Hamilton* ☎ *441/ 292–2083* ✉ *Water St., St. George's* ☎ *441/297–8363* ✉ *Clocktower Centre, Dockyard* ☎ *441/234–0959.*

Makin Waves. Warm-weather sports clothing and swimsuits by Roxy and Quick Silver, among other brands, are sold at this beachy shop. There are also sunglasses, beach bags, flip-flops, and snorkeling and dive gear. ✉ *75 Front St., Hamilton* ☎ *441/292–4609* ✉ *Clocktower Mall, Dockyard.*

The Outlet. Reduced-price merchandise from the English Sports Shop, Ashton & Gunn, Cecile, and Crown Colony are sold here for up to 75% off the usual prices. ✉ *30 Queen St., Hamilton* ☎ *441/295–0084.*

Pier-Vu. Breezy beach clothes in natural fibers are the specialty in this small store. The flowy skirts, island shirts, and small, colorful tank tops are suitable for wearing on the beach or in town. Sunglasses are also on sale. ✉ *39 York St., St. George's* ☎ *441/297–4299* ✉ *Clocktower Mall, Dockyard* ☎ *441/234–6868.*

27th Century Boutique. Khakis, polo T-shirts, and dress shirts predominate in the sizeable men's section here. A small women's section has mostly office wear. Women accompanying men tend to gravitate toward the store's large supply of nail polish. ✉ *Imperial Bldg., 4 Burnaby St., Hamilton* ☎ *441/292–2628.*

Sasch. Part of the Stefanel group, this store brings the very latest, hippest fashions in casual, business, and dress wear from Florence, Italy, to Bermuda. The clothes are high quality, made of primarily natural fibers in neutral colors. Large men may have trouble finding a good fit as most sizes are for smaller frames, and some styles are body-hugging. There's also a small selection of trendy shoes and handbags. ✉ *12 Reid St., Hamilton* ☎ *441/295–4391.*

WOMEN'S CLOTHING

Benetton. This branch of the international chain has a wide variety of casual, chic women's and children's clothing, in both brash, bright colors and more subdued tones. ✉ *Reid St., Hamilton* ☎ *441/295–2112.*

Fodor'sChoice ★

Calypso. Bermuda's fashionable set comes to this boutique to spend plenty of money on sophisticated designer wear and Italian leather shoes. Calypso has the island's largest selection of swimwear. Pick up a straw hat and sunglasses to make the perfect beach ensemble. Eclectic novelty items from Europe make great gifts. Calypso's shop in Butterfield Place, **Voila!**, carries Longchamps handbags and Johnston & Murphy men's shoes. There are branches at the Coral Beach & Tennis Club, Sonesta Beach Resort, Fairmont Southampton, and Clocktower Mall at the Dockyard. ✉ *45 Front St., Hamilton* ☎ *441/295–2112.*

Cecile. Specializing in upscale off-the-rack ladies' fashions, Cecile carries such designer labels as Basler, Pucci, and Louis Feraud of Paris. There's a good selection of swimwear, including swimsuits by Gottex. An accessories department carries shoes, scarves, jewelry, handbags, and belts. The Fairmont Southampton has a branch. ⊠ *15 Front St., Hamilton* ☎ *441/295–1311.*

★ **Cow Polly.** Phoebe Wharton's store brings together expensive hand-painted clothing from Southeast Asia; beautifully crafted straw bags and hats; and unusual pottery and jewelry. The men's ties are unlike any you'll see elsewhere on the island. ⊠ *Somers Wharf, St. George's* ☎ *441/297–1514.*

Crown Colony Shop. This English Sports Shop–owned store sells quality formal and business wear for women. Look for Mayeelok silk dresses from Paris, and two-piece skirt and pant sets, which sell for $235 to $295. ⊠ *1 Front St., Hamilton* ☎ *441/295–3935.*

Eve's Garden Lingerie. Silk and satin panties, boxers, brassieres, and nightgowns, in sizes small to full-figure, are tucked away in this discreet shop at the back of Butterfield Place. Massage oils and an adult section are also available. ⊠ *Butterfield Pl., Hamilton* ☎ *441/296–2671.*

Frangipani. Owned by A. S. Cooper, this little store sells colorful women's fashions with an island-resort look. Cotton, silk, and rayon leisure wear are the backbone of the stock. Frangipani also sells a collection of hand-strung, brightly colored, beaded necklaces, bracelets, and earrings. ⊠ *Water St., St. George's* ☎ *441/297–1357.*

Jazzy Boutique. Lots of spandex and jeans are sold at this trendy juniors' clothing store. Plastic purses, faux-gem jewelry, and other colorful accessories tempt preteens of every ilk. Fortunately, the prices are quite affordable. ⊠ *Washington Mall, Reid St., Hamilton* ☎ *441/295–9258.*

MaxMara. Prices for this Italian designer's clothing average about 20% less in Bermuda than they are in the United States, although the accessories sell at much the same as U.S. prices. While the boutique is much smaller than its counterpart on Madison Avenue, it still has a good selection of conservative-casual wear and evening attire. ⊠ *57 Front St., Hamilton* ☎ *441/295–2112 Ext. 130.*

Ray Juan's II. Here you'll find women's plus-size clothing of all kinds, from lingerie to evening gowns. ⊠ *Washington Mall, Reid St., Hamilton* ☎ *441/296–2859.*

Revelation Boutique. Cool, contemporary linen clothing is the focus of Paulette Spence's small shop. ⊠ *79 Reid St., Hamilton* ☎ *441/296–4252.*

Secrets. Come to Secrets for sometimes understated, sometimes flashy, but always sexy swimwear and lingerie. The shop also carries massage oils and adult games. ⊠ *Washington Mall, Reid St., Hamilton* ☎ *441/ 295–0651.*

★ **Stefanel.** This popular Italian chain is good for simple, stylish, modern women's clothes, mostly made from cotton and other natural fabrics. The colors are neutral, sometimes with delicate small prints. Prices are commensurate with quality, seasonal sales are particularly rewarding. ⊠ *12 Walker Arcade, Reid St., Hamilton* ☎ *441/295–5698.*

Trim's Plus Fuller Figure Fashions. An offshoot of Trimingham's department store, this shop sells plus sizes only. Brand names, like Liz Claiborne and Harvey James, are well represented in both swimwear and casual wear. ⊠ *19 Queen St., Hamilton* ☎ *441/296–1578.*

Vibe. Funky clothes, shoes, and accessories at reasonable prices make Vibe a choice shop for women who want to keep up with the latest styles. ⊠ *5 Burnaby St., Hamilton* ☎ *441/296–4883.*

Coins

Bermuda Monetary Authority. This agency issues and redeems Bermuda currency, and also oversees financial institutions operating in and through Bermuda. At its offices in Hamilton, it sells collectors' coins, including replicas of the old Bermuda "hogge" money of the early 17th

century. Tree-frog, spiny-lobster, and tall-ship coins are among the many other pieces for sale. ⊠ *26 Burnaby St., Hamilton* ☎ *441/292–5278.*
Portobello. Coin collectors will salivate over owner Richard Mutzke's coins from all over the world, including, of course, Bermuda. He also sells antique prints and ornaments, but don't get too attached to what you see—some of the pictures adorning the walls are not for sale. ⊠ *The Emporium, 9 Front St., Hamilton* ☎ *441/295–1407.*

Crafts

Bermuda Clayworks. Miniature lighthouses, customized house-number plaques, and tableware are among the brightly painted pottery pieces created in this little shop. You can even buy a plain bisque item to paint yourself. The owners fire it and deliver it to your hotel or home. ⊠ *Maritime La., Dockyard* ☎ *441/234–5116.*
Bermuda Craft Market. The island's largest permanent craft outlet is the Dockyard's old cooperage building, which dates to 1831. Dozens of artisans show their work here, and you can expect to find baubles and edibles from Bermuda-cedar hair clips to Bermuda honey and jam. Quilts, decoupage, and handpainted glassware are among the prettiest souvenirs and gifts in the marketplace. ⊠ *The Cooperage, Dockyard* ☎ *441/234–3208.*
Bermuda Glassblowing Studio & Show Room. A restored village hall in the Bailey's Bay area houses this glassblowing studio, where artists create and display examples of their hand-blown glass in vibrant, swirling colors. You can watch the glassblowers at work and purchase the fruit of their efforts. ⊠ *16 Blue Hole Hill, Hamilton Parish* ☎ *441/293–2234.*
★ **The Bounty.** The spicy smell of cedar is the first thing to greet you in this tiny shop, where owner Kersley Nanette and his staff hand-craft teak and cedar model ships. The focus is on tall ships of the 17th and 18th centuries. Prices range from $150 to $2,000. Models of the *Sea Venture* and *Deliverance* are especially popular. You can also commission the staff to make the ship of your choice. ⊠ *19 York St., St. George's* ☎ *441/297–2143.*
★ **Island Shop.** Visit in the afternoon and you may meet the friendly owner and artist Barbara Finsness, who creates brightly colored, island-theme designs for ceramics, linens, and pillows. A number of her original watercolors are also available for purchase. ⊠ *Old Cellar La., Hamilton* ☎ *441/292–6307.*

Crystal & China

Bluck's. A dignified establishment in business for more than 150 years, Bluck's is the island's only store devoted exclusively to the sale of crystal and china. Royal Doulton, Royal Copenhagen, and Herend china competes with Lalique, Waterford, Baccarat, and Kosta Boda crystal in glorious displays, while Limoges porcelain boxes sit primly in their display cases. The courteous staff will provide you price lists upon request. ⊠ *4 W. Front St., Hamilton* ☎ *441/295–5367* ⊠ *53 Front St., Hamilton* ☎ *441/295–0244* ⊠ *Water St., St. George's* ☎ *441/297–0476.*
Vera P. Card. Lladró and Swarovski silver crystal figurines are available at almost identical prices elsewhere, but this store has the largest selection, including open-edition and limited-edition gallery pieces. The shop's collection of more than 250 Hummel figurines is one of the world's largest. Limited-edition porcelain plates and vases depicting Bermuda scenes cost $59 to $300. In addition, there are brightly painted, chiming cuckoo clocks. ⊠ *11 Front St., Hamilton* ☎ *441/295–1729* ⊠ *9 Water St., St. George's* ☎ *441/297–1718* ⊠ *Sonesta Beach Resort, South Shore Rd., Southampton* ☎ *441/238–8122.*

Electronics

Electronic City. Portable CD players and MP3 players are sold in this shop next to Four Seasons Furniture. ⊠ *45 Victoria St., Hamilton* ☎ *441/ 295-8915.*

M&M. A good selection of small and large electronic devices may be found at this big store, and the owners promise to beat prices elsewhere on the island. M&M also does repairs. ⊠ *Shoppers Fair Bldg., 61 Church St., Hamilton* ☎ *441/292-8158.*

Radio Shack. You can buy a camera or just replace your batteries at this reliable chain store. ⊠ *83 Reid St.* ☎ *441/292-2920.*

Gifts & Souvenirs

All Wrapped Up. Greeting cards, wrapping paper, and little gift items like aromatherapy oils are sold here. ⊠ *Washington Mall, Reid St., Hamilton* ☎ *441/295-1969.*

Bee's Knees. This small shop has souvenir T-shirts displayed from floor to ceiling. You'll also find sunglasses, postcards, keychains, and knick-knacks of all kinds. ⊠ *61 Front St., Hamilton* ☎ *441/292-6454.*

Crackerbox. Shells, shells, and more shells are what you'll find in this adorable souvenir shop. Big bins of them invite rummaging, and you can buy just one or a whole handful. Also for sale are charms and jewelry made from shells and sea glass (bits of colored glass worn smooth from tumbling in the ocean or, machine-tumbled to look that way). The store has its own line of Tobacco Bay Chocolate Beach Stones, chocolate candy colored to look like beach stones, and Bermuda Summer Breeze candles. ⊠ *York St., St. George's* ☎ *441/297-1205.*

Fodor's Choice
★ **Dockyard Glassworks and Bermuda Rum Cake Company.** This combination micro-bakery and glassblowing shop is a favorite among locals and visitors alike. Pull up an armchair and watch as artists turn molten glass into vases, plates, miniature tree frogs, and other collectibles. Afterward help yourself to the rum cake samples. Flavors include traditional black rum, rum swizzle (with tropical fruit juices), rum and ginger, and rum and banana. You can buy the cakes duty-free for $9, $17, and $25. If you purchase glassware, the company will pack the purchase then deliver it to your hotel or cruise ship. A small outlet in St. George's sells a collection of glasswork in addition to the cakes. ⊠ *1 Maritime La., Dockyard* ☎ *441/234-4216.*

Flying Colours. This family-owned and -operated shop, established in 1937, has the island's largest selection of souvenir T-shirts with creatively designed logos in hundreds of styles. The shop also carries everything for the beach—hats, towels, sarongs, toys for playing in the sand—plus other quality souvenirs, like shell jewelry. Educational toys are a specialty. ⊠ *5 Queen St., Hamilton* ☎ *441/295-0890.*

Foreign Cargo. Candles, oils, and incense are among the offerings at this shop that also stocks larger wrought-iron home accessories. ⊠ *15 Burnaby St., Hamilton* ☎ *441/296-3054.*

The Gallery. Co-owner David Pereira is happy to explain the history behind the items in this tiny store, which houses African masks, paintings, and sculptures. Pereira is also the exclusive retailer for Scottish pallette-knife painter Celia Collin, who once lived in Bermuda. Many of her watercolors portray the island. A set of four prints sell for $15, while her originals cost up to $2,000. Pereira himself makes jewelry using natural stones and 14-karat gold or sterling silver, and he works on commission. ⊠ *The Emporium, 69 Front St., Hamilton* ☎ *441/295-8980.*

★ **Gosling's Black Seal Gift Shop.** The rum maker's signature shop sells bottles of plain and flavored rum and tins of rum cake, plus T-shirts, ties, hats, and more, all with the Gosling logo, a black seal. ⊠ *97 Front St., Hamilton* ☎ *441/295-1123.*

Hodge Podge. This cluttered little shop, just around the corner from the Ferry Terminal and Visitors Service Bureau, offers pretty much what its name implies: postcards, sunblock, sunglasses, film, and T-shirts. It also sells imported shells and shell jewelry at low prices. ⊠ *3 Point Pleasant Rd., Hamilton* ☎ *441/295–0647.*

Howe Lifestyle. A variety of modern gift items including candles, frames, and photo albums may be found inside Howe's life-style store. The shop also carries some furniture and a good stock of Designer's Guild linens. ⊠ *27 Reid St., Hamilton* ☎ *441/292–1433.*

Littlest Drawbridge Gift Shop. Bermuda-cedar bowls, pens, and sachets are the highlight of this closet-size shop. Hand-painted apparel, and handcrafted pottery and wooden games, are also on sale. ⊠ *Clocktower Mall, Dockyard* ☎ *441/234–6214.*

The Living Centre. While the Living Centre and its sister stores deal mainly in high-end furniture, visitors have been known to drop in for some comparison shopping and to pick up accessories, like china or mirrors. ⊠ *41 Victoria St., Hamilton* ☎ *441/296–5284* ⊠ *Furniture Basics* ⊠ *49 Church St., Hamilton* ☎ *441/292–1844* ⊠ *Four Seasons Furniture* ⊠ *45 Victoria St., Hamilton* ☎ *441/295–8267.*

Onion Jack's Trading Post. Onion Jack's own line of sweet and spicy sauces are sold here, along with an assortment of flip-flops, beach wear, and sunglasses. ⊠ *77 Front St., Hamilton* ☎ *441/295–1263.*

Otto Wurz. It's hard to miss this Front Street store. Joke signs proclaiming such witticisms as LAUGH AND THE WORLD LAUGHS WITH YOU, SNORE AND YOU SLEEP ALONE fill its windows. Inside is a collection of model ships, silver and pewter jewelry, children's wood toys, and English silverware. ⊠ *3 Front St., Hamilton* ☎ *441/295–1247.*

Pulp & Circumstance. If it's an original, quality gift you're after, look no further. The Reid Street store sells exquisite, modern picture frames in all shapes and sizes and from all over the world, plus candles, bath products, gifts for babies, and greeting cards. The Pulp & Circumstance stationery store in Windsor Place, just behind the main one, sells photo albums, pens, and Bermuda-theme stationery. Delicate pastel notepaper engraved with pictures of Gombey dancers or dinghies sells for $35 per box. ⊠ *Reid and Queen Sts., Hamilton* ☎ *441/292–9586* ⊠ *Windsor Pl., Queen St., Hamilton* ☎ *441/292–8886.*

Rising Sun Shop. This country store is easy to spot with its eye-catching inventory usually hanging outside the entrance. Novelty gift items may include a ship decanter, picnic baskets, and silly toilet plungers—though inventory changes frequently. ⊠ *Middle Rd., Southampton Parish* ☎ *441/238–2154.*

★ **Sail On and Shades of Bermuda.** Owned and operated by Hubert Watlington, a former Olympic windsurfer and top local sailor, this shop stocks a gigantic selection of sunglasses; outdoor clothing and swimwear by such brands as Patagonia and Helly Hanson; plus wacky toys and gifts. The store is tucked into an little alley, opposite No. 1 Shed and a cruise-ship dock. ⊠ *Old Cellar La., off Front St., Hamilton* ☎ *441/295–0808.*

Towne Crier. One of St. George's numerous souvenir shops, the small Towne Crier in the square is a convenient spot to pick up Bermuda T-shirts, windbreakers, hats, and shell jewelry. ⊠ *King's Square, St. George's* ☎ *441/297–0874.*

★ ♳ **Treats.** You'll find bulk candy in just about every flavor here. The Candygramme gift box is filled with candy of your choice and decorated with a balloon. Prices start at $15. ⊠ *Washington Mall, Reid St., Hamilton* ☎ *441/296–1123.*

Grocery Stores

Many of the accommodations on Bermuda allow you to do your own cooking. Considering how expensive the island is, this option has widespread appeal for travelers on a budget. Still, groceries are relatively expensive. A dozen imported large eggs cost about $2.50. Locally raised eggs are even more expensive, about $4 a dozen. A loaf of Bermuda-made bread is $2.50, while U.S. bread is $4. And a 13-ounce can of coffee is $8.50. Unless stated otherwise, grocery stores carry liquor. Many grocery stores offer 5% off cash purchases on Wednesday. It's customary to tip the person who bags your groceries $1 or $2 for their efforts. For a small purchase, spare change is fine.

A-One Paget. This grocery is near Barnsdale Guest Apartments and the Sky Top Cottages. Be warned, however, that the route between Sky Top and the store takes in a significant hill, which could make for a difficult hike if you buy a lot. ⊠ *Middle Rd., Paget Parish* ☎ *441/236–0351.*

Dismont Robinson. Locals turn to this convenience store on holidays or during odd hours when other stores are closed. It's open daily from 8 AM to 10 PM, and it carries a small stock of food, plus ice, wine, beer, and spirits. ⊠ *135 Front St., Hamilton* ☎ *441/292–4301.*

Esso Tiger Market. If you need sundries or munchies in the early hours of the morning, this 24-hour convenience store is the only place to go in Hamilton. Beyond cigarettes and frozen foods, it stocks film, aspirin, and coffee. ⊠ *37 Richmond Rd., Hamilton* ☎ *441/295–3776.*

Harrington Hundreds Grocery & Liquor Store. Harrington is a must for those observing special diets or seeking out unusual ingredients. It has the island's best selection of wheat-free foods, including gluten-free pastas, breads, and cookies. It's close to Spittal Pond and Angel's Grotto, but not within walking distance. ⊠ *South Shore Rd., Smith's Parish* ☎ *441/293–1635.*

Heron Bay Marketplace. Part of the island-wide Marketplace chain of stores, this one has a large selection of fresh vegetables. It's convenient to Longtail Cliffs and Marley Beach, but not on foot. ⊠ *Middle Rd., Southampton Parish* ☎ *441/238–1993.*

Lindo's Family Foods, Ltd. Lindo's is a medium-size store with a good selection of organic foods, fresh seafood, and fine imported French and Italian cheese and pâtes. It's within walking distance of the several Warwick accommodations. ⊠ *Middle Rd., Warwick Parish* ☎ *441/236–1344.*

The Marketplace. The island's largest grocery store, and the chain's headquarters, Marketplace offers homemade hot soups, stir-fries, salads, dinners, and desserts for about $7 a pound. This branch is also open Sunday 1–5. ⊠ *Church St. near Parliament St., Hamilton* ☎ *441/292–3163.*

Miles Market. Miles is Bermuda's Balducci's, with a large selection of upscale or hard-to-get specialty food items and high-quality imported and local meats and fish. Many items are on the expensive side, but the quality and selection here are unsurpassed in Bermuda. The market delivers anywhere on the island. ⊠ *Pitts Bay Rd. near the Fairmont Hamilton Princess, Hamilton* ☎ *441/295–1234.*

Modern Mart. Part of the Marketplace chain, but smaller than its flagship Hamilton store this location has all the essentials. It's easily accessible from Sky Top Cottages, Loughlands, and other south-shore hotels. ⊠ *South Shore Rd., Paget Parish* ☎ *441/236–6161.*

Rock On–The Health Store. Nutritional supplements, natural remedies, and environmentally friendly toiletries are among the goods offered at one of Bermuda's few health stores. The knowledgeable staff will guide customers in their selections, but there are also plenty of books available, too. ⊠ *The Emporium, Front St., Hamilton* ☎ *441/295–8537.*

Shelly Bay Marketplace. This branch of the Marketplace chain is the only large grocery on North Shore Road. ⊠ *North Shore Rd., Hamilton Parish* ☎ *441/293–0966.*

Somerset Marketplace. The largest grocery store on the island's western end, it's convenient to Whale Bay Inn, but take a moped or taxi. ⊠ *Somerset Rd., Sandys Parish* ☎ *441/234–0626.*

Somers Supermarket. Despite its small size, Somers has a large selection, with hot food, salads, and sandwiches made fresh daily. It offers free delivery service within St. George's, and it's open Monday to Saturday from 7 AM to 9 PM, and Sunday from 8 AM to 8 PM. ⊠ *York St., St. George's* ☎ *441/297–1177.*

The Supermart. English products, including the Waitrose brand, are the specialty of this store, which stocks all the usual groceries. You can pick up a picnic lunch at the well-stocked salad and hot food bar. ⊠ *Front St. near King St., Hamilton* ☎ *441/292–2064.*

Jewelry & Watches

★ **Astwood Dickinson.** Established in 1904, this store has built a reputation for its exquisite collection of unmounted stones; upmarket jewelry, including designs by Baccarat and Tiffany and Co.; and wide range of Swiss watches. Cartier, Oakley, and Tag Heuer watches, among other famous names, are sold for up to 20% less than in the United States. The shop's Bermuda Collection, exclusively designed and created in the upstairs workshop, ranges from 18-karat gold charms to bejeweled pendants representing the island's flora and fauna. ⊠ *83–85 Front St., Hamilton* ☎ *441/292–5805* ⊠ *H. A. & E. Smith's, Front St., Hamilton* ☎ *441/296–6664* ⊠ *Walker Arcade, Hamilton* ☎ *441/292–4247.*

Crisson's. The only store in Bermuda carrying Rolex, Curum, and Movado, Crisson's attracts well-heeled customers who come here to buy merchandise at prices 20% to 30% off those at home. Earrings are a specialty, and there's a large selection. The gift department carries English flatware, Saint Louis crystal, and imported baubles, bangles, and beads. ⊠ *55 and 71 Front St., Hamilton* ☎ *441/295–2351* ⊠ *16 Queen St., Hamilton* ☎ *441/295–2351* ⊠ *20 Reid St., Hamilton* ☎ *441/295–2351* ⊠ *Elbow Beach Hotel, South Shore Rd., Paget Parish* ☎ *441/236–9928* ⊠ *Sonesta Beach Resort, South Shore Rd., Southampton Parish* ☎ *441/238–0072* ⊠ *York and Kent Sts., St. George's* ☎ *441/297–0672* ⊠ *Water St., St. George's* ☎ *441/297–0107.*

E. R. Aubrey. Gold and tanzanite are the specialties of this Hamilton jeweler. The store also carries a large selection of certified diamonds and promises to match prices as long as they can be verified. ⊠ *19 Front St., Hamilton* ☎ *441/295–3826* ⊠ *101 Front St., Hamilton* ☎ *441/296–3171.*

Everrich Jewelry. This bargain jewelry store stocks countless styles of basic gold and silver chains, earrings, bangles, and rings. ⊠ *28 Queen St., Hamilton* ☎ *441/295–2110.*

Gem Cellar. Jewelers here make Bermuda-theme charms selling for $40 to $200, and they can turn around custom-designed gold and silver jewelry in one to two days. ⊠ *Old Cellar La., Hamilton* ☎ *441/292–3042.*

Solomon's. Manager Allan Porter and his skilled staff custom-design charming, one-of-a-kind pieces costing from $70 to upwards of $100,000. ⊠ *17 Front St., Hamilton* ☎ *441/292–4742 or 441/295–1003.*

Swiss Timing. The staff offers jewelry repairs and custom designs, as well as pieces from Germany, England, and Italy. ⊠ *95 Front St., Hamilton* ☎ *441/295–1376.*

Vera P. Card. Known primarily for crystal and porcelain figurines, this shop also carries fine and costume jewelry, including an extensive tanzanite ring collection. ⊠ *11 Front St., Hamilton* ☎ *441/295–1729* ⊠ *9*

Water St., St. George's ☎ *441/297-1718* ✉ *Sonesta Beach Resort, South Shore Rd., Southampton Parish* ☎ *441/238-8122.*

★ **Walker Christopher.** *The Bermudian* magazine has named this goldsmith the island's best for fine jewelry. You can work with a jeweler to design your own exclusive piece or choose from classic diamond bands, strands of South Sea pearls, and the more contemporary hand-hammered chokers. Walker Christopher is the only Bermuda retailer carrying the Galatea diamond and pearl collection. The workshop also produces a line of Bermuda-inspired gold jewelry and sterling silver Christmas ornaments. ✉ *9 Front St., Hamilton* ☎ *441/295-1466* ✉ *A. S. Cooper, 59 Front St., Hamilton* ☎ *441/295-3961.*

Linens

House of Linens. A wide collection of hand-embroidered table, bed, and bath linens can be found at this shop, which also sells baby linens and infant wear. ✉ *Washington Mall, Reid St., Hamilton* ☎ *441/296-0189.*
Irish Linen Shop. In a cottage that looks as though it belongs in Dublin, this shop is the place for Irish linen tablecloths. Prices range from less than $10 to more than $3,000. Antique tablecloths can cost nearly $2,000. The best buys are the Irish linen tea towels for around $10. From Madeira come exquisite hand-embroidered handkerchiefs, plus linen sheets and pillowcases, and cotton organdy christening robes with slip and bonnet, hand-embroidered with garlands and tiers of Valenciennes lace (from $220 to more than $800). The store has an exclusive arrangement with Souleiado, maker of the vivid prints from Provence that are available in tablecloths, place mats, and bags, as well as by the yard—the last at a huge savings over U.S. prices. ✉ *31 Front St., Hamilton* ☎ *441/295-4089.*

Liquor Stores

Bermuda liquor stores have a good selection of wines and spirits. Each has branches sprinkled around the island from St. George's to Somerset. Spirits are sold for the same prices in liquor stores and a bit more in grocery stores.

Bermuda Duty Free Shop. The airport store invites you to put together your own package of Bermuda liquors at in-bond (duty-free) prices. Gosling's Black Seal rum and rum cakes are among the native products. ✉ *Bermuda International Airport, 3 Cahow Way, St. George's* ☎ *441/293-2870.*
Burrows Lightbourn. This chain has a comprehensive selection and stores all over the island. ✉ *Front St., Hamilton* ☎ *441/295-0176* ✉ *Harbour Rd., Paget* ☎ *441/236-0355* ✉ *Water St., St. George's* ☎ *441/297-0552* ✉ *Main Rd., Somerset* ☎ *441/234-0963.*
Gosling Bros. Ltd. The maker of Bermuda's Black Seal rum also stocks a full selection of wines and other liquors at its stores. The helpful and knowledgeable staff provides excellent advice. Gosling's does export its products, but they are not always as readily available as rums from the Caribbean countries. ✉ *Front and Queen Sts., Hamilton* ☎ *441/295-1123* ✉ *York and Queen Sts., St. George's* ☎ *441/298-7339.*

Luggage

Harbourmaster. Tumi luggage and briefcases, among other brands, are sold here. ✉ *Washington Mall, Reid St., Hamilton* ☎ *441/295-5333.*

Music

The Music Box. Stereos and other electronics are crammed into the window of this independent store. Inside is a small but diverse collection of new CDs and DVDs. ✉ *58 Reid St., Hamilton* ☎ *441/295-4839.*
Music World. Every genre from pop to gospel to local sounds may be found at this major store. ✉ *Bermudiana Arcade, 27 Queen St., Hamilton* ☎ *441/292-8785.*

YO, HO, HO & A BOTTLE OF RUM

ONE OF THE DISTINCT PLEASURES in a visit to Bermuda is getting to sample a bit of island rum and rum-based products. Gosling's Black Seal Rum is perhaps the best-loved by locals. It's darker and thicker than the usual stuff, with a hint of a caramel flavor—especially when mixed with carbonated ginger beer to make a Dark and Stormy, a famous Bermuda drink (treat it with respect and caution).

Gosling's is one of Bermuda's oldest companies, and its Hamilton liquor shop was established in 1806. Gosling's Black Seal Rum was sold in barrels until just after World War I and inherited its name from the black sealing wax that sealed the barrel corks. In its 151-proof variety, Black Seal will test the strongest drinker. Many prefer to buy it in the standard 80 proof.

Bermuda's "rum swizzle," another popular drink, also uses the ubiquitous Black Seal Rum, along with a splash of club soda, lime juice, and sugar. Gosling also produces three liqueurs that are big favorites—Bermuda Gold, Bermuda Banana Liqueur, and Bermuda Coconut Rum. These liqueurs can be ordered everywhere, from poolside bars to late-night jazz clubs. They're even found in cakes, as you soon discover in gift shops and on restaurant menus. Classic Bermuda rum cakes are a delicious, non-toxic way to taste the island's famous export. Fear not if rum's not your thing: Guinness and Heineken are among the widely available imported beers.

Sound Stage. Small but fairly comprehensive, Sound Stage stocks new-release, mainstream CDs and DVDs. ⊠ *Washington Mall, Reid St., Hamilton* ☎ *441/292–0811.*

Photo Equipment

Jiffy Photo. In addition to photo developing, owner David Burgess sells film and a small supply of Fujifilm, Pentax, and Canon digital and film cameras. A small museum at the front of the store has a collection of cameras donated or left behind by customers. ⊠ *5 Burnaby St., Hamilton* ☎ *441/295–4436.*

Stuart's On Reid Street. Stuart's has the island's largest stock of digital and film cameras and camcorders by makers such as Nikon, Canon, Olympus, Minolta, and Pentax. Stereo equipment and other small electronics are also available. ⊠ *5 Reid St., Hamilton* ☎ *441/295–5146.*

Shoes & Handbags

Boyle, W. J. & Sons Ltd. Bermuda's leading shoe-store chain, Boyle's sells a wide range of men's, women's, and children's shoes. **Trends** on Reid Street has the most up-to-the-minute foot fashions, although the **Sports Locker** has a good stock of running shoes and flip-flops. The Church Street store specializes in children's shoes. ⊠ *Queen St., Hamilton* ☎ *441/295–1887* ⊠ *Mangrove Bay, Somerset* ☎ *441/234–0530* ⊠ *Water St., St. George's* ☎ *441/297–1922* ⊠ *Trends, The Walkway, Reid St., Hamilton* ☎ *441/295–6420* ⊠ *The Sports Locker, Windsor Place, 18 Queen St., Hamilton* ☎ *441/292–3300* ⊠ *Children's Shop, Church St., Hamilton* ☎ *441/292–6360.*

Calypso. Women looking for quirky, snazzy footwear often visit Calypso's main store. The shoe and bag section is small but with choice, super-trendy, somewhat weird styles and colors. Items may cost a little more than you want to spend, but serious bargains can be had during sales.

There are branches at Coral Beach & Tennis Club, Sonesta Beach Resort, Fairmont Southampton, and Clocktower Centre in the Dockyard. ⊠ *45 Front St., Hamilton* ☎ *441/295–2112.*

Colosseum. Pricey but gorgeous Italian shoes, bags, and leather jackets for men, women, and children are on offer at Colosseum. Prices are slashed drastically if you are lucky enough to catch a seasonal sale. ⊠ *Washington Mall, Reid St., Hamilton* ☎ *441/292–0116.*

Locomotion. Italian, Spanish, and American shoes for women and children are sold in this small store. ⊠ *Washington Mall, Reid St., Hamilton* ☎ *441/296–4030.*

Louis Vuitton. Come here to find the famous monogram on ladies' handbags, men's and women's briefcases, carry-on luggage, wallets, credit-card cases, and other items. Prices here are the same as in the United States, except there's no tax. Small ladies' handbags start at about $750. Small, soft leather carry-ons cost up to $1,000, and natural cowhide briefcases start from $3,000. ⊠ *Butterfield Pl., Front St., Hamilton* ☎ *441/ 296–1940.*

Personality Footworks. This shop offers trendy, bargain-price shoes for women and children. The store has a very good selection of formal sandals. ⊠ *Washington Mall, Reid St., Hamilton* ☎ *441/292–9317.*

Quattro. For the very latest shoe styles from Florence and Rome, check out this closet-size shoe shop. The men's and women's shoes are beautifully made, but prices can be high. ⊠ *12 Reid St., Hamilton* ☎ *441/ 295–9815.*

REPAIRS **Heel Quik.** Locals swear by this store's friendly, expert staff. They offer same-day service on shoe repair and minor luggage repair. The store also sells some luggage, plus shoe polish, laces, and umbrellas. ⊠ *35 Church St., Hamilton* ☎ *441/295–1559.*

Sporting Goods

★ **The Dive Shop.** The best prices for dive gear are found, naturally, at Bermuda's most complete dive shop. The children's mask-and-snorkel set costs $30. You'll find a large selection of wet suits, fishing gear, and camping supplies. ⊠ *7 Park Rd., Hamilton* ☎ *441/292–3839.*

Fly, Bridge and Tackle. The only island store completely dedicated to fishing supplies, Fly, Bridge and Tackle offers everything a fisherman needs except the fish. Plus, the avid fishermen on staff offer excellent advice about fishing in Bermuda. ⊠ *26 Church St., Hamilton* ☎ *441/295–1845.*

International Sports Shop. Frisbees, snorkel gear, exercise wear, and rackets all available here. ⊠ *Bermudiana Rd., Hamilton* ☎ *441/295–4183.*

Sports 'R' Us. This store has Bermuda's largest selection of running shoes, plus gear and equipment for most sports. ⊠ *Shoppers Fair Building, Church St., near Queen St., Hamilton* ☎ *441/292–1891.*

The Sports Locker. Athletic shoes, Teva sandals, and flip-flops are sold here. ⊠ *Windsor Pl., 18 Queen St., Hamilton* ☎ *441/292–3300.*

SportSeller. Big-name exercise gear, knapsacks, and running shoes are available at this shop, which also sells Speedo swimwear and some sunglasses. ⊠ *Washington Mall, Reid St., Hamilton* ☎ *441/295–2692.*

Upstairs Golf & Tennis Shop. Golf clubs, tennis rackets, and the accessories for those sports are the specialties of this store. You'll find some of the best brands available, including Ping, Callaway, and Titleist for the golfer, and Yonex and Dunlop for the tennis player. Men's and women's sportswear is also sold. ⊠ *26 Church St., Hamilton* ☎ *441/295–5161.*

Winners Edge. This store sells exercise wear, water bottles, and helmets, and it is the only store in Bermuda to sell Cannondale, Gary Fisher, and Trek equipment. ⊠ *34 Church St., Hamilton* ☎ *441/295–6012.*

Stationery & Art Supplies

Artcetera. This is where you can buy pens, paint, charcoal, pastels, sketching pads, canvases, and almost anything else an aspiring artist might need to capture Bermuda in color or black and white. ⊠ *34 Burnaby Hill, Hamilton* ☎ *441/295-2787.*

Card Cove. This tiny cottage offers a good supply of cards, calendars, toys, and party supplies. ⊠ *19 Queen St., Hamilton* ☎ *441/295-0727.*

The Royal Gazette Stationery Store. Pens, envelopes, writing paper, and note pads are plentiful at this well-stocked stationery store. ⊠ *32 Reid St., Hamilton* ☎ *441/295-4008.*

Toys

The Annex Toys. This large toy department in the basement of the Phoenix Centre has one of the best and most up-to-date selections of toys and games for all ages. There is also a good supply of kites and beach toys. ⊠ *3 Reid St., Hamilton* ☎ *441/295-3838.*

Jack 'N' Jill's Toy Shop. This cottage near Victoria Park is filled with traditional toys as well as more newer, perhaps "cooler" toys. The store is also the island's exclusive retailer of Bruynzeel art supplies. ⊠ *7 Park Rd., Hamilton* ☎ *441/292-3769.*

Magic Moments. Party planners will find gift-bag loot, balloons, banners, feather boas, and almost anything else you might need for a theme party. ⊠ *Washington Mall, Reid St., Hamilton* ☎ *441/296-8848.*

Toys 'N' Stuff. Popular with locals, this centrally located store sells toys and games for all ages, party supplies, children's furniture, and prams (strollers). ⊠ *Queen and Church Sts., Hamilton* ☎ *441/292-6698.*

UNDERSTANDING BERMUDA

BERMUDA AT A GLANCE

BASKING IN THE ATLANTIC, 508 mi due east of Cape Hatteras, North Carolina, restrained, polite Bermuda is a departure from other sunny, beach-strewn isles: you won't find laid-back locals wandering around barefoot proffering piña coladas. Bermuda is somewhat formal, and despite the gorgeous weather, residents wearing stockings and heels or, for men, jackets, ties, Bermuda shorts, and knee socks are a common sight, whether on the street by day or in restaurants at night. On Bermuda's 22 square mi, pastel cottages, quaint shops, and manicured gardens telegraph a staid, suburban way of life. A British diplomat once said, "Bermuda is terribly middle-aged"—and in many ways he was right. Most of the island is residential, the speed limit is 20 mi per hour (although many drivers go faster), golf and tennis are popular pastimes, and most visitors are over 40 years old. So are most Bermudians.

With this brings good things: Bermuda is one of the wealthiest countries in the world—average per capita income is $38,505. It has no income tax and no sales tax, though an import duty of 22.5% or more is included into almost every price tag on the island. There are no slums, and there is virtually no unemployment. Crime exists, of course, but the rate of crimes committed per capita is lower than in most other countries. There are also no billboards or neon signs, due to laws that regulate these more gaudy displays of commercialism.

A few Bermudians still speak the Queen's English, but the majority have their own unique accent, which reflects the country's diverse English, American, West Indian, and African influences. The population of just over 60,000 is 63% black, 33% white, and 4% Asian and other. Historically, Bermudians of English descent worked to recreate a middle-class England of their own. And as in so many colonies, the Bermudian version is more insular, more conservative, and more English than the original. Pubs, cricket, and an obsession with protocol are reminders of a distant loyalty to Britain and everything it used to represent. A self-governing British territory since 1968, with a parliament that dates from 1620, Bermuda loves pomp and ceremony. But the British apron strings are wearing thin. Although a referendum on independence from Britain was soundly defeated in 1995, the idea bubbles up from time to time. The first labor government—the Progressive Labour Party (PLP)—was elected in 1998, taking some Bermudians' hopes for identity and autonomy to dizzying heights—and terrifying others. In 2003, Bermudians were granted the rights of full British citizenship. Great ceremony still attends the recovening of Parliament each November. Marching bands parade through the capital in honor of the Queen's official birthday, a public holiday. Regimental bands and bagpipers reenact centuries-old ceremonies. And you can still get tea in a china cup.

Bermuda wears its history like a comfortable old coat. On a small island, real estate is too valuable to permit the island's legacy to be cordoned off for mere display. Most of Bermuda's historical buildings are well used. A traveler need only wander through the 17th-century buildings of St. George's—a UNESCO World Heritage Site—with its dozens of continuously occupied shops and private homes, to realize that Bermudian history remains part of the fabric of life. Each successive generation adds its own thread of achievement and color. Indeed, the island's isolation and diminutive size have forged a continuity of place and tradition almost totally missing in the United States. Walk into Trimingham's or A. S. Cooper & Sons department stores, and you are likely to be helped by a descendant of the founders. The names in the telephone book resemble those that populate the history books—Tucker, Trott, Dill, Zuill, Outerbridge, Butterfield—and a single lane in St. George's carries the memories and historical meaning of centuries. Even today, the love that early 19th-century Irish poet Thomas Moore had for lovely-but-married Hester Tucker—the "Nea" of the odes in which he immortalized his feelings—is gossiped about with a zeal usually reserved for the transgressions of a living neighbor. Bermuda's attachment to its history is more than a product of its size, however. It is through its past that Bermuda creates its own unique identity, drawing on its British roots 3,500 mi away and mixing those memories with the cultural influences of its giant American neighbor and its relatives in the Caribbean.

Since the very beginning, the fate of this small colony in the Atlantic has been linked to that of the United States. The crew of the *Sea Venture,* whose wreck on Bermuda during a hurricane in 1609 began the settlement of the island, was actually on its way to Jamestown, Virginia. The passenger list of the *Sea Venture* reads like a "Who's Who" of early American history. On board were Sir Thomas Gates, deputy governor of Jamestown; Christopher Newport, who had led the first expedition to Jamestown; and John Rolfe, whose second wife was the Native American, Pocahontas. In the centuries since, Bermuda has been somewhat of a barometer, registering the evolving relationship between the United States and Britain. In 1775 Bermuda was secretly persuaded to give gunpowder to George Washington in return for the lifting of a trade blockade that threatened the island with starvation. In the War of 1812, Bermuda was the staging post for the British fleet's attack on Washington, D.C. When Britain faced a national crisis in 1940, it gave the United States land on Bermuda to build a Naval Air Station in exchange for ships and supplies. In 1990, Prime Minister Margaret Thatcher and President George H. W. Bush held talks on the island.

The fact that Bermuda—just two hours by air from New York—has maintained some of its English character through the years is part of its appeal for the close to half million Americans (more than 90% of all visitors) who flock here each year. More important, however, Bermuda means sun, sea, and sand. It has a year-round mild climate, pink beaches, turquoise waters, coral reefs, 17th-century architecture, and splendid golf courses. In fact, Bermuda has more golf courses per square mile than anywhere else in the world.

Bermuda didn't always seem so attractive. More than 300 shipwrecks lie submerged on the reefs where divers now frolic. William Strachey, secretary-elect

for Virginia and a passenger on the *Sea Venture,* wrote that Bermuda was "a place so terrible to all that ever touched on them. Such tempests, thunders, and other fearful objects are seen and heard about those islands that they are called the Devil's Islands, feared and avoided by all sea travelers above any place in the world." For the crew of the *Sea Venture,* however, the 181 small islands that compose Bermuda meant salvation. Contrary to rumor, the islands proved to be unusually fertile and hospitable, supporting the crew during the construction of two new ships, in which they departed for Jamestown on May 10, 1610.

Playwright William Shakespeare drew on the accounts of these survivors in *The Tempest,* written in 1611. The wreck of the *Sea Venture* on harsh yet beneficent Bermuda—"these infortunate (yet fortunate) islands," as one survivor described them—contained all the elements of Shakespearean tragicomedy: that out of loss something greater is often born. Just as Prospero loses the duchy of Milan only to regain it and secure the kingdom of Naples for his daughter, Admiral Sir George Somers lost a ship but gained an island. Today, Bermuda's motto is *Quo Fata Ferunt* (Whither the Fates Carry Us), an expression of sublime confidence in the same providence that carried the *Sea Venture* safely to shore.

That confidence has largely been justified over the decades. Each year, many of the island's nearly 500,000 visitors, who help to fuel the economy, are repeat vacationers. However, Bermuda's very popularity has threatened to diminish its appeal. Residents have raised concerns about traffic congestion, overfishing, and reef damage. Some of the government's steps to preserve Bermuda's trademark beauty, civility, and tranquility have been successful; others have not.

Traffic jams leading into Hamilton, the island's capital, are no longer uncommon, despite the facts that each resident family can have only one car, and automobile rentals are prohibited. Faster ferries were introduced in 2002 to help relieve some of the congestion, yet locals have failed to embrace them with the gusto the Minister of Transportation anticipated. The government also restricts the number and size of cruise ships that visit the island, because the large numbers of passengers add to crowding, yet, since they need not patronize local hotels and restaurants, contribute little to the island's coffers. Still, when the cruise season begins, in April, and the first sleek liners dock in Hamilton, St. George's, and Dockyard, there is an energy and excitement that infects locals as well as visitors.

When all is said and done, however, whatever problems Bermuda has stem from a surfeit of advantages, and almost any island nation would gladly inherit them. The "still-vexed Bermoothes" is how Shakespeare described this Atlantic pearl, but he might have changed his tune had he found a chance to swim at Horseshoe Bay, or hit a well-placed chip shot to the 15th green at Port Royal. Had that been the case, who knows? Instead of a reference to a storm-wracked island, *The Tempest* might have been Shakespeare's reaction to a missed putt on the 18th.

— By Rachel Christmas Derrick

— Revised by Sue Johnston

THE HIDDEN BERMUDA

GOOD MORNING," SAYS THE POLICE OFFICER. A woman turns around, certain a guilty look has just crossed her face. She and the officer are the only two people on this stretch of grass, so he must be addressing her. She wonders immediately if she has done something wrong, though she is simply standing in a public park, watching boats go by. After all, she has heard that people could be arrested in Bermuda for such transgressions as cursing and bathing nude. Perhaps she has committed some crime unknowingly. Perhaps she missed some sign and is standing where she oughtn't to have stood. Her eyes dart around for a hint of the sign. *Oh no,* she thinks. It is her first morning in Bermuda and already she is in trouble.

Had it been her second morning, the woman doubtless would have been more at ease. As it turns out, her only mistake was ignorance of Bermuda's famous "good morning" ritual. These magic words (or their relatives, "good afternoon" and "good evening") begin every conversation conducted on the island; show up in all exchanges with waiters, bank tellers, and shop assistants; and are almost mandatory when you cross paths with someone, even a perfect stranger, on an uncrowded street. Those who learned at a young age, in another country, the don't-speak-to-strangers rule can be thrown quite off course by Bermuda's disarming social custom.

One might argue that, when 60,000 people share an island of only 21 square mi, they need to maintain a veneer of amity, but the truth is that most Bermudians are genuinely social people. And that condition can be contagious. A day or two of responding to the ritualistic greeting with a "good morning" of your own, and you are likely to lose whatever standoffish tendencies you brought with you.

Much less charming is the motorists' equivalent of the "good morning" ritual—the Honking Habit. "If I don't toot at everyone I know when I see them on the road, they'll think I'm stuck up," one taxi driver has said. Horns in Bermuda are used more for social reasons than safety. Unnerving as the practice may be, remember that they are not honking at *you,* no matter how slowly you are driving your rental scooter. Bermudians would consider *that* downright rude!

Johnny Barnes is a living example of Bermuda's national friendliness. Every weekday, rain or shine, from dawn until 10 AM, this eccentric retired gentleman stations himself in the traffic circle near the entrance to Hamilton and greets drivers on their way into town. "Good morning. I love you!" he calls, waving at one and all. Some reply, "Good morning, Mr. Barnes. Love you too, darlin'." And they mean it. So beloved is Johnny as a symbol of Bermudian friendliness, that a life-size bronze statue of him was commissioned by a group of local citizens. The statue was designed and sculpted by famous Bermudian artist Desmond Fountain, and stationed just steps from the real Johnny's corner. You can see a picture of Johnny in the Hamilton Visitors Service Bureau.

Despite the openness of the people, Bermuda isn't easy to understand. Just when you think you've got it figured out, new evidence appears. Your first impression of this perfect arrangement of rocks, sand, and greenery set in the turquoise sea may be that it's a pretty, orderly, quiet island, where you can plant yourself on a beach, gaze at the ocean, sip tea, and just get lost. Such pastimes are not discouraged, but repeat visitors discover a complex life behind the dunes and hedges of hibiscus. There's more to Bermuda than meets the eye.

Let's start with the fact that it's sitting on a volcano. When the great suboceanic eruption was finished, about 100 million years ago, the mouth of the volcano barely peeked above the sea surface. Over the centuries, millions of coral polyps attached themselves to the rock. Waves broke the coral down into fine sand, which settled on the shores. These lovely islands are really a collection of fossilized dunes. This fossilized sand, a light, porous, rock known as Bermuda stone, can be cut with a handsaw and is still quarried for the walls and roofs of houses. Though soft, the stone is very durable—some of Bermuda's homes have lasted more than 300 years.

Bermuda's first home builders arrived by accident in the summer of 1609, when their vessel, the *Sea Venture*, was shipwrecked on the reefs. Instead of their intended destination, the British colony of Virginia, Captain George Somers and his band of English traders and settlers came ashore on this uninhabited island. Settling near what is now the town of St. George's, they spent a few years building the *Deliverance* and the *Patience* to take them on to British America. They described their experience of pleasant weather and great fishing and, before long, there was a flourishing English colony in Bermuda, the Somers Island Company.

The island's British roots are clearly evident, particularly to visitors from the United States. Bermudians drive on the left. They put the "U" in "colour" and the "me" on "programme." They say "mad" when they mean "crazy." Hotels serve tea in the afternoon. Cricket is the national sport, and the annual east–west final competition, in August, even merits a statutory holiday. (Emancipation Day is really to celebrate the abolition of slavery, but to most locals, it's Cup Match time.) Lawyers, barristers, attorneys, and judges wear itchy, white wigs. The national anthem is, "God Save the Queen," sung without pronouncing the "R's." Indeed, Bermuda is one of Britain's few remaining self-governing overseas territories. The simmering issue of independence was defeated in a 1995 referendum, and today's parliamentarians have other issues on their minds, such as figuring out how a small island nation can play a significant, sustainable role in the global economy.

Despite its British accent, other cultures also have helped shape Bermuda. Its closest neighbor, the United States, has been part of its history since the wreck of the *Sea Venture*. The United States was the prime market for Bermuda's agricultural products during the 19th century, and has been the source of most of its tourism visitors since the time of Mark Twain. Its strategic mid-Atlantic location brought thousands of American soldiers to the island from the World War II era until the mid '90s. Today, in their place, there are armies of accountants, traders, actuaries,

and underwriters working in various international businesses.

At least 15% of Bermudians can trace their ancestry to Portugal. Portuguese agricultural workers began arriving on the island in 1849. It's not unusual to hear Portuguese spoken in shops and on the street. (Listen for the Portuguese version of the "good morning" ritual: "Bom dia!")

The islands of the Caribbean were also Bermuda's early trading partners, as were Canada's Atlantic provinces. As a result, many Bermudians have ancestral links to Trinidad, St. Kitts, Jamaica, and Canada.

Today, about 20% of Bermudians are alien "guest workers," whose employers must have government permission to hire them. Many have jobs in technology or financial services, and more are employed in the hospitality industry. A Bermudian restaurant might have a French chef, an Italian host, Sri Lankan and Swiss waiters, a Canadian accountant, and a Czech running the computer system—and the food, like the staff, will be an interesting fusion of the island's international influences.

As well as the people and culture, the flora and fauna are international. This is most evident at Paget Marsh, where the brilliant gardeners of the Bermuda National Trust—they might be called "horticultural xenophobes"—work hard to keep out all but native and endemic plant species. The plants are interesting, but nowhere in the four native habitats along the shady boardwalk trail is there a bright flower; a palm, citrus, or banana tree; or a trace of the exotic hibiscus, frangipani, and oleander that line Bermuda's roadways. Those are all imports, many brought by the British military from outposts around the globe. Much of Bermuda's beauty derives from these and other colorful plants, carefully sculpted by enthusiastic gardeners. "I saw a man cutting a hedge with a sword!" a five-year-old visitor announced, referring to the island's preferred garden tool—the machete. His mother had her own surprises, "What are those trees with the red and blue flowers? I've never seen blossoms in two colors before." She was referring to pink oleander which, like almost every tree or shrub in Bermuda, is often host to a constellation of blue morning glories. These, along with nasturtiums, fennel, and rosemary, so carefully tended in other countries, are considered weeds in Bermuda, they grow so profusely.

There is little endemic wildlife. The skink, an extremely rare, snake-faced lizard, originates here. And the cahow, a unique sea bird, has been resurrected from virtual extinction by naturalist Dr. David Wingate and his colleagues. But other critters have made their home on these islands. Assorted lizards, some as small as your finger, others about a foot long, were imported from the Caribbean to eat bugs. All are shy and none bite.

None of the land-based creatures can hurt you; however, some can disgust you. One such beast is the giant toad, a shy, warty, brown specimen brought from Guyana in 1875 to control cockroaches. Less repulsive is the whistling tree frog, whose song fills the night air from April until November. The tree frogs are an inch or less in length and, though the volume of their chorus suggests there are hundreds around your guest cottage, you'll be hard pressed to actually see one.

Toads, bugs, and whistling frogs are all part of Bermuda's night life. So are the frisky accountants, bankers, lawyers, and others who spill out of Hamilton's offices into the warm evening for happy hour. Bermuda offers a surprising number of unexpected urban treats. The Bermuda Arts Festival, which takes place throughout January and February, brings in dance, music, and theatrical productions from around the world. The growing Bermuda International Film Festival attracts a roster of excellent films and filmmakers to Bermuda every April. The Bermuda Jazz Festival is two September nights of outdoor concerts performed by outstanding local and international artists. It's pretty nice dancing under the stars to George Benson—live!

Still, however lively and sophisticated Bermuda may be, it is the quiet, the simple, and the beautiful that hold the island's magic. Ask a handful of locals to name their favorite leisure activity, and few mention the nightlife. But you are more than likely to hear:

"Sitting on the cliffs at Spittal Pond with my sketch pad."

"Curling up with a good book at Astwood Cove."

"Walking along the streets of St. George's."

"Climbing to the top of the Gibb's Hill Lighthouse."

"Swimming off the boat at night and watching the phosphorescence sparkle all around me."

"Driving from Southampton to St. George's along South Shore Road."

"Riding around on the ferry for no reason at all. It's a brilliant cruise."

"Snorkeling among the blue-and-yellow parrot fish at Church Bay."

"Flying a big kite at Horseshoe Bay."

"Buying and eating fresh vegetables from Wadson's stand in Southampton."

"Going to the beach in the evening to watch the sunset."

Clearly, Bermuda's natural beauty matches its cultural and social attributes. As you head for a day of sightseeing or shopping, you may just find yourself pausing to smell the rosemary and freesia in the morning dew or listen to the rumble of the rolling surf. When all is said and done, simply being here is a reason to say, "Good morning!"

— By Sue Johnston

THE GUNPOWDER PLOT

FROM THE TIME THE SHIPWRECKED Englishmen landed on its shores on their way to Virginia, Bermuda has felt a tug from both sides of the Atlantic. Today, this British territory sitting on America's doorstep finds this dual allegiance beneficial, yet there have been times when being caught in the middle was downright dangerous.

At the start of the American Revolution, Bermudians, who had strong trading and family ties to the northern colonies, were sympathetic to the colonists' desire to run their own affairs. But Bermudians are a practical people and felt that, in their own self-interest, it was best to remain loyal to the Crown and mind their own business. Unfortunately, that business—and the island's very existence—was threatened when the Continental Congress placed trade sanctions on Britain and all of its loyal colonies. Bermuda was immediately and unwittingly caught up in the conflict. Then, as now, essential food supplies were imported and, if the embargo continued, the island faced deprivation, even starvation. But then, as now, reaching an agreement on what action to take was never an easy process.

In one corner was the governor, George Bruere, a staunch royalist whose sons were fighting for the King in America. In the other corner was the leader of a powerful Bermudian clique, Colonel Henry Tucker of Somerset, whose sons, also in America, took the colonists' side. Though the families were related by marriage—Tucker's eldest son had married the governor's daughter—the hostilities drove an irreparable wedge between them. Ever the loyalist, Bruere could not give in to rebel demands. Ever the pragmatist, Tucker felt action was needed to avert a local disaster.

Through his sons, Colonel Tucker tried to gather intelligence about what it would take for the Congress to lift the embargo. He suspected they might do so in exchange for salt, one of Bermuda's important trade products. Full of hope, in July of 1775, Tucker led a delegation to Philadelphia to see what could be arranged. The response to the offer of salt was less than enthusiastic; however, the Bermudians learned that, though salt was of little interest to the Americans, any ship bringing arms or gunpowder would be free to trade. Thanks to Tucker's sons, who had friends close to members of the Congress, General Washington had already learned that the British kept large amounts of gunpowder in St. George's.

Tucker, who'd left Bermuda with no intention of being disloyal to the Crown, had been comfortable with the notion of trading salt for food. He was now quite uneasy with the treacherous suggestion of dealing in arms—and stolen arms at that. But the Americans had the advantage. Bermuda desperately needed supplies. So Tucker made a deal with Benjamin Franklin to exchange the British powder at St. George's in return for permission to trade.

Empty American supply ships were immediately sent out to Bermuda, along with Tucker and one of his sons, to fetch the powder. On August 14, 1775, a flotilla of whaleboats and other vessels formed at Somerset and, after dark, headed east to St. George's. Leaving the boats at Tobacco Bay, the Americans and a number of renegade Bermudians, supporters of Tucker, broke into the unguarded storage area and, throughout the night, loaded 100 barrels of gunpowder into the boats. By the first light of dawn, the ships and their cargo of British powder were headed back to America.

Bruere soon heard the news and issued an urgent proclamation.

POWDER STEAL

Advt
Save your Country from Ruin, which may hereafter happen. The Powder stole out of the Magazine late last night cannot be carried far as the wind is so light.
A GREAT REWARD
will be given to any person that can make a proper discovery before the Magistrates.

The governor's messengers frantically rode to each corner of the island to deliver the proclamation. The legislature was assembled and, though many in the Assembly knew a great deal about the events of the previous night, nobody revealed the secret. They simply approved the reward and wrote up a stern statement denouncing the act.

The offer of reward failed to attract the help Bruere needed to stop the ship or even to send a warning to the British admiral in Boston. In a land of ships and seafarers, it took Bruere nearly three weeks to assemble a ship and crew. When the governor's ship finally reached Boston, Admiral Howe sent His Majesty's Ship *Scorpion* to Bermuda to help maintain control. In 1778, to keep an eye on Bermudians' activities, a garrison replaced the ship.

When Bermudians reflect on the gunpowder plot, one of the puzzling questions is how it happened at all—let alone in the shadow of Government House. This is a nation where speculative discussion is an art form. Almost everyone has an opinion on almost everything and can't wait to share it. That Bermudians managed to keep the plot so secret that Governor Bruere heard not a whisper, before or during the event, attests to the desperation of their situation. The story reminds us how vulnerable a tiny, isolated island with no natural resources can be—and how critical it is for the people of that island to make the most of their relationships on both sides of the Atlantic.

— Revised by Sue Johnston

BOOKS & MOVIES

Bermuda has a large publishing industry, for so small a country. Three newspapers, several lifestyle and business magazines, and scores of books satiate the local appetite for literature of all kinds. Some volumes, such as those by respected historian William Zuill, are out of print but can still be found in book shops—and at the Hamilton public library. Those listed here are widely available.

Historical Books. *The Story of Bermuda and Her People,* by W. S. Zuill, traces the history of the island from the *Sea Venture* wreck in 1609 to the present. *Rogues and Runners: Bermuda and the American Civil War,* published by the Bermuda National Trust, is an exciting account of the island's role in the fight between northern and southern states. David Raine, a prolific Bermudian historical writer, combines painstaking research with lively storytelling. Among his popular titles are *An Irishman Came Through,* the tale of poet Tom Moore's stay in Bermuda; and *Shakespeare, an Island and a Storm,* which makes the link between the story of *The Tempest* and the wreck of the *Sea Venture.* Beautifully illustrated, *Bermuda Forts: 1612–1957,* by Dr. Edward Harris, represents more than 15 years of archival and archaeological research and is a fascinating book for history buffs of all ages. Colin Pomeroy tells two tales of bygone transportation in *The Bermuda Railway: Gone But Not Forgotten* and *Flying Boats of Bermuda.*

Picture Books. Selecting a picture book to remember your Bermuda vacation may be one of your most difficult vacation tasks—there are so many coffee-table books available. Roland Skinner's *Picturesque Bermuda* and Ian McDonald Smith's *A Scape to Bermuda* are local favorites. G. Daniel Blagg's *Bermuda Atlas & Gazetteer* is a comprehensive guide to Bermuda with more than 400 pages of historical text, 16 color maps, and 50 original watercolors by West Indian artist Luca Gasperi. *Bermuda Abstracts,* by Graeme Outerbridge, and *Bermudian Images,* by Bruce Stuart, offer an artist's view of this picturesque island.

Lifestyle. For a charming account of growing up in Bermuda during the 1930s and 1940s, see *The Back Yard,* by Ann Zuill Williams. A more recent account of a Bermuda childhood is *Nothin' But A Pond Dog,* by Llewellyn Emery, a delightful reminiscence that follows the adventures of a boy and his dog in the late 1950s. Emery continues the saga in *The Fires of Pembroke.* The island's social traditions are reflected in its special holiday meals in chef-author Judith Wadson's *The Seasons of Bermuda.* In *Fruits and Vegetables of the Caribbean,* M. J. Bourne describes the Bermudian produce you may find on your plate. Dale Butler's *Tall, Tall, True Bermuda Tales* is a collection of anecdotes, poetry, speeches, and words of wisdom about the Bermuda lifestyle. Butler, an educator and parliamentarian, may be Bermuda's most prolific author. He's produced books for both adults and children on subjects as diverse as ghosts, sporting events, and prominent Bermudians. His books, and those of his colleagues at his aptly named company, The Writers Machine, focus on the island's history, heroes, and folklore.

Novels. *The Bermuda Indenture: A Novel* is a Grisham-esque book by Strudwick Marvin Rogers, involving the search for the deed to an important property. *The Bermuda Affair: A Novel with its Roots in Wartime Bermuda,* by Alan Edmund Smith, is a love story set during World War II. Anne Newton Walther's *A Time for Treason* is set during the American Revolution. Vanessa Fox's 1994 murder mystery *Bermuda* tells of a supermodel who returns to the island to investigate the suspicious death of her half-brother. In David Manuel's mystery *A Matter of Time,* a monk struggling with a crisis of faith comes to Bermuda and is pulled into an investigation of drugs, dirty money, and murder.

Children's Books. Younger audiences will find a host of reading material, among them Willoughby Patton's *Sea Venture,* about a young boy on board the ill-fated ship; E. M. Rice's *A Child's History of Bermuda,* which tells the history of the island in terms children can readily understand; Dana Cooper's illustrated *My Bermuda 1, 2, 3*; and artist Elizabeth Mulderig's three *Tiny the Tree Frog* books. *The Bermuda Petrel: The Bird That Would Not Die*, by Francine Jacobs, tells the true story of how these rare birds (known as cahows) have been saved from extinction. *Gombey* describes the colorful and mysterious masked dancers who are part of the island's traditional folk celebrations. A picture book for all ages is Don Trousdell's charming *Dockyard Cats*, which depicts the wild and woolly felines that inhabit the island's West End.

Nature & Wildlife. *Bermuda's Botanical Wonderland*, by Christine Phillips-Watlington, contains illustrations and descriptions of the island's plants, plus wildlife-habitat information, suggested nature rambles, and vignettes, poems, and quotations about nature and life. Andrew Dobson's *Birdwatching Guide to Bermuda* offers comprehensive information on Bermuda's feathered residents and visitors. In *Bermuda's Marine Life*, Wolfgang Sterrer introduces you to creatures you may find below the ocean's surface.

Movies. Panatel VDS has produced several half-hour videos about the island, including *Bermuda Highlights*, *Dive Bermuda*, and *Bermuda Bound, Paradise Found*. Videos formatted for both North American and European systems are available at several stores around the island. A hit with locals, the "mockumentary" *Aliens in Bermuda,* is a sendup of news coverage of an alien landing. On a more serious note, Errol Williams's critically acclaimed documentary *When Voices Rise* tells the story of the dismantling of segregation in Bermuda in the late 1950s.

CHRONOLOGY

1503 Juan de Bermudez discovers the islands while searching for the New World. They are eventually named after him.

1609 An English fleet of nine ships, under the command of Admiral Sir George Somers, sets sail for Jamestown, Virginia, with supplies for the starving colony. Struck by a hurricane, the fleet is scattered, and the admiral's ship, the *Sea Venture*, runs aground on the reefs of Bermuda. The colonization of Bermuda begins.

1610 After building two ships, *Deliverance* and *Patience*, from the island's cedar trees, the survivors depart for Jamestown, leaving behind a small party of men. Admiral Sir George Somers returns to Bermuda a few weeks later but dies soon afterward, having requested that his heart be buried on the island.

1612 Asserting ownership of the islands, the Virginia Company sends 60 settlers to Bermuda under the command of Richard Moore, the colony's first governor. The Virginia Company sells its rights to the islands to the newly formed Bermuda Company for £2,000.

1616 The islands are surveyed and divided into shares (25 acres) and tribes (50 shares per tribe). The first enslaved men and women of African descent are brought here from America and the West Indies to dive for pearls and to harvest tobacco and sugarcane.

1620 The Bermuda Parliament meets for the first time (in St. Peter's Church, in St. George), making it the third-oldest parliament in the world, after those of Iceland and Great Britain.

1684 The Crown takes control of the colony from the Bermuda Company. Sir Robert Robinson is appointed the Crown's first governor.

1780 The "Great Hurricane" hits Bermuda, driving ships ashore and leveling houses and trees.

1804 Irish poet Thomas Moore arrives in Bermuda for a four-month stint as registrar of the admiralty court. His love for the married Hester Tucker was the inspiration for his steamy poems to her (the "Nea" in his odes), which have attained legendary status in Bermuda.

1815 Hamilton becomes the new capital of Bermuda, superseding St. George.

1834 Slavery is abolished.

1846 The first lighthouse in the colony, the 117-foot-high Gibbs Hill Lighthouse, is built at the island's western end in an effort to reduce the number of shipwrecks in the area.

1861 Bermuda enters a period of enormous prosperity with the outbreak of the American Civil War. Sympathetic to the South, Bermudians take up the dangerous and lucrative task of running the Union blockade of southern ports. Sailing in small, fast ships, Bermudians ferry munitions and supplies to the Confederates and return with bales of cotton bound for London.

1883 Princess Louise, daughter of Queen Victoria, visits Bermuda, launching the island as a tourist destination.

1899   Britain establishes POW camps on Bermuda during the Boer War with South Africa. Nearly 5,000 prisoners were detained on the Great Sound islands through 1902.

1931   Built at a cost of $4.5 million, the Bermuda Railway opens years behind schedule. Maintenance problems during World War II cripple train service, and the whole system is sold to British Guiana (now Guyana) in 1948.

1937   Imperial Airways begins the first scheduled air service to Bermuda from Port Washington, New York.

1944   Women landowners are given the vote.

1946   Automobiles are lawfully allowed on Bermuda for the first time.

1953   Winston Churchill, Dwight D. Eisenhower, and Prime Minister Joseph Laniel of France meet on Bermuda for the "Big Three Conference."

1959   A boycott leads to the end of racial segregation in movie theaters, hotels, and restaurants.

1968   The first election is held after the law giving landowners an extra vote is abolished.

1971   Edward Richards becomes Bermuda's first black premier.

1973   Governor Sir Richard Sharples and his aide, Captain Hugh Sayers, are shot dead. In 1976, Erskine "Buck" Burrows is convicted of the murder, as well as several other murders and armed robberies. He is hanged in 1977.

1979   Gina Swainson, Miss Bermuda, wins the Miss World Contest.

1987   Hurricane Emily hits Bermuda, injuring more than 70 people and causing millions of dollars in damage.

1994   Her Royal Highness Queen Elizabeth II and Prince Philip pay an official visit.

1995   The Royal Navy closes its Bermuda headquarters after having maintained a presence on the island for 200 years. The U.S. Naval Air Station base closes, having operated since September 1940.

   In a referendum on independence, 75% of voters say "no" to severing ties with Britain.

1996   An attempt by a local company to bring McDonald's restaurants to the island fails when Bermuda's Parliament nixes fast-food franchises.

1997   Bermuda's first female premier, the Honorable Pamela F. Gordon, is appointed.

1998   In a landslide victory, the Progressive Labour Party (PLP) is elected to power, putting an end to 31 years of rule by the United Bermuda Party (UBP). The UBP is dominated by affluent descendants of Bermuda's 17th-century English settlers, while the PLP was formed in 1963 from the ranks of Bermuda's labor and desegregation movements.

2000   The historical town of St. George is awarded World Heritage status, as the fourth-oldest municipality in the Western Hemisphere.

2003   Bermudians are granted the rights of full British citizenship.

INDEX

FODOR'S KEY TO THE GUIDES

America's guidebook leader publishes guides for every kind of traveler.
Check out our many series and find your perfect match.

FODOR'S GOLD GUIDES
America's favorite travel-guide series offers the most detailed insider reviews of hotels, restaurants, and attractions in all price ranges, plus great background information, smart tips, and useful maps.

COMPASS AMERICAN GUIDES
Stunning guides from top local writers and photographers, with gorgeous photos, literary excerpts, and colorful anecdotes. A must-have for culture mavens, history buffs, and new residents.

FODOR'S CITYPACKS
Concise city coverage in a guide plus a foldout map. The right choice for urban travelers who want everything under one cover.

FODOR'S EXPLORING GUIDES
Hundreds of color photos bring your destination to life. Lively stories lend insight into the culture, history, and people.

FODOR'S TRAVEL HISTORIC AMERICA
For travelers who want to experience history firsthand, this series gives in-depth coverage of historic sights, plus nearby restaurants and hotels. Themes include the Thirteen Colonies, the Old West, and the Lewis and Clark Trail.

FODOR'S POCKET GUIDES
For travelers who need only the essentials. The best of Fodor's in pocket-size packages for just $9.95.

FODOR'S FLASHMAPS
Every resident's map guide, with 60 easy-to-follow maps of public transit, parks, museums, zip codes, and more.

FODOR'S CITYGUIDES
Sourcebooks for living in the city: thousands of in-the-know listings for restaurants, shops, sports, nightlife, and other city resources.

FODOR'S AROUND THE CITY WITH KIDS
Up to 68 great ideas for family days, recommended by resident parents. Perfect for exploring in your own backyard or on the road.

FODOR'S HOW TO GUIDES
Get tips from the pros on planning the perfect trip. Learn how to pack, fly hassle-free, plan a honeymoon or cruise, stay healthy on the road, and travel with your baby.

FODOR'S LANGUAGES FOR TRAVELERS
Practice the local language before you hit the road. Available in phrase books, cassette sets, and CD sets.

KAREN BROWN'S GUIDES
Engaging guides—many with easy-to-follow inn-to-inn itineraries—to the most charming inns and B&Bs in the U.S.A. and Europe.

BAEDEKER'S GUIDES
Comprehensive guides, trusted since 1829, packed with A–Z reviews and star ratings.

OTHER GREAT TITLES FROM FODOR'S
Baseball Vacations, The Complete Guide to the National Parks, Family Vacations, Golf Digest's Places to Play, Great American Drives of the East, Great American Drives of the West, Great American Vacations, Healthy Escapes, National Parks of the West, Skiing USA.

At bookstores everywhere.   www.fodors.com/books